SHE DANCED ME A STORY

She Danced Me a Story

By Jeremiah T. Bannister

© Our Lady of Victory Press, MMXXIII

ISBN 979-8-9877607-3-4

Our Lady of Victory Press is an imprint of The Meaning of Catholic.

The Meaning of Catholic is a lay apostolate dedicated to uniting Catholics against the enemies of Holy Church.
MeaningofCatholic.com

Our Lady of Victory, pray for us!

TABLE OF CONTENTS

Tempus Fugit [IN THE FOG OF WAR] Part I of IV.......... 11

section i:

AS IT WAS + IN THE BEGINNING +

1. PILLOW/BLANKETS [With Super Friends].................. 15
2. TO DIRGE & DARE [On a Warped Chessboard] 22
3. THE FUN SPOT [In Sami's Garden of Eden] 29
4. MONSTERS THRIVE [In Lies of Hidden Hands].......... 40
5. ROSES & REDWOODS [Day One at Helen DeVos] 46
6. VITALS! VITALS! [Everything is Vital] 52
7. "DON'T WORRY ABOUT ME [TOO MUCH]..." 58

section ii:

AS IT IS NOW [IN HER ORBIT] + (LIFE, WITH CANCER) +

Tempus Fugit [IN THE FOG OF WAR] Part II of IV 67
8. FOX, FRIENDS, and FR. SIRICO 72
9. BIRTHDAYS & BIOPSIES [Let Cancer Eat Cake] 85
10. SHE DANCED ME A STORY 96
11. HOWLS IN THE HALLWAY 109

12. CANDY, CANES, AND CANNABIS
[Miracles at Mary Free Bed] 126

13. KILLING CANCER [With a Sonic Screwdriver] 149

14. FLURIOUS & GRUSTRATED:
[Having "The Talk" with Your BFF] 162

15. SAMI'S FRIDAY NIGHT LIGHTS 172

section iii:

AS IT WILL BE FOREVERVER
+ TO SALUTE A SUPERNOVA +

Tempus Fugit [IN THE FOG OF WAR] Part III of IV 183

16. PRINCESS SAMI'S BIG HUZZAH
[Blackrock Medieval Festival] 186

17. WHERE DID THE CANCER GO? 198

18. MAKE-A-WISH, LITTLE STAR! [Wish Ball 2015] 203

19. MEMENTO MORI [Jubilee Atop the Thames] 215

20. DOCTOR WHO'S FIRST AID KIT 226

21. #NeverGiveUp [On Christmas Eve] 243

22. HAPPY B-DAY, BABY JESUS 258

23. ANGELS IN THE VORTEX 264

24. 50 FIRST DATES [aka Love—Into A Million Pieces] 279

25. A VERY STORMY FOURTH OF JULY 290

26. FOURTH DOWN & SUNSET
[A Hail Mary at Beaumont] 296

27. THE SWORD OF MANY SORROWS 306

28. ZOMBIES & QUIET ZONES 314

29. ELLE EST BELLE EN BLEU
["She is Beautiful in Blue"] 325

section iv:

A WORLD WITHOUT END
THE BITTERSWEET: + LIFE & DEATH +

30. BIRTHDAY CANDLES AT A FUNERAL 335

31. TO LIVE (AND DIE) [Beneath the Waves] 342

Tempus Fugit [IN THE FOG OF WAR] Part IV of IV 350

32. THE SAVING SOLITUDE OF SILENCE 358

33. BATTLE ROYALE: IN THREE ACTS
[The One vs. The Many] 365

34. SOMETHING (OR SOMEONE)
[Greater Than the Sum] 378

35. THE CRUX AT THE CROSSROAD
[Christmas Eve 2017] 387

36. A Godmother's Sacred Heart [World Without End] 389

37. SETTLING SCORES [On Warped Chessboards] 399

To my family...

[Past, Present, and Future]
#TeamTinyDancerFOREVER

Tempus Fugit
[IN THE FOG OF WAR]
Part I of IV

+ In The Quiet Zone—Summer Solstice 2017 +

    A streetlight shone through the divide of the blinds, and lightning illuminated the surface of Sami's balloons, which set aglow the haze of smoke that now hovered like a ghost in the room. Papa was home, alone in his office, reading *Purgatorio* to the sounds of rain and rolling thunder, accompanied by John Frusciante's "Song of the Siren" spinning slowly on the turntable. He'd been smoking now for hours (or maybe it was weeks), but it felt like he'd been there for months, crying, thinking, plotting and scheming, pondering questions that couldn't be answered, in hopes of help that never came.

    Life had been wild since they buried their child—a mind-bending mix of delight and despair—and the family spiraled in all sorts of directions, spanning the spectrum from Mama's moderation to the polars of Papa's extremes. The boys were okay, but something was missing, and Teresa was failing in school. Then Papa got injured by visions of grandeur, and #TeamTinyDancer fell apart at the seams. It came like a tidal wave, completely out of the blue, and the family was left to grapple with the aftermath. Unfortunately, Papa wasn't much help, not now anyway, for he'd been trapped in a maze of malaise and addiction, always complaining they'd lost their way but forever unable (or unwilling) to accept a solution.

    He used to think it was clever to claim that life was a game of chess, but from his throne in the room where his daughter died, he saw the warped chessboard, scorched by the flames of unholy fire, and all his pieces were falling apart.

    So, Papa struck a match, lit his pipe, then inhaled with all his might, and, with his eyes closed, he descended into the dark of the abyss, recalling the days of love and laughter in the life his family lived before THE WAR.

section i:

**AS IT WAS
+ IN THE BEGINNING +**

I

PILLOW/BLANKETS
[With Super Friends]

+ Grand Rapids, Michigan—March 2015 +

There was a curious cadence in the pitter-patter of Sami's hi-tops ascending the stairs, but Papa knew it was her. He heard the school bus barrel down the road, and the laughter of his children echoed through the halls. But, unbeknownst to them, he'd spent the last hour or so playing chess in the attic, patiently biding his time, minute-by-minute, second-after-second, until, finally, Samantha arrived.

"Psst..." Sami whispered from the stairwell.

"Whoa! Who is that? Who's there??"

Sami covered her mouth, trying her best not to laugh, and in a ridiculous robot voice, she replied, "I. Am. Mystery Girl 5000."

"Woooow..." Papa said as he hurried to remove a stack of books from the table. "Mystery Girl 5000, huh?"

"Yes. Obviously."

"Honestly, I kinda wondered if this was a trick, but that robot voice is awesome—probably the best I've ever heard."

"Thank you. *BEEP* I have practiced all week. But now I am on a secret special mission to see *BEEP-BOOP* if you *BOOP-BOP* would love to have a Pillow/Blankets party with me, Papa."

He sat his elbow on the arm of the chair, and, with his chin resting on his palm, he scrunched his eyebrows deep in thought. "Well, it is Friday, and Pillow/Blankets is my favorite family tradition, but a sleepover? With a robot?? I dunno about that. I mean, what would Mama think of me spending the night with some chick named Mystery Girl 5000?"

"Wait! What? No!" Sami sputtered, fearing she'd sabotaged her otherwise ingenious scheme. "I mean, erm, *BEEP* Yes, that. is. true. But I am not really *BOOP-BOP* a robot."

Papa smiled like a Cheshire cat, and with a voice like the caterpillar from *Alice in Wonderland*, he asked, "Ah, then *who*, may I ask, are *you*?"

"Sorry, but I am programmed to make you guess my name... or... something. Please. Try. Hard."

"Hmmm..." Papa hummed as he rocked in his chair, studiously stroking the wild curls of his long, wavy beard. "Well, if I had to guess, I'd say you're...mmm... T-Bear." That was Sami's tongue-tied, thumb-sucking little sister Teresa, so it wasn't the worse guess in the world, but-

"Negative! That is a very bad guess, actually. Please. Try. Again."

So, that's what he did... again... and again... and again. He rattled off almost every name in the house—he even asked if it was Sami's super-fat tabby cat, Lion—but every guess was worse than the last.

"C'mon, Papa!" Sami said, stomping her foot on the stairs. "You aren't even trying."

"Au contraire, mademoiselle. I just needed to figure out if you were a real robot. You broke character twice, though, so now I *definitely* know who you are." He paused for dramatic effect, imagining the sweat beading up on Sami's brow, and he held his answer for as long as he could. But just when he thought Sami would break the silence, he sat up in his chair, and with all the fake confidence he could possibly muster, he declared, loud and proud, "I knew it was you the whole time... Athanasius."

"EXTERMINATE!" Sami yelled as she burst into the room. She loved being compared to Mama, and she didn't mind being mistaken for Teresa (at least Teresa was a girl), but her younger brother Athan? No way, José! And with her arms crossed in protest, she rolled her eyes. "Athan might be my *little* brother, but he's a *big* fat brat."

Papa raised an eyebrow. "He might be your brother?"

"Ha-ha, Papa. And nice try, Mr. Lies. But I know for a fact that you knew it was me the whole entire time."

"I dunno, you are really good at fake robot voices. It's why I've always said you should go to a ventriloquist college when you grow up."

Sami punched his shoulder, then sat on his lap, and with her left-arm wrapped around his neck, she leaned in nice and close to his ear, whispering, "You... are... A WEIRDO!" Sami sat up and rolled her eyes at him, and in a playfully sassy voice, she said, "Oh, and just in case you didn't know, ventriloquist colleges are super-duper fake news." Then she scowled at him. "And you know how much puppets creep me out, so now I'm probably gonna have scary dreams all night, thank you very much!" Sami's scowl didn't last long, though, as it was quickly replaced by that look every parent sees when their kid has a trick up their sleeve. And she had something better than a trick. She had Papa in checkmate—and in only two moves. "Hmm... actually, now that you made me think about it, there's really only one cure for those kinds of nightmares."

"Just one, huh?" Papa asked, trying his best to hide the fact that he knew what was coming next. "Alrighty, then, tell me, what is this *one and only cure* you speak of?"

Sami jumped for joy, and with her left-arm raised high overhead, she shouted, "It means a Pillow/Blankets sleepover party with Papa!"

+ At a Hole in the Fourth Wall +

First off, Sami was lying through her teeth about puppets giving her nightmares. She loved them—even the creepy animatronics ones. Secondly, Sami would say and do almost anything for a sleepover party with Papa, and that's *exactly* what Pillow/Blankets was.

It all began one fateful night, when Sami was two years old...

SHE DANCED ME A STORY

+ BATTLE CREEK, MICHIGAN (CIRCA 2007) +

Every night, after tucking Sami in bed, Papa would b-line it to the couch, where he'd fall asleep to the sights and sounds of his all-time favorite cartoon: The Challenge of the *Super Friends*. But there was just one problem: Sami loved *Super Friends* even more than Papa did. And she was a zany little zealot, always watching with the kind of devotion and raw intensity that sports enthusiasts experience when their favorite team plays against their lifelong rivals. She'd fret and fawn over her favorite good guys, heroes like Batman, Superman, Aquaman, and Wonder Woman. And she always bashed and booed those icky-gross villains who were part of the Legion of Doom, with mischief-makers like Cheetah, Scarecrow, Lex Luthor, and Bizarro. She even bit her nails when members of the Justice League were in trouble, which, like the Batman TV show from the 1960s, always happened sometime around the midpoint of the show. And like most cartoons from the '70s and '80s, there were always lessons to be learned. No matter how sticky the situations were for Sami's beloved *Super Friends*, she loved that the world's most conniving criminals could never prevail over Truth, Justice, and the American Way.

Sami didn't just love *Super Friends*, though. She was a full-blown fanatic, and this caused all sorts of trouble, especially after bedtime. Fact was, it was the nexus of all her nighttime naughties. She was a persistent little girl, always breaking out of bed, crawling on the carpet, then carefully climbing onto Papa's chest, where she'd fall asleep to the rhythm of Papa's heartbeat. Mama feared it would become a terrible habit, and that is exactly what happened. Papa was a sucker, and he loved spending time with Sami, so he always concocted some elaborate explanation as to why she just had to stay up with him. It worked often enough, but he didn't always get his way, and when Mama won, she'd make him lay Sami back down to bed.

That was until, one late and fateful summer night, when Sami did something that would change the Bannister family forever. Rather than running through the rigamarole of her regular evening ritual, Sami simply hopped out of bed, strolled straight through the middle of the room, then stood beside Papa on the couch. In her right-hand, she held a musical pillow that played "Jesus Loves Me," and in her left-hand was a teensy-weensy technicolor blanket that Mama had knit as a gift for her birthday.

"Why are you still awake?" Mama asked. "It's after midnight, Sami. Go back to bed!"

Undeterred, Sami gazed at Papa with her big, blue, Precious Moments eyes, and with a few flutters of her lashes, she held her hands out to him, and in the most adorable chipmunk voice anyone had ever heard, she asked:

"Pillow/Blankets, Papa?"

Mama shook her head. "Well, Jeremiah, you're hosed."

SHE DANCED ME A STORY

And, oh, how hosed he was, for never in human history had a father been so bewitched by his beautiful little girl.

And, for crying out loud, Papa thought to himself, *those eyelashes! Where in the heck did Sami even get those things, anyway?*

An important question, indeed, but Papa had more urgent things to ponder, for he'd fallen face-first into an ooey-gooey sea of sentimental cuteness—and he was drowning beneath its waves! Resistance proved futile, and from that night on, Pillow/Blankets was the family's most cherished and enshrined tradition.

That was seven years ago, so Sami was now 10 years old, and she wasn't the only child anymore. First came Athanasius. Sami was joking when she called him a big fat brat, but he was a snarky little guy. Ambrose came next, and just like his brother, he was a wee little man, but he was gentle, creative, and with blond hair and blue eyes, he was the spitting image of his dad. And last, but not least, there was Teresa. She was adorable and adventurous, with long brown hair and almond eyes that curled into crescent moons whenever she smiled. Teresa reminded everyone of her half-Asian beauty queen Mama.

And yet, despite all these additions, the Bannisters remained a family of super-friends, happy and hopeful that some things, like Pillow/Blankets, would forever remain the same...

... but even those things were about to change, and they would begin to change that very night.

II

TO DIRGE & DARE
[On a Warped Chessboard]

Papa read fairy tales to the kids before tucking the younger ones into bed. Sami grabbed an armful of pillows and carried them up to the attic. There seemed to be a little limp in her stride as she entered the room, but she hadn't complained of any pain, and the pile of pillows in her arms was so big, she couldn't even see where she was going, so Papa was surprised she was able to walk without tripping and falling at all.

"I'm scared you'll be mad at me," Sami said as Papa hurried to hide beneath the blankets. They'd barely settled over top of him when Sami dropped the pillows to the floor. She looked around the room, wondering if he was still downstairs, but then she saw the pillows move. Sami laughed and shook her head. "That's basically the worst hiding place in the world, Papa." She stood there, thinking back on the hundreds of sleepovers they'd had together and all the silly ways he tried to make her laugh. Memories like those always made her smile, but tonight they made her sad. "I was saying, I don't want you to be mad at me, but I wondered if maybe we could watch something other than *Super Friends* tonight..."

It took a few seconds for him to respond, and the silence made her nervous. "Are you being serious right now?" he asked from beneath the blankets. Papa didn't mean to sound sad or upset, it just came out that way. He feared he had come face-to-face with that fateful day in which Sami would come of age and say she's just too big to play his childish games anymore. He knew it would happen sooner or later (it always does), but he always supposed he'd see a sign—or, if he was lucky, maybe two or three—and that all the signs would be kind enough to permit him some time to prepare. Peeking his face out from under the blanket, he sighed, "I guess life doesn't always work out that way, huh?"

"Life?"

"Yeah, I mean, you're 10-years-old, Sam, and it's cool you're getting bigger, but I guess it's kinda bittersweet for dads." He lifted the blankets from over his head and offered Sami his hand. "I knew you'd get too big for my cartoons, but it still sorta bums me out, ya know?"

Sami frowned, then took a hold of Papa's hand. "Now *that* is cuckoo bird nonsense, and you know it, too." She struggled to the floor, looking a little like someone with a bad back or bum knee, but with a quick tuck and an awkward roll, she flopped down on the bed of blankets, where she caught her breath, then turned to look at Papa. "I'll always love *Super Friends*, you know. And when I'm married and have a bunch of kids, we'll watch *Super Friends* every weekend, and I'll make them laugh with stories of all the fun I had growing up." Rolling over on her stomach, she propped herself up on her left elbow. "I'm just in the mood for something a little more sciency tonight, that's all."

"We could watch Cosmos, or maybe Doctor Who?"

Sami squinted her eyes, and with puckered lips, she replied, "Ooo, Neil deGrasse Tyson does have an epic mustache, but we already watched Cosmos, and I promised Paul I'd wait to watch Doctor Who with him."

She wasn't wrong—Tyson does have a magnificent stache—and a promise was a promise, especially since it involved the family's favorite friend. So, Papa and Sami surfed online for something fun and sciency to watch. In the end, they settled on a docudrama, entitled, "Darwin's Dangerous Idea," and once they'd gotten settled into their fortress of pillows and blankets, Papa dimmed the lights, Sami cranked up the volume, and the two of them, together, pushed play.

The cinematography was surprisingly good, and it began with some sweet stories about Darwin and his daughter, Anne.

"Aw," Sami said as Lion settled by her side, "and just when I thought tonight couldn't get any better..."

Lion was Sami's Garfield cat, super-lazy and really fat. He'd been part of the family since Sami was seven, and she loved him like a brother.

With a mouthful of Pop-Tarts, she said, "It's his whippy tail. And his purr is like a lullaby promising to keep me safe when I'm asleep." Sami used her tongue to gather the last bits of icing from her teeth, then smacked her lips. "And ya know what else, Papa?"

"Me and you are basically the same as Darwin and his daughter."

"Pfft!" Papa sputtered, splattering sprinkles of his Irish stout all over the floor. "I hate to break it to you, Sam, but Darwin had a 165 IQ, and Papa is just an average guy."

"Yeah, that's kinda true, but Darwin loved Anne like crazy, didn't he? And Anne loved to hang out at his job, just like how I go to the radio station and roller rink whenever you go to work. Anne's 10-years-old, too, and that's how old I am right now."

"Mmm..." Papa hummed with a smile on his face, "you really are my mini-me, aren't you, baby?"

Sami blushed. "It's why we're SamiMiah forever, Papa." Then she hugged his arm and snuggled by his side to finish the movie.

The Darwin family's happiness ended abruptly though, for in a tragic twist of fate, Anne became deathly ill. It came out of nowhere, and Darwin didn't know what to do. In fact, things got so bad so quickly that he was forced to send her out of town for an emergency examination. It was a Hail Mary, but they'd tried everything, and now they were running out of time. And in a heart-wrenching display of fatherly love, Darwin carried his dying daughter, wrapped in a blanket, to a carriage in the street outside their home, where his wife and children kissed Anne and said goodbye.

As the carriage slowly began to roll away, Mrs. Darwin assures Anne that she'd come back soon. "And Papa will look after you."

But Anne only got worse. It was dreadful, and neither Papa nor Sami knew how things would end, so they held each other's hands, anxiously wondering what would happen next.

"Have we truly exhausted our options?" Darwin pleaded with the doctor.

The doctor replied, "All one can do now is pray."

Moments later, Anne's mother, Emma, was shown weeping in a storm, with thunder and lightning flashing and crashing about. She looked to heaven, and shouted with all her motherly might:

"*Why, God? Why??*"

It was so painful to watch. And the sorrow in Emma's voice could only mean one thing: *Anne had died.*

Darwin was devastated, wallowing in a valley of tears on the floor. Anne's doctor hovered over him, and with a painful reluctance in his voice, he offered Darwin one final condolence:

"The Lord gives, and the Lord takes away."

Sami's face was flush with fear and fury, her fists clenched, white-knuckled with the ache and agony that accompany defeat and despair. For though Sami was still quite young, she had developed a sagacious sense of death's permanence—and, oh, how she hated the Reaper.

"Anne is dead, Papa!" Sami cried. "She's really, really dead!"

Papa wrapped his arms around her, and with their faces pressed deep into each other's shoulder, they wept their broken hearts out. But then came Anne's funeral scene, and they had to see what happened next.

Whether fact or fiction, the movie portrayed it as a miserably rainy day. Darwin sat near Anne's deathbed, gazing, forlorn, out the window as he caressed a silver ribbon once worn by his daughter. But, alas, came the time for his family to make their way to the church. So, Darwin gathered his cane and limped alongside his wife and children, all of whom were dressed in the saddest shades of funeral black. Barely a word was said before the bang of the church bells rang through the countryside, and Darwin stood still. There was such sorrow in his eyes as he gazed up at the steeple, and after a moment's pause, he turned his gaze toward the ground.

Emma knew what troubled her husband's heart, for she'd witnessed Darwin wrestle many years with God. Still, with an outstretched hand, she begged him. "Please, Charles, please come in..."

But Darwin declined, choosing instead to remain outside the church... mourning in the rain... broken and alone.

"That would be me!" Papa growled, slamming his fist to the ground. "I'd hate anything to do with God for the rest of my life. And there's no way I'd ever go back to church—not after something like that!"

Papa explained how he agreed with the sentiments summed up by Darwin biographer, James Moore, who said Anne's death marked the end of Darwin's Christian faith. Darwin simply couldn't believe a good and all-loving God could oversee such a world, and events like these cut against the grain of claims regarding a meaningful and orderly history of mankind. Surely, Anne didn't deserve to be punished, so how much less did Anne deserve to die? Such was Darwin's dilemma...

"And he's right," Papa thundered. "Anne was just a victim, a victim to the vanity of our existence. There is no moral to the story, no grand purpose for the struggle. Everything just runs according to laws of nature, and nature doesn't care about our feelings."

Sami could feel Papa's anger, but she knew that, deep down in his heart of hearts, it wasn't anger so much as fear that compelled him to think and talk that way. So, she listened, silently petting her purring cat. Then, when he finished, she asked, "You really wouldn't go back to church?"

"Me? After something like that?? Not in a million years!"

Sami sniffled, then used her sleeve to wipe her eyes. "I get what you're saying, but would that even include Christmas Eve?"

Ah, now that was a cutting question, for Sami knew a secret: Papa used to be a Christian...

He was a Roman Catholic with a radio show when he stopped attending Church, and he was a Protestant pastor before that, and he'd spent nearly a decade debating atheists on radio, TV, blogs, and internet video sites; he had wrestled with the divine and walked with a spiritual limp ever since.

Still, and for reasons he never really talked about, Papa found himself faithfully attending a Midnight Mass or Eastern Orthodox Vigil every Christmas Eve. Sami liked that about Papa, even if all of his Atheist friends thought it was weird.

"Not even on Christmas Eve!" he snarled. "Never. Never again."

Sami lowered her head, then she grabbed hold of her right-hand, and with a tremor in her voice, she said, "I understand, but if something terrible like that ever did happen, then you gotta promise me something."

Papa shuddered at the thought. "What? If something like *that* happened?"

"Just promise me, okay?"

Papa nodded, so Sami sat up straight, looked deep into his eyes, and said, "Just promise me you'll never hate. I know it would be super-hard for you, especially because you're bipolar and everything—and nobody likes it when kids die—but most of our friends and family believe in God and go to church, especially on Christmas. And even though you don't agree with them 100 percent, I'll love them forever with all my heart no matter what." And with nothing more, Sami sighed, then rolled over to go to sleep.

"Thanks a lot," Papa muttered, half-jokingly, under his breath. He was bewildered by Sami's bizarre request, and his bones rattled with rage, but that all changed when he became transfixed on a poster that hung on his wall. It was a poster of Sandro del Prete's "Warped Chessboard," and Papa loved to look at it, especially when he was going through a difficult time. He admired del Prete's ability to transform altogether ambiguous objects into otherwise impossible images. He saw within the patterns a kind of reflection, a representation of the cryptic queries and dreadful hypotheticals that always gnashed and gnawed at his heart.

How does a parent survive the death of a child? he thought. *I've been to a few of those funerals—they're the saddest scenes in all the world. Why would God permit such evil things like that to happen, anyway? And to innocent children! And where on earth could a family turn for hope in a situation like that?* He recoiled at the thought, but he couldn't avoid wondering, *If our family ever was forced to bury one of our own, who or what would we become?*

These were macabre misfortunes to meditate upon—and they started to make him mad—but his worries withered away when he heard Sami whisper in a soft and tired voice. "Papa, when is the next time you deejay at the roller rink?"

He fluffed Sami's pillow, then slowly ran his fingers through her hair. "Tomorrow morning, sweetheart." Then he covered her feet with a colorful comforter, and said, "It's after midnight, though, so go to bed, baby."

In typical Sami fashion, she yawned, and with a smile on her face, she let out a fading "Yaaaaaaay," then closed her eyes and drifted to sleep.

III

THE FUN SPOT
[In Sami's Garden of Eden]

+ The Next Morning—In Byron Center +

Whether it was the pepperoni pizza, buttery popcorn, and nacho cheese, or the clickity-clack of rollerblades on hardwood floors, or the jingle jangle of tokens tumbling into video games, the Bannister family loved the Byron Fun Spot. Sure, it was a rinky-dink roller rink in the middle of Nowhere, USA, but that was part of its charm. And as far as they were concerned, the Fun Spot was their very own Garden of Eden, a home away from home, where folks were more like family than friends. And, of all Sami's friends at the Fun Spot, she adored no one more than the tall and pretty teenage girl named Riley.

Sami had barely even walked through the door when Riley picked her right up off the floor and twirled her around like a ballet dancer, telling her over and over just how much her friends had missed her.

"Wow!" Sami said, still dizzy from all that spinning. "You missed me that much, huh?"

Riley rolled her eyes. "Pfft. Obviously, duh. Like you even need to ask. C'mon, you have been gone for, what, like, four weeks?" Then she unwrapped a lollipop and tossed it in her mouth as she mumbled, "Not gonna lie, girl, it sorta feels like you've been gone forever." This was an understatement. Sami had been AWOL for a month, and she had been having excruciating headaches, but four weeks felt like a long time, especially for a young girl to have a headache. Papa had also been sick around the same time, and the two of them had had the same symptoms, but it was taking Sami much longer to get better, so people couldn't help but worry. "Are you feeling better, though? I mean, you're here, right, so you're at least doing better than before."

Sami shrugged her shoulders, then nervously grabbed her right-hand. "Yeah, I'm pretty good, I guess, but my head still hurts sometimes, and I'm still super-tired for some reason, so I take really long naps almost every day." Sami scrunched her face like she had smelled something sour. "At least I'm not puking anymore. Well, not *that much*, anyway. Seriously, puking is so gross! And it's weird cuz my parents thought maybe I just needed some glasses, but the eye-doctor said my eyes are perfectly fine."

That, however, was not the whole story. It's true that Sami could see the tiny letters on the chart, but she failed to mention that the optometrist noticed how the pupil in her right-eye never dilated, not even when he shined his light at it.

"I guess he's as confused as we are, but we're talking to my pediatrician tomorrow, so she'll tell me if I need glasses or not."
"That is really weird," Riley replied. Then, with the flip of a switch, Riley got very serious. She looked to make sure that no one was watching, and, using the back of her hand to hide her mouth, she pointed to Papa and his friends, and whispered, "But *nothing* is as weird as those dorky dads over there."

JEREMIAH T. BANNISTER

"Catch!" Kelly said as he tossed some Laffy Taffy to Papa. Kelly was Riley's dad, and he was the Fun Spot manager who hired Papa a few years earlier. They'd known each other for a while—or at least long enough for Kelly to get a handle on Papa's habit of always running late. "So, how is the best kids' skate DJ in GR feeling today?" he asked.

Papa laughed, but he was nervous, scrambling as fast as he could to prepare his playlist. "I dunno, bro, I've never met the guy."

Dan put his hand on Papa's shoulder. "Yeah, but that's probably because he's always late to work."

"That's a dirty-rotten rumor," Papa scoffed. And with a lift of his chin, he straightened his bowtie, and boasted, "It's also rumored he's a bona fide (and very dapper) gentleman."

"Oh, brother," Dan scoffed, and Kelly rolled his eyes.

All joking aside, Papa was predictably and perpetually late, but so long as he kept doing a great job every session, Kelly let it slide. And Dan, well, Dan was the man. At 6'2" and 300lbs, he was a huggable, loveable kind of guy. And he always sported a black and white striped shirt, the kind that made people wonder if he was a skate ref, at least until someone said:

"Nah, man. That guy?"

"Oooh, yeah, I remember. He's that dude who was slippin' and fallin' all over the place, right?"

SHE DANCED ME A STORY

Yeah, Dan was *that* dude, or at least he was when he first started skating. That was a few years ago, and Dan had become a great skater since then, but it was hard to forget a guy the size of a Pittsburg Steelers' lineman flopping and flailing around the rink. It was brutal. Kids snickered every time they saw him lying like a "dead bug" on the ground—and it went on like that for hours. Then, just when Papa worried that Dan was about to call it quits, he turned on the mic and cued up Survivor's "Eye of the Tiger."

"This one's for all you first-time skaters out there. I know skating is tough, and it's never fun to fall." With the sound of the song soaring in the background, he looked at Dan and said, "I promise, you will get better. You'll probably slip and fall, and you might even get hurt, but that's life, right? All you gotta do is give it your best, and like my daughter always says, 'Never give up—no matter what—and always remember—keep on smiling!'"

These three Musketeers were true blue buddies, all-weather friends, always waxing nostalgic about the "good old days" when songs were great, and it was still *en vogue* to skate. Most of all, they were family men, and there was nothing in the world that made them smile quite like the sight of their wives and children laughing and skating around the rink.

Kelly tossed another taffy to Papa, and said, "Well, let's hope you being dapper does the trick..." Then he walked away and shouted over his shoulder, "... because today is Tiny-Totz."

Papa froze, shocked that he had forgotten that it was Tiny-Totz! After all, it was one thing to be tardy, but it was the epitome of stupidity to be tardy for Tiny-Totz. Simply put, Tiny-Totz was the Fun Spot's special session for kids and first-time skaters, so the place would be packed with patrons and parties, all of them paying for five fantastic family-friendly hours at the Fun Spot. 'Twas the kind of crazy known to make grown men cry. Not Papa, though. No, he was made for moments like this...

... or so he thought.

"Can we have candy?" kids asked (*repeatedly*).

"No."

"Hey, mister, can you fix the arcade games?"

"No..."

"Yo, DJ, will you please play my very naughty & totally inappropriate song request?"

"No!"

It went like that for five whole hours, which would have been bad enough, but two employees called in sick, so Papa had to skip his lunch, and by the time he finally caught a break, the kitchen was closed for the day. He was so upset, and he feared he'd snap and lose his mind... but all those frustrations faded away every time he saw Sami skating.

Her clothes were a wild array of vibrant colors, and the lights sparkled like stars across the jewelry on her arms and neck. She looked like Punky Brewster, or better yet, a celestial Cindy Lauper, and today she wore some new blue blades with a golden phoenix emblazoned on the side. Sami soared wild and free. She was a diva true-to-form, her every move in harmony with the melody of the music, swinging and swaying her arms while singing along with all her favorite songs. She was beautiful to behold, with energy and elegance, gliding like a ghost across the gleaming maple floor. But she was tenacious, too, especially at the end of the day, when, like now, Kelly and Dan placed orange cones around the center of the rink, which could mean only one thing: Papa was about to say-

"IT'S TIME FOR FAST SKATE!"

Fast Skate was Sami's favorite, and she wasn't alone. True, most kids love games like Limbo, Dead Bug, and Freeze Tag—especially when you get them screaming at the top of their lungs for candy—but Fast Skate, *that* was the barn burner. Even the audience got into the action, kicking and shouting as they fought for seats along the wall, where they would cheer for their favorite in-house skaters. This was no kiddie race, either. It was the big shebang, risky business reserved for the most hardcore skaters at the rink, the real crème de la crème of the crop.

With only seconds to spare, Sami got in starting position, and with a ratta-tap-tap of her wheels to the floor, the rink transformed into an arena with a brilliant Rainbow Road, every plank aglow with colors spanning the spectrum, and each of them in sync with the sound of the song.

Then, with Dan's checkered flag raised high, Kelly nodded at Papa, who smiled to the skaters waiting for the whistle, then thundered into the microphone:

"Ready... Set... GO!"

SHE DANCED ME A STORY

The Fun Spot rocked and roared with excitement, and the building shook to its foundations when the audience leapt to its feet.

Mama worried, though, when she noticed that Sami was the only girl in the race.

"It's okay," Teresa assured her, "Sami beats boys all the time."

"Yeah, Mama," Ambrose added, "Sami is fast like Speedy Gonzales!"

"Speedy Gonzales?" Athan scoffed. "More like the DeLorean from *Back to the Future*!"

And he wasn't kidding! Sami flew like a phoenix, bright as lightning, and leaving tracks of fire flickering in the trails set ablaze in her wake. It was all so surreal... and yet it was here that something unsettling first appeared.

Papa had watched Sami skate hundreds of times, and like most rollerbladers, she had a certain style: arms held low, bent in at the elbow, always swinging in tandem with the cadence of her skates. He wondered, then, why Sami now raised her right-arm high overhead around the turns, or why her right-hand was curled-up in a funky kind of fist, all bent and turned out at the wrist.

It reminded him of something he'd seen many years before when a baby bird fell from its nest above their porch. The bird's bones were badly broken, and its little wing was withered from the fall, leaving it helpless and entirely unable to fly. The family had a funeral for it, as well as for its brothers and sisters, with five rocks being placed on their porch to honor their memory.

But quite unlike the baby bird, Sami was flying just fine, and her funny form didn't slow her down one bit, for by the midpoint of the race, Sami had flown from fifth- to fourth-, from fourth- to third-, and now a split second behind the boy in first place!

That was until...

click-clack-crack!

The crowd gasped when Sami's right-leg wobbled and slipped out from beneath her, which caused her to tumble face-first to the floor. She was so confused, and she thought she'd lost one of her wheels, but everything was fine—everything except the fact that she was now back in last place. Determined to win, she sprang to her feet, then-

CLICK-CLACK-CRACK!!

... she fell *again*, this time to her back. Tears streamed down her cheeks, though less from pain than sorrow and disappointment, and each time a tear dropped to the floor, a plank of Sami's Rainbow Road lost its glow. Everything in Sami's sight was a blur of shape and color, tracers in a world now locked in slow motion—even the cheers collapsed into a cacophony of eerie echoes, plaintive and hollow, and all of them fading so fast. Sami wiped her eyes and, looking up at the reflection in the disco ball gleaming and glimmering overhead...

... wherein she witnessed the world revolving 'round about her, and the disintegration of her dreamlike Rainbow Road.

Sami struggled to climb to her knees, and for a moment, she feared she was unable to stand, so she reached her hand toward the DJ booth and cried out in the loudest voice that her family had ever heard:

"PAPA! HELP ME!"

He leapt from his chair and into the air over the barrier, but before his feet even hit the floor, Sami shook her head, and with eyes as bright as a million suns, she yelled for him to stop. Everything inside of him wanted to help her, but Papa knew what she was thinking—and it was exactly what she needed to do. So, he waited, quietly listening for that grit of her teeth and the growling sound of grinding gears as the world between her ears returned to a shared sense of space and time.

"Get up," Papa whispered under his breath. Then he looked into Sami's bright blue eyes, pointed his finger toward the finish line, and shouted, "Don't you dare give up, Samantha Lee! Never, ever give up!"

The building shook like an earthquake when Sami stood to her feet, and the brilliant lights of Sami's Rainbow Road now shined with an almost otherworldly glow.

"You can do it!" Riley cheered, and the children chanted, "Go, Sami, go!" Then-

BOOM!!!

Sami blasted off like a fighter jet, and she must have felt like Goku from Dragonball Z, because her power level was way over nine thousand! The girl was full-blown supersonic, winding and weaving at break-neck speeds past all the other racers, who tumbled left and right and all around, being thrown to the ground by the sheer force of her velocity. She'd broken the sound barrier, so these kids didn't know what hit them, not until, moments later, the sound of her giggle finally reached their ears. And with sheets of sparkling light showering ten feet high in her wake, Sami was back, now skating neck-and-neck with a tall teenage boy. But time was ticking, and Dan raised his checkered flag, so she squinted her eyes and pressed her lips tight, taking that final turn lower than any turn she'd ever taken—so low that her long flowing hair brushed gently against the ground. And now, facing the final stretch, Sami glanced at the boy, and with a twinkle in her eye, she winked at him, then gave it all she had, pouring herself out (every drip of every drop) until, at last-

Dan shouted, "FIRST PLACE!"

The ending was picture perfect, and that rinky-dink roller rink in Nowhere, USA, roared with an applause that was heard from miles and miles away. For it was on that day that Sami did what no one thought was possible, finishing a mere nanosecond behind the teenage boy in first place.

Ambrose pushed his way through the crowd, then hugged his sister with all his might. "It was like the grand finale of everyone's favorite movie," he exclaimed.

"And you were *definitely* the superstar of the show," Teresa said.

"Really?" Sami replied, still trying her best to catch her breath. Then she laughed. "You guys know I lost, right?"

Athan scoffed and rolled his eyes. "Whatever, Sam, everyone knows you would've won if you didn't fall down." And with a menacing glare at the teenage boy who won, Athan slapped his fist and snarled under his breath, "You'll get him next time, Sami. Trust me."

SHE DANCED ME A STORY

+ One Hour Later—Back at Home +

After work, Papa went to the attic and chowed down a fistful of Cheez-It crackers. And while he sat there, thinking back to the baby bird's broken wing and the shock of Sami falling during Fast Skate, he heard, once again, that curious cadence in the sound of Sami's shoes upon the stairs.

"Speak of the devil," Papa said as Sami limped into the room.

"I just wanna tell you how much I love you before I go to bed."

"You love me, huh?"

Sami sat on his lap, then grabbed her right-wrist and lifted both hands over his head. With her fingers interlocked around the back of his neck, she cracked a half-smile, and with a lyrical and almost singsong voice, she said, "I love you, Papa... with all of my heart... into a million pieces."

"Then you gotta be real with me. I hate sayin' this, but I feel like you're hiding something from me, and it's kinda messed up, Sam."

Sami's eyes shot toward the floor, and she bit her bottom lip. "Nothing. Nothing is the matter. I guess I just fell, that's all."

"Then I guess you just fell twice, Sam. And I guess nothing made you cry for help, either, right? Everyone in the rink heard you say it. And now you're walking kinda funny."

"Yeah, well, maybe I'm walking funny because I fell. I bet you never thought about that."

Papa raised his hands in self-defense. "Whoooaaa, little horsy, you gotta slow up on that. And don't be mad at me for being worried. I'm your dad, and I love you like crazy, but I'd be lying straight to your face if I said I didn't feel you were hiding something from me."

Sami sighed. "I know... and you aren't entirely wrong. I'm sorry, too, because I don't want you to be mad at me. That is the only time I've ever fallen down that way, though, and it happened during Fast Skate, so I think I just got really confused." She reached with her right-hand for a chess piece on the floor, but she struggled to pick it up, so she switched to her left, then placed the white queen to her rightful square. "I wish I knew what was really going on," she said, still staring at the board. "At least then I'd stop being all scared and confused."

Sami tried being sly, so subtle and nonchalant, but Papa saw what she had done. He knew it was the same right-hand he'd seen earlier that day, all curled up like a broken wing. He reached out to grab hold of it, but Sami pulled away just as his fingers grazed across the skin of her wrist. Then, in an obvious attempt to change the subject, Sami swiveled on his knee and said, "Oh, my gosh, I'm such a dork! I totally wanted to show you something I learned to do. You won't believe how awesome it is, either, so I just know you'll be happy and proud of me when you see it."

Papa laughed and shook his head. "You can't even fathom how proud I am of you, Samantha." Then he tucked a strand of hair behind her ear. "You make me proud in a million different ways every single day—and you can bet I'll be proud of you forever."

Rarely had a truer truth been spoken, and yet nothing in all the world could have prepared Papa's heart for the terrible secret that Samantha Lee was about to confess...

IV

MONSTERS THRIVE
[In Lies of Hidden Hands]

+ Moments Later—In the Attic +

Sami hopped off Papa's lap, then limped to the shelf where he kept his fancy pens and leather journals. "You won't believe how awesome this is," she said as she selected what she knew to be his favorite diary. She sat across from him at the table, and with the pen cap between her teeth, she mumbled, "Look, Papa, I learned to write with my left hand."

Her writing was slow but smooth, and her penmanship was crisp and concise, even elegant, in both cursive and in print.

"Dang, girl, that's amazing," Papa exclaimed as he examined the page.

Overflowing with pride, Sami closed her eyes and smiled like a girl atop the world. "I worked so hard on that, Papa! It took me two whole weeks to do, and if you're proud of me, then that means my teacher will be proud of me again and won't be sad at me anymore."

"Pfft! You're the teachers' pet, Sam. Seriously, when has Mr. Levi ever been mad or sad at you?"

No sooner had he said those words, than a sudden and most dreadful sort of sadness cast its spell over Sami. It looked like the weight of the world was on her shoulders, and the silence in the room was broken only by the silent screams of her soft and subtle sighs.

"I'm just afraid you're gonna be surprised, Papa."

Papa was confused. "Why would you ever be afraid to surprise me?"

Sami squeezed tighter and tighter around her wrist. "I want to tell you... but I'm really scared you're just gonna be mad at me."

"I ain't mad yet," Papa laughed, anxiously. "But I'll be ticked if you don't tell me what the heck is goin' on." There was a tumultuous mix of fear and anger in his voice, and his eyes looked strained from the storm that was building deep inside. "You gotta level with me, Sam. Why do you think your teacher isn't proud of you anymore? And why do you think I'll be mad at your surprise? And what the heck does any of this have to do with you learning to write left-handed?"

Sami's chin dropped down to her chest, and her eyes vanished in shadows from the drapes of hair that hung in front of her face. "My teacher said my writing was sloppy, and he told me I should slow down, but I know that wasn't the problem because, even when I did what he told me to do, I still couldn't get the work turned in on time-and that made him even sadder about me." Sami paused a second, then shrugged her shoulders. "I guess I just thought that, if I could learn to write left-handed, then maybe all my problems would disappear."

Papa didn't reply right away, but she knew he was listening. She saw his jaw tighten as he was tossed to and fro in a torrent of fear and fury. And it was there, with Papa ensnared like a lamb in that thicket of logic and emotion betwixt the myriad reasons a father has for fighting or flying away, that Sami finally told him the truth...

"I'm so sorry, Papa... but my hand just doesn't work anymore."

"What do you mean it doesn't work anymore?"

Every one of his words were more intense than the last, and it frightened her a little, but Sami knew she had lied to him, and she had a feeling that things would only get worse—much worse—from here. It felt so good, though, for her to finally be honest, to no longer suffer in the silence and solitude of deceit. And she knew that was true, even if it meant she'd have to break Papa's heart.

"I mean... I haven't written right-handed for two weeks."

"NO!" Papa growled as he raised his fist—

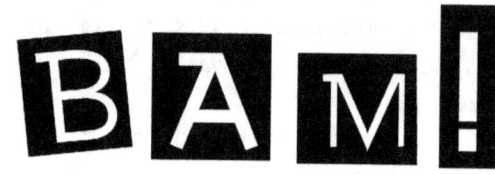

The chessboard bounced high off the table, and chess pieces flew all over the room. Sami watched them tumble, and she gazed down at a king that had fallen by her feet. "Please don't hate me," she begged. "My teacher said my new writing looks really good, and-"

"Dang it, Samantha Lee! He's not your dad. I am!" It sounded so preposterous, and he wondered if it was a prank, so he grabbed the pen and placed it on the table, demanding that Sami show him how she could still write with her right-hand.

She grabbed the pen with her left-hand, using it to place it in her right, but she held it like people hold darts or paper airplanes. He thought she was putting on an act, especially after he saw the way she wrote.

"You gotta be freakin' kidding me!" he snarled as he snatched the paper off the table. "There's no way you're being serious. Look at this crap—it's nothing but chicken scratches! This is obviously a joke, Sam, and it's not very funny."

He was right. She hadn't written a single legible word. He was frantic now, wildly searching through all his pockets. When he found his wallet, he pulled out an old and wrinkled piece of paper, tattered and torn from years of wear and tear. "Do you recognize this?" he asked.

Sami nodded. "Yes, Papa. It's the letter I wrote that told you how proud I am of stuff you do, and how you should never give up on your dreams... I didn't even know you still had that."

> Dear Jeremiah Thomas Bannister,
>
> I love you sooooooooo much I hope that you don't fail in your talking. You are really funny at times, you make really funny faces and you make funny voices. I love your singing I know I don't say that alot but I should. You are a very special person. Everyone is and you have a very special talent, and that's your voice. Your good at talking to children, talking at places, and your singing.
>
> I love you!
>
> Sincerely
> Samantha
> Lee
> Bannister

"Of course, I do—I've carried it in my wallet for years!" He slid the letter across the table. "Now look at it, Sam. Look good, too, because THAT is your handwriting." And with his finger pressed hard against the paper, he squinted his eyes, and in a very slow, demanding voice, he commanded her to write one... more... time.

Sami fought like mad to hide her fear, but her fingers had taken on a life of their own, and she knew they couldn't write anymore. She bit her lip and raised her chin, determined to do her best, but the hair fell away from her face, and now, with her eyes laid bare under the tungsten light, Papa saw tiny tears streaming down her cheeks. They were tender, and they twinkled in the light... but did they tell the truth?

SHE DANCED ME A STORY

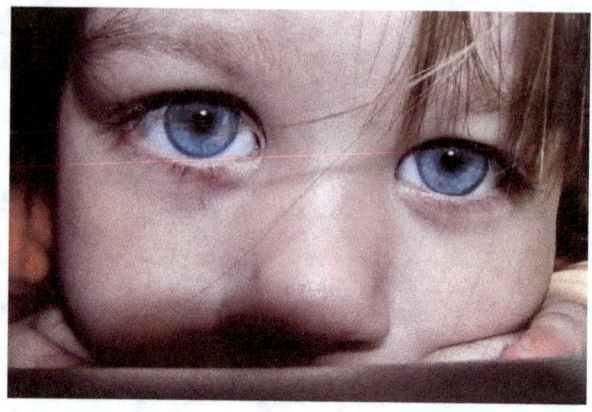

Papa looked into her eyes, as he was sure they never lied, and much to his surprise, they were sad, and they shimmered with sincerity. Worst of all, they were scared. He had been so confused, confused about the eye that wouldn't dilate, the curious cadence of her shoes as she limped up the stairs, and the broken wing of the baby bird as she flew around the turns... none of it made sense, and it had been driving him mad.

But now, in the madness of this moment, Papa stumbled upon the source of Sami's troubles—and he found it in a teardrop dangling on the end of her chin. It wiggled and wobbled as it hung on for dear life, but nothing could withstand the gravity of the situation... tugging... pulling... dragging it closer to the edge. Then... he exhaled, and his breath traveled across the table, nudging the tear just enough to make it fall from Sami's chin. And as it fell, Papa's eyes grew wide with terror. For, there, in the twinkle of that tiny tear, he beheld a terrible triad—the deadliest of all life's cruelest constellations...

BANG!

Sami's pen fell straight into the puddled remains of the tear that dropped from her chin. And with her face buried into her hand, she wept and cried aloud, "It's my fault! This is all my fault!" She begged him to forgive all those things she'd done and all those things she had failed to do. And she admitted that she was afraid. "But most of all, I just love you, Papa. And I promise I'll never lie to you or to anyone ever again."

Papa knew an act of contrition when he heard one, and he wished he had the power to absolve, but all he could offer was his heart.

He reached over the chessboard to hold Sami's hands, and in a soft and sympathetic voice, he said "Look, I don't know what's going on, but whatever it is, we can-"

GASP

Sami saw the whites of his eyes when, for the very first time, Papa felt what she was hiding. Her hand felt boneless, entirely limp, and it would have felt completely lifeless were it not for the twitch of her wrist and the spasms of her fingers... little spasms that caused her hand to curl into a fist.

"Do you know what's wrong with me?" Sami whimpered.

Papa just sat there, staring at her hand. He wished he hadn't doubted her, and he regretted making her write, but he hated himself most for having gotten mad. He slowly raised his head, and with calming breaths between his words, he said, "Go downstairs... tell Mama to get the kids ready... we gotta go..."

"But what should I say if Mama asks where we're going?"

"Tell her to call Paul..." he continued undisturbed, "we gotta go to the hospital..."

"The hospital?" Sami gasped. "If you know what's the matter with me, will you please just tell me?"

But Papa kept talking in that distant, droning tone. "Don't stop... don't fight... don't eat or go to the bathroom... just go straight to Mama. And tell her to call Paul..."

Sami limped as she rushed to leave the room, and with the fading sound of that curious cadence from her shoes on the stairs, Papa sat back in his chair, and with water welling up in his eyes, he recalled that terrible triad in Sami's tear:

RIGHT-LEG...
RIGHT-EYE...
RIGHT-HAND...

It was a monster... and it was in the left-side of Sami's brain.

V

ROSES & REDWOODS
[Day One at Helen DeVos]

Sami had never been inside of Helen DeVos Children's Hospital, but she always loved the way it looked, especially at sunset. It was huge, standing over 10 stories tall, and the whole building looked like it was made of shiny blue mirrors, allowing people to see the city in its reflection as they passed by. And best of all, that's where Paul worked.

Paul was all sorts of wild and zany, a real child at heart, and like the Bannisters, he loved TV shows like *Doctor Who* and *Sherlock*. Plus, Paul played video games, and he knew a lot about Pokémon, so life was endless fun when Paul was around. But he was a worry-worm, too, so when the family pulled into the parking lot, they found him pacing and puffing like a chimney on his e-cig.

"What's going on? Is Sami okay?? Is there anything I can—???"

"Yooooooooo, bro," Papa laughed.

"Whaaaaaaaat?" Paul replied.

Papa put his hand on Paul's shoulder, and with a cool and calming smile, he said, "I just wanna say I love you, bro." It was a blatant attempt to tranquilize Paul—even just to stop his rambling—but it worked.

Paul took a huge, calming breath. "Whew! Okey-dokey, so now that we've got all *that* craziness outta the way, will someone please tell me what the heck is going on?"

Mama helped Sami out from the car and sat her down in a wheelchair outside the Emergency Room. "We just need some help with the kids, just in case Sami has to spend the night."

"It shouldn't be hard," Papa said. "They've been crazy busy all day, so if you feed them, they'll probably pass out on their own"

"Especially if you read us a story," Teresa said as she yawned and wiped her eyes.

"It just depends on what the doctors find," Mama said, "but there's a chance they'll keep her overnight, and if they do, we'll need more help."

Paul watched with Papa as Mama wheeled Sami toward the door. "Dude, you know I'll do anything for your family, all you gotta do is ask."

"Then you better record the new episode of Doctor Who!" Sami shouted from over her shoulder. "We were supposed to watch that tonight, remember?"

"How could I forget?" Paul yelled back at her. And with a cross over his heart, he promised he wouldn't watch it until Sami got home, then he hugged Papa goodbye, and drove the kids back home.

Inside, nurses hurried to take Sami's vitals, then they placed her on a hospital bed and rushed her toward the MRI, which was in a winding maze of dark hallways deep within the underbelly of the hospital.

"It feels like a dungeon down here," Sami whispered to Mama, "all quiet and creepy."

Not everything was scary, though. Sami saw motivational messages in the halls, playful paintings of funny fish swimming on the walls, and there were huge multicolor tubes bustling with bubbles near the service desk. Still, it was kinda creepy, at least at night and in the dark, so everyone was relieved when Sami was finally assigned a room. But then, just as they were settling in, Mama got a message from one of Sami's friends.

"It's Gladys," she said as she typed her reply. "Her family drove 30 minutes to visit, and they even brought you a present." Mama paused, and in a nervous, drawn-out voice, she said, "Buuuuut..."

"But what?" Sami asked.

"Buuuuut visiting hours are over. I guess security told them that one of us has to go to the front lobby if we want to pick up your present."

Then, with the kind of precision that comes only with years of practice, Mama and Sami turned their heads toward Papa at the exact same time.

Papa looked around the room, then pointed at himself. "Who, me? Yeah, right, like I'm gonna retrace my steps through all those creepy halls. And what's up with that whole head-turn at the same time voodoo? Are you two practicing that maneuver behind my back or what?"

"Stop being such a fraidy cat," Sami said.

Papa didn't like this at all, but that's *exactly* what he was: a fraidy cat! He feared things like the dark... and lightning... and spiders... and tornadoes... and deep water... and of being lost and alone. And being alone was the worst of them all: he hated being alone, especially in the dark. It was ridiculous, but whenever he found himself spending the night alone in the house, he'd open every closet, check behind all the curtains, and turn on every light in every room just to make sure that no one else was there. Then, at bedtime, he'd play a G-rated movie or cartoon just so he could sleep.

"Yeah, you're totally a fraidy cat," Mama said while playfully petting his head.

"You two are so rude."

"Pretty-please, Papa?" Sami begged with puppy dog eyes.

"No way, José! Not after you guys just made fun of me!"

Papa thought he'd thrown down the gauntlet, but he ought to have known better, since Sami was sure to wage an all-out-war. In the arms race between little girls and their dads, the dads are always one step behind—and Sami knew that. But she also knew that Papa would do almost anything not to leave her side, so she just cut to the chase and, unleashing the biggest guns in her arsenal, she fluttered her extra-long lashes, and said, "But you know I love you soooo much." Her pouty lip was unreal, and there was a cute little whimper in her voice, but it's what she said next that was the nail in the coffin.

"You know I would, Papa... *if I could*."

Mama didn't need to look up from her knitting to see that Papa was bleeding out all over the place. He pretended to be terribly unimpressed, but there was no coming back from that. Sami went for the jugular, and all that was left for Papa to do was to stand up and head out the door.

As he was leaving, Papa turned around, and with a smirk on his face, he winked, and said, "Honestly, Sam, you had me at 'pretty-please.'"

The lobby was dark, lit only by those bubbling multicolored tubes, and the only sound around was that of a security guard, who was laughing with a woman at the front desk. But even if the place was pitch black and packed with people, it wouldn't have been hard to know that Gladys was around. It never was. A tall Native American girl with an award-winning smile (and the most boisterous laugh in town), Gladys was one of a kind. She always managed to find herself at the center of attention—or if she was lucky, right smack dab in the middle of some good old-fashioned mischief.

"Hey, Mr. B," she said as she stood from her seat. "Is Sami okay?"

Papa waved for her to sit down, then sat across from her at the table. "That's what we're here to find out, but we won't know anything until at least tomorrow morning."

SHE DANCED ME A STORY

"Ugh. Why does everything have to wait until tomorrow?" Gladys cast a grumpy glance toward the security guard, then made an icky face and stuck her tongue out at him. "Only family after 10 p.m. Hmph! That security guard is such a rude jerk..." A rascally smile crept across her face. "You know, you could always tell them I'm your *other* daughter."

Papa waved to her family, who were sitting on a couch about twenty feet away. "I'm pretty sure the security guard figured out who your parents are."

"Grrr..." Gladys groaned as she dropped her head to the table. "Oh, yeah, sorry, I guess I forgot just how *not* fun you are, Mr. B." She raised her head, and without saying a word, she reached her hand into a decorative bag on the floor by her feet. "I bought it from a store on the way here. I even paid for it with my own money." It was a pinkish-red rose, still in maturation, and it was bundled in Baby's Breath. "Sami loves flowers, and she's as beautiful as a rose to me." Her voice cracked from getting all choked up. "It's Sami's favorite color, too, so I thought it was perfect."

Gladys looked so helpless and sad, and Papa knew she was scared for her BFF, so he tried his best to comfort her. "Sami loves this color, Gladys. It's perfect." Then he chuckled. "You know, it always reminds me of Sami's cheeks whenever you make her laugh."

"I thought that same thing," Gladys said. The thought made her laugh a little, but it didn't last long. "I need to go back home, Mr. B, but I need to tell you something first, and you have to promise to tell Samantha."

"I promise," he replied with his fingers raised in Scout's Honor.

"No, Mr. B, I know I can joke around a lot, but I'm really serious right now..." Tears welled up in her dark brown eyes, and her emotions made it hard for her to talk. "Sami is my best friend in all the world, and I'm just scared, you know, and I just hope she'll be okay." She used her sleeve to wipe tears from her face, then looked at the moon shining brightly through the window. "So... I mean... well... will you just tell her that no matter what happens, I promise with all my heart to always love her, and that I'll always be her friend?"

Papa nodded, then the two of them stood to their feet, and after a tearful hug, he waved and said goodbye to Gladys and her family. He was almost to the exit when Gladys turned around, and shouted, "I know you're scared, too, but you're Sami's dad, and she loves you and the family like crazy, so you gotta be like a redwood tree, cuz they're strong and tall. It's what your family wants to see... and it's what Sami needs."

"You're more than a friend, Gladys," Papa shouted back. "You're ohana!"

Gladys smiled. "Ohana forever, Mr. B."

Walking back toward that dark and dreary hallway, Papa stumbled upon a sign, and the headline grabbed his attention. It read: *U.S. News & World Report ranks Helen DeVos Children's Hospital in Three Specialties*. Then his eyes scrolled to the bottom of the sign, where he saw three words: *Urology, Nephrology, and Cancer*. That third one hit him hard, and he shuddered at the thought. He'd never met a kid with childhood cancer before, and he couldn't even imagine what life would be like for families that had to deal with that, but he'd seen them on TV, and the commercials always made him cry. *That'd be the scariest thing in all the world!* he thought. Wiping his head, he let out a sigh of relief, and said, "I bet all those families are so grateful to have a hospital like Helen Devos right here in town..."

With these thoughts in mind, Papa closed his eyes, then smelled the rose one last time, and with a smile in his heart, he bravely re-entered the dark labyrinthian halls that would lead him back to his daughter...

VI

VITALS! VITALS!
[Everything is Vital]

+ The Following Morning—at Helen DeVos +

Beams of light splashed through the shades, showering warmth and light across Mama's extravagant Asian eyes. The sun had served her faithfully for many years, and its silent song never failed to summon her from a full night's sleep. But this morning was different... and Mama was already wide-awake.

"Get up, Jeremiah," she whispered. "You gotta hurry and get dressed. The nurse said the doctors will be here any minute."

"Oh, trust me, I know," Papa yawned, propping himself up on his elbows. "I was too tired to get undressed, and I was so nervous, I struggled to stay asleep..."

"Yeah, me too..."

"Meeeee threeeeee," Sami whispered, playfully.

"Oh, come on!" Mama laughed. "How can you be awake right now?"

"Probably for the same reasons you guys are. And how am I supposed to sleep, anyway, with all those nurses waking me up every hour?"

"They woke you up *every hour?*" Papa asked.

"Yes, and it was terrible, too. They just kept saying, 'we gotta get your vitals, we gotta get your stupid vitals.'"

Papa's back hurt from sleeping in that chair, and he felt like an old man trying to stand up. "At least you have a comfy bed. Seriously, what kind of sicko made these chairs? They're the worst. And for hospitals? No way, that ain't even right!" It's true, hospitals should stop buying such terribly uncomfortable chairs. Papa began to tell a crazy story he had concocted about the kind of weirdos who think those chairs are perfect for hospitals, but his diatribe was interrupted by a soft and subtle knock on the door.

"Did we catch you at a bad time?" a woman asked as she peeked into the room. She was short, blonde, and very pretty, and a tall and smartly dressed man accompanied her. "My name is Dr. Kurt, and this is Dr. Pridgeon. If you wouldn't mind, we'd like you to join us in the conference room to discuss the results of Samantha's MRIs."

"Am I allowed to go, too?" Sami asked.

"I'm sorry, Samantha," Dr. Kurt replied, sympathetically, "but I think your nurse needs to take your vitals, and-"

"Vitals? Aw, come on! Give it a break already, why don't ya."

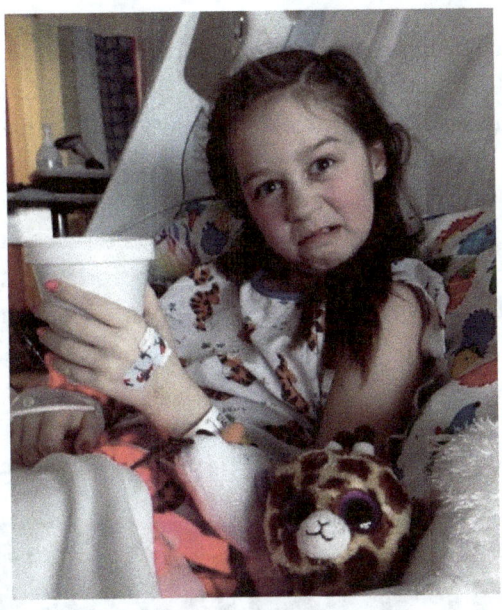

Dr. Kurt scrunched her face a little. "I know vitals are no fun, but they let everyone know how you're doing, so they're very important."

"That's right," Papa said. And with an overly dramatic seriousness, he added. "Cuz vitals are VITALLY important."

"Woooow," Sami scoffed, "you just won the 'Worst Joke of All-Time' award in the Guinness Book of World Records."

"If it makes you feel better," Dr. Kurt said as she opened the door, "while we're gone, food service will find out what you want for breakfast. But if you're not in the room when they get here, they'll think you just want some icky oatmeal."

SHE DANCED ME A STORY

Sami squinted her eyes. "Hmmm... I'll believe you this time, Dr. Kurt, but they better get my order STAT, cuz I'm dyin' over here!"

The walk to the conference room was a hustle and bustle of sound and commotion as nurses huddled with doctors for morning rounds, kitchen staff delivered their meals, and Child Life volunteers roamed room-to-room with gifts boxes—a few of them even had therapy dogs. Unlike the night before, the hospital felt so happy, so bright, and so alive...

... then Dr. Kurt sighed and closed the door to the conference room.

"We have Sami's results," she said, "but first let us express how truly sorry we are."

"And rest assured that our very best doctors will work with Sami and your family throughout this entire process," Dr. Pridgeon added.

Mama grabbed Papa's hand, terrified by the implication underlying their assurances. "What's wrong? Is Sami going to be okay?"

Dr. Kurt pressed her lips as she unwrapped the string from around the seal of a manila envelope. She removed Sami's scans and placed them neatly on the table. Mama and Papa had never seen an MRI before, or at least not one like this. Dr. Kurt told them that the image on the left was from another patient. "This is an image of what we'd expect to see in a healthy brain," she said. Then she directed Mama and Papa's attention to the image on the right.

"And these are Sami's results..."

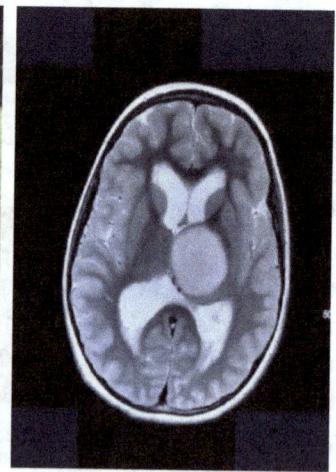

"As you can see, a rather large mass has developed in the base of Sami's brain. It's in a region of the brain known as the thalamus."

Mama's eyes grew wide, and she squeezed Papa's hand so tight that it started to hurt him. "The thalamus? What is that? And what do you mean by a mass?"

Papa knew what those words meant, though...

"It means Sami has a brain tumor," he sighed.

Her nostrils flared as she whimpered, "Cancer? But how is that possible?!?! Sami's only 10-years-old!"

"Childhood cancer is very rare," Dr. Pridgeon assured her, "but Sami's not alone."

"The mass is very large," Dr. Kurt continued, "about the size of a golf ball, but until we get the biopsy report and follow-up MRIs, we won't know for certain. When we get the reports, our Tumor Board will decide how best to proceed."

"But I cook healthy food at home!" Mama protested, her lips trembling with the disbelief of denial and despair. "And it's not like she smokes or anything! I mean, c'mon, she's just a kid!!!"

Dr. Kurt consoled her, assuring them that Helen DeVos had some of the best childhood oncologists in the United States.

"And we'll introduce you to our neurosurgeon later today," Dr. Pridgeon said.

"Jeremiah?!" Mama howled. "Tell me this isn't real! Please, God, tell me Sami doesn't really have cancer!"

"I know this is hard," Dr. Kurt said in a kind and comforting voice, "but I promise that we will do everything we can to help Sami and your family." Dr. Kurt passed Mama a box of tissues. "I'll break the news to Sami around lunchtime, okay?"

Dr. Pridgeon nodded in agreement, saying, "Dr. Kurt did her residence at St. Jude's. She's very good with children, so-"

"No!!!" Papa interrupted with a grizzly growl. His teeth were grinding, and he clenched his fists so hard that his fingernails almost cut through the palm of his hand. He took a breath, trying to maintain his composure, and softly said, "What I mean is, please... I think we should be the ones to tell Sami about her results." The doctors were reluctant, but Papa wasn't really asking their permission, and there was no way he would budge, so they wrapped up their meeting and gave Mama and Papa some privacy.

SHE DANCED ME A STORY

When they were gone, Papa wiped away Mama's tears, and with their hearts and hands entwined, the two re-entered those bright and joyous halls of Helen DeVos.

+ The Hallway Outside of Sami's Room +

"Mama! Papa!!" the kids shouted as they rushed to hug them.

Papa knelt on one knee, and with all the kids in his arms, he asked them how their evening went.

"Athan kept asking if you guys had any updates," Paul replied, "and all of them said they were too sad and scared to sleep alone, so I just let them sleep on you and Ang's bed."

Ambrose chuckled. "Yeah, but Paul is so good at reading stories to us, we just fell asleep right away."

"Paul even stood on the bed to take a picture of us," Athan said. "He thought it would make you and Mama happy to see that we were okay."

Teresa pulled her thumb out of her mouth and wiped it on her jeans. "Yeah, but now we're having fun with Sami in her room," "And it's a lot of fun in there because tons of people sent Sami a bunch of toys and flowers and stuff."

"What are you guys doing out here in the hallway, then?" Mama asked.

"Sami told the nurse she had to use the bathroom," Paul replied, "so she asked for some privacy. I think I heard the door open, though, so you guys can probably go in." Then he looked more closely at Mama. Her face was flush from crying, and she was still wiping her tears. "Hey, man," Paul whispered to Papa, "what did the doctors say? Is Sami gonna be okay?"

Papa didn't say a word, but the sadness in his eyes told Paul more than enough. He told the kids and Paul to wait outside for a few minutes, then reached for the door, but before he could turn the handle, Mama began to weep and sob aloud. Everyone in the hallway agonized for her, and the sudden outburst left the kids scared and confused, so Papa hurried and wrapped his arms around her, and Paul and the kids did too.

"I just don't think I can handle it," Mama cried as Papa ran his fingers through her hair. "I'm just afraid I'll make things worse because of all of my emotions." She looked at Papa, and pleaded with him, "Can you do this, Jeremiah? I'm begging you, please..."

He looked her in the eyes and nodded in agreement, which made Mama cry even harder. She thanked him over and over again, hugging and kissing him all over his face. Then, with one last sniffle, Papa told her he loved her, then reached for the door, and calmly entered Sami's room...

VII

"DON'T WORRY ABOUT ME [TOO MUCH]..."

+ Alone With Sami—in Her Room +

Teresa wasn't kidding! Sami's room really was filled to the brim with bright and beautiful presents. Near the window were red roses, pink carnations, and Sami's favorite flower, Stargazer lilies. And her bed was covered in stuffed animals, including a pink and purple owl with a bow and bright green eyes, as well as a rainbow-colored cat from the Build-A-Bear Workshop—the cat even had two hearts like Doctor Who.

"I guess people really love me," Sami laughed as she exited the bathroom. "A bunch of 'em said they read about me on your Facebook."

"It looks like Toys-R-Us in here," Papa laughed. His laughter turned to terror, however, when he realized the real reason Sami asked for privacy. Her limp had worsened dramatically, and her spine looked like it was the shape of a question mark. She could no longer walk on her own, either, so, with her left arm slung over the nurse's shoulder, Sami slowly dragged her foot across the floor... one small and very difficult step at a time.

The nurse helped her to the bed, and as she left the room, she promised Sami that she'd be back in an hour to check her vitals again.

"Vitals??" Sami shouted at the door. "Seriously, Papa, vitals are even worse than the eggs here—and let me tell you, the eggs in this place are icky gross!" Then Sami smiled and licked her lips. "But they can do vitals all day for all I care, at least as long as they keep bringing me Pop-Tarts."

Papa stood by her bedside, quietly looking at Sami. She smiled so big, and her eyes were filled with light. They looked so innocent, so fragile, and yet so filled with childlike faith, that Papa feared they'd shatter like snow globes under the pressure of what he had to say. He sat on the edge of the bed and took hold of Sami's hand...

"Hey, Papa, what did Dr. Kurt say about my MRI?"

A deluge of dread rained over his head, and his heart wished to whisk her away, to cast off in an ark to that pleasant place where love and life remain unscathed. But Fates are brutal, and they'd cast their lots, so he closed his eyes to remember what he must be: a redwood tree, for Sami and the family. He envisioned a trunk so big and so broad that a B-52 could fly through. And with roots deep and branches wide, he was sturdy and stable, and now as tall as the sky. So, he kissed Fate's die, then held Sami's hand, asking, "Do you trust me, Sam?"

Her chin quivered as she said, "I trust every word you say, and I trust it all the time because you never lie..." Then she giggled. "Well, you don't lie to me, at least not on purpose, anyway."

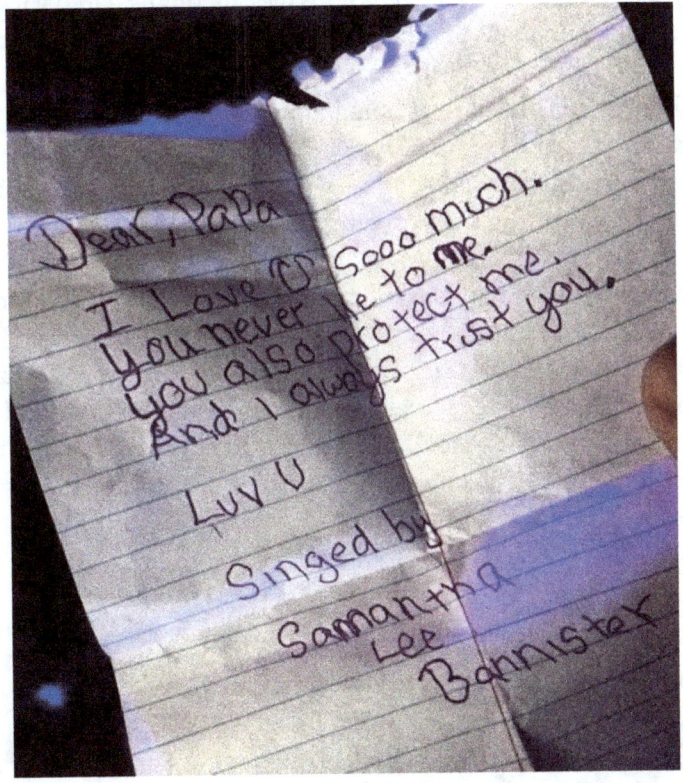

Papa tried to contain his emotions, but tears poured out of his eyes, and with the most gut-wrenching pain in the timbre of his voice, he uttered the words:

"You have cancer in your brain, Samantha."

Sami's eyes trembled, and her face paled with terror.

He pointed toward the base of his neck, saying, "It's in the back of your brain, in an area called the thalamus."

"What is the tha-la-mus?" Sami asked, nervously.

"It's a part of your brain that controls a lot of things, like the way we move our bodies, even stuff our bodies do without thinking about it."

"Do you think that's maybe why my eye wouldn't dilate?"

Papa nodded. "And it's why you had a hard time writing. I think that's why you fell at the rink too... and why you needed help walking to the bathroom." Papa hated every word that came out of his mouth, but he hated what came next even more. "It can mess with our memories, and it can affect stuff like sight and sound, taste and touch, even breathing and sleep."

"But that stuff is just part of being a person—just part of being alive—and my memories help make me who I am."

"I know," Papa groaned through his teeth. "And it's getting worse, Sami... cuz your cancer is growing bigger really fast."

Sami breathed heavily, and for a moment she felt aware, even sensitive to those things she had always taken for granted. She listened closely to every one of Papa's words. He talked about brain surgeries, as well as her future with chemo and radiation. Then, when he said there were different kinds of cancer, her eyebrows raised. "Well, I really hope my cancer isn't one of those bad kinds!" she said. But through it all, there was really only one thing on her mind, so when it sounded like Papa was finished, she squeezed her Build-A-Bear cat and asked him the saddest question he had ever heard:

"Papa... am I going to die?"

He growled and shook his head. "You better not die, Samantha Lee! Don't you dare! You hear me?? Not on *my* watch!"

Sami wiped her nose on her wrist. "I believe you, Papa, and I really believe every word you say to me, so make me a promise..."

Then, with tears streaming down her face, she begged, "Just promise you'll always be by my side. And no matter what, you're not allowed to lie to me—not ever, okay? Promise! Cuz this is my life, you know, and just because I'm a kid doesn't mean I'm not allowed to know the truth about stuff like this."

Papa raised his right-hand and swore a solemn oath. "You have my word, baby—forever! Scientific honesty, no matter what."

"Even if it's super-scary and really hard to talk about?" she insisted.

"*Especially* if it's super-scary and really hard to talk about."

Sami laid the pig on her lap, then tucked a tress of hair behind her ear. "Alright, then just one more thing. You're a warrior person—that's why I tell people you're the Hercules of radio—so you gotta swear you'll never stop fighting for me."

Papa laughed a little, and he playfully thumped his chest like King Kong, but then he got serious, saying, "You can't even imagine the great and terrible things I would do, Samantha... the dark and dreadful depths I would descend to try and help you. I mean, you're my daughter, obviously, but you're more than that, ya know. You're one of my all-time favorite friends, and I promise I'll prove it to you every day."

She trusted every syllable that came out of his mouth, but she saw Mama hugging Paul and the kids in the hall, and it broke her heart. She saw their fear in their chins, which quivered with dread for the 10-year-old girl dying of cancer in the hospital bed. She thought of others too, even the people who sent the presents, and she imagined what they'd feel like when Papa told them she had cancer. So, just as Papa reached for the door, she asked him for one last favor.

"Can you make a video of me saying thank you to everybody? You know, just to thank everyone for all the stuff they sent me?"

She wanted to make it look like that scene where E.T. hides a mountain of stuffed animals in Elliott's closet, so Papa worked hard on the set, then started to record...

The whole thing felt so strange, and with Sami smiling through his camera, he couldn't help but be blown away. Here she was, having just discovered that she had cancer, and yet her cheeks were rosy with cheer, and her big blue eyes beamed with delight, grateful to just be alive. But then, without warning, Sami paused... and with a soft squeeze to her hand, she did something that would forever change the course of their lives:

SHE DANCED ME A STORY

She went off-script.

"I hope you're not too worried about me, everyone. I'll do okay, I promise. And I'll make sure... that I'll do fine."

"A lot of people love you; you know."

"Mm-hm," Sami hummed with a smile on her face.

"And you love a lot of people, don't you, baby?"

She nodded, and with a peace that surpassed all of Papa's understanding, Sami waved, and said, "Goodbye!"

The kids came rushing in, and Mama and Paul sat with Sami on the bed while Papa told everyone on Facebook what they had learned. He struggled to convey the profundity of their predicament, and there were no words that could truly express how he felt. It was infuriating, so unjust and unfair, yet there she was, smiling and carrying on, loving life and caring for others. And, so, he typed:

I JUST TOLD SAMI SHE HAS CANCER, AND WHAT DOES SHE DO? SHE SMILES AT THE SHADOW OF DEATH, ONLY CRYING OVER THE PROSPECT OF LOSING HER HAIR, AND EVEN THEN, SHE MERELY ASKS TO MAKE A VIDEO EXPRESSING HER GRATITUDE, AND TO ENCOURAGE PEOPLE NOT TO WORRY TOO MUCH. IT WAS BEYOND BAFFLING—IT WAS A WHOLE NEW LEVEL OF AWESOME! AND NOW, COME TO THINK OF IT, SAMI NEVER ONCE ASKED, 'WHY ME?'

"What are you typing?" Sami asked as she tossed a shiny "Get Well" balloon into the air.

"I'm writing a warning to everyone."

Sami froze for a second, but then the balloon bonked her on the head. "A warning?"

Papa laughed. "Yeah, I'm warning everybody that they better have a box of tissues when they watch your video."

Sami bounced the balloon on her index finger. "Do you really think that people will see my video, Papa?"

"Oh, you don't even know," he replied beneath his breath. Then, just when he was about to press Enter, he glanced up at Sami, watching as she smiled and pet her Build-A-Bear cat, then he typed:

ACTUALLY, YOU BETTER MAKE THAT *TWO* BOXES OF TISSUES!

Once it was posted online, he put his phone in his pocket, and with a paradoxical peace pounding like a jackhammer in his heart, he smiled, and thought to himself...

And thus, it begins...

section ii:

**AS IT IS NOW
[IN HER ORBIT]**

+ (LIFE, WITH CANCER) +

Tempus Fugit
[IN THE FOG OF WAR]
Part II of IV

+ In The Quiet Zone—Summer Solstice 2017 +

Papa's exhale was painful, and he coughed so hard, he almost puked. He'd been adrift for so long, and he'd tried his best to smile, but life just wasn't the same... and now he was lost in a sea of sorrow and smoke.

The books in the room provided him solace, with titles filled with words penned by the likes of Homer, Dante, Keats, and Marcus Aurelius. He considered them his personal friends, sages of the ages always crooning his favorite tunes. But, like Sami, they were dead, so they weren't singing new songs anymore. The drugs helped a little, or at least that's what he thought. Every hit was like a fresh gust of wind in his sail, bringing back to life those faithful friends, all dead and gone, who'd long been buried in the depths of his heart. But his head was tattered, there were holes in his jib, and he'd been adrift without a compass for years.

He exhaled again, blowing the smoke at the drooping balloons in the corner of the room, and the sight of their flight made him smile, but these moments were as fleeting as his breath, and the gravity of the situation weighed heavy on their hull. The whole thing made him laugh, imagining them to be even worse off than his boat, but then he sighed, for unlike the balloons, Papa was a man, and thinking back to a conversation with Mama, he cried, recognizing that his woes were the work of his own hands...

+ Six Months Prior –the "Great Spring" of 2017 +

"You know you're gonna be late," Mama said. He had an important speaking engagement that night, but he had gotten distracted with a debate he'd been having online. Then he spent an extra fifteen minutes with a lively interviewer, so now he was running late. "They're paying you, too, Jeremiah, so maybe you should be more punctual."

"Meh," he replied, still trying to fix his tie, "at least I'll look good."

SHE DANCED ME A STORY

Mama stood behind him, resting her chin on his shoulder as she watched him in the mirror.

"Ugh!" he grumbled as he furiously unraveled his tie. "That's gotta be, like, the fifteenth time I've done that! Seriously, what's wrong with me?"

Mama spun him around and started working on his tie. He'd been in the Navy, and he was the kid with ties and briefcases in grade school, but once he got a good knot in a tie, he'd leave it there for years, always afraid he would be unable to tie another one just as good as the last. When she was done, she looked at him and noticed his hair was unkempt. She used her finger to pull back a wavy lock of hair that hung wildly over his eyes, then whispered, "You always need my help, don't you?"

"I do that on purpose, you know."

Mama pressed her hands against his chest and gazed up at him. "Oh, you do, huh?"

"Mmm..." he hummed, flirtatiously, as he wrapped his arms around her waist. "Of course, I do. It's a ploy to get you to run your fingers through my hair."

Mama laughed half-heartedly, then patted his chest. "Well, I worry about you, Jeremiah."

"What? About my hair??"

"No," she laughed. "I mean, yeah, your hair is always a wreck, but that's just you. No, I worry because it's like you always have something going on—and I'm worried that it's getting the best of you."

"Whatchu talkin' 'bout, woman?" Papa laughed as he laced up his tri-tone wingtips. "Life is freakin' dope right now. Seriously, Ang, just think about it. The radio show is rocking like crazy, our Facebook is on fire, and our calendar is packed with public speeches."

He wrapped his laces around the ankle of his boot, then double-knotted them through the loop on the back of his Docs, leaving the strings to hang near the middle of his heel. "Seriously, how are we not doing better than ever right now?"

SHE DANCED ME A STORY

Mama draped her arms around his neck, and with her ear pressed close to his heart, she sighed. She knew those things he said were true, and all of it was well and good, at least insofar as it went.

"But there's more to our lives than that stuff, Jeremiah. I mean it, too. I'm worried about you. And it isn't just you. I worry about all of us... me... you... the kids... even Sami... it just feels like–"

"I know what you're saying, Ang. And, trust me, I get it. Okay, so we're runnin' around with our hair on fire, but you gotta believe me, there isn't nothing wrong. I mean it, there ain't nothin' to worry about, Ang."

Mama heard what he said, but she couldn't bring herself to believe him. And while she knew that the sudden squeeze of his hug was meant to emphasize the underlying certainty of his assurance, there was a terrible tremble in his arms, and beneath the soothing timbre of his voice, Mama heard the bipolar rhythm in the war drum of his heart, and she shuddered at the sound of his double-negatives...

+ BACK IN THE QUIET ZONE +

With plumes of smoke in the room and the memory of Mama's loving embrace consuming him, Sami's balloons bobbed like a sinker with a fish on the line, begging him to "Get Well Soon!"

VIII

FOX, FRIENDS, AND FR. SIRICO

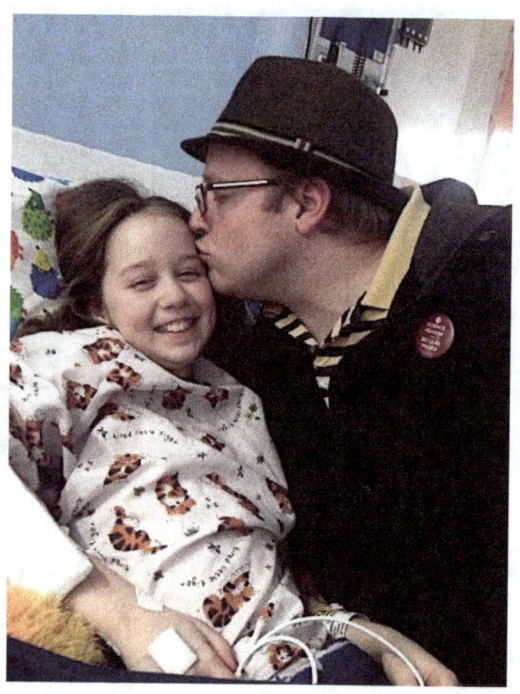

+ The Day After Telling Sami She Had Cancer +

Paul burst through the door like a bat out of Hades. "Um, you won't even believe how many people are in the waiting room right now—it's total pandemonium... and I love it!"

"Oh, I can believe it," Mama replied as she helped the nurse clean up Sami's breakfast tray. "Jeremiah was up half the night responding to people on social media, even one of his old classmates from journalism school. I guess she works at Fox 17 now, and she said Sami's video is one of the biggest local stories trending on Facebook."

"Yeah. I guess they wanted to talk about it on the morning news."

"What?" Sami asked as Pop-Tart crumbs tumbled out of her mouth. "Did you say yes, Papa?"

Papa put down his phone and walked with Paul to the door, then winked at Sami, and said, "I told her the same thing I'm gonna tell everyone in the waiting room: you gotta wait your turn."

+ In the Waiting Room +

Papa stood there, mouth agape, shocked by what he saw in the room. He'd been up all night, plotting and scheming, and he thought he had a handle on how the day would work... but he wasn't expecting this.

Paul laughed, then ribbed Papa with his elbow. "What? You thought I was joking?"

The room was a flurry of the family's favorite friends, and it was abuzz with a tragicomical blend of laughter, tears, and nostalgic conversations. He saw family friends, as well as associates from Center for Inquiry–Michigan, who had come with boatloads of food. Sami's teachers were there, too, along with 20-30 people from the school, and a bunch of folks came from the roller rink.

How are we going to manage so many people? Papa wondered.

"And *this* is where I come in," Kelly said into his ear.

"Dang it, Kelly! You almost gave me a heart attack, dude."

Riley laughed. "We've been standing here next to you the whole time, Mr. B."

"How was I supposed to know that? And why didn't you tell me your dad was Professor X, reading people's minds like that all the time?"

"Cuz she'd never blow his cover," Dan said into Papa's other ear.

"Seriously, what the heck is wrong with you people?" Papa laughed with his hand over his heart. "Creepin' up to spook me like a bunch of weirdos." He looked around the room to make sure no one else was trying to surprise him, then he laughed. "You guys can't do that kind of thing to me. For real, I'm already freaking out over here. The last thing I need is a heart attack."

"Well, at least you'd be in a hospital," Riley replied.

Dan tugged Papa by the sleeve, then pointed toward the far side of the room. "Now take a good look at *that* and tell me you don't feel a million times better already."

"Is that–?"

"Yup," Kelly nodded.

"And you know, he never does this sort of thing for anyone," Dan said.

Riley packed her mouth with some Big-League Chew. "It's a big deal cuz I guess his dad has cancer. It's in his lungs, but I heard it's pretty bad."

Dan sighed. "I hate cancer so much right now."

Papa pressed his lips, and his nostrils flared. "Trust me, bro, you aren't alone on that one."

"And neither are you, Jer," Kelly said. Then he wrapped his arm around Papa's shoulder and hugged him like a chum as the five of them looked out over the room, marveling at the massive crowd of friends and families patiently waiting to see Samantha Lee.

+ Back in Sami's Room +

"How many people came to visit me?" Sami asked with yet another Pop-Tart in her mouth.

"Five or six," Papa replied, trying his best to hide the lie. "And you better cool it on all that sugar. For real, you're like a chain-smoker with those Pop-Tarts, unwrapping a new one before you're even done eating the one in your hand." Then he laughed, saying, "You just watch, we'll be rolling you out of here like the Oompa Loompas rolled that Violet girl out of the Chocolate Factory."

"Ha-ha," Sami said in a sassy voice. "I could eat Pop-Tarts all day."

She wasn't joking, either. Sure, she was a freak for Kellogg's Pop-Tarts, but the doctors had her taking tons of steroids for the swelling in her brain, and those meds made her hungry all the time. She later hated the "moon face" that the steroids gave her, and the weight that she gained on account of them, but in that moment, her only focus was fulfilling her unquenchable desire for more food. Her focus on Pop-Tarts disappeared, though, the moment she heard a familiar voice from in the hall.

"Watch out! C'mon, let's make some room! Sami's besties comin' through!"

Sami's eyes welled with tears. "Emilie! Get in here right now!"

"Oh, you didn't think I'd let her come alone, did ya?" Gladys asked as she and Emilie entered the room.

Sami cried the happiest tears, then reached out her arm as far as she could, and said, "I want to hug you so bad right now, but I'm sorta stuck in this bed, so you gotta come here!"

Emilie and Gladys raced over and leapt onto the bed, where they wrapped their arms around their friend, laughing and crying their hearts out.

"Hey, now, c'mon you guys!" Clara sang in a quirky voice. "You better not forget about me." Then, just as she walked into the room, she tripped and tumbled onto the floor. It would've been a stupendous entrance, except Clara forgot to let go of the handle connected to the red Radio Flyer wagon she was pulling behind her. It was filled with mountains of goodies... mountains of goodies that had just now spilled out all over the floor. "Ooh," Clara said, nervously. "Now *that* is embarrassing." She used her finger to push her glasses back up her face, then turned to look at the girls, who were smiling and shaking their heads in utter amazement over the whole thing. Clara blushed and bashfully used her shoe to kick some candy out of the way, then slowly walked backward toward the door, waving her hands like she was trying to distract them. "You never saw this, you neeeever saaaaw thiiiis." She did that until she was back in the hallway, then she hurried to hide around the corner, but only for second before—

Boing!

She bounced right back into the room, arms outstretched, and cheered, "See! Ta-da! It's me! Your good pal, Clara!"

SHE DANCED ME A STORY

These cutie-pies were the "Peter, James, and John" of Sami's Best Friends Forever Club, and (much to Papa's dismay) they brought that Radio Flyer full of sweets for Sami.

"Oh, you'll have a sugar rush all day every day while you're here," Emilie cackled as she ogled fistfuls of candy.

Gladys glanced at Papa and shrugged her shoulders. "Sorry, Mr. B, but we even brought a bunch of Pop-Tarts."

Sami grabbed a box and shook it at him. "Ha! And you and Mama thought you could actually stop me? Nevuh! Mwahahahaha!"

Clara wagged her finger at him. "Yeah, Mr. B, and don't even think about flushing 'em down the toilet, either." Then, with one eye squint shut, Clara glared, menacingly, through her Coke bottle glasses, and said, "I mean it, too, cuz I got my best eye on you."

Papa didn't like Sami eating so much junk food, especially since people were sharing links with him about the dangers of sugar for kids with cancer, but, for the first time since Sami was admitted into Helen DeVos, she wasn't worried about the IV in her arm or even that she needed help to the bathroom. She didn't even complain when the nurse came in to take her vitals. No, the love and laughter of her friends had left no room for fear, much less for the humdrum of being a bed-ridden kid with cancer—even boredom was banished by girly gossip about "all those dumb boys!" He knew it was fleeting—that, at some point, everyone would need to go home—but for the time being, Sami was smiling... and cancer had lost its sting.

Hour after hour, Sami's room was packed to capacity, and the room overflowed with hugs, laughter, and an ocean of tears, as well as heaps of stuffed animals and enough Pop-Tarts to last two lifetimes. Sami was overjoyed when students and faculty from her school stopped by with balloons, letters, and Santa-sized sacks jam-packed with "Get Well" cards created by her classmates at Campus Elementary. Her teacher Mr. Levi was there, and Sami cried when he said she was a leader of the class, even of the whole school, and that everyone was proud of her.

And just when no one thought it could get any better...

Sami's room rumbled with the resounding sounds of "In Summer," from Disney's *Frozen*. The children cheered and squealed with delight as Anna and

Elsa walked through the door. They were so beautiful, and their costumes were perfect. But it was the silly snowman, Olaf, who stole the show.

The man in the costume was the owner of the Fun Spot, the one Riley said had a father dying of lung cancer, and in that suit, he was free to release those childhood fears and adult emotions that left him feeling helpless in the face of his dad's battle with cancer. He twirled and danced about the room, swinging his arms to and fro. And just when the song came to an end, Olaf curtsied, sat on the edge of Sami's bed, and gave her the biggest hug any snowman has ever given a child.

"Oh. My. Gosh!" Clara exclaimed. "This is basically the perfect cherry on top of the most delicious cake ever made."

As the night wore on, Sami's friends said their goodbyes, and when they had left for the evening, the room was quiet again…

"Two or three people, huh?" Sami laughed.

Mama plopped down on the couch, then chuckled at the thought of Papa's lie. "In fairness, I'm pretty sure he said there were only five or six."

"Meh," Papa shrugged, "so maybe I was off a little…"

"You were off by, like, one thousand," Athan replied.

SHE DANCED ME A STORY

Teresa turned down the lights, then sat up on the bed next to Sami, and said, "You guys gotta be nice to Papa. You know he isn't very good at math."

"Well," Sami replied, "for once, I'm actually glad Papa's so bad at math, cuz today was the best surprise I've ever had in my whole entire life."

Papa relaxed on the chair near Sami's bed, then leaned back and extended the leg rest. "I'm actually really good at math, thank you very much." He put his hands behind his head, and with his eyes closed, he smiled, and said, "In fact, I'm so good at math, I can assure you, with absolute certainty, that that was the last of all my surprises."

Papa was a tricker, though, and he had a super-sneaky secret up his sleeve, for unbeknownst to anyone in the room, he'd been on a mission from the moment he woke up. It's true that he knew very little about childhood cancer, but he was a pro when it came to media and journalism. So, when Fox 17 requested permission to cover Sami on the morning news, he said they'd have to wait until evening. It wasn't that Papa was ungrateful—he wanted everyone in the world to know about Sami—and he wasn't being rude, but they only had a few photos and Facebook posts, and that just wasn't much for Fox 17 to work with.

That would be fine for newspapers or radio, Papa thought to himself, *but not TV.*

And the reason was simple: TV is all about sound and moving images. (Those are their bread and butter.) So, like a clever little monkey, Papa spent the whole day quietly roaming the room, being all sorts of subtle and sneaky, snapping tons of pictures and videos of Sami with her visitors. And now, with everyone gone, the sunset was on the horizon, and that meant two very important things:

1. It was almost time for the evening news, and...
2. His classmate at Fox 17 needed that footage—pronto!

No sooner had Papa sent the material, though, when Ambrose ran like The Flash across the room toward a mysterious visitor standing by the door.

"Ambrose!" the woman cried as he wrapped his arms around her waist.

Papa couldn't believe his eyes, for the woman at the door was someone Ambrose hadn't seen since he was two years old. A short and beautiful Italian woman dressed in modest black apparel, she was a blast from the family's Catholic past, being none other than Ambrose's godmother, Marijo...

... and she didn't come alone.

"I hope we're not intruding," said a man in a black cassock and cappa cloak.

The intonations of his voice resonated with the remains of an accent that developed during an Italian childhood in Brooklyn, New York. He looked like his older brother, who played "Paulie Walnuts" Gaultieri in HBO's *Sopranos*, so Papa knew exactly who (and what) they were dealing with—and he didn't like it one bit! He felt like a rabbit caught in a trap, and his mind was muddled by a bundle of memories and emotions. He scrambled for an excuse to escape, but he failed to formulate a fitting response before Sami sat up in her bed.

"Hey, I remember you!" she said. "You're Fr. Sirico. I know because you used to call me Fire Toes."

"I did, didn't I," Fr. Sirico replied.

"Yeah! You called me that because my sandals lit up with little red lights whenever I ran around the church."

He laughed and sat his biretta on the table. "I see you have a really good memory, Samantha."

Sami sighed. "Yeah, but I have cancer, too, you know."

Fr. Sirico folded his cape over his arm, and in a very kind and fatherly voice, he said, "I'm so sorry to hear that, Samantha, but that's actually why I'm here." Then he turned toward Mama and Papa. "Do I have your permission to pray a blessing over your daughter?"

It's a funny thing, simple questions, for they contain the capacity to create such complex conundrums. And this was a doozy of a dilemma, especially since the particulars of this predicament were compounded by so many competing and even contradictory calculations.

Consider... On the one hand, Mama and Papa no longer believed in God, and they'd neither seen nor heard from Fr. Sirico since they stopped attending his parish in Kalamazoo nearly a decade before. Add to that the fact that

SHE DANCED ME A STORY

Kalamazoo was nearly an hour-drive from Grand Rapids, and it just seemed kind of odd he'd even be in town. Plus, Sami was in preschool the last time she darkened the door of a church, meaning prayers (and the pious priests that pray them) factored in as nothing more than distant memories. On the other hand, Sami wasn't a preschooler anymore—she was an overachieving 10-year-old girl with brain cancer—and Fr. Sirico wasn't *just* their priest. He had been the family's confessor, their spiritual director, and someone who'd been concerned about Papa's ever-increasing lack of faith. He even gave him a statue of Our Lady of Mt. Carmel from the sacristy, as well as a personal copy of a big yellow book, entitled, *Enthusiasm*, by a certain Msgr. Ronald Knox. Fr. Sirico said it was bursting with stories from the wild side of Christian history, detailing the lives and lessons to be learned from those with a tendency to take everything too far—which, for some, proved far enough for them to find themselves abandoning the Faith altogether. Papa never read that big yellow book, and he wondered where he'd placed both the book and the statue, but just seeing Fr. Sirico at Helen DeVos reminded him of just how lost they were.

These were very vexing variables, after all, so painful and problematic, and he felt so divided. Even so, he was forced to admit that there was simply no way to subtract that Sami was embroiled in a battle with brain cancer... and though he didn't have the answer, he figured it wasn't really his problem to solve.

Begrudgingly, Papa deferred to Sami. "What do you think, Sam? You want Fr. Sirico to pray for you?" He supposed it was a safe bet, especially since Sami would surely decline the offer...

... but the kids were right: Papa really was bad at math.

"Of course, you can pray for me. I'd like that from you."

Mama helped the kids to the hall, where Marijo stood, hand-in-hand, with Ambrose. Papa was the last one out the door, but before he even had the time to close it all the way, he was surrounded by his kids, all of them fighting for a front-row seat at the window, hoping to catch a glimpse of the mysterious priest praying mysterious prayers over their sister.

Through the glass, they saw Sami, shining with serenity, as Fr. Sirico kissed his purple stole, hung it around his collar, and performed the Sign of the Cross.

"What is he saying?" Athan whispered.

"I dunno," Papa replied. "I can't hear anything through the door."

"Why don't you just read his lips, then?" Teresa wondered, aloud.

"Read his lips? Are you kidding me, T?" Honestly, Papa sucked at reading lips, but he knew that Fr. Sirico loved the Traditional Latin Mass, and having spent countless hours in confession with him, Papa knew he liked to pray in Latin, so he thought back to those olden days and gave it his best. "Well, if I had to guess, I think he just said, '*In nomine Patris, et Filii, et Spiritus Sancti.*'"

"Wooow," Teresa blurted out, "Fr. Sirico talks fancy!"

"It means, 'In the name of the Father, and of the Son, and of the Holy Spirit.'" Papa replied.

"Why is he sprinkling water on Sami's bed?" Ambrose asked.

"Yeah," Athan added, "and what did he just rub on her head?"

"That's holy water, Ambrose, and he anointed her with the *Oleum Infirmorum*. It's sacred, though, so be quiet."

"Why is he doing all that stuff, Papa?" Teresa asked. "And how do you know all about it, anyway, even Fr. Sirico's fancy talk stuff?"

Papa growled and grumbled, "Why are you guys asking so many questions? What do you think I am, some play-by-play announcer or something?" Shaking his head, he returned to watching through the window. He regretted getting grumpy, especially since his kids had never heard him or Mama pray—not even when Papa's best friend Scott died in a car accident—so their curiosity was to be expected. And Fr. Sirico was the first priest they'd ever seen face-to-face, so everything was new to them, even a little bizarre. And as any parent can attest, a mix like that is bound to stir up some serious questions in curious children. "Martha Stewart couldn't have come up with a better recipe," Papa whispered to himself.

"Is Martha Stewart a saint or something?" Ambrose asked.

"No," Papa laughed. Then he sighed. "But neither am I, so I'm really sorry for snapping at you guys."

Athan grabbed ahold of Papa's hand and pressed his head against his arm. "It's okay. We know you're just really scared about Sami's cancer, so we forgive you."

Then, with one last touch to Sami's head, Fr. Sirico closed with a Sign of the Cross and said, "Amen."

Fr. Sirico thanked Sami and the family for letting him bless her, and he expressed that if they ever needed anything, they only had to let him know. Then he bent down to the ground and bundled the kids in his cape. "And that goes for all of you little munchkins too."

SHE DANCED ME A STORY

"Thank you so much for coming," Sami said with a wave from her bed. "I hope we get to see each other again someday."

"Me too," Fr. Sirico replied. Then he picked up his biretta, and with a nod of his head, he smiled. "And I have faith we will... li'l Fire Toes."

Papa walked with Marijo and Fr. Sirico into the hallway, but before they reached the exit, Marijo stopped and pulled a small pouch from her purse. It was filled with wooden prayer beads and a double-sided photo of a girl. It was vintage, maybe early-1900s, and on one side, she was young and beautiful, rich, and dressed in dainty clothes, while the other side showed her, maybe 10 years older, dressed in the habit of a Carmelite nun. It was St. Thèrése of Lisieux, and the beads were a devotional known as "The Little Flower Rosary."

"The love you share with Sami reminds me of the love St. Thèrése shared with her father," Marijo said as she placed the pouch in the palm of Papa's hand. "It warms my heart to see you two together." She folded his fingers over the pouch, then began to cry. "I don't know if you remember when my son died, Jeremiah, but this chaplet helped me through that."

Papa didn't just remember; he was at the funeral. In fact, he'd thought about it only a few days before, after Pillow/Blankets, when he was gazing up at the poster of del Prete's "Warped Chessboard." The boy's death surprised everyone, and his family was devastated, but especially Marijo. Papa had been in the narthex, not far from the pallbearers, and he could see her through the windows of the door to the sanctuary. Dressed in funeral black, with a veil draped over her face, Marijo stood in the aisle, weeping with her friends. And that's when a little boy made an innocent mistake. He'd been playing with the other kids outside when they heard the bells. He rushed to the door and swung it wide open. What Papa saw next had stuck with him ever since, for with the door wide open, Marijo beheld her son's casket. People tried their best to stop what came next, but it was too late, for Marijo dashed past the ushers and through the door, then hurled her body atop the casket, crying out in the most gut-wrenching voice anyone has ever heard:

"My boy! My boy! My precious baby boy!"

It was a dirge, so painful, so raw, and so surreal that it haunted Papa for years... and even more now that Sami had cancer.

"Thèrése died when she was 24-years-old," Marijo said, "but she said she'd spend eternity doing good for people on earth, and she vowed to let fall from Heaven a shower of roses." Her words made Papa cry, but she could see that they were angry tears, for the despair of doubt and death had devoured his heart. "I know it's hard to believe. Trust me, I know. But God loves Sami, Jeremiah. He loves Ang and the kids too... and He loves you." Marijo placed her hand on Papa's cheek. "And I love you too, ya hear?" Then she squinted her eyes at him, and with a quick wag of her finger, she said, "And don't you ever forget that, either. Never."

Papa wanted to say something skeptical, but he was savvy enough to foresee the futility of getting into an argument with an old-school Italian godmother—especially with one who claims to be compelled by the Blessed Virgin Mary—so he accepted her offering and placed the pouch and wooden beads into his pocket.

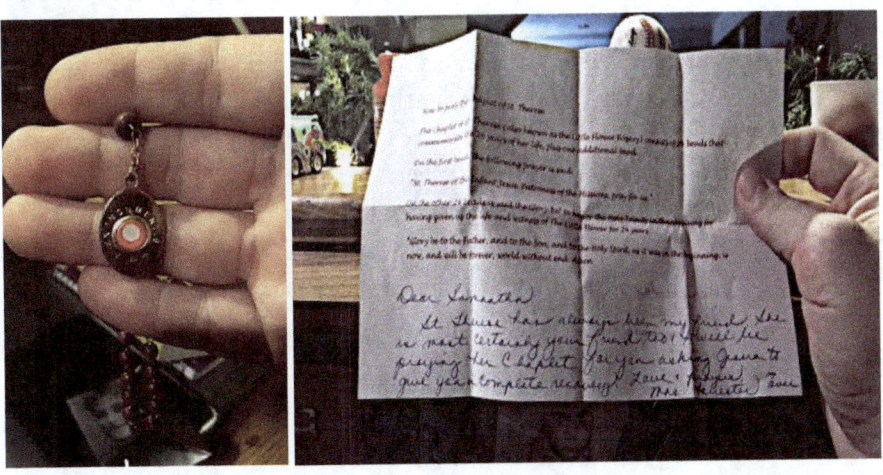

Mama asked him to help her carry the kids to the car, and when they were all buckled in, he gave Mama a kiss, waved goodbye, and walked, silent and alone, back to Sami's room. Sami was fast asleep when he returned, so Papa sat in the chair and turned on the TV.

"Can you mute that, please?" Sami asked in a soft and sleepy voice.

"You don't want to see what's on the news?"

"I do," she laughed, "but how am I supposed to watch the news when I can't even open my eyes? I'd rather hear you play guitar, anyway."

Papa picked up his Fender, tuned it to 432Hz, and softly picked its strings. The sound of his strums made the room feel like a monastery, a holy place and sacred space where ruminations ran wild, and where reflections resonated throughout the emotional tones embodied by the melancholy key of E minor. Papa poured his heart into the strings of that guitar, and his soul surfed atop the oceanic soundwaves of its soaring octaves.

Is this a dream? he wondered. *It feels like a nightmare, except-*

Papa's thoughts were interrupted by a fascinating feature on Fox 17. He chuckled at the sight of charming little children, and he shook his head as they grabbed fun toys and fruity treats from a wagon full of presents. And teachers conveyed their condolences with gobs of "Get Well" cards created by students from a local public school. The presentation was perfect, and it made Papa so proud that he almost started to cry, until he saw a silly snowman from a local roller rink, and he was overcome with joy. Then, alas, came the star of the special. She was banged up and bedridden, but she was brave and very beautiful—so beautiful that the words on the banner at the bottom of the screen began to bother him. It said that she was staring down the barrel of a deadly disease, and reporters described her as suffering. Yet there was something about her, something that told an altogether different tale: a story of life and love, of friends, family, and the grace to be grateful for every guest—even those whose presence was their only gift to offer.

So, with the residual remains of his guitar's root note reverberating in the room, Papa curled-up beside Sami on the bed, and with tears in his eyes, he thought in his heart, *That girl on TV is more than a hero to me. She's...*

**A stem from my seed...
a bud from Mama's blood...
she's our firstborn Little Flower.**

IX

BIRTHDAYS & BIOPSIES
[Let Cancer Eat Cake]

+ March 27–a Few Days After Fox 17's Special +

Psst... psst... psst... psst...

    It was an hour before dawn when Papa heard the chirpy sounds of girly whispers. He tried to wake up, but his eyelids were as heavy as hammers laid down on the anvils of those periwinkle bags that sagged beneath his eyes, so he peered through his lashes, and, in the soft blue haze of the hospital room, he saw Sami speaking with the nurse. They were covering their mouths like they had something to hide.
    Sneaky secrets? Papa thought quietly. *Those are never good...*

Crinkle... crinkle... crinkle... crinkle...

    What the—? Papa wondered as he re-awoke from his slumber. He didn't remember falling back to sleep, but he must've been out for a while because the nurse had time to fetch a noisy paper bag.
    "Uh-oh..." the nurse whispered, looking over at Papa. "I think your dad is awake."
    "Shhh..." Sami replied. "Be veeeery quiet... and don't move... that way he won't notice us..."
    Ah, the old 'Pretend to be a Statue' trick, huh? More like deer caught in headlights. Oh, they were so busted. But before Papa could roast them for being shady little schemesters, Mr. Sandman sprinkled his last dash of dreamy dust into his eyes, then gently blew on the nape of his neck, and rocked him back to sleep...
    That was until Sami cried out in a very loud voice:
    "Papa, get up! I need you! Help me—FAST!"

Papa jumped out of bed, but he was barely awake, so he staggered around the room like he was drunk. "I'm awake, Sami! I'm awake! Oh, my gosh, okay, what the heck is going on?"

Sami giggled. "Oh, nothing much, I just need help getting something out of this paper bag."

"Are you serious?" Papa groaned as he wiped his eyes. He scoffed, then buttoned his shirt and put on his slippers. "You freaked me out over a paper bag? Darn it, Sam, I'm tired, and you scared the daylights out of me!"

In a super-sneaky voice, Sami said, "It's not just any paper bag, Papa." She struggled to open it, then peeked inside and grabbed ahold of something squishy. "Ta-da!" she said. "HAPPY BIRTHDAY, Papa!"

It was a French cruller smothered in vanilla icing, and *that* was Papa's all-time favorite donut.

"I need your help to light the candle on the cake," she said, pointing to candles and matches on the nightstand. "Well, it's a birthday donut, but you know what I mean. I guess they didn't have any birthday cakes in the kitchen, but they had these, and it was your favorite one, so I thought it was maybe even more perfect than a cake."

"Ah, so that's what you and the nurse were whispering about!"

"Papa!" Sami giggled, punching him in the arm. "I knew you saw us."

He laughed and said, "I see everything." Then he raised his eyebrows. "Well, everything except the calendar, I guess, cuz I totally forgot today was my birthday."

"I never forget your birthday. It's kinda hard to forget, actually, cuz you always say it's basically a national holiday and all." She paused for a moment and pressed her lips. "That got me thinking, though. You know how you always sing 'Happy Birthday' to kids at the Fun Spot? Well, I kinda wondered if maybe it would be nice for someone to sing it to you for a change." Then, with a quick clearing of her throat, Sami started to sing. It was lovely, heartfelt, and bursting with gusto! She even tried her best to use both arms, waving them around like a maestro at a symphony. And when it was over, Sami had him light the candle, then told him to make a wish. "You gotta close your eyes first, though, *then* you can blow out the candle."

He thought he had a perfect idea, but before he had time to close his eyes, he saw something that broke his heart:

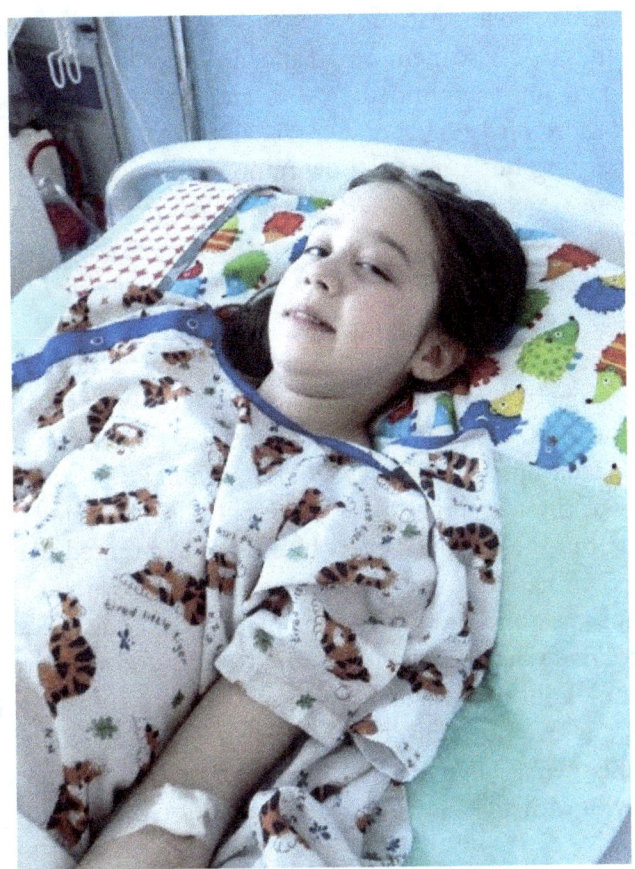

Sami could no longer hold her head up, and her right-shoulder shrugged toward her cheek. Even worse, he saw a droop on the right-side of her face, and it made him wonder if she had had a stroke in the night. It was obvious she knew, at least about her neck and shoulder, and he could tell that she was trying very hard to hide it, but even in the dim light of dawn, Papa could clearly see the spasms. He wanted to cry, but he saw how hard Sami tried, and he knew she didn't want him to be scared, not for her, and not on his birthday. So, he closed his eyes and thought...

What I wouldn't give for Doctor Who's time-traveling TARDIS! I'd bring her back to those good old days, to a time—anytime at all—before the cancer came. He envisioned early mornings playing chess with the kids before they scampered off to school, and he fantasized about fun-filled afternoons rocking out at the rink. He even dreamed of dinners distracted by the kids doodling in his favorite diaries, as well as sleepovers with *Super Friends* within a family-sized fortress of pillows and blankets. These memories made him so happy, but when he opened his eyes, he saw Sami surrounded by IVs and hospital monitors. And even though she sat there with a smile on her face, Papa sighed inside, afraid that his visions were nothing but a mirage now trapped in the rearview mirror of his life. *I wish my family was here. I wish this room was flooded again with love and laughter. And I wish today would be a picture-perfect day, exceeding anything we could ever hope for—one that we'd always remember... and, oh, yeah, lest I forget, screw you, cancer.*

"C'mon, already!" Sami laughed, impatiently. "It's a donut, not a magic genie." So, with an elfish grin sprawled across his face, Papa took a deep breath, then blew out the candle. "Finally, Mr. Slowpoke, took you long enough." Then she licked her lips, and said, "Now, let's dig in!"

The smell of the match had barely dissipated by the time Sami and Papa finished eating, but they enjoyed every bite. They even acted all rich and fancy, daintily using their napkins to wipe the icing from the corners of their lips. But when the donut was gone, Sami told Papa that she had one more gift to give.

"I want to give you a special two-armed hug, but you gotta sit by me on the bed." It took a lot of effort, and it looked so terribly clumsy, but it was a labor of love, and even though it took a few tries, Sami finally got both her arms around his neck. Then she pulled him close and whispered in his ear, "Papa, I love you with all of my heart... into a million pieces."

Mama arrived an hour later, and the family came bearing gifts.

"We wrapped them ourselves," Athan said, handing him a present.

"I bet you did," Papa chuckled, staring at the chaotically taped paper bag in his hands. "This is, um, quite the accomplishment, buddy."

Mama kissed Papa on the cheek. "Oh, you don't even know, baby. We got you a bunch of surprises today."

Papa sat there for a while, quietly watching his wife and children, and he was content. "Honestly, you guys, I wouldn't be sad if I never got a birthday gift again... as long as I have all of you in my life."

"Welp, sorry you two," said a woman at the door, "I guess Jeremiah doesn't want to see us today."

Papa's eyes grew wide at the sound of her voice—the first voice he had ever heard...

"It's Nana!" the kids shouted.

"And Uncle Isaac too!" Athan cheered.

Papa's mom and brother lived in Pennsylvania, and no one had told him that they would be there for his birthday...

... but he needed them now more than ever, so he shot up like a lightning bolt from his chair, then dove head-first into the arms of his mom, weeping like he did when he was still a kid, and his brother kindly patted him on his back.

Nana grabbed Papa's shoulders. "Okay, let me look at you, son." She examined him for a moment, then patted his cheek. "Well, you look alright. Not a day over 40."

"But Papa turns 37 today," Teresa replied with a confused look on her face.

Uncle Isaac nodded his head in agreement, but he didn't say any words—he rarely ever did, at least not since the car accident. He was only six when it happened, and it left him with a closed-head injury, but he was Papa's bro, and the kids loved him like crazy, so everyone was happy when he was around.

Nana rolled her eyes and made a goofy face, then pointed toward the door. "I hope you don't mind, but this goofy goober wanted to tag along, so I let him ride with us."

toot – toot – to – tooooot!

The goober burst in like a wild man, dancing around like some drunken jester, and he played a terrible tune on what sounded like a cheap recorder. It was Celine Dion's *My Heart Will Go On*, except it was really, really bad. Still, the mere sight of him made Sami bounce up and down with excitement.

"Uncle Dustan!"

He was a burly and bearded redhead, covered in freckles, and always a bellyful of laughs. Like Papa, he was a bona fide prankster, and he always told a ton of silly stories, especially about the crazy things that he and Papa did in Bible college.

"Tell the one about Batman & Robin," Ambrose begged. "The one where they broke into you guys' dorm room."

Athan was already cracking up just thinking about it. "No, no, you gotta tell the one about that time Papa crushed Uncle Brian's Butterfinger into tons of tiny pieces, and how it fell all over the car when Brian tried to eat it!"

"Why not tell both of 'em?" Dustan replied. And with a wicked grin hovering over his chin, he promised to tell them about the time Papa pooped his pants in an all-you-can-eat buffet.

"Aw, c'mon, man!" Papa complained. "That's so messed up."

"Buuuuut, I won't tell you any of those stories unless you let me do what I came here to do." Dustan reached into a bag and grabbed a handful of books. "I actually wanted to spend some time reading to your sister."

"Aw," Sami replied. Then she squinted her eyes nice and mean, saying, "I'll only let you read to me, though, if you promise you'll never play that stupid flute thing ever again for the rest of your life. Seriously, that thing sounds really terrible."

"Yeah," Athan grumbled, "I kinda made me puke in my mouth a little bit."

Sami watched as Dustan fumbled through the books in his hands. "What did you bring to read to me?"

"Well, let's see here... I brought a little *War and Peace*, by Leo Tolstoy, and... erm... ah, I've got *The Brothers Karamazov*, by Fyodor Dostoevsky."

Sami rolled her eyes and shook her head. "Yeah right, Uncle Dustan, nice try, weirdo, but those books are huge, and I bet they're really boring for kids."

Dustan looked surprised. "Oops! Sorry, those are just my light daytime reading." He hurried to put the big books back in his bag, and his face lit up with a smile when he grabbed hold of a much smaller book. "Hmph. That's weird, I guess all I've got left is *The Velveteen Rabbit*. Hm, my bad."

"You're such a jerk," Sami laughed. Then she glanced toward Nana. "However, I wouldn't even care if it was 2,000 pages of pure boredom... as long as Nana promised to play with my hair while I listened."

"Ugh," Nana playfully protested. "I guess... if I have to."

Everyone knew Nana was lying. Truth is, there were few things in the world Nana loved more than playing with hair, even her own. It was her specialty, her most prized of personal pastimes, and she had a horrible habit of it. But of all the hair she'd ever encountered, Sami's was her favorite. Her hair was long and luxurious, and soft as a bunny's bottom, so Nana spent hours twirling it, swirling it, and kneading out the knots. This time was different, though, for Nana knew that beneath that hair was a beautiful brain that was fighting for its life. And like Samantha, it grieved Nana's heart that the doctors would dare to cut it, and that Sami would be bald by the morning. So, she sat on the bed, curled up close to Sami, and played with her hair, crying quietly as Dustan read the story.

Friends and family stopped by throughout the day, even Papa's dad, Pa, who rode his motorcycle all the way from California. Papa's sister, Aunt Curly, also came, and she brought her vintage Caboodle with nail polish for Sami's big biopsy in the morning. Great Gramma stopped by too.

SHE DANCED ME A STORY

"You're really getting up there, Jeremiah," she laughed, limping around like an old man. "I almost bought you a cane for your birthday."

But time wore on, and people got tired, especially Sami. Her pre-surgery meds were starting to kick in. So, everyone said goodbye, bidding "Get Well!" and "See you in a few hours!" to Sami and the family.

"Ahhhh," Papa sighed as he sat in a chair, grabbed a blanket, and closed his eyes. It felt so good, like a perfect ending to a perfect day...

"Don't even think about it, Mr. Sleepyhead," Mama said as she puffed some powder on Sami's cheeks. "We still have to meet Cathy in the chapel upstairs."

"Cathy? Like, Cathy from Center for Inquiry?"

"Yup," Mama mumbled with a bobby pin between her teeth, "she's getting everything ready in the chapel upstairs right now."

Right now couldn't have come quickly enough as Sami's spasms were off the charts, and the headaches made her feel like her brain was exploding. Doctors tried to keep things under control, but that meant pumping her full of pain pills, muscle relaxers, seizure meds, and those dreadful steroids—and now she was stoned out of her mind. So, as soon as Mama was done getting her ready, the family rushed through the halls and into the elevator.

+ In the Chapel at Helen DeVos +

The sanctuary was simple yet serene, and the walls were painted with Autumn colors of red, brown, and yellow, as well as orange, and evergreen. The kids made shadow puppets on the walls under the lights from the setup, and Cathy's husband ran around the room, moving this or that here or there as his wife called out commands. They were friends of the family, and part of CFI, a largely Atheist group that Papa belonged to.

"Hey," Athan said, pointing at Cathy, "you're the lady who took pictures of me and Teresa for all of those Old Orchard juice ads online."

"That's me," Cathy smiled as she adjusted the lens of her camera.

Athan frowned. "You made me dress up like a silly bunch of grapes!"

Cathy laughed. "You were cute, and I paid you fifty bucks." Then she peered through her camera, and said, "I've got an adorable apple costume in the bag over there... if you really want to wear it."

"In your dreams," Athan replied. "Not even for another fifty bucks!"

Then, just when they were about to begin, Papa pulled Cathy aside.

"Sami's really tired," he whispered, "and her shoulder spasms are practically nonstop. We'll do our best, but I just wanted you to know."

Cathy understood. And with a final layer of lipstick, a bit of blush, and a couple curls in Mama's hair, the girls looked gorgeous. Teresa even got some glitter for her cheeks. And with another "No, here!" and a final "No, there!" to her husband, Cathy was ready to roll.

Sami sat front and center, and Teresa was tucked in close to Mama, while Athan and Ambrose took their spots on either end. It was picture perfect, or at least it would have been, but Sami's spasms got worse and worse, always shrugging and jerking her shoulder. It was so spontaneous, so unpredictable, and Sami hated how it made her look in all the pictures. It all felt hopeless, and the family feared that all was lost...

... but that's when Cathy had an idea.

She pulled Sami's arm to lower her shoulder, then wrapped it tight around Papa's back. "You gotta clamp it hard!" And with the sound of tears welling up in her voice, she told him, "No matter how much it fights, Jeremiah, you gotta fight it even harder. Do you hear me?"

"Thank you," Sami slurred with a yawning smile. "I wish I could stop all these spasms right now because I just want this picture to be perfect for everyone."

"Move the light to the left," Cathy told her husband as tears streamed down her face. She hurried to wipe her eyes with her sleeve, then said, "No, your other left—yes, there! Okay, now hold it steady." She was amazing to watch in action, and just when the shoot was about to end, Cathy ran to the wheelchair and grabbed Papa's scarf. "Hurry up, Jer. Put it on!"

SHE DANCED ME A STORY

It was colorful, twelve foot long, and an almost perfect replica of the scarf worn by Tom Baker in Doctor Who.

"That's Papa's special scarf," Sami said. "Mama knitted for him it with love."

Papa wrapped it around his neck, and with a few final clicks from Cathy's camera, she said she had only one more picture left to take...

"I want to see Jeremiah holding Sami in his arms, with Sami's head and hands resting on his shoulder."

Sami was heavy, and she wasn't able to help very much, so Papa knelt, wrapped his arms around her waist, and with the biggest bear hug he'd ever given, he pressed her against his chest, then lifted her off the ground.

Sami giggled like a drunkard. "This makes me feel like a little girl again!"

Papa thought the same thing. It reminded him of those times long ago when Sami would fall asleep in his arms during his sunset walks with Mama around the block. It's hard to explain, but in the sanctuary of the Upper Room in Helen DeVos, he felt as though the two of them had commandeered Doctor Who's time-traveling TARDIS, and that the Doctor's "bright blue box" had landed in a perfect space in time, to those good old days when Papa was young, and Sami was cancer-free...

+ Moments Later—Back in Sami's Room +

Aunt Curly tucked the kids into their makeshift hospital beds, while Dustan told them funny stories, and Nana twirled Sami's hair. Mama got a phone call, but the doctors were administering anesthesia in the room, so she talked out in the hall. Then, just when everyone had settled in, Mama burst back into the room...

"You won't even believe who I just talked to!" she exclaimed.

"Ugh," Athan grumbled as he wiped the sleep from his eyes. "And just when we were all getting comfortable."

"Hmph," Mama scoffed, playfully. "Then I guess nobody cares that Make-A-Wish is sending us on a special trip!"

Everyone shot up from their sleep.

"Is it just for me," Sami asked, "or can the whole family go with me?"

Mama sighed, pretending to be sad, then smiled, and shouted, "They said it's for the whole family, so all of us can go!"

The kids leapt from their beds and danced around the room, laughing and cheering at the top of their lungs. Then, amid all that craziness, Papa felt a soft and sleepy tug on his sleeve.

"I'm really sorry, Papa," Sami said.

"Sorry?" he laughed. "Sorry for what?"

Sami's meds were getting the best of her, and she was fading fast. "Well... today is your birthday... but for some weird reason... I'm the one who got all the best presents."

Papa sat next to her on the bed, where the two of them watched the family celebrate the news about Make-A-Wish, and he assured her that it was the best birthday he'd ever had. Then, just when Sami closed her eyes for the last time before her biopsy, Papa kissed her forehead, and with the whiskers of his mustache tickling her ear, he whispered...

"Believe it or not, I got way more than I even wished for..."

X

SHE DANCED ME A STORY

+ The Following Day +

Sami's neurosurgeon was Dr. Foody, but everyone at Helen DeVos called him "The Energizer Bunny." And after Sami's biopsy Mama and Papa knew why. He navigated the nooks and crannies of Sami's brain for six long hours, and when everything was said and done, he had gotten exactly what he was aiming for. He submitted the samples to the Tumor Board, where the hospital's best experts dissected the details.

"Sami's cancer is very rare," Dr. Kurt said. "And it's very, very aggressive."

"She has an anaplastic astrocytoma," Dr. Pridgeon added. "These account for about 10 percent of childhood brain tumors around the world."

Mama pressed the side of Sami's head to her chest. "What caused this to happen??? None of this makes any sense!"

Dr. Kurt told her it could've started only recently, but it was also possible that it had been there for a while, especially given its size.

"Truth is," Dr. Pridgeon added, "there's no way we could ever know for sure what caused this."

Sami looked at them, and said, "You told me that cancer has grades, and you said that some of the grades are scarier than others." Her lip quivered, and her eyebrows raised with worry. "I guess, well, I'm just wondering what kind of grade the Cancer Board thinks my cancer has..."

"We think it's Grade III," Dr. Pridgeon replied, "but there's a possibility it's a Grade IV. And Grade III tumors can become high-grade glioblastomas with time, so it's important we start treatment right away."

Sami looked around the room at her family and the presents from all her friends, and after a moment of silence, she looked up at the doctors, and asked, "Dr. Kurt, is my cancer gonna kill me?"

Sami's question sucked the air out of the room, but Dr. Kurt was calm. "We're gonna do everything we can to prevent that, Sami, but we're gonna need your help, okay?" Sami nodded, so Dr. Kurt told her about the surgery she needed, and about the kind of treatments she should expect, as well as how long it might take her to heal.

"And rest assured that Sami's quantity and quality of life are our top priorities," Dr. Pridgeon promised.

Sami thanked them for being honest with her. "It's gotta be really hard talking to kids about cancer," she said, "especially cuz cancer kills kids. But you're really nice about it, and your voice helped me not be so scared."

"We're in this together," Dr. Kurt said. "I promise."

The days that followed flowed a little differently—and this was by design. Since Sami arrived at Helen DeVos, her room had been flooded with visitors. They poured in from diverse currents, and they came from all over the country. There were waves of young people, old people, single and married people; White, Black, and Asian people; and most of them were Christians, but there were also a lot of Atheists, and a few of Sami's Jewish and Native American friends. It was awesome, at least for a while, but it started to feel like a tsunami—and there was no sign that the outpouring would subside anytime soon.

SHE DANCED ME A STORY

Making matters worse, Sami was drowning in an ocean of opiates, and she struggled to stay afloat, so Mama and Papa stemmed the tide by closing the floodgates, reducing the never-ending stream of friends, fans, and followers to a more sustainable trickle of close friends and family. This made Sami sad, of course, but Surgery Day was quickly approaching, and she knew she needed some quiet time with her team. Still, in those rare moments when Sami was awake and alert, she was grateful for the guests, especially Nana and Aunt Curly. They pampered Sami with Pop-Tarts, spoiled her with bedtime stories, and Nana sang soothing songs while Sami slept. Best of all, Nana played with Sami's hair for hours and hours on end.

"Maybe if you ask Mama, she can give you some of my hair when the doctors cut it off. You know, like she did when all of us kids got our first haircuts."

"Some of it?" Nana laughed. "I want all of it." Then she held out a brown paper bag with the words "Sami's Hair" written on it. "I came prepared."

The whole night was tranquil, and when the younger children had fallen asleep, everyone quietly gathered their things and whispered their goodbyes, leaving the perfect amount of time for Papa and Mama to spend alone with their daughter.

+ Pillow/Blankets (At Helen DeVos) with Mama & Papa +

"We're sorry for squishing you so much," Mama giggled as she snuggled next to Sami under the blankets.

"Speak for yourself," Papa laughed. Sprawling his leg across the bed, he said, "I hope you don't mind, Sam-Jamz, but I'm gonna use you like a body-pillow."

Sami didn't mind at all—after years of Pillow/Blankets, she was kind of used to it—but she especially didn't mind right now. She was scared about the surgery, and she worried about what her life with cancer would be like, but now, swaddled by her parents and the soothing sound of *Super Friends* on the TV, Sami was safe... at peace... and before long, fast asleep.

Time flies when you're dreaming, though, so it wasn't long before the sun had risen, and everyone was wide awake.

"Psst..." Sami whispered in Papa's ear. "Get up. It's Surgery Day."

Papa yawned, then wiped the sleepy dust out of his eyes. "Where's Mama?"

"She went to get you guys some Starbucks."

Papa walked to the bathroom sink and started to brush his teeth. "Is Mama grabbing us anything?" he asked with a mouthful of foam.

"No, I'm not allowed to eat, remember? But I need something from you. Well, two things, actually. First of all, do you remember that story you wrote about me when I was a little kid? The one where I wore a tutu and was dancing in front of the mirror in your office while you worked?"

"Of course," Papa replied as he spit out his toothpaste. "How could I forget?"

"Will you read it to me this morning? And can you share it on Facebook, that way people can think happy thoughts and not super sad ones when I'm having my surgery." Papa splashed some water on his face, then grabbed his MacBook. "Oh, and I want you to include 'Tiny Dancer,' by Elton John, with it. I like that song so much, and he wears some super-cool clothes. Plus, it goes perfectly with the name of the story."

Papa smirked as he typed. "That's three requests, you know?"

"Then let's make it four," Sami laughed. "See, last night I learned that a lot of kids with cancer have things called 'teams,' and they use hashtags too, that way people can find them online. There's this one kid in the hospital who has a team called #RickerStrong, and another kid named his team #TeamKeegan. There's even a cool kid in England who named his #TeamReece."

Papa typed those hashtags into Facebook, then scrolled through some pictures of the kids and their families. "That sounds awesome, but what do you want to call your team? #TeamSamantha? #TeamSamiLee?"

"I thought about all those, but I thought of one better." Then she smiled, and said, "I want our team to be #TeamTinyDancer."

"Because the song?"

"No—I mean, yeah, that song is obviously awesome, but no, I picked it because that's what you called me in your story." Then she smirked and shrugged her shoulders. "Elton John's song does make it easy to remember, though, doesn't it?"

"Hmm..." Papa replied with a doubtful look on his face. "I dunno, Sam. Honestly, I'm just not sure Elton John would like that very much." Sami looked devastated... that was, until Papa said, "Because I think Elton John would totally love it. Duh."

SHE DANCED ME A STORY

Sami punched his arm. "Ugh! You're so mean to me sometimes! Seriously. You really had me going. Now read that story to me before I get mad at you for real."

So, Papa put on his glasses and started to read...

Sami loved listening to Papa read his stories. He wrote from his heart, so they weren't just words to him, and he read them like an actor reads his lines, which made his words come alive with an artistic mania that painted pictures in her mind, like movies playing right before her eyes. And it didn't matter that she'd heard the story dozens of times or even that she remembered all the details. Sami hung onto every word... especially today.

Then, after he read the final line, Papa posted his story, along with the song and Sami's new #TeamTinyDancer hashtag, to Facebook.

Doctors had already administered anesthesia when Mama returned with the coffee, so it wasn't long before the family was standing outside of the operating room, where Dr. Foody was getting prepared.

He warned them this would be a very long operation—maybe upward of 12 hours—and he apologized for his team running late. That last part didn't bother them, though, as it meant they'd have a few extra minutes with their daughter. It wasn't much, but it was enough for the anesthesia to start working... and for the grim realities of their situation to kick in.

"I hate that they're gonna cut all of my hair off," Sami slurred. "And what if my scar is really huge? People are gonna say I'm ugly." Mama and Papa tried to comfort her, but no matter what they said, Sami simply couldn't shake the fear that this surgery would leave her with other scars, and that these would be scars that may never fully heal.

The nurse was at the door, so Papa hurried for his phone, and, with their fingers interlocked, he and Mama placed their hands at Sami's hairline, covering her hair, then took a picture...

The droop in her face was still there, but her eyes did all the smiling. "I do look beautiful, don't I?"

"The prettiest princess in the whole world," Mama promised as she rubbed her thumb across Sami's forehead.

Those were the last words Sami heard before she fell asleep. And once the doctors were ready, they gave Mama and Papa an alarm.

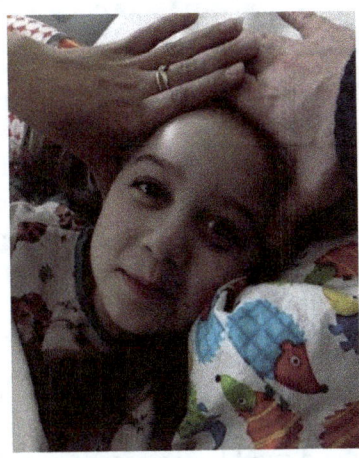 

"It buzzes and beeps really loud," the nurse warned, then she pushed a button, which caused the device to shake and make noise, and red and blue lights flashed all around it. "It's really annoying," she laughed, "but it'll get your attention, that way you'll know when we're done with Sami's surgery." And with that, the nurse wheeled Sami's bed into the operating room, where Dr. Foody and his team stood masked and at the ready.

+ "The Long Wait" Back in Sami's Room +

The hours that followed were some of the saddest (and most silent) of their lives. Nana and Curly were along for the ride, but everyone was on pins and needles, and hardly anyone said a word. Curly and Nana just quietly prayed, while Mama knit Sami a hat, and Papa played chess by himself. Every second felt like an hour, though, and Papa's mind was reeling.

CRASH!

In a fit of rage, Papa used his arm to clear the board, and all his pieces tumbled to the floor! The women were startled by the outburst, but they didn't ask why he did it, and no one dared correct him. They just sat there, watching as Papa glared, angrily, at the pieces, then rested his head on the now empty chessboard.

SHE DANCED ME A STORY

He was traumatized—certainly in a state of shock—and like a man in a trance, he started seeing things—and these visions appeared to come alive. Papa feared he'd gone mad, but he was mesmerized, in awe of apparitions hovering like holograms atop the glass checkered squares of his board. He saw so many shapes and symbols, things like stairs, candles, large doors, and a fiery heart pierced by swords and dripping with blood. None of it made sense, but that was the least of his concerns, as the board suddenly transformed into a sheet of melted glass.

The board ran like ooze along the ground, then crawled up the walls and spread across the ceiling, until, alas, Sami's room was covered in the black and white squares of Papa's chessboard. Gigantic bubbles expanded in the ooze around the room, and he cried for help, but all the women were gone. He dashed to the door but slipped on a rook and tumbled to the floor, where he laid like a man dead-alive in a tomb, watching in horror as the huge oozy bubbles popped around the room. They were like wrecking balls, obliterating the floor, ceiling, and walls, and every burst was a breakthrough, revealing an altogether different dimension—a realm of realities beyond the physical confines of material existence. In time, everything was subsumed, leaving Papa in a world of mystery, where clocks ticked backward and everything foreign felt so strangely familiar...

It was a nave, opulent and ornate, lined with pillars, and plumes of incense hung like clouds in the air. Papa struggled to see, but the tender twinkle of twilight in the nighttime sky seeped through the stained-glass windows, and the glow of votive candles danced across a simulacrum of copper sparrows perched in a dome over the apse.

Papa gazed up at a golden canopy in the center of the dome, and he had so many questions, but the people in the pews had nothing to say, and he wondered if they even knew he was there. He turned to take a seat, but when he did, his foot bumped into a kneeler…

BANG!

The sound echoed throughout the nave, and Papa worried he'd disrupted something sacred, so he sat there, in fear and trembling, as though he'd awoken the angels in the architecture…

Suddenly, Papa was blinded by a brilliant light. It was a golden canopy, which was no canopy at all, but a chandelier—and it shone like the sun. Then, with his eyes closed, Papa heard a piano…

Dun-dun-dada-dah-dun-dun-dada

He remembered that song, and he knew it by heart, but he couldn't recall what it was or when he'd heard it. It sounded like something from long ago, back when life enjoyed the quiet and calm of the womb. And while he pondered these things, the light dimmed down, and he opened his eyes, just in time to see a little girl emerge from the shadows.

She was young, dressed in a cute pink tutu, and she was pushing a large magic mirror across the stage. Then, when she got it where she wanted, she whispered and waved at the reflection, then angled the mirror to face the pews, and made her way to the center of the stage, where she danced to the sound of that charming childhood tune.

I know that girl, Papa thought to himself, but just as it was with the song, so it was with her: a mystery concealing an answer, and an answer that required time and reflection. She wasn't really a dancer, and most of what she did wasn't even ballet, but what she lacked in posture and form was more than made up for by her grace and her innocence.

Then someone (or something) turned off the lights...

Papa gasped, entirely unable to see. He longed for a lamp or even a candle—any light at all—but there was only the sound of the music, and Papa started to get scared.

"Are you still there, little girl?" Papa cried aloud. "Can you hear me? Can anyone hear me at all??"

❊SHUNK❊

His pleas were answered by a spotlight that turned on just as the chorus came to the crescendo of its coda. And there she was! She'd been dancing all the while, even in the dark. Then, just as the music was about to end, the little girl turned toward the mirror, raised her hands high up to heaven, then curtsied, and dropped fistfuls of flower petals to the floor.

When she finished, she returned to the shadows, and everyone quietly left the nave... everyone but Papa. He remained there, sitting in the pew, pondering those things that he had seen and heard.

Could she feel the coolness of the floor through the soles of her ruby red shoes? he wondered. *Was she sad that there were so many empty seats? Did it matter either way? And what did she see? What did she see that I didn't?*

Papa bowed his head, pondering and storing these things in his heart, but then he saw something out of the corner of his eye. There, within the pane of the magical mirror, Papa beheld a man, hunched over with grief, his head resting flat on a chessboard while his mother ran her fingers through his hair.

"She saw me!" he shouted. "She saw me in the mirror!"

He'd witnessed so many spectacular things since being subsumed by the chessboard, but it was there, in that mysterious moment, that he began to see things rightly. More than that, he'd seen the whole for what it truly was: a story that only his tiny dancer could tell. And unlike any other tale Papa had ever read, hers was best told without a single word. For such was a daughter's love, displayed, as it were, through a simple song and dance.

BZZZ-BEEP-BEEP...
BZZZ-BEEP-BEEP...
BZZZ-BEEP-BEEP...

It was an alarm, and it shook the sanctum. Icons on the walls cracked and crumbled as sparks rained down from the chandelier, and laser beams of red and blue light flickered and flashed like lightning bolts out of the mirror.

"Come back, little girl!" Papa cried. "Please, someone help me!"

Then, through the frightful sounds of the nave collapsing around him, Papa heard a faint, albeit familiar voice. It was a woman, and she was pleading with him: "C'mon, Jeremiah. Sami is waiting..."

Her call was irresistible, and it came from the mirror, which now pulled at him like a star being sucked into a black hole, stretching his body into skinny spaghetti strings, all of them swimming and swirling safely through a firestorm of falling debris.

It was inexplicable, like being in multiple places at the exact same time. And just when he feared he would crash into the mirror, Papa's noodle-like appendages bundled back together like a ball of yarn, and—

CRASH!

Straight through the glass, twisting and turning through a tunnel of light. It was a timeline, a passageway from the future-present to the present-past, and like a comet, Papa whirled around planets, moons, and galaxies. Then, as he broke through the Earth's atmosphere, he burst into a blazing ball of fire.

"Geronimo!" he cheered. And with a mighty roar, he shouted, "Hold on, Sami! Papa's comin' home!"

BOOM!

He barreled through the roof of the hospital, and the blast of his impact was like an atomic bomb, but time stood still, and like two rivers running into one another, Papa's ghost softly and quietly spiraled its way back into his body.

Mama shook his shoulder. "Jeremiah, wake up! We gotta go!"

SHE DANCED ME A STORY

"I'm awake!" Papa shouted as he sat up in his seat. He looked around the room, patting his chest and face, laughing as he said, "The room is normal! And I'm back! I'm back! I'm really, really back!"

"Normal?" Curly laughed. "You're definitely not normal. And you've been here the whole time, you goof. Trust me, I know, cuz you've been snoring our ears off for hours."

"You drooled all over your chessboard, too, baby," Mama said as she wiped the saliva from the side of his face.

"How long has she been in surgery?" Papa asked.

"Nearly twenty hours," Curly replied.

The alarm rattled and flashed again, and they knew what that meant. The four of them raced through the hallways, down the elevator to the room where they'd last seen Sam. And there she was, in recovery... but as they approached her bedside, they were rocked by reality. Sami's nostrils were filled with breathing tubes, and another protruding from her mouth. She was surrounded by a bunch of monitors, and there was a drain tube in the top of her head... a head the doctors had shaved completely bald, and which now bore the marks of a massive incisions.

"Your daughter did amazing," Dr. Foody assured them, "but she needs to rest, and we'll have to watch her very closely for the next few days as they are absolutely vital to Sami's recovery and ultimate outcome."

Nurses transported Sami to the Intensive Care Unit, so Nana, Curly, and Mama returned to the room to gather their things, while Papa stayed by Sami's bedside. And when the nurses were finished, they left the room, leaving Papa and Sami... together... yet alone.

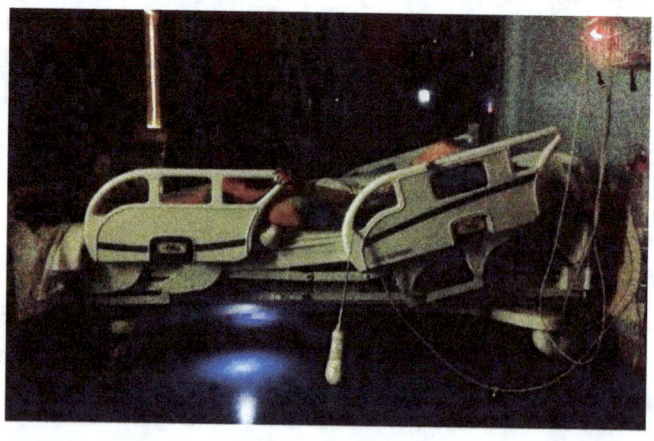

"I'm so proud of you," Papa wept, kissing and caressing her cheeks.

Sami's face was so swollen from the surgery, and doctors said she wouldn't wake up for hours, but Papa pampered her with praise, speaking as though she were wide awake and as if nothing on earth was wrong. He pressed his lips beside the incisions on Sami's scalp, and began to hum a tune…

Dun-dun-dada-dah-dun-dun-dada

It was an age-old melody, a song he hummed through Mama's pregnant belly, long before Sami knew the meaning of the words… and like lightning on a clear day, it hit him:

That song! It's the one from my dream! I sang it to her when she was still a baby. And he remembered that there were lyrics…

With tears streaming down his face, Papa sang into her ear:

WHO IS MY BABY? WHO IS MY GIRL?
WHO IS THE PRETTIEST PRINCESS IN THE WHOLE WORLD?

SHE DANCED ME A STORY

Sami moved and moaned like she'd heard her father's dirge, so he stood for the final stanza, and in a voice so loud the whole world could hear, he sang with all of his heart:

S<small>AMI IS MY BABY</small>! S<small>AMI IS MY GIRL</small>!
S<small>AMI IS THE</small> P<small>RETTIEST</small> P<small>RINCESS IN THE</small> W<small>HOLE</small> W<small>ORLD</small>!

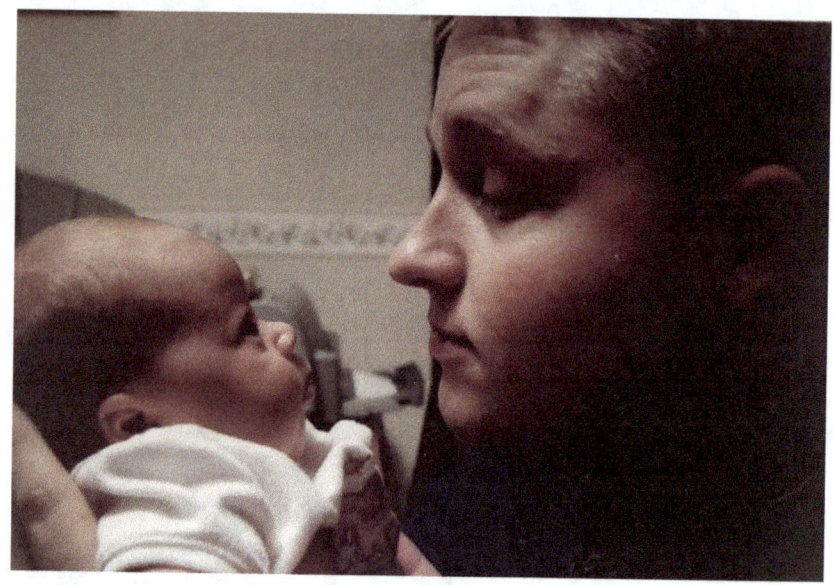

XI

HOWLS IN THE HALLWAY

+ 10 Days Later—Still in Recovery +

"HELP ME!!!"

"Is there nothing you can do for her?!" Papa snarled.

The room was full of nurses, but the blank stares of terror in their shell-shocked eyes revealed a tragic truth: they were as scared as he was. Worse yet, the great people at Helen DeVos were as utterly horrified by what they heard and what they saw as they were helpless to do anything about it at all. It was strange, too, because Sami's surgery seemed to go according to plan. Dr. Foody had removed 80 percent of the tumor, and Sami's facial droop and shoulder spasms entirely disappeared. She didn't have blood clots either, so doctors were confused by the sudden onset of "seizure-like" symptoms. They were so sporadic, so severe, and so terribly scary. They weren't short, either, as some of her "episodes" lasted upward of 120 seconds... 120 seconds of Sami crying out, begging for help, and in, what seemed to be, excruciating pain.

"It's inexcusable!" Papa growled, pointing his finger at all the nurses in the room.

"We're trying, Mr. Bannister," one of them said, "but we honestly don't know what to do."

Another chimed in, "And even if we did, we wouldn't have the authority to intervene."

Papa's face turned beet-red, and his cheeks trembled with rage. "Then get out of here! Leave! All of you! NOW! And don't come back unless you've got answers!"

Nurses apologized and sped out of the room.

SHE DANCED ME A STORY

Mama closed the door behind them, then sat next to Sami on the bed. "You went too far this time, Jeremiah," she said.

Papa just sat there, staring at the floor and trying to stabilize his breath. "I know I did, Ang."

"These are some of the best doctors in the country, and you know they're trying their best. We've been here for over three weeks, so people have gotten to know Sami and the family, and it really hurts them to see her like this."

Papa sighed. "I think I made a few of them cry."

Mama rubbed the nape of his neck. She knew he was grateful for Helen DeVos, and he knew they'd be lost without them, but she also knew he was trying his best to advocate for Sami, and these episodes were just too much.

"I dunno, Jeremiah, I guess all I'm trying to say is that you're doing what you have to do, but you gotta know that the doctors are doing their best, and these nurses hate seeing her like this."

"I'm so sorry, you guys. I just hate feeling so helpless. And these episodes—whatever they are—they're the worst. I really don't expect some magical answer... I just want help."

Sami placed her hand on Papa's shoulder, and in a soft and soothing voice, she said, "Well, if you really wanna help me, you could always give me some of your ice cream."

Mama looked confused. "Um, Sami, we don't have any ice cream."

"Yeah, I know we don't have ice cream—obviously—because you two keep eating it behind my back, which wouldn't be so bad except that you come back to my room with mint chocolate chips all over your lips all the time! And that is so rude because Dr. Kurt keeps telling me, 'No, Sami, you just gotta keep eating Jell-O and drinking water.' It's bad enough I have cancer, but they don't even have real Jell-O. And just water every day? All while you meanies eat ice cream?? No way! That is so not fair."

She made some good points. For starters, Mama and Papa were bad at wiping away the "ice-creaminating evidence," and Dr. Kurt did have Sami on a restrictive diet, at least until things were more stable. So, to smooth things over, the three of them concocted a plan...

The nurse at the desk was hard at work when Papa strolled up to the counter. "Hey, Mr. Bannister, what can I help you with?"

Papa looked around the room like he didn't want to be seen, then he leaned over the desk, and whispered, "I think Sami has a bad case of cabin fever."

"Really?" the nurse replied with her eyebrows raised, "Why do you think that?"

"Well, just look at her," Papa said, pointing back to Sami, who was sitting in her wheelchair near the door to her room. Sami didn't know what cabin fever was, so she had no clue what it made people look like, but she figured it involved puppy dog eyes, so she put out her pouty lip and gave it her best.

"Oooooh," the nurse replied, sarcastically. "Yup, it looks like Sami's got the fever."

"That's what we thought too!" Papa said as he rested his elbows on the desk. "And we read somewhere online that ice cream from the cafeteria downstairs is the best treatment for..." and leaning in close, he covered the side of his mouth with his hand, and whispered, "The Fever."

"Somewhere online, huh?" the nurse replied. She sounded doubtful, and she thought about it for a moment. The suspense was intense, and Papa started getting nervous, but then she smiled, and said, "Yup, sounds good. See you soon."

Papa was so convinced she was going to say no, he already had his rebuttal ready, but just as he was about to say it, he caught himself mid-sentence. "Wait, you said yes??" Then he turned toward Mama and Sami, and shouted, "She said yes!!!"

They couldn't believe it—their plan actually worked! (Okay, so maybe the nurses just wanted to get Papa out of their hair for a bit, but who cares.) Then, just as they were about to leave, the nurse stopped them.

"Keep your phone with you," she said, "just in case we figure something out."

"Uh-oh..." Sami laughed, sarcastically, "figure something out?!?! It sounds like they're on to our top-secret plan! We better book it out of here before they bust us!"

Mama pushed Sami's wheelchair as fast as she could, while Papa pretended to be Secret Service, looking around in every direction to make sure no one was trying to stop them—and they laughed the whole way there. They laughed in the hall, they laughed in the elevator, they even laughed while standing in line. It felt so good, and they started to think they'd never stop laughing, but things cooled off quickly once they approached the cold glass window of the ice cream stand in the cafeteria.

"They have so many flavors," Mama said as she ogled the ice cream. "Mmm... they have Superman, Cookie Dough, and Blue Moon."

"Yummy-yum-yum," Papa sang, "they even have Bubble Gum."

"Is that what flavor you're gonna get, Papa?" Sami asked.

"Pfft! No way, babycakes. It just sounded good because it rhymed. Plus, my doc at the VA said this hospital is making me fat, so I gotta cool it on all the ice cream and candy."

"Aw," Sami sighed, "well, I'll make sure you don't steal any bites of mine, you know, cuz I don't want you to get more fat and stuff."

"Me? An ice-cream robber?!?! What an outrageous accusation!"

Sami promised to keep an eye on him, which would have been fine and dandy, too, but after a few seconds to settle on a selection, Sami smiled at the lady behind the counter, and said, "Mint Chocolate Chip, please."

Mint Chocolate Chip?!?! Papa thought to himself, now biting his bottom lip with worry. *But that's my favorite flavor!*

Enter: The Understatement of the Century.

Truth is, Mint Chocolate Chip was to Papa what Pop-Tarts were to Sami: pure kryptonite. Papa didn't just love it, either—he looooved it!

So rich... so sweet and creamy! he said to himself as the woman behind the counter pressed scoops of ice cream into Sami's waffle cone. He licked his lips and thought, *No, I can't... I can't... I can't resist!* Such was his internal battle, anyway, for as far as anyone else could tell, he was just an overweight dad looking all sorts of desperate to get his paws on his daughter's Mint Chocolate Chip ice cream cone.

Sami played tough, but Papa looked so pitiful, pouting like a baby over an ice cream cone. After a while, he was drooling all over himself, and people started to stare.

"Okay," Sami said, "I'll give you one bite—but only one, you hear?"

Oh, Papa heard, alright—loud and clear! And in a genius dad move, Papa grabbed ahold of Sami's ice cream, and with a sinful smirk in his smile, he opened his jaw as wide as he could and shoved a massive mound of ice cream into his mouth. "See? One bite," he said with a mouthful of Mint Chocolate Chip.

Sami was not impressed, and she worried that Papa would figure out a way to steal more bites, so she never let him leave her sight. It wouldn't have mattered, anyway, as Sami was fiending so badly for some sugar that she devoured her cone in a matter of moments. She ate that cone so fast that she got a huge ring of green ice cream all around her lips.

Papa was laughing hysterically, and Mama said she looked like she was in a pie-eating contest, but Sami wasn't laughing, not even when Mama said the green lips made her look like the Joker, or even when Papa said the chocolate streaked on her cheeks looked like Mel Gibson's war paint from Braveheart. Then she saw herself in a mirror, and all those uncontrollable giggles from their trip to the cafeteria came flooding back into her belly.

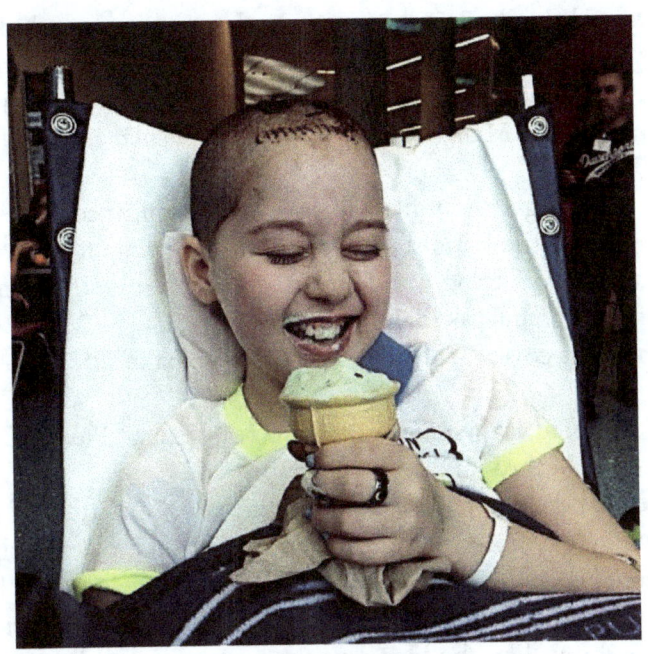

The laughter faded fast, however, as Sami started to complain of stomach pains.

"That's what you get for eating so fast," Mama laughed as she wiped ice cream from Sami's face. "You're lucky you don't have brain freeze."

Ice cream wasn't the culprit, though, and her pain was no laughing matter. It's easy to overlook—and even easier to forget—but kids with cancer are prescribed an enormous amount of medication, and sometimes that makes it tough for people to keep track of things. That's not good, either, especially when the regiment includes narcotics. Every medicine has their pros and cons, of course, but narcotics are risky, and not just because they're habit-forming. They also happen to be notorious for causing constipation, so it was a real oopsie-doopsie when Sami's doctors forgot to prescribe some stool softeners.

"Her belly is really big!" Mama told the nurse as Sami continued to scream and scratched at her stomach. "Just look at it! It's bulged-out like she's pregnant!"

"I just gave her some meds for her tummy, but they'll take a while to work, so for now, we'll need to get Sami in a diaper-"

"A diaper?" Sami cried, anxiously. "But that's so gross and embarrassing! And I'm not a baby anymore."

The nurse felt badly, but she also must have been a psychic in her spare time, for it wasn't long before Sami needed to use the bathroom. And just as she worried, no one was free in that urgent moment to assist Sami.

"C'mon already!" Mama complained. "I've pushed the 'Help' button so many times!"

"I really have to go, though!" Sami said as she squirmed in her bed.

Then, just when the Bannisters were about to give up hope, a nurse they'd never seen raced into the room and began to unwrap something in her hands.

"What is that?" Sami asked, impatiently.

"It's a mattress cover," the nurse replied, "to make sure you don't make a mess on the bed."

"No!" Sami cried as the nurse lifted Sami's bottom. "Please! Can't you just help me go to the bathroom like a normal girl???"

Papa tried his darndest to control his emotions, but after all the week of episodes, crying, icky hospital food, and constipation... *this* was the straw that broke the camel's back. "Stop!" he growled as he put his hand between the nurse and Sami. "If you can't carry her to the bathroom, then I will."

The nurse didn't like the idea, but she knew she couldn't stop him. Plus, Papa knew what he was doing. He had worked all different kinds of jobs, one of which was as an in-home assistant to a quadriplegic hippie in Minnesota. That meant Papa knew how to transfer people out of beds, as well as how to help with shower and bathroom duties. Sami was much smaller than Papa's 6'6" quadriplegic friend, too, so carrying her was going to be easy-peasy-lemon-squeezy.

"It's all just part of the job, anyway," he said as he carried Sami.

Just as he sat her on the potty, she groaned and made an icky face. "No offense, Papa, but you better get your butt outta here—STAT!"

She wasn't in there long, and she took care of herself just fine, but when she was done, Sami asked for Mama's help back to the bed.

"Everything go alright in there?" Papa asked.

"That's private," Sami laughed, "and kinda gross too, you sicko… but if you really need to know, yes, I feel much better, thank you very much."

She wasn't exaggerating, either. Not only had Sami's gut-busting discomfort practically disappeared, but her stomach also shrank back to its normal size. This relief was only momentary, though, as Sami continued to suffer from those awful and erratic episodes, and their world continued to rock and reel like a rollercoaster, tossed back-and-forth between bliss and fear. It was so dizzying, so disorienting, and so disappointing that it started to feel like emotional whiplash.

A few days later, Papa's cousin Derek brought some clippers for Sami to shave his head. Paul and Papa got in on the action, and hair went flying all over the room. Everyone laughed at the men's shaven heads, and for the first time in days, Sami hadn't experienced one of those screaming episodes.

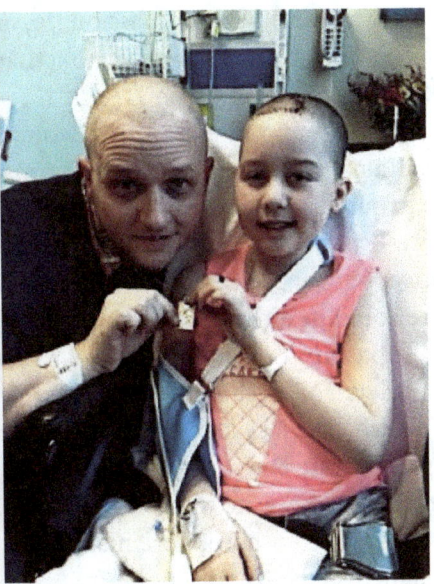

When day turned to night, Sami's narcotics hit her hard, so Derek packed up his clippers, and he and Paul let Sami kiss their heads one last time before saying goodbye before heading back to their homes.

Sami wanted to stay up and talk, but she passed out fast, and in the quiet calm of the hospital room, Mama noticed something: with the kids at Great Grammas and Sami fast asleep, she and Papa had some alone time.

The two of them put on their slippers and quietly snuck out of Sami's room. They walked around the hospital, stopping only every now and again to sob on one another's shoulder. When they arrived at the glass enclosure of a street top bridge, they sat on a bench, holding hands and admiring the view of downtown Grand Rapids, while an ambulance with its lights flashing passed under them.

They looked at each other, searching for a sign, some assurance that things would be fine. They were madly in love, and they often lost track of time, especially when they were alone, but Mama was nervous leaving Sami like that, so she stood up and told Papa they had to go back.

Papa wasn't quite finished, though. "Oh, no, you don't," he said as he grabbed her hand. And in a valiant effort to be all smooth, Papa twirled her toward him, then held her tight, and with his arm around her back, he dipped her toward the ground, gazed deep into her eyes, then howled like a wolf and kissed her - and, yes, he kissed her a lot!

It was so sudden, so passionate, and so hilariously ridiculous that it took Mama's breath away. "You've held that in for a while now, haven't you?" Mama asked, flirtatiously.

"Oh, you don't even know, woman."

Mama was still dipped in his arms, with her peacock blue hair splayed on the ground, and her view of the world inverted. She could clearly see several nurses passing by. They were professionals about it, and they pretended not to notice, but the smirks in their smiles said something different. "You knew they were coming, didn't you?" Mama whispered.

Papa didn't care, though, and with the warmth of her breath still on his lips, he smiled. "Meh, let 'em be jealous."

With one last kiss, he lifted her back to her feet, and the two of them hugged... but this time was different. Mama was squeezing him so hard, it almost hurt, and she was weeping worse than she'd wept in weeks.

"It's just so hard, Jeremiah," she cried. Then she clenched her fist, and screamed at the top of her lungs:

I HATE YOU, CANCER! I FREAKING HATE YOU!

Then she took a breath and shook her head. "It's just not fair, and I just wish it was me in there! I wish I could take her place, Jeremiah, to take away all her pain and all her fear." She grabbed hold of his shirt and squeezed it in her fists. "We've lived life, ya know? We went to college, we got married and had some kids. But Sami? She's only ten years old! She isn't even in high school yet!" And with her eyes cast down toward the ground, Mama sighed. "Sometimes I feel like I can't take it anymore, and I hate myself for it! Part of me just wants to run and hide, especially with all these episodes. They're evil, Jeremiah, and I just feel so helpless... I just hate feeling so completely helpless, ya know, especially when I know Sami needs me."

Papa held her in his arms, gently stroking her hair as she sobbed on his chest, and he promised her that she was doing better than anyone could have imagined. "You're a superhero, Angela Lee, especially to Sami." He wiped the tears from beneath her eyes. "We're in this together, you know. No matter what happens, we're in this together. And if you get down, that's okay. It's gonna happen, anyway, but I ain't goin' nowhere." Then he held her face in his hands. "There will be times when I need you like you need me right now. I know they're coming, Ang, and so do you. But I know *this* even more..." He raised his pinky in the air and told her to swear. "We're a team..."

Mama wiped her nose with Papa's shirt, then chuckled and nodded her head. And with her pinky interwoven with his, she swore a solemn oath. "I promise, Jeremiah. We're in this together... and we're together forever."

SHE DANCED ME A STORY

The stroll back to Sami's room was short and sweet, but when they got back, they discovered that Sami was experiencing the tail-end of yet another one of those episodes.

"They're getting worse," the nurse admitted, anxiously, as she used a wet towel to wipe the sweat from Sami's brow. "It's over now, but this one lasted for nearly five minutes!"

Sami looked exhausted, but even that paled in comparison to the devastation in her eyes. She hadn't experienced an episode all day, and part of her hoped they'd be gone forever, but they weren't, and this one tore her apart. Doctors upped her narcotics, hoping it would help, but they only made her really drowsy and confused. Her eyes rolled around in her head, neck-deep in delirium, but no amount of morphine or madness could stop her from loving on an alpaca plushie Mama bought before her surgery.

"It's soft like Lion," she said, hugging it and rubbing it against her face. "It's cuddly like Lion, too." Sami smothered that alpaca with hugs and kisses, and her eyes closed-shut with contentment as she felt its fleece on her cheeks. Then she paused, and with a confused expression on her face, she asked, "Lion doesn't have a pink bow in his hair, does he?"

"Not yet," Mama laughed.

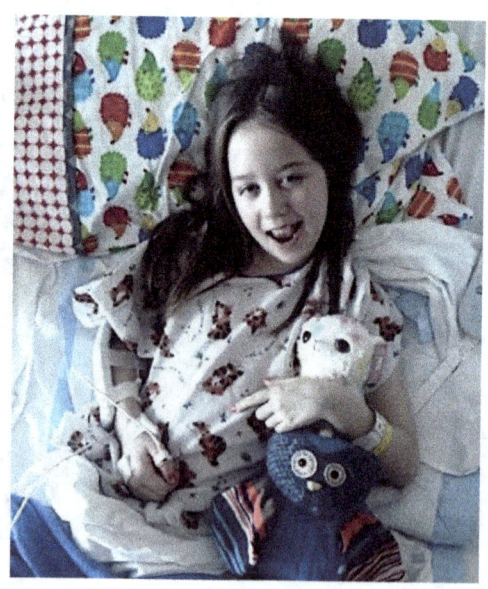

Sami had that look a kid gets when they've concocted a clever plan, and with the alpaca in her hand, she wagged her finger in its face. "Hmph, hear that? Mama said not *yet*..."

Sami named him Jake, and he was a godsend. Every time she had an episode, Jake was there, and he was always willing to be squeezed to death over and over again. And when her episodes would end, his curly fur was always there to wipe her tears or just to be petted. But Sami's episodes only got worse—and experiencing them was a living hell! Mama was right: they were evil, excruciating experiences, and they took enormous amounts of energy and emotion to endure, both from Sami and from everyone witnessing them, especially now that they were lasting nearly ten minutes at a time...

Then came 2 a.m.

The episode was so sudden and so severe, but this time was different.

"Mama! Papa!" Sami cried. "I can't see anymore! And I can't hear!" With the dread of death in her heart, Sami cried aloud what she worried would be her final words...

"Please tell my parents I loved them!!!"

Papa tried everything, but nothing worked, so he did what he always did when he felt helpless: he turned to Mama... but Mama was so traumatized, so tortured by Sami's blood-curdling epitaph, that she reached the point she feared the most, and with tears in her eyes, she curled up on the bed, and pulled the blanket over her head.

Papa's eyes grew wide, and he fell to pieces inside... horrified and heartbroken at the same time. And that's when it happened. In a sudden burst of rage, Papa did the unthinkable:

"ENOUGH!" he yelled at the top of his lungs. He rushed to the door and opened it wide, allowing Sami's cries to howl in the hallway. It was a daring move, and maybe kinda dumb, but her screams were dreadfully loud, and something had to give.

"Can you please close the door, Mr. Bannister?" a nurse asked, politely. "Patients are trying to sleep."

"I bet they are!" he snarled. But he didn't budge—and Sami only got louder—so it wasn't long before other nurses came running to her room.

"Now will you close the door, Mr. Bannister?"

"Are you going to make this go away?" Papa replied.

"There's nothing I can do, only a doctor-"

"Wait!" Papa rudely interrupted. "Hold on, so you're not a doctor?"

"No, but-"

"Oh, so you can't diagnose patients or prescribe medicine?"

"Um, no, but-"

"Then what the heck are you doing here?!" Papa growled, then he walked close to the nurse and stared into his eyes, scowling in the meanest voice he'd ever used, "You need to get me a doctor right now, or I take Sami elsewhere."

"It's 2 a.m. Mr. Bannister. We have docs on call, but-"

"So, call them."

"But I've already called them a few times about this, and they said they don't have any answers for you yet."

"Well, then you're gonna call them one more time, aren't you?"

"But, but I... I-"

"But there ain't no buts about it, cuz I'm about five seconds from getting my daughter the heck out of this place!"

"I-I-I can try, but what if I can't get him on the line?"

Papa gasped, sarcastically. "If you can't get 'em on the line?! You guys blew past that line hours ago, so don't be talkin' to me about some measly lines you can't cross." Of course, Papa knew that wasn't what the nurse meant, but he was on a roll—and he was done messing around. He was a deadly debater too, even when he was out of his mind, and good ol' Mr. Nice Guy was no longer in the room.

The nurse looked nauseated, caught between a rock and a hard place, and part of him hoped that Papa would have pity, but he knew that they were past the point of no return, and he could see no mercy in Papa's eyes. So, after a vain attempt at a calming breath, the nurse looked at Sami, and with tears in his eyes, he whispered, "I'll rattle every chain I can, li'l Sam. You hear me? I promise."

His hands trembled as he pulled the cell phone from his pocket, and his fingers shook, violently, as he dialed the number. A doctor answered, but before the nurse could say anything, Sami cried out for help.

MAMA! HELP! PLEASE! IT'S COMING BACK!

Mama threw off the blanket and raced to the bed, where she hurled daggers of death stares toward the nurse as she howled like a Luna Wolf:

"DO IT! DO IT RIGHT NOW!"

Tears streamed down the nurse's face, but he pressed his lips, shook his head, and said, "I'm sorry, sir, but you need to hear this," then he held his phone close to Sami's face...

Within a few hours, Sami's room was packed with doctors. Sadly, even now, none of them had a clue as to what was going on.

"No way," Papa snarled. "That ain't gonna fly, not anymore."

A brave and daring soul spoke up, insisting that Helen DeVos had some of the most brilliant medical minds in the world on the case.

"*Some?*" Papa replied. "No doubt! But that means, by your own admission, that you aren't the only ones." He looked around the room, asking whether any of them knew anyone outside of Helen DeVos... but no one spoke up. "Seriously? No doctor friends? No classmates from med school?" He stood there, shocked and at least a little offended. "I'm sorry, but there's simply no way this is happening right now."

"We obviously know people outside this facility, Mr. Bannister, but we'd have to make some calls, and that would take time."

"Then call them, dang it! Call 'em up, order tests, prescribe meds, do whatever you've gotta do! But I swear, if you don't figure this out, we'll take Sami out of here faster than you can explain to insurance why you let limo-loads of cash waltz right out the door."

Sami had been sitting there, quietly listening to Papa rant and rave at the doctors. She normally hated to see Papa so angry, and she knew he hated it too, especially since they were so grateful for Helen DeVos, but at this moment, he was fighting tooth and nail, and she was proud of him.

"I love you so much," she said. "And thank you for fighting for me."

Papa nodded, but he didn't say anything. He didn't have to. She knew he was giving it everything he had. He may have been mean as a Sun Bear, but life and death—and all these episodes—do crazy things to people. Even so, he knew when enough was enough, so he closed his eyes, and with his head bowed, he exhaled. And in a calmly stern voice, he said, "Y'all have heard me loud and clear tonight, amirite?"

They heard him all right, and after a few final words (many of which Papa wished he'd never said), the doctors ordered tests, promised to make those calls, and left the room.

The next 96 hours were tough, but doctors were on the ball. They even made calls, one of which was to a doctor who knew what Sami was experiencing. It took a while for the new prescription to work, but, with the episodes becoming less frequent—and less intense—things were finally getting better.

Childhood cancer is a zero-sum game, though, so if it wasn't one thing, it was probably another.

"I can't move it!" Sami cried, frantically. "I can't move my right-leg at all!" She grabbed it, yelled at it, and even hit it, hoping that something would make it work... but it backfired, serving only to reveal something so much worse: Sami wasn't only unable to move her leg, she couldn't even feel it anymore. In a weird way, that was worse than anything that had happened thus far. She could handle the shoulder spasms and the stroke-like droop in her face, and she could even endure the fear and pain of those terrible episodes.

"But this?!" she wept, angrily. "I won't ever be able to skate again!"

And *that* was a nightmare.

+ Sami's Last Day at Helen DeVos +

When the day came for Sami to be transferred to a rehab clinic in town, Mama gathered their things while doctors got her ready for the road. Papa tried to help, but they told him to wait in the hall, so that's where he stood, biting his nails while watching through the window.

"Are you her father?" asked a woman standing next to him.

"Oh, my gosh!" Papa gasped. "Wow. Holy cow! I didn't even see you there." In fact, Papa had never seen her anywhere. That threw him for a loop, too, because after a month at Helen DeVos, Papa thought he'd seen everybody, and there's no way he would've missed seeing this woman, not with her purple glasses, purple blazer, and purple pants and heels—she'd have stood out in any crowd! "Yes, the girl in that room is Samantha... she's my daughter... and she has cancer."

"I'm sorry to hear that, Mr. Bannister," she replied, still paying close attention to the people in the room. "Samantha seems very sweet."

That's when one of the people examining Sami nodded to the doctor in purple, then gave her a big thumbs up. It must have been something important because the doctor in purple clapped and clasped her hands.

"Excellent! Just as I thought!"

"What is just as you thought?" Papa asked.

The doctor turned toward Papa, and with a confident nod, she smiled, and said, "Your daughter will walk again, Jeremiah."

Papa was so shocked by her words, he covered his mouth with his hands, and he choked up so badly, he could barely talk. "What, I-I, I mean, how could you possibly know that? And I don't mean to be rude or anything, but I don't even know who you are."

"Oh, goodness," she said as she reached out to shake his hand. "I'm Dr. Kuldanek."

Papa opened his mouth to reply, but they were suddenly surrounded by a crowd of people and the sound of very loud music.

+ Moments Earlier—Back in Sami's Room +

Sami was glad to be leaving, but she was embarrassed by the scar on her head, and she worried that people would stare and make fun of her.

A Child Life volunteer named Reese brought her some fancy shades, and nurses sat a boombox on her lap.

"What is this for?" Sami asked.

SHE DANCED ME A STORY

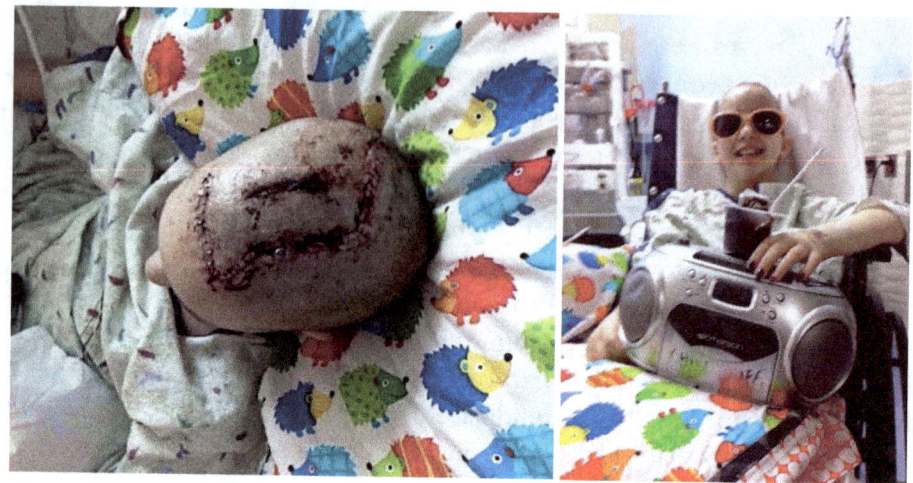

Reese smiled. "How else do you expect to play 'What Does the Fox Say?' loud enough for everyone in the hospital to hear?"

"But why would I do that?" Sami laughed, nervously. "Won't that just make more people stare and make fun of me?"

Reese winked, and said, "Oh, you'll see."

Unbeknownst to Sami, people had already assembled throughout the halls, and others were spreading the good news. So, when Sami pushed play on the boombox, everyone was ready... everyone but Papa.

He was surrounded by doctors, nurses, patients, and passersby, all of them singing and dancing to the music, and everyone was cheering for his daughter. People ran from different rooms, even different wings of the hospital, just to be there when the little girl with the big incisions and an even bigger smile rolled by them in her wheelchair. And when any new person caught up with her, they'd join her entourage, singing and dancing with everyone else, all the way to the exit doors.

Papa was determined, though. He wanted to know—he needed to know—how Dr. Kuldanek was so sure that Sami would walk again.

He pushed and shoved his way through the crowd, but there were just too many of them, and Dr. Kuldanek was walking away. He shouted her name, but she didn't turn around, and he worried she couldn't hear him over all the commotion. He yelled again; this time as loud as he could:

"Dr. Kuldanek!!!"

It took a second, but she stopped, then turned around.

"How do you know Sami will walk again?" he shouted.

She shouted back, "The same reason I knew how to stop those episodes Sami was having." Then she smiled. "It's also how I knew your name without you telling me... and it's the same reason I gave your parents 25 years ago when I told them your brother Isaac would walk again..."

XII

CANDY, CANES, AND CANNABIS
[Miracles at Mary Free Bed]

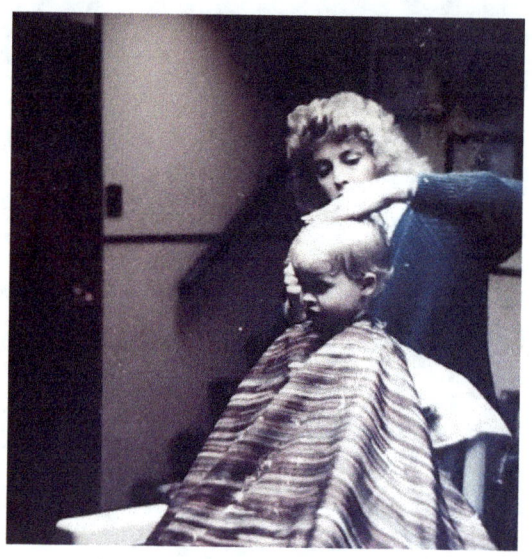

+ Winter 1988—Battle Creek, Michigan +

    Hues of red and blue flickered and flashed in the night, casting galaxies of sparkling light onto the icy branches that wept in the willow near the wreckage. The car was crumpled like an accordion, and it was cloaked in unholy smoke interwoven with a layer of freshly fallen snow. EMTs shouted through shattered windows as the Jaws of Life opened the door, where they found a six-year-old boy barely breathing on the floor, and a father, helplessly trapped, crying to God for help.

    Help came, and her name was Nana, then known as Mommy. She had gotten the call ten minutes before, while at home with Jeremiah and Curly, who were laughing and dancing along to a song booming through Pa's beloved

McIntosh ML-1oc speakers. The party quickly came to an end, though, when the children saw their Mommy drop the phone to the floor...

Pa and Isaac had gone for a haircut, but while they were there, it began to snow. The roads were slicker than they were before, and the flurry of snowflakes made it hard for drivers to see, but Pa and Isaac were so happy, so happy that they even forgot to-

"Put on your seatbelts!" Nana yelled as she started the car. The click of their buckles was music to her ears, but it was the song of a specter, sung by the fear that their family would be facing years of tears and pain.

Turns out, Pa and Isaac were almost home when a truck backed out in front of them. Pa swerved out of the way, but then he almost hit a telephone pole, so he quickly steered the tires back toward the road, where he and Isaac came face-to-face with oncoming traffic. And in the blink of an eye, they collided head-on with a Cadillac three-times the size of their Honda—and crashed at 45 mph!

Just before the impact, Pa realized what he'd done. In the haze of the fun back at the barber shop, he forgot to put on his safety belt... and he failed to have Isaac do the same.

"Isaac!" he screamed. Pa reached across the seat, pressing his palm as hard as he could against Isaac's chest, but there was nothing he could do.

Isaac's six-year-old body flew like a ragdoll through the air, and the impact of his head to the glass caused the windshield to shatter. Pa was knocked out for a while, and he was in a lot of pain when he woke up, but none of that mattered once he saw Isaac. For there he laid, crumpled-up on the floor... blue, unconscious, and blood flowed from his ears and nose. It was the darkest and thickest blood that Pa had ever seen, and he knew Isaac was in trouble. The shattered glass of the windshield said it all: Isaac's head had almost gone through it, and the impact on his head from the collision caused a clot in his brain, which left him unconscious and near death. Making matters worse, Isaac's trachea and left lung had collapsed, so he was barely breathing...

After an emergency craniotomy, the doctors shared with sadness, "We can't promise that Isaac will survive, or even come out of this coma, but even if he does, he will unlikely be the same boy you knew and loved before today..."

+ April 2015—Mary Free Bed +

"Hey, Sami, look what I can do!" Jana said as she hopped and hobbled around the room.

"Wow! You really did it. You're walking again!"

Jana was a spirited and carefree six-year-old girl, but her war vet dad told the Bannisters that she suffered from terrible seizures. Like Sami, Jana needed brain surgery, and she'd been at Mary Free Bed for a while, even longer than the other boy in the therapy room. He was from Marshall, Michigan, and he'd been hit by a driver who ignored the red, blinking stop sign lights on his school bus. Jana was a hard worker, though, and with her stickered-up helmet and customized cane, she was the cutest little thing at Mary Free Bed.

Sami re-stacked her therapy blocks. "I wish I could walk again."

"You'll walk again," Dr. Kuldanek said. "It'll just take some time."

Papa handed Sami her last therapy block. "That, and some hard work."

"Maybe," Sami grumbled, "but then why is it that all I ever do is play fun games and bounce basketballs around the room?"

"Oh, my!" Mama replied. "That sounds downright miserable!"

Sami gave Mama one of her world-famous death stares, but she knew that the best things in life came with time, so she had to be patient, and she accepted that it was gonna be hard getting back on her feet again. It made sense, then, that "a lot of hard work" is exactly what Dr. Kuldanek ordered.

Sami had some time to spare, anyway, as her doctors didn't have her scheduled for chemo or radiation until later that month. Dr. Kuldanek also ordered a prescription to deal with Sami's episodes, which made it easier for Sami to function throughout the day. Turns out, those episodes weren't seizures at all. They were neurostorms resulting from hypothalamic stimulation directly affecting Sami's sympathetic nervous system. Add some stimulated adrenal glands into the mix, and you've reached the root of Sami's neurostorms. It explained her involuntary body positioning, her hyperventilating, her abnormally rapid heart rate, and the enormous amounts of sweat she secreted whenever she was experiencing an episode.

"Yeah, and I'm glad those meds make all those crazy brain zappy storms go away," Sami said (with a hint of reluctance), "but now that I'm feeling better, Dr. Kuldanek has me doing therapy like crazy every day!"

It's true, Dr. Kuldanek had Sami doing crunches every day, as well as leg exercises to rebuild the muscle that had atrophied while lying in a hospital bed for over a month. She had speech therapy, too, where they played games, put puzzles together, and learned some fun brain-twisters. Those therapies were aimed at opening new mental pathways, but some of Sami's therapies were purely practical. She needed help regaining a semblance of the self-reliance she enjoyed before her surgery. And that meant some "down to earth" day-to-day routines, stuff like eating, showering, getting in and out of her wheelchair, and dressing herself for the day—they even taught her how to brush her teeth left-handed. All of it was basic, even intuitive to able-bodied people, so they tend to be taken for granted. But cancer sucks, and it messed Sami up, and she couldn't take anything for granted anymore, so they pushed her hard every day, then let her rest with a well-deserved nap.

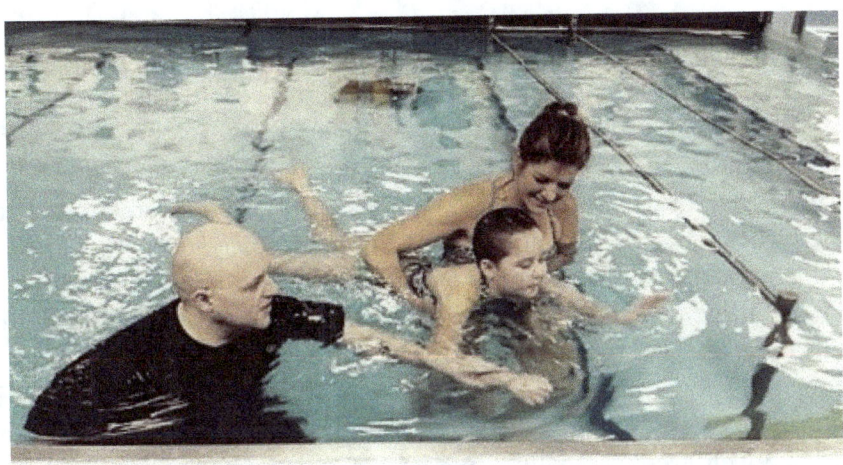

That nap came as a godsend today, and in more ways than one. Papa had a super-sneaky scheme up his sleeve, and once he did it, Sami would need lots of sleep.

It was no secret that Papa and Mama hated cancer, and there was no hiding how much it hurt their hearts to see their daughter suffer, but Papa grew tired of disguising just how much he loathed the pill-poppin' smorgasbord of Vicodin, Morphine, Xanax, and Valium the doctors had her on. She was blown-out 24/7, and by mid-afternoon, she was a zombie, and sometimes she drooled like a dog.

"It's so embarrassing," Sami complained.

Papa was listening, but he was also filling a gel cap with oil from a syringe. It was dark golden brown, sticky icky, and had a funny smell that made Sami scrunch her nose.

"I mean, I know I need meds to help me and stuff, but sometimes I think the meds these doctors give me make my life even worse."

Papa agreed, and that's what got him thinking. He was a journalist, and he'd been influenced by the drug-fueled writings (and lifestyle) of Hunter S. Thompson. Like Thompson, Papa lived on the wild side. Time took its toll, though, and Papa was now a 37-year-old man with a wife and four kids, but, thankfully, it wasn't all for naught. He had learned a lot through his many manic misadventures, especially things having to do with the medicinal benefits of otherwise illegal "street drugs," and the medical benefits of marijuana.

Michigan was a medicinal marijuana state at that time, and Sami's cancer made her a shoo-in for a medical card. The law required two doctors to sign off on her prescription, but that was easy-peasy. However, things got kinda risky when it came to the type of cannabis Sami needed.

"It's called RSO," Papa said as he held up the gel cap. "And it's a whole other level of weed."

Mama's brow furrowed with suspicion. "What do you mean by 'a whole other level'?"

Papa stopped for a moment, wondering how best to phrase this. Then he handed Sami the capsule and a cup of water, saying, "Well, it's stronger than the Maui Wowie Cheech & Chong were smokin' in the '70s, that's for sure."

Mama crossed her arms and gave Papa one of those looks wives give their husbands when they're onto their schtick. "How much stronger, Jeremiah?"

"I mean, you know, it's medicinal, so—"

"And didn't the doctors say *that* stuff was illegal?"

Sami popped the gel cap in her mouth, then took a swig of water.

Papa stared into the distance, thinking through the many ways Mama could respond to what he had to say. Three things were certain, though: Mama loved Sami, she absolutely hated cancer, and, like Papa, she would be willing to do almost anything to add to the quality and quantity of Sami's life. "Honestly, Ang? You wanna know?"

"Of course, honestly. I'm not asking you to lie."

Sami made an icky face. "YUCK! Seriously, Papa, I heard you say cannabis tasted awesome, but I can tell you, that flavor is totally not awesome in my mouth right now!"

Mama glared angrily at Papa. "Wait! You told Sami that cannabis tasted awesome?"

Sami shoved a Pop-Tart in her mouth, hoping to get rid of the flavor. "He also told me that RSO was strong enough to put down an elephant."

"Jeremiah!" Mama said, scornfully.

"Wait! What? No way! I never said it could put down an elephant."

Sami shrugged. "I dunno, maybe he said a horse, I forget."

Mama was upset, but she was really just scared. She didn't want Sami to be so high that she couldn't do her therapy, and she couldn't help but fret over the fact that what they were doing was illegal. After all, as bad as cancer is with all the meds she'd been taking, it would be much worse if she was taken away because of weed, only then to be put back on the very meds they're hoping the cannabis could replace. "And Sami's a ten-year-old girl, Jeremiah, not an elephant."

"A horse," Sami corrected her.

"Whatever. Either way, you're neither of those things."

"I know," Papa sighed, "but her cancer is a beast." Then he paused and got very, very serious. "And about the other part... yes, we could get in trouble."

"What we're doing isn't just illegal, Jeremiah. It's, like, illegal big time."

"I'm dying, though, Mama," Sami sighed from her bed. Her words tore at the heart, but they also cut to the chase. "And I hate that, ya know. You're right too, though, Mama, because I'm just a kid, but I wanna live the best life I can. And I'm the one with cancer, anyway, right? Plus, like Papa said, it's not like people are gonna turn on the news and hear, 'Today, a little girl with brain cancer died from some weed.'"

Sami reached over and grabbed the syringe, looking closely at its dark, gooey content. "No matter what, I trust you guys, and I know we can keep this a secret, that way people won't get mad or take me away. So can we all just be okay now?" Then she giggled and shoved the rest of her Pop-Tart in her mouth. "I'm starting to feel, like, erm, you know... mmm, this Pop-Tart is amazing... whew... yeah, so, um, Mama, it's definitely too late for me to change my mind, even if I wanted to."

SHE DANCED ME A STORY

The next few days at Mary Free Bed ran like any other, except that Sami was taking "Papa's Meds" three or four times a day, which meant Sami was as high as a kite. Nurses in the therapy room even wondered why she was always giggling and carrying on about the munchies.

"Um, duh, obviously," Jana said in a punky voice, "'cuz girls love eatin' food!"

"Yeah!" Sami giggled, all spaced-out. "And we love eating fried chicken too!"

Jana raised her forearm crutch high to the sky, just like She-Ra did whenever she raised her magical sword. "YES! Fried chicken," she declared, "cuz it's food! And Twinkies too!"

Sami laughed so hard she practically fell out of her chair. "Twinkies and Pop-Tarts!" she said with a thunderous voice. But then she paused, looking around the room all sorts of confused...

"Wait... did somebody just say something about Pop-Tarts?"

"YOU DID!" Jana thundered in a big dinosaur voice.

"Oooh, yeah," Sami giggled. "I guess that was me, huh?"

"Of course, it was!" Jana replied. "And you wanna know why?!" Then Jana stomped her sparkly Velcro shoes and used her crutches like little T-Rex arms, roaring, "Cuz you are MUNCHY-SAURUS REX!"

Jana was just being Jana—all sorts of adorable and hilarious—but her time with Sami at Mary Free Bed helped more than she or her family even knew, and not just because she provided cover for Sami's medicine-induced goofiness.

Jana was Sami's first "hospital friend" since the whole thing began, and it wasn't all just laugh and play. Jana encouraged her, too, inspiring Sami to take things in stride and to try her best all the time, especially in therapy.

Sami's life wasn't just sunshine and rainbows, though, and Dr. Kuldanek was saddened by something Sami said at the end of their last session, so she told Sami's therapist to take a detour on the way back to Sami's room...

"What are we doing?" Sami asked as the therapist wheeled her past her room.

"Yeah, Sami's room is back there," Jana said.

The therapist just smiled. "Well, I've got one more exercise for you." Once they stopped, she locked the brakes on Sami's wheelchair and told Mama and Jana to stand at the other end of the hall, then she took the blanket off Sami's lap, and said, "Alrighty, then, you're going to need to stand up for this one, Samantha."

"Stand up?! That's crazy talk! And what if I fall?"

The therapist sat on a roller chair, then wheeled it next to Sami. "That's why I'll be with you the whole time." Grabbing the harness around Sami's waist, she added, "And, look, if you get nervous, you can always balance yourself with the rail on the wall."

Sami's jaw dropped in disbelief. "Wait, you want me to walk?!"

"Obviously," she laughed. "And you want to walk too... right?"

"Yeah, but-"

"Well, then that's what you're going to do." Then she pointed toward the far end of the hall, saying, "And you're gonna walk aaaaaall the way over to Mama and Jana."

"All the way over there?!"

The therapist nodded. She was aware that Sami was petrified, but that sort of thing just came with the territory, and if therapists at Mary Free Bed were good at anything, they were good at making even the most hardened skeptics doubt their doubt.

Sami's hand shook like a leaf as she reached for the rail, and her knees knocked with fear when she stood to her feet...

"You can do this, Samantha!" Jana shouted from down the hall.

Sami scoffed under her breath, but then she saw the faith in the therapist's eyes, and when she looked at Jana standing strong on her braces, and Mama with her arms opened wide, she remembered a story that Nana told her when she was still a little girl...

SHE DANCED ME A STORY

+ Hershey's Chocolate World (circa 2012) +

The smell of milk chocolate made Sami hungry, and she couldn't wait to get the free sample at the end of the tour, but she didn't want the ride at Hershey's Chocolate World to end because she was sharing a seat with Nana, and Nana was telling her all about what happened to Uncle Isaac when he was a kid.

"The doctors said he was gonna die?"

"Uncle Isaac almost did die," Nana replied.

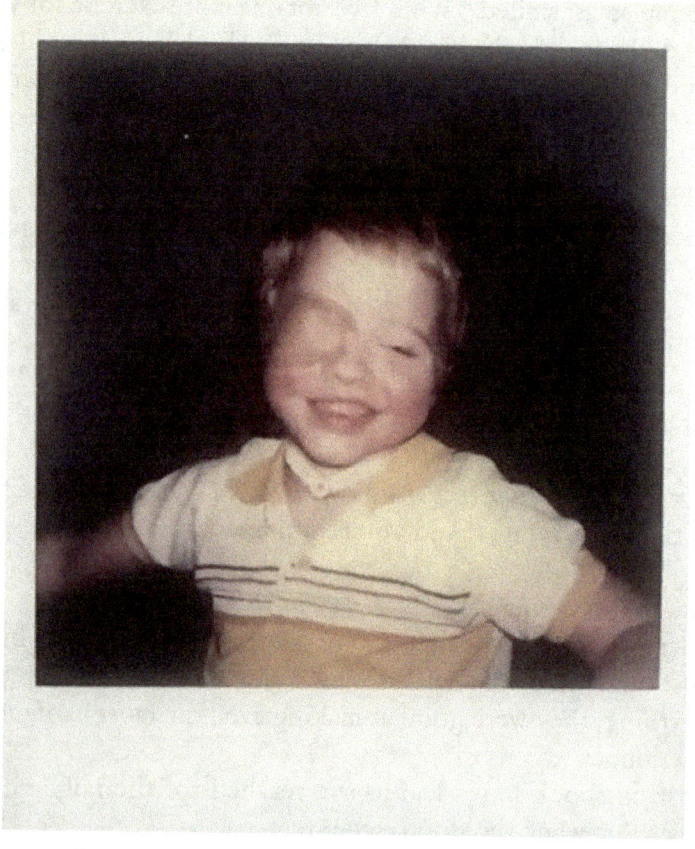

Sami's eyes opened wide. "Well, I'm glad THAT didn't happen, that's for sure."

Nana nodded her head. "It was scary, and we had to make some really hard decisions—things I hope and pray you'll never have to face—and for a while, the doctors thought that even if Isaac did wake up, he wouldn't be able to walk or talk, and he probably wouldn't remember a single thing from before the accident... not even me, and I'm his mom."

Nana's voice cracked with the pain of the memories, and she pressed her lips tightly together. She didn't want to cry—she'd already cried enough for ten lifetimes—so she wiped under her eye, and with that bittersweet joy that flows from the pain of the past, she laughed and shook her head in disbelief, saying, "But those doctors were wrong... Oh, how God proved them wrong so many times."

But it didn't come without a cost. Isaac not only had a tracheotomy tube that he would live with for the next twenty years, he was, among many other things, still unable to walk.

"So, what did you do, Nana?"

Nana leaned her elbow over the back of the chair to twirl her fingers through Sami's hair. "Well, that's when we met a doctor... a doctor who loved the color purple."

Dr. Kuldanek was younger back then, but her love for all things purple was the same, and she was just as hopeful that miracles really did happen at Mary Free Bed, so she was always optimistic about Isaac, and she worked with him every day. But, Isaac's progress was glacially slow, and with every passing day, success seemed to drift further and further away...

"...until one evening, we grabbed some McDonald's for dinner. Everyone was eating in Isaac's room, laughing and carrying on, when I saw something miraculous."

"A miracle? What was it?"

Nana leaned in close to Samantha, and whispered, "Uncle Isaac was standing up."

"What? Did he just do that all on his own??"

"Yes!" Nana replied as she made the American Sign Language sign for walking. "And there he was, just strutting through the room like there was nothin' to it."

"Whoa! What! He was just walking around like nothing ever happened?!"

Nana laughed. "No, Isaac took baby steps, but at least he was walking." Nana cocked her chin to the side and thought back. "Actually, come to think of it, there was something weird about the whole thing."

SHE DANCED ME A STORY

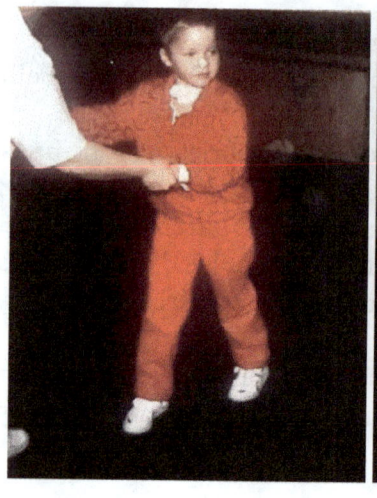

"Weird?" Sami asked with a quizzical smile.

"Kind of. I mean, imagine, there he was, walking across the room, right in front of everyone, and yet for some weird reason, Isaac was licking his lips like he was hungry, and he was reaching out his hand and wiggling his fingers like he was trying to grab something."

"Did you ever figure out why he did that?"

Nana pointed to Isaac and Papa seated ahead of them. "It was your dad."

"My dad was weird and made Uncle Isaac walk again?!"

Nana laughed and shook her head. "No-well, yeah, your dad *is* weird-but that night, all he was doin' was sittin' down on the ground eating his food. I guess Isaac just saw those fries and wanted some, cuz he got right up outta that seat, walked right over to your Papa, and snatched that fry right up out of his hand."

"That's amazing!" Sami cheered.

"Uncle Isaac must've thought so, too, cuz after he grabbed that French fry, he sat on the ground, stretched out his legs and nice and cozy, then *plop* right down on his back..."

"Why did he do that?"

Nana winked, then wrapped her arms around her granddaughter. "Cuz, he earned that French fry, and he knew it tasted even better than it looked."

The tour came to an end, so Sami and Nana finally got their free Hershey's Kisses, but as they entered the souvenir shop, Sami asked Nana one more question. "Well, two actually. First, what ever happened to that doctor who loved purple? And what did it feel like to finally have Uncle Isaac back home with the family?"

"I don't know what ever happened to that doctor," Nana replied, "but I bet she's helping people just like she helped Isaac. She might even be helping lead the next generation of therapists who will do the same thing that she does, that way the miracles at Mary Free Bed just keep on rolling." She paused for a moment, thinking back to the day that Isaac returned home. There were signs and balloons all over the place, and there was a big poster of Goofy welcoming Isaac home. "It's kinda hard to answer that second one, Sami. It felt good, but 'good' just isn't good enough to tell you how I felt in my heart."

"Maybe you felt like the way Uncle Isaac felt eating that fry?"

Nana laughed and ruffled Sami's hair. "Yeah, it felt a lot like that."

+ Back in the Long Hall at Mary Free Bed +

Sami squinted her eyes and pressed her lips, then gripped the rail and started to walk.

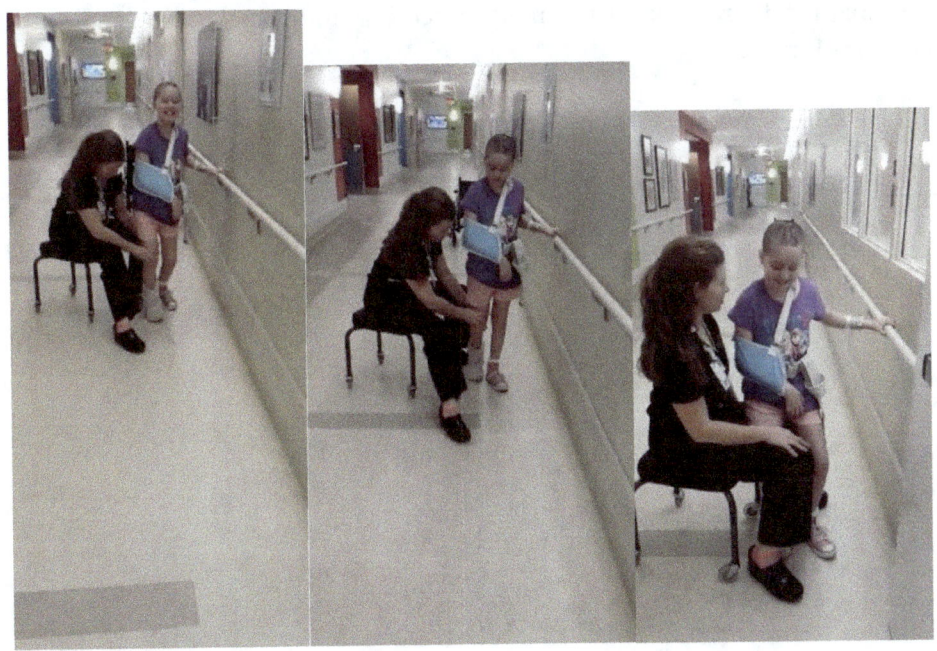

SHE DANCED ME A STORY

Mama wanted to cheer her on, but the sight of Sami walking the halls of Mary Free Bed made her laugh and cry at the same time-and Jana did more than enough cheering for both of them, anyway.

"You're doing it, Sami!" Jana shouted. "And you better not quit! You can make it all the way here-just believe in yourself!"

Sami's steps were clunky, and she took one teensy-weensy step at a time, but she grew braver and bolder with every step, and with Mama, Jana, and the therapist cheering her on, she started to believe. Then, halfway to Mama, Sami decided to give it everything she had. So, with her eyes closed, she licked her lips, then released her hand from the rail.

The therapist saw what Sami did, and it made her so proud. So, just like a mother helping her child to ride a bike without training wheels, she slowly let go of Sami's safety belt, and let her walk on her own.

Sami made the hugest "Sami Face" she'd ever made, then she shouted, "Look, Mama! I'm doing it—I'm walking, Mama! I'm walking!"

Mama was weeping with joy, and as Sami got closer, she reached out to her daughter. When Sami saw that, she used all the strength she had left to raise her right arm, entirely unassisted, then she reached as far and as hard as she could, wiggling her fingers like she wanted something, until finally, her hands took hold of Mama's.

"And Munchy-Saurus WINS!" Jana shouted.

The four of them hopped up and down, giggling like little girls. And after some huge hugs and high-fives, Jana said goodnight, then danced down the hall, twirling one of her canes like a magic wand, singing, "Do you believe it's magic? I sure hope you do! Cuz you'll always have a pal in these sparkly shoes."

 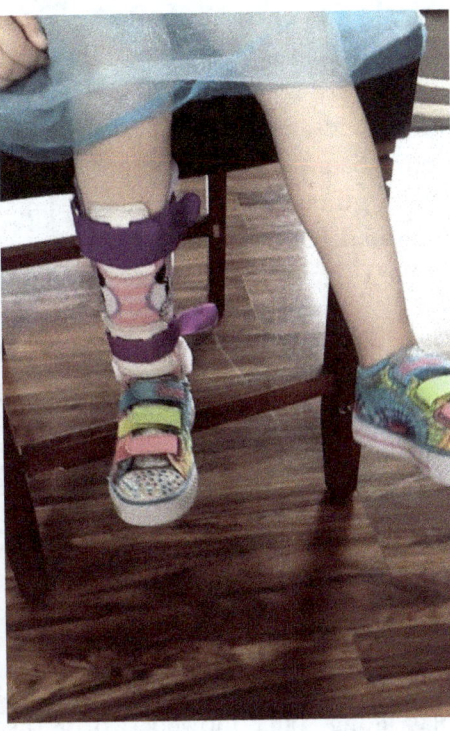

"Ahhhh," Sami sighed with a smile as she plopped down on the therapist's lap. "Thank you for believing in me."

"Who? Me?" She ruffled the hair on Sami's head, and said, "No, *that* was all you, And maybe a little of Dr. K, too. All I did was wind you up and let ya go."

"Well, then I know just what you need." Sami grabbed tightly to her wrist, then raised both arms up and over the therapist's neck and gave her the biggest family-sized two-arm hug that any therapist had ever received.

From that night onward, Sami was different. Every day was so intense, with Sami pushing herself harder in therapy than she ever pushed at anything before. That was until something entirely unexpected happened…

"Going home?" Sami asked (with a hint of jealousy).

Jana was spinning around in circles, mesmerized by how her new tutu whirled through the air. "Where else would I go?" she laughed. "My mom and dad wanna throw me a party, though, that way I can say goodbye. So, c'mon!"

"What? Right now??"

"Duh! Of course, my party is right now. Sheesh."

Streamers hung from the ceiling, and the sound of music filled the air. The smell of pizza was everywhere, too, and the place was packed with doctors, nurses, friends, and family, and all of them wore fun party hats. It was epic... so epic, that Sami started to feel sorta bummed.

"I'm gonna miss you a lot," Jana said as she handed Sami a slice of pepperoni pizza.

"Aw, I'll miss you too. But now who's gonna hang out with me when you're gone?"

"You can hang out with the present I got you," Jana replied.

"You got me a present? But it's your special day, so I should be the one getting you a present, not the other way around."

"Yeah, but all my days are special days," Jana said with a punky flare. "And I got tons of presents already, so I'm not sad one bit." Then Jana bounced like Tigger over to a chair, where she grabbed something out of a bag, then hurried to hide it behind her back. "I'm not tellin' what it is, though, so you gotta guess the surprise."

That probably would've been hard if the stuffed giraffe's head wasn't sticking out over Jana's shoulder, but the whole thing was so cute, Sami decided to play along. Jana allowed two or three wrong guesses before she simply couldn't take it anymore, and pulling the giraffe from out behind her back, she said, "Ta-da! It's *this*!"

"A giraffe!" Sami cheered as she pet its fluffy hair. "She's really soft. But I don't know what her name is."

"Um, hello!" Jana laughed. "Her name is Jana, obviously." Then she sat on the bench and rested her head on Sami's shoulder. "I thought that could help you remember me forever... cuz I'll never forget you, you know?"

Sami chuckled, and with Jana the Giraffe in her hands, she rested her cheek on the helmet of that little diva in sparkly shoes, and said, "And I promise I'll always remember you, too."

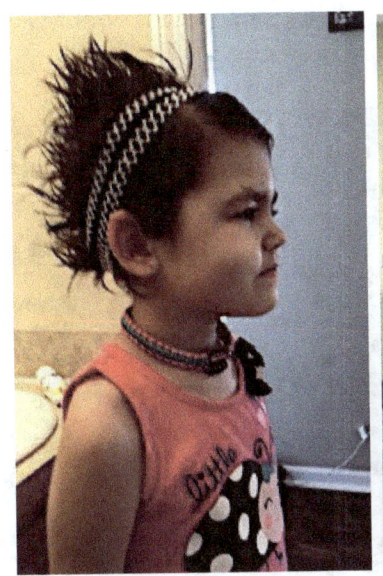 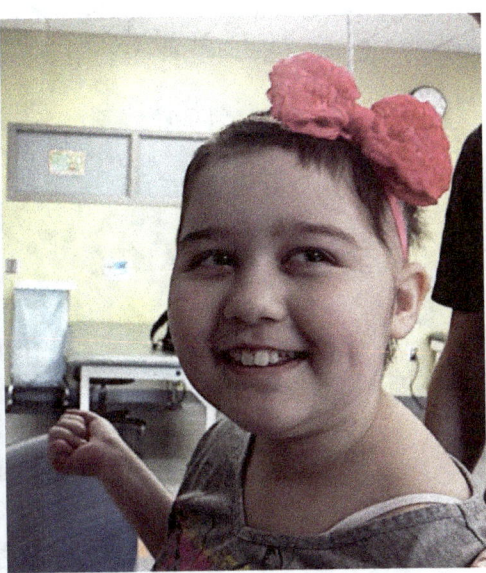

    Sami loved that sparky little spitfire, and she hated to see her leave, but Sami made good on that promise, and she kept her in mind every day after that, even sleeping every night with that super-soft giraffe. The family was relieved to see Sami keep making progress, and now more than ever before. For though Jana was no longer at Mary Free Bed, her love was, and that magic she helped Sami believe in was finally working its wonders.

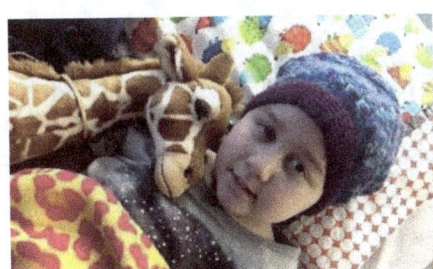 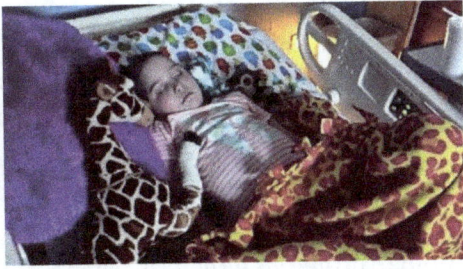

    Then, one dark and delightful night, Papa bought some fried chicken from a local takeout. Sam was getting used to cannabis, but it still made her laugh a lot, and she talked kinda funny, but she wasn't a zombie, and she hadn't complained about pain for weeks. In fact, she hadn't complained about anything at all. No nausea, no depression, no sleepless nights, not even about the fake hospital Jell-O—nothing at all. Sami even started walking with a cane, got back to doing homework, and watched educational videos about cancer, radiation, and even the history of prohibition in America.

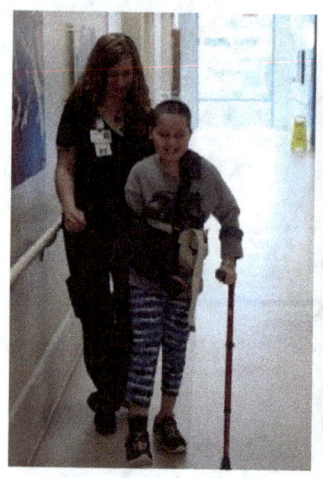

"That movie was ridiculous," Sami said as she turned off *Reefer Madness*. "Seriously, I really hope America changes the laws about that stuff, especially for people with cancer—and even more for kids with cancer!" She shoved a fistful of chicken in her mouth, mumbling, "Maybe I can help them... yeah... mmm... I'm definitely gonna do that..." She was still chewing when she wiped some barbeque sauce off her lips, and with a twinkle in her eye, she giggled. "But you're gonna have to wait, United States of America... at least until after I take a nice looooong nap."

What was true for America wasn't true for Dr. Kuldanek, though, and what she had to say must've been important because she called Sami and the family into her office right away. This worried Mama and Papa, especially since Sami wasn't scheduled to meet with Kuldanek's team for another two weeks-

"Three weeks, if you want to be exact," Dr. Kuldanek said. She was flipping through a bunch of papers, shuffling them around to be in a certain order, then she jogged them on the table, and looked at Sami.

"Is everything okay?" Mama asked.

Dr. Kuldanek shifted her glasses to the end of her nose and looked at Sami. "Well, I'm going over all the notes here-"

"I've been trying really hard," Sami interjected.

"Apparently," Dr. Kuldanek replied. Then she removed her purple glasses, allowing them to hang on the string around her neck. "It appears that Sami's therapists say that she has met all of her goals."

"That's good, right?" Sami asked as she bit her nails.

"It means you've exceeded all of our expectations," Dr. Kuldanek replied. The Bannisters just sat there, looking very confused, so Dr. Kuldanek put it as plainly as she could: "You'll still have radiation and chemo with your team at Helen DeVos, but as far as Mary Free Bed goes... it means you can go home, Samantha."

"Wait, I don't have to stay here another three weeks?!"

"I mean, if you really want to stay, you can-"

"Nooooooooo!" Sami squealed with excitement. Then she caught herself, and very calmly said, "I mean, yes, ma'am, please and thank you."

Dr. Kuldanek chuckled and waved for Sami to follow her into the hall. Once there, she pointed to something, and said, "Consider it a goodbye present for a job well-done."

It was a brand-new wheelchair, and it was a bright and beautiful shade of pink, just like her cane and leg brace. The wheels were super skinny, too, so Sami knew it was faster than the ones at the hospital. Best of all, the little wheels in the front lit up all different colors as it cruised around the hallway. She was so grateful, the emotion nearly overwhelmed her, but that emotion only got heavier during the drive back home...

Children from the neighborhood hadn't seen Sami since she first went to Helen DeVos, and that was two months ago, so when they saw her in the backseat of the van, everyone ran over to greet her. No one stared at her scars, and everyone loved the lights on her wheelchair, but Sami couldn't help that she was nervous. Sure, many things had remained the same, but life was different now... and Sami was different now too.

Mama wheeled Sami's chair down the sidewalk toward the house, and when they reached the stairs, Papa reached down to help lift her, but Sami told him to stop, then asked him to help her stand to her feet. Papa reached for her cane, but, again, Sami said no.

"Papa, this is something I've gotta do."

The steps were daunting, and there were more of them than she remembered, but Sami meant what she said a few weeks back, on the first night without Jana at Mary Free Bed...

SHE DANCED ME A STORY

+ Flashback: Sami's Room—Mary Free Bed +

"I want to go home, Papa."

"I know you do, baby. And trust me-"

"No, you don't!" Sami sharply interrupted. "I'm sorry, Papa, but you don't know at all! I mean, when I was at Helen DeVos, you and Mama got to go home sometimes. But I couldn't go home! I was stuck in that stupid bed the whole time!"

"I'm sorry, sweetheart," Papa replied, "I didn't mean to-"

"And stop that too!"

"Stop what, Sam?"

"Stop saying sorry! It's not your fault—none of this is. And I know that you and Mama are helping me the best you can, but there are some things that I must do, and I have to do them myself, even for myself."

Papa tried consoling her, assuring her that she was doing her best.

"But that's the thing, I haven't been doing my best. Not really. I just lay in bed, eating Pop-Tarts and watching cartoons all day. Okay, so maybe I do good in therapy, but so what? I know I'm not doing my best. I'm not even trying as hard as when I was a cheerleader, and I'm definitely not trying as hard as when I skated at the Fun Spot."

"So, you don't want to hurt yourself," Papa replied, "I get that-"

Sami slammed her hand on the bed. "No! Are you even listening to me?! It's more than that! It's about me being afraid. I hate being sick and tired, but I'm even sick and tired of being sick and tired. Yeah, life is hard, and people fall, but they have to get back up, ya know? That's true for me too! I might fall down sometimes, and I'm probably gonna get hurt sometimes too, but I need to feel my heart pumping again, Papa. I need to get all sweaty. And most of all, I just need to be brave!" Then she paused for a moment, breathing and taking it all in. She'd said a lot, but she'd been holding it in for a while, and she had to let it out. "It's the only way home, Papa... I just want to go home... and when I do, I need to do it my way."

Papa worried what this would mean, but there was a storm in her eyes he hadn't seen since that last time at the rink. She was going to do it, because she knew what she had to do, and she knew she was the only one who could get it done.

"Your way?" Papa asked.

Sami nodded. "Yes, Papa, my way."

JEREMIAH T. BANNISTER

+ Back at the Steps in Front of Their Home +

Sami reached for Papa's hand, and Teresa assisted on the other side, while Mama stood recording on the porch. Once she was stable standing on her feet, she began her ascent. It was hard going up those steps, and she feared more than once that she would fall, but then she saw the balloons by the door and a cute and colorful sign that read, "This Is Our Home!" Ambrose and Athan were fighting over the mail, and Lion whipped his tail as he waited patiently near the door. It was perfect, and, finally, after all these years, Sami understood what Nana said at Hershey's Chocolate World. More than that, she knew why Isaac's French fry tasted even better than it looked.

"The only thing missing is Goofy," Sami thought to herself.

Athan ran to the door, and yelled, "You better get your lazy butt up here, Sam. You've got mail!"

Sami rolled her eyes, and laughed, "Oh, brother."

SHE DANCED ME A STORY

In the house, she sat on the couch, petting Lion and looking through the mail. There were handwritten letters, drawings, poems, and gift cards, and Sami loved every one of them.

"I think you got a fun box too," Teresa said.

Sami held the big box in her hand, shook it a little, and put it to her ear like someone trying to hear the ocean in a seashell—she even tried to smell it—but the only clues were the tiny sounds of tiny objects bouncing and banging around.

"What do you think it is?" Teresa asked with her thumb in her mouth.

"I dunno, sounds like jellybeans, or maybe shiny stones for my rock collection." Then, when Sami opened the box, she saw weird stickers that made her wonder, and she yelled to the other room, "Hey, Papa, why are there scary WARNING and BIOHAZARD stickers on my fun box?"

XIII

KILLING CANCER
[With a Sonic Screwdriver]

"It says CHE... MO... CALS," Ambrose said, trying his best to read the words on the label.

"Let me see that," Papa said, grabbing it from Ambrose's hands. He didn't need to see it, though—he already knew what it was. Doctors told him they'd send Sami's chemo in the mail... he just didn't expect it so soon—and definitely not on Sami's first day home. Papa sighed and shook his head, whispering under his breath, "No moment's rest for cancer kids."

"And look at all the POISON symbols!" Athan said.

"Poison?" Sami replied. "Is this gonna poison me to death, Papa?"

"You won't die from the chemo," he assured her, "but it's a dangerous drug for a deadly disease, so they gotta put warning stickers on the box, that way people who don't have cancer won't play around with it." He read the label, then tossed the papers back into the box. "It's kinda like fighting fire with fire, and that's good and all, but playing with fire is risky business, so we gotta be careful."

"Yeah, but do I really have to start my chemo today?!"

"Are you kidding!" Papa replied, hurrying to put the bottle back in the box. "Today? Pfft! You just got home!" He looked at Mama, and he was relieved when she nodded at him, letting him know that what he did was the right thing—or that even if it wasn't, they were going to do the wrong thing together.

"And there's no way we'd want you to feel all tired and icky on your first day back to school tomorrow," Mama added, "especially since it's gonna be Special Person Day."

Sami was glad she didn't have to start chemo, but she was ecstatic to finally get back to school. And why not? She was a star student, she had a cool teacher, and she was friends with almost everyone. There was the rub, though, for whether running at recess, dancing during lunch, or doing cartwheels in the gym, Sami was an active girl... or at least she used to be.

"But now I have a cane and a wheelchair. And what about my hair?!"

Mama unloaded a huge box of hats that people sent while Sami was away. There were so many to choose from, and everyone tried them on. She had aviator hats with furry flaps, a chicken-shaped hat with a beak and wings, and a pretty hat with leopard print that matched her leg brace. Sami loved them all, but her favorites were a fuzzy blue hat shaped like a monster and a furry brown hat with long rabbit ears that you could bend to stand or sit in all different ways.

"The one with the rabbit ears reminds me of Bob's Burgers," she said as she pulled a pink unicorn hat out of the box, "but unicorns are beautiful, and they're magical too, so I'll look super-cute... plus, I think it'll make me feel like my wheelchair is riding on top of rainbows."

A most ingenious plan, for sure, but when morning came and Mama wheeled the chair up the handicap ramp, Sami started to doubt.

"Hey, Mama, do you think kids will still want to be my friend?"

"Why would you even think that way?" Mama replied. "Everyone misses you, and you're a class leader, so they look up to you."

"That's true," Sami chuckled, nervously. Then she sighed, and said, "But now they'll be looking down at me in a wheelchair."

Mama pushed the handicap button by the entrance. "It's always possible, I guess. I mean, they are kids." Then she patted Sami's unicorn hat, and said, "But, if they see what I see, then they'll see a very special girl standing strong and tall in a fight against cancer."

Her words made Sami blush. "You always know the right things to say to my heart, Mama."

Inside the classroom, students were huddled around their desks, talking about boys and basketball, while others sat quietly reading books, and Mr. Levi was wiping down the chalkboard when he saw Mama wheeling Sami down the hall. His heart leapt with joy, and he smiled as he cried. Then, just as Sami's wheelchair entered the room, everyone stopped what they were doing. It was awkward for a moment, as no one said a word, but then it hit them...

"SAMANTHA!!!" they cheered.

Kids jumped over desks and ran through aisles to reach her, where they smothered her with hugs and high-fives. Everyone was talking at the same time, telling her how much they had missed her, and how much they loved her unicorn hat and wheelchair with the little wheels that lit up.

Mama waved to Mr. Levi, then she kissed Sami goodbye, but before she left, she saw a poster on the wall. It was written with colorful markers, and little handwritten notes were pinned everywhere. In the middle were big, bold words that read, "Special Person Day," and right beneath it was a photo of Samantha.

The whole day turned out totally awesome. Kids opened doors for her, took care of her tray during lunch, and some of them carried her books. Even the bully had a change of heart. He used to be mean to Sam, but now he helped her in the hallways, and he stood guard near her chair at recess—just in case anyone dared to treat her badly. It was the best day of school Sami had ever had, so she was especially sad when the bell rang, and even sadder when she remembered about Lemmen-Holton...

+ Lemmon-Holton Cancer Pavilion +

Lemmen-Holton stood directly across the street from the children's hospital, and it was made of brick and looked very drab, at least compared to Helen DeVos. And it was after regular business hours, so the place was empty, which made the dim lighting and self-playing piano even more unnerving. Sami had places to go, though, and there were important things to do, so the family hurried toward the elevator that led to the Radiology Department.

"Samantha?" asked one of the technicians. "The doctor will be with you shortly, but we have a few special things for you first."

"Oooooh," Sami replied with a mouthful of cannabis caramels, "I love special things!" And with a big smile on her face, Sami added, "Especially when they're for me."

They'd heard that she liked Pokémon, and they knew she loved Doctor Who, so they made her a Radiation Appointment Calendar, then covered it with tons of stickers.

"Look, Sami," Athan said, "it's the 10th Doctor, David Tennant!"

"And they even have Matt Smith!" Ambrose cheered.

SHE DANCED ME A STORY

Sami smiled at the technician and, using the back of her hand to hide her mouth from her brothers, whispered, "Matt Smith is the 11th Doctor, and he's my heartthrob."

The tech explained that Sami would have 30 sessions in the Radiation Zone, and that she'd be there every weekday, but she'd get every weekend off. And whenever she was there, she'd get to put another sticker on her calendar.

"Plus, when you're all done with your treatments, you can take the calendar home with you."

Sami thought that was cool, but she was still kind of confused about something. Looking around the room, she asked, "Didn't you mention Pokémon earlier?"

The tech's smile faded a little. "Well, actually, we have to make that, and that's why we needed you here."

She led the family to the Radiation Zone, where other technicians were waiting. The Bannisters had never seen a radiation machine before, so they were blown away by how large it was. It looked like one of the robots from Star Wars, and it even had an "arm" that roved back-and-forth above a platform where Sami would lay.

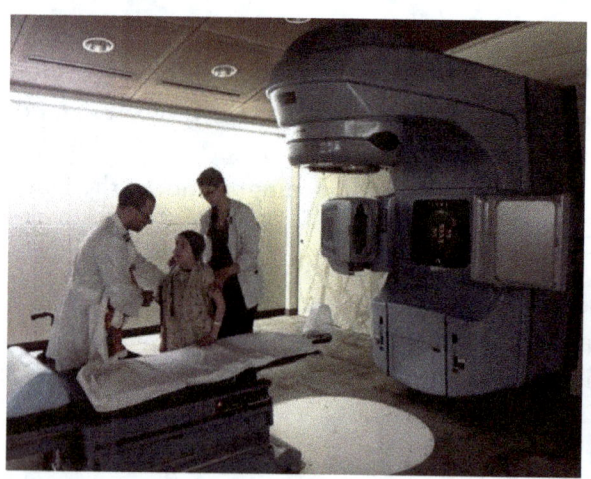
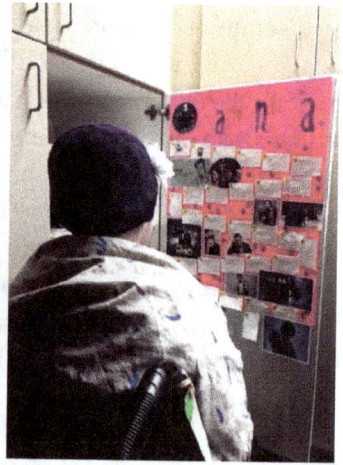

"Okay, now this is the part that isn't very fun, but it's really important, and I promise it won't take long." She grabbed a display mask from the shelf, then handed it to Samantha and told her to pass it around. "So, this is what your mask will look like. Well, it's what it looks like without all the Pokémon stuff, but it gives you a good idea of what you'll wear every time you're here."

"It looks kinda like a hockey mask," Sami giggled. "What's not fun about that?"

"Well, hon, we must make yours, and it has to be the perfect shape of your head and face, so we're gonna need you to remain very, very still. It only takes a few minutes, though, so you'll be in and out of here in a jiffy." Then she made an unpleasant face, and said, "But, I gotta warn ya, it might feel kinda weird, at least for the first few minutes."

"Is it going to hurt?" Sami asked, nervously.

"No, but it might be kinda hot at first, and it will feel sorta wet, but it cools off pretty quick, so you don't have anything to worry about." Once the family was done looking at the mask, she put it away, saying, "It'll get tight for a minute, but we gotta make sure it fits perfectly and that it's long enough to lock you in during radiation."

"Lock me in? But how will I be able to move my head?!"

The tech remained remarkably calm, and she smiled the entire time, but everyone knew she hated this part, especially when she had to say it to a kid. "You won't move your head, sweetheart. In fact, you'll need to keep your head as still as you can, that way the radiation only hits the parts of the brain with the cancer." She spread a sheet over the bed where Sami would lay. "It might make you feel a little claustrophobic, at least at first, but you'll get used to it after a while."

Sami hated the sound of that, and she started to panic. "I don't want to be here anymore," she cried. "I just want to go home!"

Everyone promised she had nothing to fear, but after all Sami had been through, she wasn't in the mood for all their half-truths. Everyone felt helpless, and no one knew what to do... that was, until Athan had an idea.

He took the bag off his back, then unzipped it as fast as he could. Reaching inside, he grabbed his Tigger doll, and placed it on Sami's chest.

"Tigger is stuffed with fluff," he said, "so you can squeeze him as hard as you want, and he won't even get hurt one bit. And if Tigger can guard The Hundred-Acre Wood from heffalumps and woozles, then he can definitely protect you from that scary claustrophobia."

"Don't be ridickerous!" Sami laughed. "Winnie is the one who is stuffed with fluff."

So, when the techs laid the mesh over Sami's face, Athan nodded at her, and Sami rested her hand over top of Tigger, and held him tightly to her heart.

SHE DANCED ME A STORY

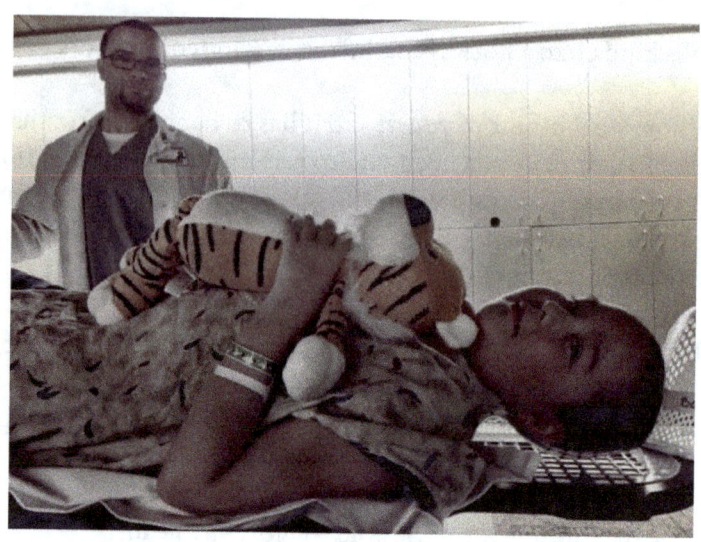

It didn't take long, and once the mask was molded, the techs placed patches of tape with Xs drawn on them across the forehead and temple—they marked where the machine's laser lights would land, indicating the exact place where radiation would enter Sami's brain. And once the Xs were all lined-up, the techs told her that Child Life would decorate her mask overnight.

"And don't forget," the tech shouted as Mama wheeled Sami down the hall, "you'll get a sticker for your calendar tomorrow! It's Day One of radiation, so we'll make it fun—I promise!" She smiled and waved, waiting patiently for Sami and the family to enter the elevator, but when the doors were closed and the family was finally out of view, the happy technician sighed and sobbed in her hands.

+ BACK AT HOME +

The family tried their best to be optimistic, but as the night wore on, Sami got sadder and sadder. She was scared about Radiation Day, wondering what kind of side-effects she'd experience, and her hair had only started to grow back, so she hated the idea of losing it a second time. And Sami's doctors were upset that Papa postponed the chemo, so they told him to start her treatment right away. Suffice it to say, Sami and the family had a lot on their mind… that was, at least until Paul stopped by.

"I got something for you guys," Paul said, waving a DVD in his hand.

"Just what I wanted! A new WWE DVD!" Athan exclaimed.

"Ha-ha, in your dreams," Paul replied. "I've actually had this for a while, and since today is Radiation Eve, I thought it would be a perfect time to make good on an old promise."

Sami gulped down her chemo, and with another fistful of Papa's cannabis caramels in her mouth, she mumbled, "What's on the DVD?"

Paul ejected the tray, then inserted the DVD, and with the glow of the TV screen shining on his face, he closed his eyes and waited for the Main Menu to appear…

"*DOCTOR WHO*!!!" the children cheered.

"Is it the one we were gonna watch on my first night at Helen DeVos?!" Sami asked.

Paul looked over his shoulder and grinned. "Duh, I kinda promised, didn't I?"

Sami sat with Paul on the couch while the rest of the kids brought bean bags from their rooms, and Mama and Papa made some popcorn, as well as hot cocoa with marshmallows in it. And once they were nice and settled in, they spent the next fifty minutes glued to the screen.

SHE DANCED ME A STORY

Sami watched with wonder as Doctor Who jumped out of an exploding airplane, and the adults were blown away by how his Sonic Screwdriver helped him escape some sticky situations, and everyone was fraught with fright when he, with his companion, Clara, "The Impossible Girl," dared to challenge his archnemesis, The Master, and her evil army of Cybermen.

"Do you think Doctor Who will save the day?" Ambrose asked as he bit his bottom-lip.

"Doctor Who never loses!" Sami replied. "I believe in him with all of my heart."

Doctor Who was in a jam, though. Worse yet, The Master and her evil army of Cybermen appeared to have the upper hand. The kids were sitting on the edge of their seats, worried that, maybe, just maybe, this might mark the death of Doctor Who!

"Who is going to stop The Master?!" the kids cried aloud.

At that very moment, #TeamTinyDancer heard what they'd been waiting for! It was subtle, but it was there, and it got louder and louder with every frame-per-second! It was the song that played whenever The Doctor had a plan—and not just any plan, but the plan that would inevitably lead him and his companion to victory.

Turned out, while The Master was busy boiling-up an evil scheme to pour down rain that would turn humans into Cybermen, one of her minions went rogue. It was Clara's boyfriend, who had been captured and turned into a Cyberman early in the episode. His transformation wasn't complete, though, since he didn't delete his emotions—and he still had his heart!

"There will be no rainfall today," Clara's Cyberman cried aloud. "The sky will burn, and the clouds will be set ablaze with it."

The Master laughed. "And who on earth do you think has the power to do that?"

He looked her in the eyes, and replied, "Me."

"And how, exactly, do you plan to do that?" she scoffed.

With his head held high, Clara's boyfriend replied, "BECAUSE I WILL BURN."

"You? One fiery Cyberman? Ha! How will that save your precious Planet Earth?"

Clara's boyfriend turned toward his fellow Cybermen, who had assembled in a graveyard overlooking London, and with a loud, commanding voice, he shouted, "Attention! Today is one of tremendous tragedy—one of mankind's darkest hours! And just look at us, we're a miserable bunch of misfits. Worse yet, we are dead men walking. But today, we're transformed, entirely new creations, and the dead shall bring salvation to the living!"

Tears welled up in Sami's eyes. "He's gonna sacrifice his life for Clara!"

He sighed. "And people might call me crazy, but I've not gone mad. No, what you have is a promise... the promise of a warrior... to never stop fighting for life and for love!" Then he turned to Clara, and with his hand over his heart, he assured her, "You will sleep in peace tonight."

The Master was furious, and she frantically tried to regain control of her army, but her commands were no match for the power of love. And after Doctor Who gave Clara's boyfriend the bracelet that The Master used to control the Cybermen, the robotic army ignited the rockets beneath their feet and blasted-off into the sky.

Popcorn flew through the air as #TeamTinyDancer leapt from their seats, and their eyes shimmered as the clouds were set ablaze! Best of all, everyone breathed a sigh of relief when, city after city in countries across the globe, the sun once again shined down upon the earth.

"See, Ambrose," Sami smiled, "I told you things would work out."

Ambrose felt silly for doubting Doctor Who, but he felt even worse for doubting Samantha. "It's just really hard to believe sometimes," he sighed, "especially when you don't even know the plan."

Sami smiled at him, then mussed his hair. "I know what ya mean, but sometimes you just have to believe—and trust he has a plan, even when you don't understand."

After the credits, Paul gathered his things, and the kids crawled off to bed, but Sami was too scared to go to sleep, at least by herself. She remembered the dreadful things her doctors said about chemo, especially about how it made kids feel sick and uncomfortable, and how it even made a bunch of people puke.

"Can you sleep beside me, Mama?" Sami asked from beneath the blankets. "You know, just in case things get really bad."

Mama and Lion slept with Sami, and they never left her side. The cannabis worked wonders, too, helping her to sleep right through the night. And when morning came, she was alert, well rested, and had the munchies like crazy. Mama made the family a big breakfast, and when everyone was nice and well stuffed, they hopped in the van and drove to Lemmen-Holton for Day One of Sami's radiation.

SHE DANCED ME A STORY

"Look at all the people, Papa!" Sami said as he wheeled her through the revolving door.

"Wow! There's a bunch of 'em, huh? Way more than yesterday."

"Yeah..." Sami replied. Then she looked over her shoulder and asked in a sad and lonely voice, "but where are all of the other children?"

It's weird, the kinds of questions kids with cancer ask. Papa hadn't even thought of this before, so he certainly didn't know what to say. Sure, there were people in the building, and it's normally better to be with someone than it is to be alone. But, people were only there because they were sick, and unlike Sami, all the other sick people had some wrinkles and gray hair. Papa was relieved, then, when Sami's tech greeted them.

It was the same girl from the night before, and she helped Sami with her gown, then wheeled her over to the Radiation Calendar, and let her pick a sticker to place overtop of Day One.

"Really?" Papa asked. "Winnie the Pooh?"

"Of course," Sami replied. "Pooh Bear is cute, and he isn't scared of bees or blustery days, even if they hurt him and wreck everything."

The doctors and technicians wrapped up their last-minute prep, then they helped Sami up onto the platform, gently laid her down onto the table, and with the newly designed Pikachu mask fitted over her face, they pulled and locked it on to the table. That's when Sami started to get nervous again, so she asked Athan for his Tigger... but Athan forgot to put it in his bag!

"I'm sorry," the tech said to the family, "but everyone needs to wait outside the room."

Sami told Athan it was okay that he forgot Tigger, and she even pretended not to mind, but after the family wished her good luck and turned to walk away, Ambrose heard her whimper and say:

"I hate that I have cancer... And I wish I wasn't in here alone."

Ambrose turned around and saw tears streaming down the side of Sami's mask. Her words broke his little heart, and he hated seeing Sami locked in like that... so sad and alone.

"Wait!" he shouted as he ran back to the room. "I, um, I think I must've forgot something. I'll be right back." That was a lie, but no one seemed to notice, and that gave him just enough time to do what he knew he had to do. "Don't be scared," he whispered. Then he looked around the room. "Trust me, I have an awesome plan." That's when he pulled something out from his pocket and placed it in Sami's hands.

"But that's your Sonic Screwdriver!" Sami exclaimed.

"Shh..." Ambrose replied with his finger to his lips. "I want you to have it today, that way if you get scared, all you gotta do is push the button." He looked around one last time, then leaned in close to Sami's ear. "They're making me stay outside, but I promise I'll help you fight those scary feelings away, okay?"

Sami wanted to nod, but she couldn't move her head, so she smiled, and said, "I know sometimes I'm mean to you, Ambrose, but I really hope you know I don't mean it. You're my brother, and I love you with all my heart. Never forget that, okay?"

Ambrose blushed and waved his hand. "Nah, you're just being a big sister, that's all." He stood there for a moment, wiping the tears from the side of Sami's mask, then he ran to the door, and just as it was about to close, he turned around and assured her, "You're the best big sister I've ever had, Sami!"

She watched the doors close behind him, and in the lonely silence of the Radiation Zone, Sami thought about what Ambrose said. His words made her smile, but then she laughed. "I'm the only big sister you have, you silly goose."

Ambrose stood outside the door, patiently waiting in eager anticipation, and when he saw the "Caution: Radiation Zone" sign light up, he did what he promised he would do. Everything was on the line, so he didn't waste any time racing to his backpack, where he grabbed every stuffed animal he had, and with all his comrades accounted for, Ambrose began to play "Imagination."

SHE DANCED ME A STORY

He pretended that his family was in the Doctor Who episode they watched the night before, and that they were fighting off the hazardous horde of scary feelings that were attacking Sami. Ambrose scampered around the room, hiding behind chairs and rolling on the floor, ducking and dodging hundreds of laser beams from all their blasters, and he did it with the world's most sensational sounds:

Whoosh!

RATTA-TAT-TAT!

Zzzzwip!

PEW-PEW-PEW!
KA-POW!

The battle was intense, with injuries and fatalities all around, but bit by bit, Ambrose blasted Sami's fears to smithereens!

Then, just when he thought everyone was in the clear, he saw Mama and Papa sitting by themselves, holding hands, war-torn and woefully forlorn. He was reminded of the scene in the cemetery, just after the Cyberman had foiled The Master's plan...

The storm clouds had disappeared, and the world was free from doom, but for some reason, the Doctor was depressed. That part confused Ambrose, and he wondered why the Doctor was sad, but now, on the frontlines of Lemmen-

Holton, he began to understand, for that's when Ambrose heard a frightening but familiar voice behind him.

"Tell me, boy, why do you fight?" The Master asked. "To save Sami's soul? If so, then who do you think is going to save yours?"

Ambrose scrambled for an answer, but he didn't plan for this. Worst of all, his stuffed-animals were out of ideas and ammo!

For a moment, he felt the hopelessness he saw in Mama and Papa, and the kid in him wanted to run and hide, but then...

The "Caution" light went dark, and the doors to the Radiation Zone swung open as Sami bursted into the room.

"I did it, you guys!" Sami cheered. "And all those scary feelings really did go away—just like you said it would!"

Ambrose watched from a distance as the family hugged and gave high-fives. He'd fought so hard for his sister, and though the moment was fleeting, he needed to see all of them together, a snapshot of all he was willing to live and to die for. And just when he thought he'd seen all he could see, Ambrose noticed something that melted his heart! For, there, within the huddle of his family's happy hugs, Sami raised her hand high to the sky, then pressed the button of the Sonic Screwdriver, which lit up the room with the most victorious hue of TARDIS blue. And looking one last time at the enemy in his mind, Ambrose laughed, and with a smirk on his face, he answered The Master's question:

"Sami will save our souls. Because *she* is #TeamTinyDancer's Impossible Girl."

XIV

FLURIOUS & GRUSTRATED: [Having "The Talk" with Your BFF]

+ Midsummer 2015—In The Attic +

"Are you even listening to me, Jeremiah?!"

"I hear you, Ang," Papa replied as he plugged his mic into the interface, "but what are you, some kind of psychic or something?"

Mama knew he wasn't trying to be rude, and she normally didn't mind his sarcasm, but this was serious. And Papa knew how much Mama hated when he talked to her through mics and headphones. So, at this point, Mama's blood was boiling. "No, Jeremiah, I'm not a psychic. I'm her mother! And it doesn't take a magic crystal ball to see that Sami is depressed. It just takes paying some actual attention."

"I pay attention..." Papa replied, pausing mid-sentence to analyze the volume bar on the screen, "but Sami's never said she's depressed."

"You don't see it in her face or hear it in her voice? And, what, do you think she's just gonna hop on a mic and broadcast it to the world??"

Papa stared at the computer, confused about how Mama's voice was coming in so loud through the mic. He had turned it down way lower than normal, and he almost asked her to back away a little bit, but when he looked up, he realized she wasn't anywhere near the mic. "Look, all I'm saying is that she seems happy to me. And she's having fun playing video games, right?"

Mama's face went flat. "Jeremiah, she's playing games like Minecraft, Pokémon, and Five Nights at Freddy's."

"So? She likes those games. And Teresa is always around, so it's not like she's ever alone. Plus, if she ever gets bored, she just plays on Chess.com with me."

Mama groaned. "Yes, I know, but that's my point. Teresa is her little sister, and those games are things you can do with one hand. And be honest, how many times has Sami played chess with you?"

"She plays it all the time! Is that a problem?"

Mama shook her head. "Do you even hear yourself sometimes, Jeremiah?" Then she scoffed, and sighed, "You really don't see it, do you?"

"See what, Ang??"

"That her whole life is spent on devices now! She doesn't go outside, she doesn't play with friends, and you don't even notice…"

Papa took his headphones off and sat them on the desk. "She hung out with friends on her birthday."

"It's July, Jeremiah—Sami's birthday was back in May."

"Okay, so what are you saying? Do you think she's embarrassed or something? Ashamed?? Which one is it, Ang?"

"She's *both* of those things *and more*. I think she's really scared, but she doesn't want to admit it because she doesn't want to let people down."

"Who?" Papa scoffed.

Mama sat there, shocked. She was blown away by how a man so bright could be so slow. "You, Jeremiah! She's scared of letting *you* down."

"Oh, c'mon," Papa scoffed.

"Do you really think I like saying stuff like this? I'm her mother, and I know she loves me, but you're her idol, Jeremiah. I think she's afraid of letting you down, and that's why she always plays it safe. She knows you're far-sighted, too, at least when it comes to stuff about life. All she has to do is stay close, losing herself in the blur a little, that way you won't notice any of her imperfections."

Ding-dong-ding-dong-ding-dong-ding-dong!

"Who in the heck is ringing our doorbell like that?!" Papa grumbled. It annoyed him, but after debating with Mama for the past twenty minutes, he was more than glad to greet the crazy maniac beating the daylights out of their doorbell.

Before Mama and Papa even made it to the steps, the kids yelled up the stairs, "It's Emilie! And she has a suitcase with her!"

"Well, well, well..." Papa said as they walked down the stairs, "I guess that settles the whole 'Sami has no friends' portion of our debate."

Sami had no idea Emilie was coming over, but she missed her more than the world, so she leapt from her bed, then raced down the stairs as fast as her leg would allow. And no sooner had she reached the bottom of the steps, than she lunged straight into Emilie's arms.

Emilie was tall and skinny, with a frame like Ichabod Crane, but her heart was huge like a hot-air balloon. She and Sami didn't go to the same school anymore, and they hadn't seen each other since the early days at Helen DeVos, so a super girly slumber party was long overdue.

"It feels like forever since I saw you!" Sami exclaimed. "And I didn't even know you were coming over today."

"That's because I kept it a secret," Mama said as she reached the bottom of the steps. Then she turned and smirked at Papa, and with her eyebrows raised, she shrugged. "Now what is it that you were saying about the whole 'Sami has no friends' portion of the debate?"

"Oh, don't even get me started," Emilie said. "The past few months have been so bonkers, and I'm basically bummed every day because we don't even go to the same school anymore, so I can't tell you about all the…" Emilie froze for a moment, then squinted her eyes at the boys, who were listening on the edge of their seats for whatever it was she was going to say next. "Hmph," she scoffed, "it looks like we're gonna have ourselves an itty-bitty problem here, huh?"

Ambrose and Athan looked at each other, confused by what Emilie meant.

"What did we do?" Athan asked, indignantly.

"Yeah, we were here first," Ambrose said. "This is our house, remember?"

Emilie crossed her arms and raised her nose at them. "No, no, no, this just won't do." Then she smiled mischievously, and raised her hands like cat claws, saying, "Because the whole ride over here, these hands kept tellin' me how bad they… WANT TO TICKLE YOU!" She leaped through the air like a kangaroo, and the boys tried to run, but Emilie was tall and had really long legs, so there was no way they could escape.

"Papa!" Ambrose laughed hysterically. "Help us!"

"Don't even think about it, Papa!" Sami said as she hurriedly hobbled to get in on the action.

"Oh, c'mon!" Athan begged. "This is torture! This is TORTURE!"

No one dared come to their rescue, but they eventually escaped, quickly fled outside, and hopped on their bikes. Sami and Emilie went to the door, where they giggled and mocked the boys.

"You know I only did that to get them out of here, right?" Emilie asked with a smile on her face.

Sami smiled. "Yeah, me too." Then she shook her head, and said, "I love 'em, but boys are still dumb boys."

Emilie glanced over at Sami, and with eyes as wide as the sky, she nodded her head, saying, "And dumb boys are *exactly* what I need to talk to you about." Then she made a duck face, and said, "But that's 'Girl Talk,' so we needed privacy."

SHE DANCED ME A STORY

The two of them peeked their heads out the door and looked down the road. "Let's just stay here a little bit longer," Sami said, squinting her eyes to see as far as she possibly could, "at least until we know they're gone all the way."

Emilie smiled, then wrapped her arm around Sami's shoulder, and the two of them watched until the boys and their bikes were out of sight.

The rest of the night was pure joy, cracking round after round of ridiculous jokes, and sharing secrets with girly whispers about "all those dumb boys," but Emilie was a good helper too. She accompanied Sami up and down the stairs, helped to scooch her wheelchair close to the table during lunch, and she held Sami's hand when it was time for her shots. Seeing them made Emilie cry, but only because Sami was scared.

"And these shots always burn," Samantha said as Mama inserted the needle.

"It'll be okay," Emilie replied, wiping beads of sweat from Sami's brow. "You're the bravest and strongest girl I've ever known. You didn't even cry when you got that shot, and there's no way I could do that!"

Then, when dinnertime came, Mama made pizza, and after a cheesy chick flick, the besties fell asleep beside one another on Sami and Teresa's brand-new bunk bed.

Everything was perfect...

... or at least it was until it wasn't—and that switch came sooner than anyone could've ever imagined.

Papa had a radio show the next morning, and when he returned home, he found everyone playing and having fun outside... everyone except for Sami and Emilie. He asked Ambrose where they were, and Ambrose used his fireman puppet's arm to point toward her room, where Papa saw Sami sitting down, sulking near the windowsill.

"I guess Emilie went home, huh?" Papa asked.

"Nope, she's still here," the puppet replied, "but she's the one who went and made Sami all *grustrated*."

"Grustrated, huh? And what the heck is that supposed to mean?"

Ambrose's puppet shook his head. "Everyone in the universe knows it's a portmanteau, Papa, but I'm just a puppet without a brain, so you gotta look it up in a dictionary."

Papa was blown away that Ambrose's puppet knew how to pronounce portmanteau, but he didn't need a dictionary to figure out that "grustrated" was Ambrose's word for that terrible condition where frustration makes someone grumpy. And when Papa arrived in Sami's room, he understood exactly why Ambrose used it.

"I'm so *flurious* right now!" Sami complained.

"Flurious?" Papa asked as he sat down beside her.

Emily crossed her arms and shook her head in exasperation. "Wow, Mr. B, really? *Flurious* is just a portmanteau that means she's *flustrated* and furious at the same time."

"Oh, c'mon already," Papa replied. "Seriously, did you guys watch some stupid show about portmanteaus before I got back home? I mean, for real, where did any of you even learn that word, anyway?" He wasn't even going to mention the fact that she used a portmanteau in her definition.

Emilie scoffed and rolled her eyes, "Everyone in the world knows what those are."

"And now everyone knows I can't ride my bike!" Sami replied.

According to Emilie, the two of them were having the best morning they'd had all year, but then Emilie thought it would be fun to go outside and play with kids from the neighborhood.

Sami shot the meanest death stare at Emilie. "Why don't you tell my dad the whole truth, huh?"

Emilie looked nervous as she tucked a tuft of hair behind her ear. "I dunno... I mean, you know, I said we should go outside to play, but Sami doesn't want to."

"I do want to, but what were they doing? Just say it!"

SHE DANCED ME A STORY

By this point, Emilie started to cry. She was a strong little girl, and she could hold her own in an argument, but Sami was the closest friend she'd ever had, so hurting her (in any way at all) was the last thing in all the world that Emilie wanted to do. "You know it was an accident," she whimpered, wiping tears from her face. "Like, why would I even say something to make you sad on purpose? Do you really think I would do that to you? That doesn't even make any sense, Samantha, and it's not even fair."

"I'll tell you what doesn't make sense," Sami grumbled, "it doesn't make any sense why you said we should ride bikes when you know I can't ride bikes anymore! *That's* not fair!"

And, alas, the floodgates opened, and everything came pouring out...

"I'm not even mad at you, Emilie!" Sami shouted, angrily. "I know you didn't do it on purpose, and I'm just really ticked off about the situation, but it's terrible, and I hate it—I hate it with all of my heart! I can't ride bikes or roller skate, and I can't swim or swing on the monkey bars—I can't even climb up a slide by myself. And my hair isn't long and pretty anymore. Instead, I'm just an 11-year-old girl going bald. And I have chemo and radiation, plus therapy and all my MRIs. And then there's some meds I take every day, like shots in my stomach that burn, but if I don't take them, I could die of a blood clot, so I don't really have a choice. And cannabis helps, but sometimes at school I get really spaced out, so I don't always know what's going on all the way, and that's embarrassing. But people just all walk around, living their lives like normal, acting like I'll always be okay..."

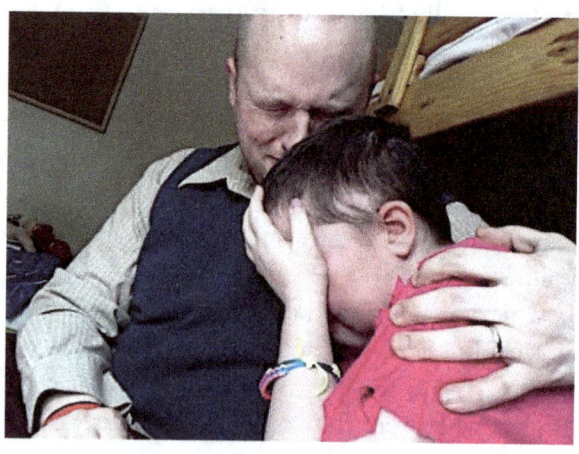

Papa and Emilie were a blubbery mess, weeping so hard, it hurt. They wanted so badly to tell her she's wrong, that her words were nothing but dirty-rotten lies, but they weren't, and even if they had something to say, where on earth would they even begin?

"Cancer wants to kill me," Sami shouted, "and I might die a painful death! I am still in fifth grade, too, you know, so I definitely don't want to die. But, no, cancer won't let me have what I want… cuz all I really want is to live."

Sami's words stung like scorpions, and for a moment they couldn't even move, but then they hugged and pressed their heads together, like a team does in a huddle, where they cried as loud and as long as they wanted. And just when it felt like they'd cried themselves dry, Papa put his hand on Sami's cheek, and said, "There's nothing we can do about the bikes, and I don't know what to do about the monkey bars, but you told Mama you didn't want that spray-hair in a can they sell on TV-"

"Papa!" Sami laughed, pushing him out of the huggle.

"Buuut…" he replied, "we did talk to your therapists about skating."

"Yes, but they said they didn't want me to do it."

"Aaand?"

"Hmph…" Sami grumbled with her arms crossed. "You said it's what I wanted and if they didn't do it, you'd just teach me to do it at home."

Emilie shook her head in astonishment. "Not gonna lie, Mr. B, but that's kinda crazy, you know."

"Oh, it's crazier than crazy," Papa laughed, "but that's how I knew they'd do it."

"No offense, but that doesn't really make any sense."

"Neither do your jokes," Papa chuckled, "but they get people laughing, so they've done what you needed 'em to do." He looked at the date on the face of his watch. "Plus, we still have the football game this weekend."

Sami groaned, "I know you said that, but I don't even know anything about football, so why would I want to be there?"

Papa looked so confused. "I dunno, probably because it's a football game for you."

"No, Mama just said it was a fundraiser."

Papa shook his head in disbelief. "Um, yes, that's true, but that's what I'm saying. It's a football game and a fundraiser at the same time, and the whole thing is for *you*."

"Whoa! Hold on. The football game is for me?"

"Duh! Your face is on the program, Sam, and they said there will be games and even zoo animals there. I'm not lying, you really are the star of the whole thing."

Emilie and Sam stood there like deer in headlights, then they looked at each other, staring with their jaws dropped for nearly ten seconds before the two of them started squealing and jumping around like crazy little monkeys. They got so worked up, they were practically hyperventilating, but with all that fresh oxygen to the brain, they had a brilliant idea:

"Oh, we definitely need to celebrate now!" Emilie exclaimed.

"Yeah, we'll party every day between now and next weekend!" Sami replied. She could see the white of Papa's eyes when she said that, but she didn't care. "We gotta start this party ASAP, like, right now!" Then she stopped, and with a confused look on her face, she asked, "But what should we do first?"

"Hmm..." Emilie thought aloud. "Aha! We should go downstairs and watch the new Hotel Transylvania 2 movie, or maybe the Goosebumps movie with Jack Black in it."

"No!" Sami replied, sharply. It was so sudden that it scared Emilie, and she could see that Emilie was afraid she'd said something wrong yet again. "Listen," Sami said in a reassuring voice, "you were honestly right about something, Emilie..."

Emilie wiped her forehead with the back of her hand, and whistled, "Whew. That's a relief. You really freaked me out for a- Wait! I was right?"

Sami limped over to the window and peeked outside. She saw her neighbor friend Markia riding her bike up and down the sidewalk, and Annabelle was performing cartwheels with Teresa, while Athan and Ambrose played "pretend" with their plushies and puppets. "It's time for me to start living, Emilie. I mean, yeah, I've got cancer and stuff, and who knows, maybe I'll beat this thing. But even if I don't, so what? I mean, sure, that's kind of the worst, obviously, but no one lives forever, right? We're all gonna die one of these days. Honestly, I could die today, or maybe tomorrow, or maybe when I'm old and wrinkly like Papa."

"For crying out loud!" Papa chuckled, nonchalantly using his hand to hide the sprawling crow's feet along his temples.

"No matter what, though, I know this for sure: I'm alive right now." And pointing her finger toward the front yard, she said, "So, you were right, Emilie, adventure is *out there*." Then she paused, looking very serious, and slowly turned her head toward Emilie, where, with a smirk that spread from ear to ear, she shouted, "And the last one to the yard is a rotten egg!"

Papa watched from the window as the girls rushed into the yard. He was so proud of his girl, and he was really proud of Emilie too. Like Gladys and Clara, Emilie was faithful, even to a fault—the sort of friend that legends are made of—and Papa knew she would remain Sami's friend forever. Seeing them play under the warm Michigan sun made him smile, but he chuckled, nervously, at how quickly life's tables can turn.

Things got tense, though, and awfully fast once neighbors saw Sami on the sidewalk.

"Hey, Markia," Sami said in a bashful voice, "I like your extensions. And the beads in your hair make you look really gorgeous."

"Thanks," Markia replied, fiddling with a strand of beaded hair. "I like your hair too."

Sami blushed, and she tried to hide the part of head where the radiation made her go bald. "But my hair is-"

"It's really pretty," Markia interrupted. "All of it. I promise." She hopped off her bike and smiled so big that cute little dimples emerged on her cheeks. "I'm just glad that you came outside to play," she said. "We missed you a lot, you know."

Sami wished there was a way to say sorry for sitting and sulking in her room, but she didn't need to. Being there was much more than enough. Her friends didn't judge her—not one itsy bit—and they spent the rest of the day playing with plushies and blowing dandelions in the wind, drawing with sidewalk chalk, and dancing with Markia. Sami was so happy, and from that moment on, she never stopped playing outside, only coming in when the moon was out, and Mama called everyone inside for bed.

XV

SAMI'S FRIDAY NIGHT LIGHTS

+ Less Than a Week Before the Game +

"It's such a lie," Sami complained as she hung her coat up.

"A lie?" Mama replied.

"Yes! Supposedly, time flies when you're having fun, but I'm having fun every day, so I don't get why it's taking so long for Friday to finally get here!" Then Sami squeezed the bunny ears on her hat, grumbling, "And that totally suuuuuuucks!"

She was right—that really did suck—but nothing sucked as badly as the never-ending litany of questions and complaints the kids hurled at Mama and Papa every day. Some of them were real doozies, too:

"Why can't Friday just get here already?"

"Can't you just fast-forward the time on the clock??"

And Teresa's personal favorite, "How much more minutes until football happens?"

It was a relief, then, when Sami's Friday Night Lights finally arrived.

+ Harper Creek Football Field—Battle Creek, Michigan +
+ Home of Coyote Football +

"Heeeeey!" Jefferson said with a strong radio voice. "You made it!"

Sami laughed and gave him a hug. "Duh! We wouldn't have missed this for the world."

"That would've been a disaster," Jefferson chuckled, then he twirled the propeller atop Sami's colorful cap. "You're kinda the whole reason I put this together."

Sami always liked Jefferson. He was a big, cuddly fella with a huge heart, and he'd known Sami since she was just a little kid. He and Papa were classmates in college, and both of them were radio hosts on the campus station, so they went way back. And Jefferson always loved whenever Sami tagged along to the station, so it broke his heart to learn that Sami had cancer. He called a few times, reading her stories, but he wanted to do something big, and as the play-by-play announcer for the Coyotes, he had a perfect plan.

First, he introduced Sami to the team. They were huge, especially with all their pads, so Sami felt like a rabbit in a redwood forest when she got in the huddle. And though they were only minutes away from transforming into monsters scaring the daylights out of the grown men on the other team, they were nothing but sweet and kind to Sami. They laughed with her, shook her hand, gave her hugs, and promised to play their best for her. But when the team made their way to the 50-yard-line, one player stayed behind.

He was tall, mega buff, and like Sami, he had cancer.
"Wait! You have cancer, too?" Sami asked, utterly amazed.
"Just like you, Sam. And I'm in treatment too."
"Hmm..." she hummed, thinking of how strange it was to see a man like him with cancer. She wasn't sure what words to use, but she knew how she felt,

so she spoke from the heart. "I'm really sorry you have cancer, and I know how scary it is, but I know you're gonna do your best, and I believe with all my heart you're gonna win."

"Amen!" he replied as he made the Sign of the Cross. And with a quick kiss of his fingertips, he pointed to heaven. "With God, anything is possible. And even if cancer gets the best of me, if God is for me, who or what can be against me?"

She'd never heard those phrases before, and she'd only seen the Sign of the Cross from Fr. Sirico and some actors and athletes on TV, but something about the sound of those words made her smile. She was also proud of how brave he was, even while knowing that he could lose his life. And then, just before he reached his team, Sami cupped her hands around her mouth, shouting, "Never give up! And keep on smiling, no matter what!"

The player stopped, took off his helmet one last time, and with a smile on his face, he replied, "With my every breath, Li'l Sam." Then he gave her a quick salute, and said, "And the same thing goes for you."

No sooner had Sami sat down when Jefferson announced that she was needed at the mic on the sideline. The place was packed with people, and no one else was at the mic, so she was really nervous, and she wondered what she was there to do.

"Tonight's National Anthem will be sung by a very special guest," Jefferson said over the loudspeakers. "She drove all the way from Pennsylvania, so let's give a big Coyote applause for-"

"Nana!!!" Sami shouted. The family couldn't believe it, and Sami hopped up and down when Nana walked out to meet her. "I can't believe you're here!" Sami exclaimed. Then she whispered in Nana's ear, "But I hope you know how to sing the National Anthem because I can't sing very good, and I don't really know what I'm supposed to do here."

Nana grinned, and said, "Trust me, Sami, we'll do great." And handing her the mic, Nana said, "All I need you to do is hold the mic while I sing."

A quiet calm came over the crowd as everyone stood to their feet, and people crossed their hearts and saluted the flag, but no one in that stadium could've imagined what they were about to see and hear. Nana's voice soared through the air, and people were blown away by the raw power of her range. Sami stood there, utterly enthralled, as Nana used sign language as she sang. Her form was perfect, and her movements matched the tempo and the tone of the anthem. It was theatrical, entirely mesmerizing, and people throughout the stands began to cry. Nana's voice could be heard from miles away when she nailed that final note, and her voice was only drowned out by the roar of the crowd, with everyone chanting, "USA! USA! USA!"

Then Jefferson flipped on the mic and thundered, "It's time for Coyote football!"

Sami cheered with all of her might that night, and she never grew tired of hearing the crunch and crack of players' pads. She wasn't the only one having fun, either. Athan shot squirt-guns while Ambrose and Teresa played cornhole, and all of them stuffed their faces with hot dogs and elephant ears. And when the game approached halftime, the Coyotes' mascot invited the family to join him in his golf cart for a ride around the field.

"They're chanting your name, Samantha!" Papa shouted over his shoulder.

She heard them loud and clear, and it made her feel like an all-star. She waved like a diva to everyone in the crowd, and she gave high-fives to all the kids lined up along the fence. She wished it would've lasted longer, but the mascot said it was their final turn, so everyone got ready to hop off. But that's when Teresa saw some very curious new arrivals in the crowd.

"Look at those costumes," she said. "They look like they're from olden days."

"Whoa!" Ambrose exclaimed. "I see a king and queen-and elves and Vikings too!"

SHE DANCED ME A STORY

"And look at those guys in shining armor," Athan said. "I've never seen a real-life knight before!"

The mascot parked near the people in-costume, and a gentlemanly duke approached the cart and bowed before the family. And in an accent so good that Sami wondered if it was real, he said, "M'lady, I am Sir Cavendish, and these are the people of BlackRock Medieval Festival. We are here for you, Sami, and we are entirely at your service."

"You're here for me?" Sami asked, bashfully—for he was a very handsome duke! "But, I'm just a normal girl, so I'm not rich and fancy like all of you!"

"Don't say such things," Cavendish begged.

"You are a mighty warrior!" said a man they called "The Hound," as he flexed his manly muscles.

"And you're a beautiful maiden too," added one of the commoner girls.

"Well, I am a warrior," Sami replied. Then she glanced at Papa, and with a smile on her face, she said, "And my dad tells me how pretty I am all the time... but he's my dad, so I think he's kind of biased."

"Ah, take heart, then," Cavendish said, "at least you can rest assured that your father hasn't gone blind."

"Or entirely mad," an elf laughed as she ribbed Papa with her elbow.

"We must make haste, though," said a powerful Viking named Thora, "for mid-game has commenced, and we are beckoned to the battlefield!"

Cavendish and Thora escorted Sami to the 50-yard-line, where knights and others battled one another. She was bedazzled by the cling and clang of their clashing metal swords, as well as by the sparks that flashed atop their shields. It looked and felt so dangerous, but the actors were trained, and all of them were brave. Sami cheered for the victors, and she never failed to console all those poor souls who lost. "Don't despair, sir knight!" Sami assured them. "You fought valiantly! And I'm very proud of you."

When the last fight was over, and the third quarter was only minutes away, Cavendish knelt next to Sami, and with a most charming and kindly voice, he asked a very special (and life-changing) question. "Lady Sam, would you please grace us with your presence at BlackRock this weekend?"

"Of course, I will!" she exclaimed. Then she sighed and shook her head in shame, saying, "I just don't have a pretty outfit to wear."

"Do not fret!" Thora assured her. "Our seamstress shall ready a royal dress for you, and our metallurgist shall craft a crown for your beautiful brow."

"And we must be honest," Cavendish said, "for the truth is, our land has been long without a leader, and it's our desire to crown you 'Samantha, Princess of BlackRock!'" All the people in costumes smiled, and some of them even cried. Then Cavendish said, "But this, only if you wish..."

Silence came over the stadium as people eagerly awaited her answer. The whole ordeal felt so surreal, but their request sounded strangely sincere, and Sami beheld an earnestness in their eyes. So, after a long and dramatic pause, Sami smiled, and shouted, "Yes! Yes! I'll be your princess! I'll be the Princess of BlackRock!"

The stadium erupted with applause, and the people from BlackRock raised their fists, swords, and battle axes into the air, shouting aloud with all their might:

"HUZZAH! HUZZAH! HUZZAH!"

The rest of the night was nothing but limelight, and though Sami had always felt like a diva, she was about to become a princess. Her entourage pampered her, and Cavendish carried her food, while Thora's Vikings served as bodyguards, and all the cast sat with her to watch the second half. The game was awesome too, and when the sun started to set, Jefferson turned on those Friday Night Lights. And even though the Coyotes didn't win, everyone did their best, and thanks to them, Sami had the night of her life.

When the game was over, the family gathered their things, but Jefferson said the team wanted to say goodbye, and the coach asked if the family would join them for prayer. At centerfield, the team took a knee, and when everyone bowed their heads, the player with cancer held Sami's hand. Then Jefferson pulled a piece of paper from his pocket, and read the prayer he had written for the event:

"Father God, thank You for Sami. Her smile testifies to that uncomplicated, free-spirited draw of inspiration, the kind that renders everyone she meets with a renewed sense of purpose and conviction, as well as a guarantee that the universe remains full of faith, love, and endless possibility. For we see within the glimmer of Sami's effervescent eyes a theater of hope, an adorable assurance that, no matter how rocky life's roads may get, the boulevard ain't really all bad." The words made him choke up, and tears cracked through his voice. "And while we cannot predict the mystery of Your providence, You know our hearts' desire: that Sami will see and do more than she ever imagined, and that no matter what the future may hold in store for her, she will live like the L.A. lady from 'Tiny Dancer,' singing her songs while dancing in the sand, always and forever refusing to call any of it the blues."

And with that, everyone shouted, "AMEN!"

The team gave Sami a last round of hugs, and everyone said goodbye, but the football player with cancer had something on his heart...

"I'm sorry we lost tonight," he said as he wiped black smudge from his cheeks.

"That's okay," Sami assured him. "It only matters that you did your best." Then she blushed, and with a bashful look, she said, "You're the true champions in my heart."

"Then I'll count it as a win."

"And you're gonna win the battle against your cancer too," Sami said. "I just know you will, and I believe in you."

He pressed his lips and shook his head. "I wish my docs were as sure about that as you are, Sam. They tell me I might die."

"Hmm..." Sami hummed. "Well, cancer is an archnemesis, and it's really good at killing people, but we're not dead yet, that's for sure. And like my best friend taught me: even if cancer does kill us one day, it can't ever stop us from dreaming."

He wrapped his muscular arms around her, just holding her and gazing out at the field. "Football's my dream, Samantha. And I'm really blessed to have a great team helping me through."

Sami pressed her cheeks deep into the sweaty mesh of his jersey, taking a moment to absorb the significance of her surroundings. From the corner of her eye, she saw Athan and Ambrose celebrating a touchdown, while Teresa tossed a balloon back-and-forth with Thora. She also noticed Nana was speaking to Aunt Curly through sign language, while Uncle Brian's wife gave a quilt that her grandmother had made for Sami to Mama. And there was Papa, who stood next to the exit, bidding farewell to the friends and family that made it out for Sami's Friday Night Lights. And a smile danced across her face when she said, "You do have a really great team helping you through... and I know that I do too."

section iii:

AS IT WILL BE FOREVER
+ TO SALUTE A SUPERNOVA +

Tempus Fugit
[IN THE FOG OF WAR]
Part III of IV

+ In The Quiet Zone—Summer Solstice 2017 +

The flash of sparks from the flint of the lighter crackled like fireworks, and the cherry burned as bright as Roman candles in the room. He wondered how long he'd sat there, dreaming and wasting away, or even if he'd been dreaming at all. He felt he'd gotten blubbery, and the balloons began to droop. He wasn't surprised (at least not by his weight), but he glared in disbelief, grumbling and complaining like a lunatic demanding answers from two old and steadily deflating balloons.

And then, just as they began their final descent, he remembered...

+ One Week Ago—the "Upward Spiral" of 2017 +

"Oh, my gosh, Jer! Are you okay??"

Papa laid flat on his back, moaning and groaning on the floor of the Fun Spot. It was hard to hear over the clickety-clack of the skates, but even with his eyes closed, he knew he made a mistake—and now he couldn't move! Dan and Kelly saw the whole thing, too, so they raced onto the floor to help him.

"Oooooow..." Papa groaned with his hand on his head.

"C'mon, Jer, stick with me, buddy," Dan said as he knelt down to the ground.

Papa chuckled, then grunted in pain, "I'm hurt, but I'm not dying, dude."

Kelly knelt down on the opposite side of Dan, just in case they needed to help him up. And when Kelly saw Papa open his eyes, he made a peace sign, and asked Papa how many fingers he was holding up.

Everything was blurry, so Papa squinted his eyes, and in a strained and raspy voice, he groaned, "Move a little closer... no... closer... even closer..." Then, just when Kelly's hand was a mere inch from his face, Papa raised his fist, then slowly flipped his middle finger, whispering, "I think it's this many..."

"Oh, ha-ha, really funny," Dan scoffed.

Kelly didn't like it, either, so he stood up and began to walk away, saying, "C'mon, Dan, he doesn't need our help."

"Whoa-whoa! Wait, you guys!" Papa cried. "Don't go." He wasn't joking around anymore, either. "Seriously, guys, I don't think I can get up on my own."

Dan and Kelly looked at each other, wondering whether it was a setup to some stupid joke where Papa would say, "I've fallen and can't get up!" and then laugh at them for being tricked twice in 10 seconds. He struggled to sit up, though, and he seemed to be in excruciating pain, so they wrapped his arms around their shoulders and helped him to a seat along the wall.

"You gonna be okay?" Kelly asked. "Be honest, man."

Dan put his hand on Papa's shoulder, and said, "Cuz if you can't, we can probably get one of the girls in the kitchen to call 911 for a *wah*mbulance."

"A wambulance?" Papa laughed. "Nah... not yet, anyway." He removed his skates, then put on his shoes, and with a sigh in his voice, he told the guys he had to get home. He gave them some lame excuse, and he promised his back was fine, but they knew he was lying, especially after Papa asked for their help out to the van.

He walked slowly, and he grunted with every step, but they knew it was pointless to argue with him, so Kelly opened the door while Dan helped him into the van, where they told him that they loved him like a brother. And when Papa left the parking lot, they waved goodbye, watching until the van disappeared in the distance....

XVI

PRINCESS SAMI'S BIG HUZZAH
[Blackrock Medieval Festival]

+ The Morning After Sami's Football Game +

Nine a.m. came quickly, and so did the scorching sun, but Sami had to be there bright and early for the Grand Opening of BlackRock Medieval Festival.

"Clara's here too, Mr. B," Sami's friend Clara said, "and she always keeps things cool."

Clara's use of third-person normally made Papa laugh, but he was much too hot for that. The temperature was just an excuse, though. Truth is, Papa didn't want to be there. He'd never been to a Renaissance Faire, and he didn't know how or why they differed from a Medieval Festival, but the whole idea just seemed weird to him. "It's role-playing," he grumbled. "And people who attend these things remind me of my old high school friends who played *Dungeons & Dragons*."

Mama laughed as she handed the kids some fans that she made from paper plates and popsicle sticks. "You do know that most of your best friends are into Role-Playing Games, right?"

"Yeah, and they're into euchre too," Papa scoffed, watching with wonder as people dressed like Hercules and Xena passed by. He shook his head in amazement, then scrunched his face, and murmured, "Oh, and yet they wonder why I'm always too busy for game night."

"Okay, Old Man Grumpy Pants," his cousin Derek interjected, "now how much you wanna bet you'll end up loving this place by the time it's over?"

He wanted to say something snarky, but before he had time to come up with a comeback, dozens of people assembled around them. There were elves, fairies, monks, and Vikings, even heroes and villains from comic books, and all of them fixed their eyes on a large wooden gate. There were a few photographers too, and they were carrying some really fancy cameras. One of them was a photojournalist for the Michigan Geek Scene, but at least he was dressed like a normal, everyday guy. And the other fella looked like a real-life cowboy, sporting a leather vest, pointy steel-tipped boots, and a massive belt-buckle big enough to eat a T-bone steak off of. As weird as it sounds, Papa thought these two were the safest bet of the bunch, so he moseyed on over and tried to strike up some good old-fashioned small talk.

"What are people waiting for?" Papa asked the cowboy.

"Y'all are 'bout ta see the Grand Openin' of BlackRock," he replied with a classy tip of his brim.

Mr. Geek Scene switched the mode on his camera, then looked through the lens, and said, "Facebook is all abuzz with rumors of something huge goin' down this morning, so I'm here to document what all the hubbub is about."

Do-Doot-Da-Doo

Their conversation was interrupted by the blast of a trumpet, or maybe it was the sound of a shofar, but whatever it was, it was enough to gain the attention of Mr. Geek Scene and the Cowboy. The two of them raced as fast as they could, then stood in front of the crowd, eagerly awaiting whatever it was on the other side of the wooden door.

Crreeeaaaak...

The gate sounded like it hadn't been opened in years, and the squeak made Papa wince. *Whoever is pushing those doors is taking their grand ol' time*, he thought. *And what on earth could be so special to require this super-cringe, overly-dramatic grand opening, anyway?*

"Whooooaaaa!" the kids exclaimed. "It's Sami!"

There she was, front-and-center, a star surrounded by dozens of adoring subjects. Her long, flowing dress was regal blue, with embroidered seams of gold, and it danced only inches above the ground, which helped to hide the little limp in her stride. The top rested along the outside of her arms, exposing her porcelain shoulders to the heat of the morning sun. And she'd been equipped with a wooden sword that neatly sheathed beneath an illustrious leather belt.

SHE DANCED ME A STORY

"She looks like a real-life princess, Papa!" Ambrose exclaimed.
"I bet she feels like one too!" Clara added.

Cavendish waved his hand to alert the crowds, then said in a loud voice, "BlackRock has been without a royal for many moons, and it has pained our people. Our scouts have traveled long and far in search of the perfect princess, but, alas, there has been no one worthy to sit on the throne..." Then he turned toward Sami, and said, "That was, until we met you."

A metallurgist emerged from the back of the crowd. He was tall and burly, and his outfit was made of heavy metal and animal skins. And he had large and leathery hands, hands that held an illustrious pillow, which served as the seat for a crown. The crown was gold, glistened in the sunlight, and it was enshrined with row after row of precious stone. He was careful to hand the pillow to the duchess, and after a surprisingly graceful bow, he signaled for everyone to kneel, and no one dared disobey—not even Papa.

"Olde World Village is a most modest place," Cavendish continued, "and we are a very humble people, but we have heart, and we never lost hope that we'd one day find a lady, nay, a princess, and one who was worthy of our love and loyalty. So, when our scouts brought word of your courageous battles, we insisted on witnessing it ourselves. But what we saw on the Field of Football was unlike anything we'd ever seen—more than anything we could've imagined—for it was there that we beheld such beauty, such sincerity, and this maiden's loving-kindness surpassed even our highest expectation." Cavendish took Samantha's hand, helping her back to her feet, then took the crown from atop the pillow, and held it high over her head. "So, it is with joy unspeakable that we coronate you, now and forever, Princess Sami of BlackRock."

The whole spectacle was shocking, and Papa could barely believe his eyes. There were dozens of people, all of them on their knees, kneeling before his firstborn, overwhelmed by joy, and with hearts crying hopeful tears. Papa couldn't believe it, and he tried to doubt what he had seen, but then he felt tears running down his cheek, and hurried to wipe them away.

Cavendish turned toward the crowd, triumphantly declaring, "Behold, all ye of Olde World Village, the brave and the beautiful Princess Sami of BlackRock!"

Applause echoed through the grove as knights and Vikings wielded their weapons, and jesters juggled while peasants threw flowers in the air. It was glorious, even rapturous, but most of all, it was authentic. And while Papa continued to wonder about a weekend spent in a wonderland of weirdos, he started to sense that BlackRock was serious, and he worried that maybe Derek was right. And with the crown on her head, Sami raised her sword, and said, "C'mon, everyone, stand up," then led her loyal subjects to the world within the walls.

The roads inside were rocky and made of dirt, and there was plenty of walking to do as booths and venues were scattered across the land. Artisans and amateurs peddled products like handcrafted leather boots, otherworldly outfits, and chalices made from precious metal. They had food vendors too, with items like a "Pirate's Energy Drink" known as RootJack, a vicious "Viking Mead," and the hugest turkey legs that the family had ever seen.

"It's kinda like a carnival," Mama said as she tried on some jewelry.

SHE DANCED ME A STORY

"Yeah, but a billion times better!" Athan exclaimed. Then he swung a quiver around his back, and asked, "Hey, Papa, what do you think? Is BlackRock the coolest place on the planet or what?"

Papa knew he'd get flack for his answer, so he tried to be all quiet and nonchalant about it, saying, "Yeah, I guess it's pretty cool."

"What's that, Sergeant Scrooge?" Derek laughed. "Surprised by the joy of a Ren faire?"

"Ahem," Papa replied, with his finger in the air, "It's a Medieval Festival, actually, and don't get your hopes up. I'm just saying that maybe it's not the dorkiest thing since the laugh track on Full House."

"It isn't terrible at all, Papa," Teresa scoffed, rubbing a super-soft and silky rabbit's foot up and down her cheek. "It's my favorite place in aaaall the woooorld."

"Meh," Papa replied, "different strokes for different folks." Then he raised his glass into the air and squinted his eyes as he looked through the bottom. "And, hey, if this mead gets me nice and drunk, I might actually end up liking this place."

Teresa didn't think that was very funny, especially since everyone was having such a great time. And what was there to complain about, anyway? Sami was a walking highlight reel, with fawning fans who followed her all around the grounds, and everyone bowed whenever she passed by. Heck, the gentlemen even tipped their hats to Sami's friend, whom they'd decided to call "Lady Clara." Magicians mesmerized the kids with their tricks while singers serenaded Mama with song, and a hairy horde of Vikings endowed Princess Sami with a medallion of Thor's Mjölnir. Even better, Sami got to sit on the throne overseeing the joust, watching as knights sparred in a tour de force of death-defying displays.

"Oh, my gosh!" Sami gasped as their jousts snapped into pieces. "I get so scared every time that happens."

Princess Sami liked the clip-clop sound of the horses' hooves whenever they would pound on the ground, and she enjoyed congratulating the knights for their bravery, even the ones who lost. And Thora the Viking spoiled the kids with candy and ice cream, as well as pockets packed with "Thora Bucks," which gave them more than enough money to buy, well, even more candy and ice cream.

It was the jail, though, that most captivated the children's time and attention.

JEREMIAH T. BANNISTER

"Hey! You!" shouted a red-haired man in a kilt who everyone called BooBoo, "yes, you, Are you Princess Sami's father?"

"Why, yes, yes, I am," Papa boasted. "I am Princess Sami's Papa."

BooBoo waved some people over, and all of them surrounded Papa. "Ah, then arresting you was even easier than we imagined."

"Arresting??" Papa cried as BooBoo grabbed hold of his arm. "What for?"

"Quiet, criminal! We've got a warrant for you."

Papa was so confused, but then he saw his children laughing and hurling insults, so he knew who was to blame. "Papa's going to ja-il! Papa's going to ja-il!" they cheered.

"How dare you?!" Papa shouted, playfully. "Why, I oughta! All of you are gonna regret this—you just wait and see!"

The Jail was made from wood and vine, and it sort of looked like a big bird cage, but the inside was furnished with a rickety bench and an array of fake feet and hands, the kind you see in stores every year around Halloween. Outside the jail was a stage, where a judge and his crew of jerky jailers made prisoners perform a series of silly and embarrassing stunts. There were crowds of people too, all of them laughing and mocking the poor prisoners as they performed their punishments.

"At least you're not alone," Papa's cousin Derek said as he played with one of the props.

"Aw, man, your kids got you arrested too, huh?"

"Dude, this is my third time in this place," Derek laughed.

"Really? What did they get you for?"

"I think the first time was for not buying more candy, and the second time was for making them go to school."

"What is this time for?" Papa asked.

"Quiet, you scallywags!" growled a beautiful woman dressed like a pirate.

Derek leaned over, and whispered, "For not even knowing BlackRock was a thing until Sami's football game."

Just then, the judge stood up from his large wooden throne, and with brilliantly dramatic rolling R's, he shouted, "Bring us Jeremiah!"

His voice echoed into the woods, and blasts from bagpipes blared in the background as the pirate lady grabbed Papa by the arm. And people chanted, "Walk of shame! Walk of shame!" as he crossed the deck and stood before the judge.

SHE DANCED ME A STORY

The rosy-cheeked judge was Flynn, and he wore a feathery capitano hat along with baggy blue pantaloons that were tucked into a pair of knee-high leather boots. "Are you guilty?" he asked.

"I don't even know the charges!" Papa replied.

"Oh, dear me," Flynn said, sarcastically, with his hands on his cheeks. "Where are my manners?" BooBoo grabbed Papa's warrant, which was rolled-up like a scroll and tucked in his kilt, then he handed it to Flynn.

"Hold on," Papa cried at BooBoo, "you knew my charges the whole time?!"

"Quiet, dog!" BooBoo scoffed, then he smiled and winked, just to remind Papa that this was all in good fun.

"Ah, let me see here," Flynn said as he scanned the scroll. "Apparently, Princess Sami and the #TeamTinyDancer crew accuse you, Papa, of, and I quote, 'being the best dad... EVER!'"

THE CROWD GASPED

"It's true!" Sami shouted.

"Yes! He is the best dad!" Athan hollered.

To which the crowd sneered and jeered, "Punish him! Make him pay!"

"Are you kidding me?!" Papa laughed. "This is rigged! Nothing but a kangaroo court!"

"Kangaroo, huh?" Flynn replied. "Hmm... yes, I think that will do just fine." And with a naughty grin on his face, he said, "I think we have the perfect punishment for you."

Everyone already had their cameras recording when a woman named Mother started punishing Papa. "All right, wretch," she snarled. "You gotta say and do whatever I tell you to, got it?" Papa nodded, so she commanded him to make a unicorn horn with his index finger, then to use his other hand like a tail. "And you gotta hop up and down like this," she said as she pranced around the stage. "And you better do it every time you sing the song."

The song was called *I'm a Happy, Happy Unicorn*, and the two of them sang so loudly that everyone in Olde World Village could hear them. Papa hopped up and down, neighed like a horsey, and echoed Mother's lyrics, belting out the words:

I'M A HAPPY, HAPPY UNICORN!
I RUN THROUGH THE FOREST ALL DAY.

JEREMIAH T. BANNISTER

I RUN THROUGH THE FOREST ALL NIGHT.
AND FAIRIES GET SCARED AND RUN AWAY.

And with puppy-eyes, he sobbed:

AND THAT MAKES ME SAD.

Then he perked up, and shouted aloud:

BUT THAT'S OKAY. YOU KNOW WHY?
CUZ I'M A HAPPY, HAPPY UNICORN!

Parents laughed while children danced around, and people took photos of Mother and Papa as the two of them neighed, stomped their hooves, and galloped around the stage. Sami and the kids couldn't believe it, either, because after all that complaining he did in the morning, there he was, acting completely ridiculous on the stage, and it looked like he was loving every second of it.

"Okay, okay," Flynn said in a loud voice. "Settle now, you peasants!" Then Flynn looked at Princess Sami, and asked, "So, Princess Sami, what say you? Has your father endured enough?"

All eyes turned toward Sami, who pretended like she was thinking long and hard, but then a smirk cut across her face as she said, "Nooooot quite yet."

SHE DANCED ME A STORY

Flynn asked for ideas, and suggestions were flying from every direction. "Make him battle with a sword!" one said. "Make him walk around the village with the Cowbell of Shame," laughed another. But Sami had the final say, so, when she declared her answer, Flynn's jailers dragged Papa kicking and screaming to the stocks.

The stocks were made of wood, and (for some weird reason) there was a big tub of water near the base. BooBoo was more than glad to place Papa's head and hands into the holes, then he mocked him as he closed and locked the latch.

"Have mercy, Princess Sami!" Papa cried.

Sami was merciless, though, dumping cup after cup of ice-cold water on Papa's neck and head. He protested every time, pretending to be indignant that he was forced to suffer such a terrible injustice, and at the hands of such a lovely girl. But through the water that poured over his eyes, he saw something that made even the coldest water delightfully bearable. Mama was taking pictures while the kids gave each other high fives, and Sami and Clara laughed so hard that they almost started to cry! Sure, the water was freezing, and now his clothes were wet, but none of that mattered, not anymore, for it was here, in this mysteriously magical moment, that Papa was baptized into the bedlam of BlackRock. And now, like the rest of his family and friends, Papa was utterly and entirely hooked.

After they were done, Papa dried off, but no sooner had he finished, than everyone was summoned to the venue near the gate. Knights, Vikings, magicians, and jesters, as well as royals, peasants, and jailers lined-up along the main stage, so the place was packed, and it was hard to find a seat. People toward the back of the crowd scooched to make room on a bench for Princess Sami while cast members on the stage filled their cups with wine. And with nostalgic music playing in the background, Cavendish signaled for the crowd to quiet down.

"The time has come, my friends, for once again, we must part ways. So, allow us to wish your journey well, and to raise our glasses for toast to the health of the company."

Friends and family joined in rhyme, raising their voices in a chorus meant to curb the grief of bidding farewell. It sounded so sad, but everyone smiled. Then, just before the second verse, Cavendish and a visiting queen stepped forward from the stage, walked toward the back of the crowd, and knelt profoundly at Princess Sami's feet.

"Join us, Princess Sami," the queen beckoned as she offered Sami her hand. Sami stood up from Papa's lap and walked through the crowd to join the people on the stage where the cast, with all of their eyes on their newfound princess, raised their glasses high, and sang with all their might:

Here's a health to the Princess / that we love so well
Her glamor and beauty / no maidens excel
There's laughter in her heart / when she rests on my knee
And none on God's green earth / as happy as me
Now her boat lies at anchor / she is ready to dock

SHE DANCED ME A STORY

*I BID HER SAFE SAILING / KEPT SAFE FROM THE ROCKS
AND IF AGAIN I GREET HER / ON BENDED KNEE
I'LL SING IN PRAISE / OF HER KINDNESS TO ME...*

The lyrics pierced Papa's heart, and he bawled like a baby. It was only a few days ago that Sami sat near the window, all flurious she couldn't ride her bike, and terribly frightened by a potentially perilous and dreadfully painful death. Yet here she stood, singing, smiling, and shining like the sun. Papa regretted being judgmental, and he reflected on all he would've missed if he'd actually gotten his way. The cameras and the crown at Sami's coronation, the clomping of horses' hooves as knights jousted in Sami's honor, and the jollity of injustice at the jail... he would've missed it all. And it made him think back to the conversation he had with Sami only hours earlier in a gazebo near the joust...

+ HOURS EARLIER—AT THE GAZEBO +

"BlackRock truly is a magical place," Sami had said as she kicked stones across the floor.

"It is pretty awesome, isn't it?" Papa had replied.

"Whaaaaa-?!" Sami exclaimed, her mouth wide open. "But I thought you said you hated this place!"

"FAKE NEWS ALERT! FAKE NEWS ALERT!" Papa replied in a robot voice.

"But you-"

"But you need better sources," Papa scoffed. "Who's peddling that propaganda, anyhow?"

"Hmmm, let me think..." Then she pointed her finger in his face, and with playful daggers flying out of her squinted eyes, she replied, "You did, Papa! I heard you!"

Papa gasped and placed his hand on his heart, then he puffed his chest like a rooster, and with a funny British accent, he cried, "How dare you?! Why, I nevah!"

"Yes-huh! You said, and I quote, 'This looks dorky, I hate it, and I want to go home.'"

Papa rolled his eyes. "Hmph. Now I know you're lying." Then he smirked, and mumbled, "I said it was weird, not dorky."

Sami shook her head, then rested it on Papa's shoulder. "I knew you were tricking me."

"Well, it's true, isn't it? I mean, c'mon, you gotta admit, this place is a little weird."

"Yeah, but we're weirdos too, you know. And these weirdos made me feel like a real princess all day. They even made Clara feel like royalty with me, and that made me so happy."

"They made you *feel* like a princess? Maybe you missed it somehow, but these people *made* you their princess! They crowned you the real-life Princess of BlackRock!"

Sami grinned so big, and when she saw Thora and Flynn playing and carrying on with the family, she said in the sweetest voice, "Honestly, Papa, today was the greatest day of my life… and I hope with all of my heart that these people will be my friends forever."

+ Back to the Grand Finale of BlackRock +

Papa snapped out of his flashback, only to find himself at the grand finale of BlackRock's closing song. He hopped up, then stood on the bench, and with his daughter in view, he raised his mead into the air, and with a voice he hoped would echo into eternity, he joined them in chorus, singing:

Here's a toast to the village / and that BlackRock above
To dance and make merry / from one glass, our love
So, let's dance and be merry / all woe to restrain
For we might or may never / all sing here agai

XVII

WHERE DID THE CANCER GO?

Mid-November 2015—Helen DeVos Chemo Clinic

"No way!" the nurse said as she spread disinfectant around Sami's port. "I think you're just trickin' me."

"Nuh-uh," Sami replied. "It's true 100 percent."

"So, wait, you're tryin' to tell me that Make-A-Wish Michigan is paying for you to have the time of your life in England?"

"Yes! And they're sending my whole family."

"Get outta here!"

Sami crossed her chest. "Swear on my love for my mom. And Make-A-Wish is sending us to Cardiff, too!"

The nurse raised one of her eyebrows. "Cardiff, Wales? What on earth is there to see in Cardiff, Wales?"

"Oh, I dunno, just the greatest place in the whole entire universe, cuz that's where I can finally see the official Doctor Who Experience Museum."

Mama sat next to Sami and unwrapped a sleeve of Pop-Tarts. "You aren't even telling her everything, Sam. You gotta tell her about Detroit too."

"Detroit?" the nurse replied.

Sami shoved the Pop-Tart into her mouth. "Oh, yeah, I almost forgot." Then, with crumbs flying out of her mouth all over the place, she mumbled, "I'm gonna be the highlighted ambassador at this year's Make-A-Wish Michigan Wish Ball, and that's at the MGM Grand in Detroit."

"You almost forgot to tell me about the MGM?!?! Now I know you're bustin' my chops."

"I'm tellin' ya, there's not a single lie in any bit of it."

The nurse wiped blood and excess numbing cream from the infusion port. "Well, you are a superstar, so I guess I'll believe you... this time." Then she clapped her hands, and said, "And, see, lookie there. You didn't even need Buzzy Bee this time."

Sami looked down at the cute butterfly bandage the nurse put over her port, then she scrunched her face. "Oooh. You're so sneaky!"

The nurse flipped her hair all fancy, and with her hands on her hips, she said with a punky flare, "Oh, I know. I'm pretty much a pro."

Once the infusion was finished, Papa grabbed their things while Mama helped Sami to her wheelchair. However, just when they were about to exit the hospital, Dr. Kurt came flying through the door, and she had a manilla folder in her hand.

"Samantha!" Dr. Kurt exclaimed, keeled over and all out of breath. "Whew, I am so glad to see you."

Sami laughed, and said, "I'm always so glad to see you, Dr. Kurt."

Dr. Kurt smiled and shook her head, then she stood up straight, and in a very serious voice, she said she had some news. The family followed her to a nearby viewing room, but Sami wasn't scheduled to meet with Dr. Kurt for another few weeks, so whatever it was that she wanted to talk about must have been urgent. This made Sami and the family kind of nervous, so it didn't help that when they got to the room, Dr. Kurt closed the door. Then, without saying a word, Dr. Kurt opened her manilla folder and pinned some MRIs to the viewing light.

"Are those my scans?" Sami asked.

Dr. Kurt nodded. "Do you notice anything different about these images, Sami?"

The family definitely recognized the one on the right. It was the first scan from Day One at Helen DeVos. And the scan in the middle was done after Sami's Surgery Day, and it showed how much of the tumor Dr. Foody was able to remove. It didn't take a neurosurgeon, then, to figure out that the one on the left was Sami's post-radiation scan, but it probably took a radiologist to figure out what it revealed. Still, Sami sat there, staring at the scans, trying to figure out what they meant.

Dr. Kurt got very serious, and she spoke in a very grave tone. "What about the new one? Look hard, Sami. Take your time. Tell us what you see... or what you don't see."

The family gasped!

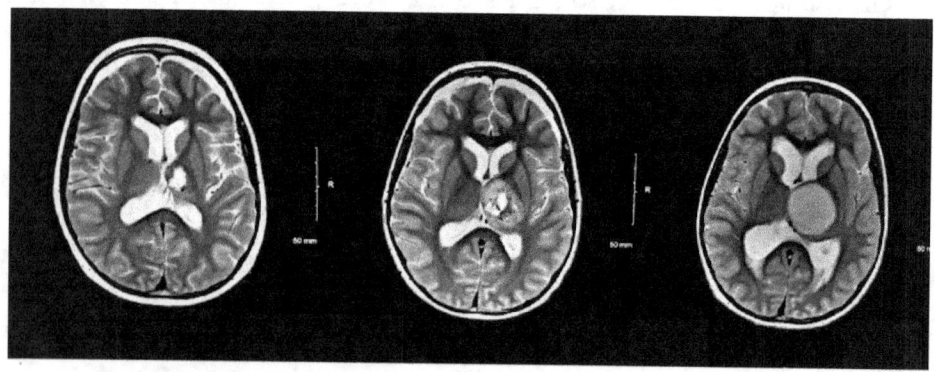

"Where did my cancer go?"

Dr. Kurt shrugged her shoulders. "I dunno, Samantha, you tell me."

Everyone was in shock, and Mama admitted that she was still unsure of what any of this meant.

"It means that there is no evidence of disease," Dr. Kurt replied.

Mama's eyes grew wide, and with an uneasy excitement in her voice, she admitted, "I'm not sure if I should laugh or cry right now."

"With news like this?" Dr. Kurt laughed. "I think it's okay to do both."

Papa watched as everyone gave hugs and high-fives, but he was conflicted—not that there was no evidence of disease (that was the greatest news in the world) so much as what Dr. Kurt meant by "no evidence of disease," and he wanted to know how on earth Sami's cancer disappeared.

Papa stood next to Dr. Kurt, then whispered discreetly, "Do you mind if I ask you something?" She leaned in toward him, that way no one would hear what they were talking about. He was nervous, though, and he rubbed his hand on the back of his neck, and he feared that he'd look like an idiot, but he wanted to know, and he needed to hear it from her. "Is this a miracle, Dr. Kurt? You know, Sami's cancer going away like that?"

Dr. Kurt looked very confused. She knew Papa was an Atheist, as he'd been open about his beliefs concerning science and religion, so this was the last question she ever imagined hearing from him. "Miracle?" she said, shaking her head. "No, I wouldn't say that."

Technically, she couldn't say that. Well, she could, but it would be as irresponsible, as it would be practically impossible to determine what was doing what. So, even if he were a man of prayer, how could he, or anyone else, determine whether it was this percent chemo and radiation, that percent cannabis, or this-or-that percent full-blown miracle? Papa knew all of this (he'd said it to Sami's prayerful supporters hundreds of times online) but deep down inside, he wanted it to be a miracle.

"The radiation treatments worked, Jeremiah. Honestly, anaplastic astrocytoma is often very receptive to radiotherapy, so we were hopeful. Sadly, it doesn't always work out that way, which means some kids and their families leave the office with broken hearts. So, whenever we see that a tumor 'melts' after radiotherapy, we're excited, and we want the patients to be excited too." She knew it's what he needed to hear, but he still looked so deflated... and once he asked his next question, Dr. Kurt knew why.

"So, Sami isn't cured?"

"No, Jeremiah. I'm sorry, but there is no cure for her kind of cancer. And just so you know, when I said that there was 'no evidence of disease,' that's kind of a technical term, and it means that the cancer is no longer visible in MRIs. Cancer cells can be microscopic, though, and tendrils often go unnoticed, but the mass is no longer visible. That's what I meant."

"But will she still have to do chemo?"

Dr. Kurt sighed. She'd heard this question so many times, and it pained her to have to break the news, but she was good at her job, and she was as good when talking with parents as she was when talking with kids. Even so, there was no way for her to soften the blow, and she knew, no matter how badly it hurt, Papa preferred straightforward scientific honesty.

"Jeremiah, Sami will need to be on chemo for the rest of her life, and recurrence is common, but this gives us time." Then she pointed to Mama and Sami. "Just look at them. Do you see how they're responding to the results?"

Papa bowed his head, then glanced over the glasses that hung low on his nose. He saw Mama stroking Sami's hair, and a nurse was holding the Child Life prize box, allowing Sami to choose a gift before she went home. All of them were so happy, just laughing and carrying on. They looked like there wasn't a care in the world. "She's so happy," Papa whimpered. "And they're all so full of hope."

Whatever the context, Dr. Kurt and Papa didn't know, but Sami said in a loud voice, "Well, I know what I'm thinking..." And with her arms raised high overhead, she cried aloud, "Ha-lle-lu-jah!"

Dr. Kurt smiled. "She is happy, Jeremiah. And you're right, everyone is full of hope..." And with the sight of tears trickling down his cheeks, she put her hand on his shoulder, saying, "and you should be too."

XVIII

MAKE-A-WISH, LITTLE STAR!
[Wish Ball 2015]

+ One Week Later—Back at Home +

    The weeks leading up to the Wish Ball were awesome. Make-A-Wish Michigan sent a series of gift packages, and they were always thematic, filled with candy, presents, and something special related to Sami's Wish Trip. Their Wish Coordinator, Ashley, even scheduled a photo shoot and TV interview with Fox 17, where they asked questions like:
    "Why did you choose the Doctor Who Experience?"
    "What activity are you most looking forward to doing?"
    "And what message do you want viewers to take away?"

SHE DANCED ME A STORY

That last one was something Sami thought a lot about, so she had her answer right away. "I want people to dream bigger thoughts," Sami said. Then she fidgeted with the "Dream Big" necklace she made during chemo, adding, "I want to encourage people to never give up, and to keep on smiling-no matter what!"

Then, with less than one week remaining before the big day, Sami received what was to be her final package...

"It's a lot smaller than the other ones," Teresa said, waving the flat envelope around in hopes of hearing some candy.

It was a voucher, though, and it was for dress clothes from a tailor in Grand Rapids. The family would've made do with what they had, but they weren't wealthy, and none of them owned any church clothes. But the Wish Ball was a gala, and it was Make-A-Wish Michigan's premier annual fundraiser, so people would be wearing all sorts of fancy and expensive clothes. Mama and Papa worried about that, as there was no way they would have enough money to rent suits and dresses for everyone, so they were especially grateful that they had been given more than enough money for all of them to buy what they needed.

Mama grabbed some high-heels and a shimmering sequin dress, while Sami selected a red dress with a cute little bow for her hair, and Papa matched the boys with some handsome tuxedos. Mama even bought the boys some colorful Chuck Taylor Converse sneakers, that way they'd look a little like David Tenant from Doctor Who.

+ The Day of the Wish Ball +

When the day arrived, everyone scrambled around the house, hurrying for last minute things. They were spending the night in the MGM Grand's Presidential Suite, then flying from Detroit Metro to London early the next morning, so-

"You guys better hurry!" Mama yelled up the stairs, her arms draped with clothing for the kids. "And don't forget, we still gotta pack the van!"

The kids raced down the stairs, bags-in-hand, but just when they reached the front yard, they saw something that made them stop dead in their tracks...

"Look at that fancy rich person's car!" Teresa exclaimed, pointing toward the beautiful black limousine parked in front of their home.

A chauffeur stepped out of the limo, opened the back door, and said, "Samantha Bannister, welcome to your limo for the Wish Ball."

JEREMIAH T. BANNISTER

The kids had never seen a limo in real life, so they wasted no time at all hopping into the back, while the chauffeur packed their luggage in the trunk.

"This is even funner than the McDonald's Play Area," Ambrose said. Then he sprawled out on a super-soft and fuzzy bucket seat, saying, "It might be even cooler than Santa's Sleigh."

Teresa unwrapped a Tootsie Pop from the ice chest overflowing with colorful candy, and scoffed, "How in the world could you even know that, anyway, Ambrose?"

"Duh," Athan replied, "probably because Santa's Sleigh doesn't have a tinted window you can roll up and down whenever you want to talk."

"Pa-paaaaa!" Teresa said in a nagging voice with the lollipop still in her mouth. "Can you please tell the stupid boys that that is the dumbest thing you've ever heard in all your whole entire life?"

It was pretty dumb, but Teresa underestimated the ridiculous things that Papa had heard. So, after taking three licks off his lollipop, he shrugged, and answered, "Honestly, T, the world may never know."

"Okay, no more arguments, you guys," Mama said. "It doesn't matter, anyway, so just cut it out already."

"Yeah, see, Athan," Teresa scoffed.

Mama cracked a half-smile, and said, "Of course, because everyone in the world knows how coooool Santa's sleigh is."

SHE DANCED ME A STORY

"Ugh," Athan grumbled, "you and Papa are so dorky sometimes."

That was indisputable, but like usual, Mama had a way with ending arguments, and from that point on, their three-hour trip to Detroit was nothing but pure fun.

The MGM Grand was an illustrious 401 room hotel and casino, and with a reflective glass structure that sparkled under the sun, it was a highlight of inner-city Detroit. The interior of the hotel was even prettier though, dashingly decorated with exotic antiques and artwork that must have cost a fortune. The place was loaded with rich and famous people too, and all of them were dressed to the hilt. Make-A-Wish had hired a photographer to take professional pictures of Wish Kids and their families. Sami was endowed with a beautiful sash indicating her induction into the Make-A-Wish Michigan Ambassador Program. She mingled with volunteers and fellow ambassadors, hearing awesome and inspiring stories about Wish Trips and Wish Balls of the past. Time flew fast, though, and before they knew it, the event was about to begin.

Dinner tables were positioned all around the room, and each of them were teeming with twinkling candles, top-of-the-line silverware, and drinking glasses made of crystal. The stage was gigantic, too, and it featured a movie screen, as well as a diverse array of musical instruments. And there was a 15' poster of Samantha on the wall. The whole scene was surreal, even enchanting, but none of these trappings were nearly as captivating as what Sami saw on the main stage.

"Oh, my gosh!" she exclaimed. "The TARDIS!!!"

There it was: Doctor Who's bright blue box, and it was all lit up. The kids weaved their way through the aisles, politely saying, "Excuse us!" as they dashed past people in their race to the front of the room. Once they reached the stage, they gazed up at the TARDIS, but it was so unbelievable that they felt they needed to touch it, even if only for a second, to prove that it was real.

"Yup, it's the real one, all right," Sami cheered as she patted the side of the TARDIS. Then, when she took her seat at a table, she leaned over to Mama and Papa, saying, "I just can't believe it, I actually got to touch Doctor Who's real-life TARDIS!"

The event was labeled, "Journey of Imagination," and it was loaded with themes and images inspired by Sami's wish. There were a variety of different acts, and a Make-A-Wish ambassador even played an original score on the piano, but it was the video featurettes of Wish Kids that moved everyone the most. People met a little boy who got to shoot pucks with Detroit Red Wings goalie, Jim Howard. And they saw a little girl who was head-over-heels about a Doughnut Shop Playhouse, and a teenage boy talked about how happy he was to finally own the red accordion he always wanted. Story after story, each one as emotional and inspirational as the last. The children were charming, adorable, and bursting with innocence, and all of them had at least two things in common: each of them suffered from the scariest of deadly diseases and Make-A-Wish Michigan was doing whatever it could to grant them a wish in hopes of providing joy amidst their fears and suffering.

When dinner arrived, the keynote speaker made his way to the podium. He was an ordinary man. He wasn't a professional orator, but he spoke from his heart. And with the power of choreographed pictures flashing across the screen behind him, he told the tale of his beautiful teenage daughter. Like Sami, she had been diagnosed with cancer, and like #TeamTinyDancer, he and his family were committed to living and loving life to its fullest. He recalled how they first discovered the signs and symptoms, and he talked about that fateful moment when doctors first told them she had cancer, as well as the many amazing, life-changing experiences they had together ever since.

Everyone loved the man's story, but Papa loved it the most. He was captivated, sitting on the edge of his seat from beginning to end, awed and inspired by the life and lessons of this beautiful girl and the family that loved her. He hoped to meet this man and his daughter, just to tell them how much he loved their story, but when he looked at the table where the man had been seated, he didn't see the man's daughter anywhere... and there wasn't a second vacant seat at the table.

Where is she? Papa wondered as he scanned the room.

Then the man continued, "My baby girl was so excited when Make-A-Wish contacted us, and she was overjoyed when she got the news that they granted her wish. Cancer is so hard to deal with, ya know, and every day contains its own set of challenges, but Make-A-Wish gave her hope, and she loved life." Then he paused...

Loved? Papa gasped.

After a painful moment's silence, the man began to cry. "My daughter never made it to Disney. She died weeks before her wish was granted..."

No! No!! No!!! Papa cried in his heart. He didn't expect this—not at all—and now he was weeping. "It's not supposed to end that way," Papa whimpered. "She wasn't supposed to die..."

The dad said a few more things, and when he was done, Papa was the first to stand to his feet, leading everyone in a standing ovation that lasted almost five minutes! He wanted to clap even harder, but he was afraid he'd break the bones in his hands. Even after people returned to their seats, Papa stayed standing, at least long enough to see the man walk away from the stage. He walked alone along the outer wall, and just as he stepped beneath the large poster of Sami, Papa realized something: the man never looked up... not even for a moment. There was no smile, no wave, no nod of recognition, nothing at all. He was broken beyond words, and with his eyes cast toward the ground, he marched his way past his empty seat at his table, to the back of the room, out the door, and toward his suite, where Papa imagined he'd spend the rest of the evening weeping himself to sleep.

Will that be me? Papa worried. *Will I be that man? That dad crying himself to sleep?*

It was a terrible thing to ponder, but it didn't last long as the emcee from WDIV-TV suddenly called the Bannisters to the stage. "And now, the moment you've all been waiting for, Make-A-Wish Michigan proudly introduces our highlighted ambassador of Wish Ball 2015, Samantha Bannister!"

It was jolting, a mind-bending segue, like going from breaking news about a war zone to a feature covering cute and cuddly kittens, but that was exactly the kind of jounce Papa needed to return to the reality of the moment.

Sami peered out over the sea of smiling faces, but the spotlight was bright and blinding. She was beautiful, even stunning in her rosso corsa dress, and she knew all eyes were on her, but she loved every second of it. And she was shocked when the emcee said they had an even bigger surprise for her.

SHE DANCED ME A STORY

"How can anything get bigger than all of this?!" she asked.

The emcee grinned, then snapped her finger, causing the doors of the TARDIS to swing open. The kids' jaws dropped in astonishment as the room was filled with applause. Then the emcee turned toward the crowd, and said in a proud and commanding voice, "All right, everyone, show Sami and #TeamTinyDancer some love as we give them a big Make-A-Wish Michigan sendoff... into a journey of imagination!"

Music from Doctor Who soared through the speakers as dozens of laser lights flashed in every direction, and the applause was so intense that it caused the stage to shake. Teresa and the boys dashed into the TARDIS, but just as Sami and her parents were about to enter, Sami turned around, and with the biggest smile and diva wave she could manage, she shouted, "Bye-bye, Make-A-Wish Michigan, we love you!"

When the door was shut, Make-A-Wish showed a video of the TARDIS flying off to London, and Ashley opened a secret hatch in the back.

"Wow," Sami said as she took Ashley's hand, "this is like a magic trick!"

There was a sparkle in Ashley's eye when she replied, "Yeah, we're magical like that."

Once the kids were out, Ashley closed the secret hatch, and when the video was over, Make-A-Wish re-opened the TARDIS, showing everyone that the family had disappeared. The audience loved it, but for the trick to stick, Sami and the family had to stay gone. They tried their best, and they would've gotten away with it were it not for the CEO of Make-A-Wish Michigan. She wanted to introduce them to a family. The mom and dad were on the Wish Ball steering committee, and they had something really important they wanted to say.

The dad stepped forward, then knelt, and, with his whole family crying behind him, he told Sami how inspired they were by her story.

"Aw," Sami replied, bashfully. "It's nothing, really. I'm just being me with my family."

"Oh, it's definitely something, Samantha," the father replied. "You've impacted our hearts in ways we could never repay."

"We wanted to do something, though," his wife said, using a tissue to wipe teary mascara from under her eye. Then she looked at her family, who were all nodding and smiling. "We had to do something, so we came up with an idea... together."

The dad smiled. "So, what did you guys think of that TARDIS up on the stage? Pretty cool, huh?"

"It's the best!" Athan replied.

"Even the size and color are perfect," Sami said.

Teresa squeezed between the kids, then stood in front of the dad. "It even had a light on top, and that reminded me of the TV show."

The dad looked around like he was being sneaky. "Do you mind if I tell you a secret, then?" The kids nodded, then leaned in close, and with one last look at his family standing behind him, the man cupped his hand beside his mouth, and whispered to the kids, "We made that TARDIS for *you*."

The kids looked at each other in disbelief. "For us?!"

"Yes," the mom said, still wiping tears with that tissue, "our family made it for #TeamTinyDancer."

One of the boys in their family spoke up. "You can put it anywhere you want at your house, and we'll get it all set up when you get back from London."

The kids were crying and giggling, jumping up and down like little maniacs in the hall, but Sami stood there, looking at the dad on his knee. "This is like the greatest dream come true!" Sami cried. "I wish I knew how to show you what it means to my heart!"

SHE DANCED ME A STORY

"I'll settle for one of your famous two-armed hugs," he replied.

"Oooohhh, you're definitely getting one of those!" Sami leapt so fast and so hard at him that she almost knocked him over. And with a ginormous two-armed hug, she cried tears of joy on his shoulder.

#TeamTinyDancer had to hurry, though! The Wish Ball was about to end, and the team didn't want to ruin the illusion of the TARDIS taking them to London, so the CEO led them to a secret passage. They raced through the halls, laughing and dancing like a bunch of weirdos, until they were safe and sound in their suite.

"The Wish Ball was epic," Athan said as he fell back on the bed.

Ambrose unclipped his bow tie, and replied, "It was better than epic, it was perfect."

Sami gazed out the huge window overseeing the city, watching the cars pass by, then sighed, "Well, it was almost perfect."

"Really?" Ambrose scoffed. "What else could you ask for??"

Sami removed her sash, then turned around, and with the most irresistible puppy face, she looked at Papa, and begged, "Buffalo wings?"

Papa thought she was joking, but Sami was serious—seriously suffering from a bad case of evening med munchies—so Mama ordered room service, and twenty minutes later, with a belly full of buffalo wings, Sami was asleep with the other kids on the bed.

Papa told Mama he needed to think, so he took the key to their suite, grabbed a copy of the *New York Times*, and made his way to a quiet place in the lobby. The lights were dim, but the fireplace spanned the entire length of the room, providing just enough light for him to read. The *Times* were riddled with raging controversies over election 2016, but not even that could keep his attention. For no matter how much he wished to distract himself with the news, and no matter how much he enjoyed reading about "Republicrat" outrage, he was insufferably distracted. Even if he weren't, there was no way in all the world he could've continued reading through the tears overtaking his eyes. He was furious inside, and in a fit of frustration, Papa crinkled the newspaper, then walked to the ledge overlooking the fireplace.

A melancholy piece of music played overhead, with instruments like the trumpet, flute, and harp, and the harmony seemed to hover atop the flit and flicker of the flames.

Where are You?!?! Papa scoffed at God. *No miracles, huh? No guardian angel to put out the fire?? No cure for all those cancer kids???* He felt like a crazy man, shaking his fist at holy ghosts and raising his voice in the wind, but he couldn't free himself of the fear or the fury that he'd felt ever since hearing the dad up on the stage. *And what's up with that, anyway, huh? Is it punishment for our sins or just the price of being born? And is it true what some of Sami's supporters say? Are you waiting for me to bend my knee? To pray?? To You???*

A gentle breeze swirled throughout the room, and it caused Papa to shiver. He had no idea where it came from, but it was tranquil, refreshing as dew before the dawn. And while he could still feel the warmth of the fire, his heart stopped overheating, and his mind, once red-hot, finally began to cool down.

He looked again at the flicker of the flames, but this time it was different, for he imagined a mysterious man, as old as time, and the family stood beside him in an old, rugged TARDIS made of wood. All of them were engulfed by fire, yet they were clothed in comfy coats, winter hats, and bulky boots. And though they looked battered and bruised (and in desperate need of a good

SHE DANCED ME A STORY

night's sleep), they were safe, entirely unscathed, and they were together, protected by that man and his old, rugged TARDIS. More than that, they were dancing, laughing, and singing songs with a single voice. It was so sacred, and for a fleeting second, Papa pondered whether he ought to lay prostrate on the floor, but he had his pride... and his hardened heart.

Then... he blinked.

And just like that, the vision vanished into oblivion, leaving only fire, darkness, and that symphony of sad and sorrowful sounds resounding from his weeping and gnashing of teeth.

XIX

MEMENTO MORI
[Jubilee Atop the Thames]

Jet lag was brutal, but the view of London through the windows of the Black Cab was riveting. Papa went to college in Canada, and he'd been to Mexico before, but he'd never been outside of North America, and the rest of #TeamTinyDancer had never stepped foot out of the United States. They were enthralled by the bigness of London, by its sprawling roads, and the myriad of monuments they spotted throughout the city. They had tons of questions too, so it was good they had taken a Black Cab—those cabbies know London like the back of their hand. And on those rare occasions when the cabbie didn't have an answer, Ambrose had it covered, as he'd committed to recording their Make-A-Wish trip in his journal.

The hotel was in Waterloo, right across the street from the Coca-Cola London Eye, but they were blue-blooded Americans, so they began their journey by turning on the TV.

"The cartoons and kid shows are pretty crappy," Athan said as he flipped through the channels. "I mean, no offense, but their CGI looks like some kindergartners did it, and their acting is even worse!"

Ambrose wrote down some notes, then put his journal under his pillow. "Plus, most of the other channels are all about queens and castles, just boring stuff."

"No," Teresa scoffed with her thumb in her mouth, "I saw some shows that we have on our TV at home."

"Yeah, like 'Walker: Texas Ranger,'" Sami laughed.

"Are we really talking about this right now?" Mama complained, "We only have a few days in London, so why are you wasting time on TV?"

SHE DANCED ME A STORY

+ Out and About in London +

The first day in London was rough, and the few that followed weren't any easier. Everything the family wanted to see was within a mile or two of the hotel, but the winds of Waterloo were hard to handle. And although Sami brought her cane, she'd complained about feeling exhausted, even kinda dizzy, so #TeamTinyDancer took turns wheeling her chair through the winding web of London's cold and rainy roads.

"This is so worth it!" Sami cheered as Papa stood behind her, bent over at the waist, with his hands on his knees, trying like mad to catch his breath. She was right, though, London *was* totally amazing. The family was entranced by the pantheon of imperial sculptures and ancient arches in Trafalgar Square. They were in awe of the otherworldly architecture of Westminster Abbey and mystified by the mysterious markings on the 4,000-year-old Cleopatra Obelisk. Everyone loved the street performers too, as well as the stroll atop Tower Bridge. And Sami waved at the Ecuadorian Embassy, wishing Wikileaks' Julian Assange good luck from a two-tier bus that later stopped at 221B Baker Street, where she snagged an authentic deerstalker cap from the Sherlock Holmes Museum.

It was insanely busy, and there was so much left to see, but the family was tired and out of time, so they made their way back to Waterloo and hopped aboard the tallest "cantilevered observation wheel" in the world: the Coca-Cola London Eye.

"I can see the whole city of London from here!" Sami exclaimed as the kids pressed their faces against the glass. In fact, at 135 meters above the River Thames, Sami could see much more than that. They saw the Gherkin, the Shard, and the Tower of London, as well as Buckingham Palace, the Queen's Palace Gardens, and the world-famous Big Ben. Once the Eye had reached the top, it stopped, just long enough for Mama and Papa to kiss. And with their children held tightly in their arms, #TeamTinyDancer stood for a moment of silence in a solemn salutation to the sunset, with its ecclesiastical colors of gold, purple, red, and white. Then they waved and bid sweet dreams to the loyal and royal denizens of this nearly 2,000-year-old city.

The walk back was cold, rainy, and blustier than a windy day in "The Windy City" of Chicago. And like every day before, the family was so exhausted that they practically dragged themselves through the doors of their hotel. They couldn't help but laugh, though, for there was no amount of bad weather or physical exhaustion that could compare to the pain and suffering behind the week's most constant and enduring conundrum:

SHE DANCED ME A STORY

"WHERE ARE WE GONNA EAT, PAPA?"

Sami's tummy rumbled with hunger, and the gang grumbled over England's apparent dislike for American fast food.

"That guy in the cab was right," Teresa complained with a gross expression on her face. "British food is icky nasty."

"Obviously!" Athan said with an overexaggerated gag reflex. "And for some really stupid reason, the waiters always promise they have lemonade. And even when I ask if it's the kind squeezed from lemons, they still just bring me some dumb old cup of Sprite every time!"

"Maybe that's why there aren't fat people in London," Ambrose wondered aloud.

It was a profound observation, no doubt, but it didn't solve the riddle of where to find delicious British food, so they contented themselves with prawn, bread and butter pudding, and some meat pie, as well as another "lemonade" from room service. And when the kids were nice-and-half-full, they turned on some Texas Ranger and fell fast asleep...

... everyone except for Sami, that is.

She wanted to go on a walk with Papa, but it was really late, and the family needed to wake up early to catch their train to Cardiff. "Papa's sleeping, anyway," Mama said, glancing over at the mound of blankets on his bed.

"No, he's not," Sami chuckled. "He's pretending, but I know the trick." Then, in a cute and practically irresistible voice, Sami begged him to show her the London Eye at night.

"Yeah-yeah," Papa groaned as he got out of bed, "I hear ya." He was so tired that he had fallen asleep in his clothes with his shoes still on. He rubbed his eyes, and with a big yawn, he said, "That was my super-secret plan, anyway."

Mama smiled, charmed by how quickly Papa caved to Sami's whim. "You'll need this," she said, handing him his coat and scarf. Then she kissed him on the cheek. "It's freezing cold out there."

That was an understatement. The wind was so intense that it flipped the flap of Papa's jacket right into his face, and it smelled like rain, which posed a problem since they didn't think to bring an umbrella. Papa ran, brisk as the breeze, maneuvering Sami's wheelchair around a stone courtyard, through a cloud of smoke from cigars near a row of late-night pubs, then by a rink aglow with purple lights, where couples ice skated to Christmas music near the River Thames.

"The London Eye looks so much different at night," Sami said with a shiver in her voice.

"Almost intimidating a little bit, isn't it?"

"Yeah, but it's decorated in red, white, and blue, just like the United States."

Papa scrunched his nose, then held out his hand to catch the first few drops of rain. "It's actually in honor of people who died in a recent terrorist attack in Paris," he told her, but before he could add another word, it began to rain—and it was a downpour!

"Papa," Sami whimpered, "I'm really cold..."

He heard the chattering of her teeth, and, making matters even worse, Sami was soaking wet—and that spelled "pneumonia." Kids with cancer are immune deficient, so getting sick is always kinda scary. But pneumonia? That was a killer! It's why she needed Pentam treatments, and it's why Papa was looking desperately for shelter, but there was nowhere to hide, and he had nothing to shield her from the storm. He found a blanket in the bag on the back of Sami's chair, but it only covered the top of her legs, and it definitely wasn't waterproof. And though his mind imagined a million things to do, only a few were in reach, and all were a dead end. So, with the rain streaming down his face, he looked at Sami sitting in her wheelchair...

... so helpless... so trusting... and dangerously sopping cold.

Papa hurried to take off his coat. It was the Navy pea coat he had been issued in basic training, and while it wasn't waterproof, it was the best chance they had at keeping her warm.

"No!" Sami cried. "You'd only have your shirt!"

SHE DANCED ME A STORY

Then he unwound the long Doctor Who scarf Mama had knit, wrapping it as fast as he could around Sami's head and neck.

"Papa! Stop!! Please? You're gonna freeze to death!!!"

He tucked the scarf under the collar of Sami's coat, then he ran his fingers through his beard, which had grown wild with curls under the weight of the rain. "I'm bigger," he assured her, "and I have fat to keep me warm. It's gotta be good for something, right?"

Papa chuckled at his own joke, but Sami knew he was lying. She saw the tears that hid behind his fierce resolve, and they betrayed a beautifully tragic fact: Papa wasn't just cold, he was terrified, and for right now, making sure she was okay in the rain was the main thing on his mind.

"If that's really what you want to do, then there's one more place I want to go," Sami shouted through the pouring rain. Then she pointed toward a bridge up ahead.o "I want to go there!"

It was the Golden Jubilee Bride. Papa took a deep breath, then pushed Sami's chair as fast as he could through the storm until, at last, with the doors shut, they were safe in the silent confines of an elevator. Papa was still out of breath, so he waited a minute, enjoying the shelter from the storm, then he chuckled and shook his head in resignation, pressing the button for the Upper Level...

DING

The doors creaked open, and Papa closed his eyes, preparing himself to re-enter the bitter cold and pouring rain...

"Um, Papa... this is weird..."

He peeked with one of his eyes still shut, then popped his head out the door, looking side-to-side, just to make sure they weren't imagining things. But they weren't imagining things at all, for in that short time that they were in the elevator, the rain and the wind just stopped.

The difference between life on the bridge and the storm of the world below was as vast as it was inexplicable, but they didn't care (or even wish to know why), and they wasted no time strolling out onto Jubilee Bridge.

Boats floated beneath their feet, and the River Thames twinkled with colorful reflections coming from London's nightlife.

"There are tons of people up here!" Sami exclaimed. Then she smiled, and looking over her shoulder, she whispered, "Even some fat people, Papa."

They wore matching fanny packs, as well as matching shirts, the ones people wore in the '90s with Bugs Bunny and Tasmanian Devil "criss-crossing" their clothes. All of that was bad enough, but the worst was yet to come, as it appeared that the couple was approaching them.

The man said "Howdy" in a curiously non-British accent, then asked if Papa could point them in the direction of the nearest Taco Bell or Arby's.

"Wait!" Papa replied, "are you from the United States?!"

"Bet your bottom dollar we are!" the woman boasted.

Her husband nodded, then said, "We're from the great state of Ohio!"

Sami grinned. "Ah, the Buckeyes!"

She knew Papa loathed Ohio State, but after everything they'd been through, she enjoyed seeing the flicker of maize in the fire in Papa's azure eyes, and she giggled when she heard him mumble under his breath, "Of course they are."

The two Buckeyes were excited to tell Papa all about Ohio, and they were even alumni of OSU, so Sami left him high and dry, wheeling herself over to the wall facing out toward Big Ben. Then, after a few more discomfiting words, Papa pointed the Buckeyes in some random misdirection, then shook his head and walked over to Sami, where he leaned his elbows on the wall and gazed out at Thames.

SHE DANCED ME A STORY

BONG... BONG... BONG

Sami cheered as the colossal clock chimed the time, but then she was struck by the fact that it was midnight. "Awww," she said in a naughty voice, "Mama's gonna be so mad."

Papa knew it was true, and he could already hear her nagging in his ear, but he had heavier things on his mind. It was easy to shake that whole conversation about Ohio State, but his brain was now a rush of ruminations powered by the river and the echoing remains of Big Ben's rumbling reminder to bide the time.

"It's a precious thing, you know," Papa said. "Time, that is." He held out his hand, hoping maybe to catch some last drops of rain. "It's alive, and every moment is ever-present, but it's only present here and now, cuz today is always getting torn into shreds, like being trapped between the wolf of the past and the edge of a cliff that everyone calls the future." Papa brushed the mist from his hands, and with a fatalistic ring in his voice, he said, "Whether we like it or not, the present is always getting eaten by the wolf and shoved over the cliff at the exact same time. It's paradoxical, but it's true every moment of every day of our lives."

"At least we have each other, though," Sami replied. She looked down over the edge of the wall, watching how bubbles emerge from underwater, thinking about their short lives spent cruising the current before bursting into oblivion. "I know that that wolf is gonna get us someday, but that's cuz we're born, so it's just part of being alive." Then she looked at him, and said, "We have friends and family too, though, and they can help us fight that wolf. That way, when we are stuck on the edge of that scary cliff, at least we can know we're not alone... and, sometimes, maybe we can all just jump together."

"Maybe..." Papa whispered. "Sometimes."

He didn't look at Sami, but she could see the sadness in his eyes.

"But then a day comes," he told her, "when people are eaten for the very last time. Then, what's done is done and over with... and they're just gone forever."

"Hmm..." Sami hummed. She knew what he was talking about, and she was nervous to say what was on her mind, but then she looked at Big Ben. "I know I'm just a kid, but cancer made me think a lot about this stuff, and I really think people should try not to waste their time anymore. I mean, it's pretty stupid if you think about it because we only have one life to live, and no one knows when or how they're gonna die."

"Or what happens after death..." Papa sighed.

"Yeah," Sami chuckled nervously, "that too. And I know that's a hard one for you."

Just then, a supply ship sailed beneath them, and it captured Sami's attention. She was fascinated by all the different colors, and she wondered what was in all the boxes, as well as where all the boxes were heading.

"I wish I could tell you the answer to that one," she said, "but I always think of it like a movie or a really good play. People get really excited in the beginning when the curtain opens up. It's like when you're a kid, or when you graduate or get married or something, or even when you have a baby. People love the stories, and a lot of times they like the characters, even some of the bad ones..." She paused, squinting her eyes to watch as the supply ship sailed away. "It's weird, I think, how we get bored and take stuff for granted. We even take our friends and family for granted. It just feels wrong to me, especially because we know how sad we'll be when it's all over and gone." And when the ship was out of sight, Sami sighed, then looked at Papa. "We do all that stuff even though we know that, sooner or later, every story has to end."

"Vanity of vanities," Papa murmured.

Sami wondered if Papa even heard her, or if he was still thinking about the wolf. She squinted up at the stars peeking out from the clouds. They were beautiful, and they reminded her of the stories Papa told about the constellations, but then she saw Corona Borealis, and almost started to cry. "Maybe," Sami replied, "but I wonder about that..."

Papa glanced over at Sami, surprised by what she said. "You wonder about God?"

Sami pressed her lips, then shrugged a little. "It's kinda hard not to wonder about stuff like that when you're a kid who has cancer."

"Kids with cancer and an all-loving God?" Papa scoffed. "Nah, I don't think so."

"Hmm..." Sami sighed. "Maybe you're right." Then, after an otherwise safe moment of silence, Sami said, "But maybe you're wrong, too, Papa."

"Wrong about God???" (She definitely had his attention now.) "You're right! I was wrong—I was wrong for a long time!" He paused for a second, then shook his head like a man in defeat. "I was wrong for most of my life, Sam..."

She knew what he meant, but something about Papa's answer made the corners of Sami's mouth smile just a bit. "Well, it's a bummer, but I don't have the one hundred percent answer to give you right now, that's for sure." Then she grabbed her wrist, and said, "I do know one thing, though, and that's that even if you *are* right about God and heaven and all that stuff, I just love being alive, and I love all my friends, and I even love my pets, too." Then she reached to hold Papa's hand, and with the sweetest eyes she could muster, she said, "And I especially love you and Mama, and the whole entire family, cuz you guys really do mean the world to my heart."

Papa smirked as he lifted his elbows from the rail. "We do have those things, don't we?"

"Of course we do. And they're the greatest gifts of all time, too." Then she raised her eyebrows, and said, "It's a lot, actually, at least if you really stop to think about it, especially because the universe is so huge and stuff."

Time was starting to sink in, though, and Papa could hear the shiver in Sami's voice, so he wrapped the scarf back around her neck. Then, just when he was about to head off to the hotel, he stopped...

"Okay, Sam, tell me, given all the stuff we know and all the stuff we think we know and all those things we definitely don't know-"

"And maybe what we know but think we maybe don't know?" Sami asked.

"Maybe," Papa chuckled. "Given all of that mess, what do you think people should do?"

"What, you mean with their lives and time and stuff?"

Papa nodded. "Yeah, what should people do with their lives and time and stuff?"

Sami scrunched her brows and put her finger by the side of her mouth, like Sherlock Holmes. "Well, I guess if I had to give an answer, I'd say that they should do what they'd want to do if they were at the end of their life and all out of time. That way they'd live the best life they could, never wasting time, and they'd love people for all the right reasons. And if they were old and gray, they could be proud of the life they'd lived... and they wouldn't be afraid to die... I mean, not too afraid, anyway."

"*Memento mori?*" Papa replied.

Sami giggled and shook her head. "I have no idea what that even means, Papa."

"It's Latin for 'Remember Your Death.' And trust me, Sami Lee, you know the meaning of 'memento mori' better than anyone I've ever met."

"Even though I don't know the words?"

Papa knelt down beside her wheelchair, then pulled the scarf tight around her, and said, "Especially because you don't know the words."

"Hmm," Sami hummed with a sense of accomplishment, "then here's me wishin' a 'Happy Memento Mori' right backatcha, Papa."

With that, Sami kissed Papa's hand, then pressed it hard against her cheek as the two of them looked out over the river, watching as ships sailed by, keeping count of the time it took for them to sail out of sight, and for any trace of their wake to no longer trouble the waters.

XX

DOCTOR WHO'S FIRST AID KIT

"Hurry up!" Mama yelled, "We're gonna miss the train!"

"We're running as fast as we can!" Athan replied.

"Yeah, Mama, stop being so mean!" Teresa complained as she struggled to drag a heavy bag along the ground. "It's just really hard to run with all this luggage!"

"Stop lollygagging," Mama scoffed. "And it's just one suitcase, T, so c'mon."

Teresa huffed, then mumbled under her breath, "but it's heavy cuz all my dolls."

"And these crazy tunnels aren't helping much, either," Papa said. He stopped for a second, then removed a map from his coat. It was wet from the night before, and the ink bled on the paper, which would've been bad in almost any situation, but the tunnels to Paddington Station were a maze, and #TeamTinyDancer was lost. Londoners were more than glad to help, but their accents were tough to understand, and they talked like rural Americans giving directions to out-of-towners, rambling on about left-turns at this or that landmark, followed by two right-turns here and there. It was confusing, and at this point, it almost felt hopeless.

Then came the sound of a flute...

Everyone thought it came through the speakers, but the more they walked, the closer they got to the source—and the music got louder and lovelier with each and every step. Without even knowing it, the Bannisters picked up their pace, being irresistibly drawn by the soft and free-flowing flutters of the flute. And the closer they got, the faster they ran, until, finally, they were standing face-to-face with the man behind the music.

He was tall, thin, and neatly-dressed, and his name was Mauro Uselli. Critics hailed him as one of the most original flute soloists to ever play Bach, and he was known for popping up in random locations all across Europe, like today, in a tunnel leading to Paddington Station.

Sami was utterly amazed by the tempo of his allegretto, and the family was flabbergasted by the speed and precision of his fingers on the keys, which clicked and clacked like the ratta-tat-tat of a machine gun. And you could see the whites of Sami's eyes as Mauro knelt on one knee before her wheelchair, playing as though she was the only person in those busy tunnels, or even in the whole world.

"That's the prettiest song anyone has ever played for me," she said, blushing as Mauro bent over to give her a hug.

Mama reminded them (for the millionth time) that they were running late, so they got a picture and said goodbye, then ran in stride with Mauro's music, which only faded as it merged into the background sounds coming from the Paddington Station.

It was a three-hour eastbound train to Cardiff, but the kids didn't care. They were the only riders onboard, so they had free reign of the train. Athan played with his toys, and Teresa with her dolls, as Ambrose wrote about Mauro in his journal, and Sami and her parents gazed out the window, seeing all the sights along the way. They saw the suburbs of Reading in the town of Berkshire, and the dry valleys of North Wessex Downs, as well as the hills of Bristol, and at long last, they saw Cardiff, their final terminus. They hailed a cab, and, less than 10 minutes later, they approached the shorelines of Cardiff's Mermaid Quay, where they beheld 22 big blue letters that boldly read:

"THE DOCTOR WHO EXPERIENCE"

The building was plain, square, and made of brick, but passing through the doors felt like entering an entirely different dimension. It looked like something out of the distant future, and the foyer was decorated with Whovian paraphernalia. They saw Daleks made from Legos, Cybermen standing watch at the door, pictures of the TARDIS, and a display that featured the handprints and signatures of all the actors who'd played the role of Doctor Who.

With a mix of fear and excitement in his voice, Ambrose said, "It's really dark in here."

"Everybody knows that already, Ambrose!" Teresa scoffed from her hiding place behind Papa. Ambrose wasn't really talking to her, but she wasn't wrong. The floors, walls, and ceiling were covered in soft black carpet, and the only light came from glass enclosures glowing around the room. Each one contained an artifact from the show, which would have been cool, except... "This place is so super-duper creepy!" Teresa complained, gazing up at a cracked Cyberman helmet. "What are they trying to do, anyway, scare everybody like crazy? Sheesh!"

"This is heaven to me," Sami replied, "cuz it's even creepier than I thought it would be."

CREEEAAAK

Billows of smoke suddenly poured into the room as a large stone door opened from top to bottom, and an eerie green light in the hands of a mysterious man caused the smoke to glow as it crawled along the ground.

"My name is Forculus Phantasos," he said in a very strong voice. His robe sparkled, and his collars towered over the back of his head. He said that he guarded the ancient doors that lead to fantasy and dreams, and that, today, he was going to be our guide. "All of you must wear the protective badge of Gallifrey," he said, passing out the glowing green lanyards in his hand. "They come from the planet of the Time Lords, the birthplace of our good, dear friend Doctor Who." Then he warned that they'd be entering a trans-dimensional world, one filled with all sorts of brilliant lights and worrisome sounds. "So, stay near me, and always listen closely."

Foculus led them into the pitch-black unknown on the other side of the door, and when the last one was in the room, the door quickly shut behind them. The smoke was still thick enough to obscure the litany of luminescent orbs around the room, but after a few moments, the fog dissipated, and everyone knew exactly where they were.

"Where the heck are we?" Papa asked.

(Okay, so almost everyone.)

"Are you serious?" Sami replied. "You don't recognize the ARS?" She hoped he was joking, but Papa just stood there, shrugging his shoulders and looking like a dummy. "Ugh," she scoffed. "This place is obviously the Architectural Reconfiguration System." Then she shook her head, and with a face letting him know he let her down, she said, "Seriously, Papa, everyone in the world knows that."

In the middle of the room stood a tremendously tall tree. With tube-like branches that dangled and drooped to the ground, it looked like a weeping willow, and the glowing teardrop orbs that blinked at the bottom of the branches made it look like the tree was actually crying.

Suddenly, a woman spoke over the loudspeakers...

"I am Romana," she said. Her voice was strong and elegant, fitting for a Time Lord. "I come to you from the Last Days of Gallifrey, speaking to you from a past you've forgotten. And all of you here are from a future that I won't live to see." She talked about the Time Lords and their home planet of Gallifrey, as well as the rise and demise of their civilization. A war had broken out, and there was a dreadful darkness cast over their land, so by the time her message reached us, their war had ended, and she and her people were dead. "There is only one who was destined to survive, and he's gone by many names: the Man in the Big Blue Box, John Smith, and even Merlin, as well as the Time Trotter, and the Oncoming Storm. But to you and to me, his name shall forever be..."

"The Doctor!" everyone cheered.

"He's different from all the other Time Lords," Sami whispered to Mama. "He's an adventurer, and he needs to experience things for himself. That's why he stole the TARDIS and ran away—even though I personally think the TARDIS stole him. He's really humble, and he's super-smart too."

"But he's encountered many enemies," Romana thundered, "as well as many friends and companions. You must wish carefully, then, for when the Doctor takes you on an adventure, he has many lives to live... while you have only one."

Romana's voice faded into silence, and the room began to rumble. Lights went wild, and the tube-like branches of the tree began to tremble. The curator promised he had it under control, but then the lights went out. The room was still cloudy with smoke, and for a moment, the only light in the room came from the glowing green lanyards. All of that changed, though, when the light from a screen filled the room. And, there, on the screen, was the TARDIS, spiraling through space. It was under attack by Time Serpents, who were using their tentacles to crush the Doctor's blue Police Box.

"Oh, no!" Athan said. "The Doctor's in trouble!"

Suddenly, static shot across the screen, and something—no, *someone*—appeared.

tap-tap (fingers rapped on the screen) *tap-tap*

Then... he spoke. "Hello? Hello?" he asked in that all-familiar voice.

"We're here, Doctor!" Athan shouted.

"Oh, there you are. Hello." Then he stopped, and with a look of annoyance on his face, he peered deep into the camera, saying, "Wait! Hold on just one second! Are all of you in my TARDIS? How did you get in here?!"

Forculus tried to explain, but it was no use.

"Ugh," the Doctor growled, running his fingers through his wild gray hair. "You've all put me in a terrible position, you know. I mean, I can't just abandon you here, now, can I?" Then he paused, startled by his own question, and started speaking out loud to himself. "Or can I? Hmmm... No, no, I mustn't leave them here. They'd be no match for the Time Serpents—they'd kill them—and we can't have that now, can we?"

While he was busy plotting and scheming what to do with his uninvited guests, the Time Serpents were attacking the TARDIS, which was now shaking and falling apart all around him! The Doctor ran like a wild man to the control panel, pushing buttons and pulling levers, but nothing seemed to work. Then he slammed his hand on the panel, and grumbled, "Darn!" His eyes were sharp, searching hard for an answer, but it was obvious to everyone in the room that their beloved Doctor was helpless.

"We want to help you!" Sami shouted.

"Ah, yes, what a brilliant idea!" he replied. Then he raised his eyebrows, almost like it was his idea. "Yes, ol' boy, brilliant indeed—if I may say so myself." Looking back toward the guests, he continued, "Go, now! You must follow that boy, I mean, girl, well, whatever, the one in the silly robe. Follow *that* into the next room. And when you make it, I'll tell you what you must do next." He had hardly finished speaking when a hidden door opened from behind them. Then, as everyone rushed into the next room, he shouted, "But you must hurry!" Then he sighed, "The fate of the world depends on it..."

SHE DANCED ME A STORY

Once there, everyone stood in awe of what they saw...

"It's the TARDIS, Mama!" Sami exclaimed. "We're inside the actual TARDIS!"

It was huge, and if people didn't know better, they'd imagine it was a factory, but with a chalkboard smattered with the scribblings of a mathematical madman, a library arrayed with ancient books, and orange power tanks protruding from the center of a hexagonal control board, there was no doubt that they were standing smack-dab in the center of Doctor Who's control room.

"But where is the Doctor?" Ambrose asked.

"I had to run," the Doctor said from another TV screen. "Damage had been done to the symbiotic nuclei in a separate wing of the TARDIS. I'm certain you'll forgive me." Then he paused, and with panic in his voice, he, again, began speaking aloud to himself. "Oh, my, these humans are clueless—they don't know what to do! Yes, of course it's on account of their being very stupid, but, my, my, we're doomed!"

"Doctor!" Forculus interjected, nervously. "Just tell us what we must do, and I promise we shall do our best..." And everyone laughed when he said, "even if we are very stupid humans."

The Doctor told them of three green crystals scattered throughout time, and he warned them of great danger. "But it's easy-peasy," he said as he brushed debris off his black velvet coat. "Just hold onto the levers on the control panel, and no matter what, do not let them go." Then, with the sort of sarcasm his fans knew and loved him for, he shook his head, and said, "'Cos it's not like we're dealing with life and death here, now, are we?"

BOOM-BOOM-BOOM

Lights flashed everywhere, and everything started to shake!

"It's like an earthquake!" Athan shouted to Sami.

The Doctor raced around, barking commands, and everyone held on to levers like their lives depended on it. "Steady now!" he shouted over the noise. "Hold her steady!"

The ground shook so badly, it was hard to stay balanced, and the lights were now out of control. Sami grit her teeth, and even though her right-hand couldn't grasp the handle, she used it the best she could, pulling on that lever with all of her might!

Forculus cried out, "Don't stop! Keep trying! We can do this—but we must do this together!" People were grunting and groaning, pulling as hard as they possibly could, when Forculus shouted, "Three... two... one!"

ZZZZEEEEW—SHUNK

The lights stopped flashing, and the only sound was that of the guests catching their breath, as well as the gentle vwoorp-vwoorp sound the TARDIS makes when it lands. Forculus was certain they were on another planet, and he spoke through a monitor, asking aliens to forgive their unannounced arrival. But there was no reply, only silence... too much silence. Even so, they didn't appear to be in danger, so Forculus told everyone to look around the room in hopes of finding one or more of the Doctor's glowing green crystals.

It was dark, and the room was cluttered with old machinery. And cobwebs hung like sheets along the walls. Teresa was terrified, so she stuck with Papa, while Mama and the kids searched the area. They looked in every box and pile of parts in the room, but all of them came up empty-handed. That was until Sami poked her hands through a cobweb, only to activate a dim red light at the end of an antenna...

...and the sight of it nearly paralyzed her with fear!

"WARNING! WARNING!" growled a Dalek as it burst through the cobweb.

Everyone ducked and ran in fear, but there was nowhere to hide, as nearly a dozen other Daleks reactivated around the room! Daleks were a ruthless race, and they vowed to exterminate anything and anyone daring to get in the way of their worldwide domination. That meant that Doctor Who was their most feared and hated enemy, and that anyone who sided with him was in terrible and immediate danger.

"DAAAAALEKS!" the rest of the machines screeched simultaneously. "YOU ARE ADVISED TO LEAVE AT ONCE, OR..."

For some reason, the Dalek stopped mid-sentence, then all of them powered down and fell back to sleep.

Everyone stood still as statues, afraid that any movement might reawaken the monsters. And in that moment of silence and stillness, Sami saw something deep in the casing of the Dalek she found in the shadows. It was glowing, and she was certain it was one of the crystals. She tip-toed toward the sleeping beast, and with one last look around, she closed her eyes and held her breath, then reached and grabbed the crystal.

A sense of elation showered over her, and she was so happy, so lost in the moment, that she held the crystal high, and shouted, "Look, everyone, I got it!"

"EXTERMINATE!" the Dalek screeched, as its systems kicked back on.

"EXTERMINATE! EXTERMINATE! EXTERMINATE!" all the other Daleks screeched.

Froculus hurried everyone to the door, but he struggled to find his key. Everyone begged him to hurry as the Daleks were closing in, and just when they feared that all was lost, Froculus found his key!

"Hurry!" he shouted as he rushed them through the door. And just before they were destroyed by the death march of the maniacal machines, he slammed the door shut, then locked it with his key.

Everyone was relieved, and for a second, they thought they were in the clear... but they should've known better.

JEREMIAH T. BANNISTER

CRACK-CRASH-BOOM

The new room roared with thunder, and lightning bolts flashed overhead, revealing a new [and even more nefarious] menace. For this wasn't a room, it was a graveyard, and they were surrounded by hundreds of-

"Weeping Angels!" the kids shouted.

These were undoubtedly the deadliest, most powerful and malevolent lifeforms the cosmos had ever seen. They looked like cherubim and seraphim, and they were lovely to behold, but behind their stony smiles, there were rows of sharp and jagged teeth. Their facial expressions were haunting, too, and their hands revealed that these angels were on the hunt. Making matters even worse, Weeping Angels were faster than the speed of sound.

"And remember," Froculus shouted, "Weeping Angels only move if you blink! You must be brave, but you must never, ever blink!"

Sami and Athan were valiant, weaving and winding their way through risky rows of growling, howling, and scowling demons scattered throughout the graveyard, but the other kids were too scared to go through it alone, so they held tightly to Mama and Papa, and all of them tried their hardest not to blink. Then, after a few terrifying twists and turns, another child in the group found the second crystal, and Froculus led them to theirnext destination—far away from those evil Weeping Angels.

This was their final room, and it was much different from the others. There were lights all around, but they were dim, and speakers were everywhere, but the room was very quiet. And there, in the center of the room, was a big blue door with a sign that said "Private: Keep Out."

Doctor Who appeared again on the screen. "You'll need those 3-D glasses your guide is handing out, for you are about to enter a most remarkable time distortion. And on the other side, you shall find yourself in the curious land... of Cardiff, Wales."

The big blue doors blew open, revealing mountains of rubble. This wasn't just any rubble, either. No, it was the remains of that place the First Doctor and his time-traveling TARDIS once called their home.

"It stinks like nothing else, I know," the Doctor complained as he waved his hand in front of his nose, "but that mustn't matter, as this is where you'll find the third and final crystal. And when you do, place all three in the glowing receptors, that way you can be transported to the gift store deep within the TARDIS."

"The gift store??" Athan whispered to himself, wringing his hands like some kind of villain with an evil plan. But no sooner had Athan done that, when the room lit up with emergency lights and the sounds of sirens filled the air. Everything in the room started shaking, and the Doctor tumbled to the floor of the TARDIS.

"The TARDIS is under attack!" Sami screamed.

"This is it!" the Doctor shouted as he climbed back to his feet. "You must find that crystal—and fast! We're almost out of time!"

Everyone scattered, searching as quickly as they could. Teresa looked in boxes, while Ambrose checked under the chairs. Time was running out, though, and no one could find the crystal. It felt hopeless, and people worried the TARDIS was lost, but that's when Sami looked up toward the ceiling, and there, high atop a mountain of harpsichord boxes, she saw a gentle green glow. She limped as fast as she could, and she tried to climb the mountain, but her hand couldn't grab onto anything, and her leg was far too weak. She tried and tried, over and over and over again, but each time got worse and worse. "Come on, stupid hand!" she cried. "Come on, you dumb leg! Can't you just work this one time???" But neither of them were listening to her, and after a few attempts, she accepted that she couldn't do it... and her heart began to break.

Athan was pulling Styrofoam peanuts from a plastic bag when he noticed Sami sulking, and he wondered why she was sad. Then he saw the green glow for himself, and he realized what was going on.

"Don't worry, Sami!" Athan shouted as he scrambled up the scrap. "I'll get it for you!"

"Are you crazy?!" Sami cried aloud. "You don't need to do this!"

"Yes I do!" he replied over the blaring alarms. And with a smile on his face, he promised her, "We're a team, Sami, cuz we're family!"

"But you're afraid of heights!"

That was true, and he kind of wished she hadn't reminded him, but he pressed his lips and used that fear to push harder and faster than he'd ever pushed before.

"Hurry, mate!" Froculus shouted. "The Doctor needs us!"

Athan climbed and climbed, and even when he almost slipped, he never looked back, and he refused to give up. He was on a mission, a mission fueled by the duty and devotion of a brother who loved his sister. And with every step up that mountain, he thought of things he'd said and done that he wished he could take back. He knew he was a pain in Sami's butt sometimes, and he knew that's what younger brothers do, but he hated that Sami was dying of cancer, and he wanted nothing more in the world than to make it disappear... but he couldn't make it disappear, and he was afraid that, one day, cancer would Sami disappear.

"Grrrr!" he growled as he reached for one of the last boxes. His arms and legs were shaking, and sweat poured down his brow, but just as he approached the top, Sami shouted:

"You can do it, Athan! I believe in you!"

And with her words still ringing in his ears, Athan reached as hard and as far as he could, and with the crystal in his hand, he raised it high to the sky, and yelled down to his sister, "I did it, Sam! I got the final crystal!"

"Hurry!" everyone insisted. "The Doctor's running out of time!"

Athan scrambled down the mountain, and when he finally reached the floor, he looked at the green glowing glass, and with a smile on his face, he handed it to Sami. "I did it for you, Samantha, cuz I think you're a true hero, and I think you're the perfect person to save the Doctor and the TARDIS."

Sami blushed and hugged him, then she ran to Forculus, and with both her hands, she slammed that final crystal into the third and final receptacle.

ZZZZEEEEEW_SHUNK

All the flashing lights and all the blaring sirens suddenly stopped.

"Whodathunkit!" the Doctor said. "You defeated the Daleks, you defied the Weeping Angels, and, now the Time Serpents, they're vanquished-and all because of you." Then he stopped, and with an arrogant smile, he said, "And maybe a little help from me, too."

Froculus opened the final door, and the kids ran off to the gift shop, where they wandered about, looking at blankets and posters, sweaters and scarves, even diaries shaped and colored like the TARDIS. But Athan wanted figurines, as well as a little TARDIS for them to fly in—that way, even from his home far across the Atlantic, he could always reenact their special adventure at the museum, helping him always remember the day he helped his sister save Doctor Who.

+ On the shores of Mermaid Quay +

The family spent the rest of the afternoon walking the windy pier, from whence they could see the BBC, and they ate at Eddie's Diner, where one of Sami's favorite scenes of Doctor Who was filmed. Then, just when they thought the day couldn't get any better, the server assured the kids that they served authentic lemonade.

"Yeah, you know, the kind you squeeze from lemons," he said.

Everyone was blown away, and they probably looked silly getting so excited over lemonade, but of all the places they'd been, it was the iconic Eddie's Diner that finally promised to pull through on some good ol' fashioned American-style lemonade.

"So, Sami, an episode of Doctor Who was recorded here?" Ambrose asked as he wrote down notes in his journal.

"Duh!" Sami laughed. "Actually, I'm sitting in the same seat of the same booth that Matt Smith sat in during that episode!"

Athan took his Doctor Who figurine out of its box, and asked, "How cool would it have been if Make-A-Wish made it so we could've met Matt Smith?!"

"I wondered about that, too," Papa replied as the server brought their food and drinks to the table. "Trust me, if I knew someone—anyone at all—who said they could actually connect us with Matt Smith, I'd have done anything to make it happen."

However, as with many things in life, some assurances are simply too good to be true...

"Sneaky little tricker!" Athan grumbled moments later as he sipped on his "dumb old Sprite."

+ On their last night in the Cardiff Centre City Hotel +

Mama was exhausted, and she wanted the train ride back to go more smoothly than the train ride there had been, so she was hoping everyone would get some sleep. Sami was wide awake, though, and Teresa wanted to cuddle with Papa, so Mama took the boys with her, kissed Papa and the girls goodnight, and went to bed.

"Doctor Who was so scary!" Teresa said as she snuggled under the blankets.

Papa leaned his head out the bathroom door, and with a mouthful of foam, he said, "Make-A-Wish really is the best, isn't it?" Then he spit out his toothpaste, washed the foam from his mustache, and turned off the light.

Sami was sitting in the bed when Papa got there, and she was looking something up on his computer. She'd heard a song at Eddie's Diner, and she liked it so much that she wrote the lyrics on a napkin. It was "My Silver Lining," by the Swedish duo known as First Aid Kit, and there was something about that song that summed up so many of the thoughts and feelings she'd experienced along the way. And so they laid there, sharing the blankets and listening to Sami's special song.

"Make-A-Wish really does make dreams come true, don't they, Sam?" Papa asked.

"Yeah..." Sami sighed, "...dreams come true..."

Teresa was half asleep, but she could tell Sami was sad. "Are you okay?" she asked with her thumb in her mouth.

It was a simple question, heartfelt, and even kinda cute, but that's all it took. For, unbeknownst to them, Sami had more than Make-A-Wish on her mind, and by this time, the pressure of holding it in had become so overwhelming, so utterly unbearable, that the only remedy was to let it all out... and to let it all out at once.

"I'm never gonna get married. Am I, Papa?" Sami cried aloud.

The question shocked him, and he tried his best to console her, but there was none of that... not here, not now...

"Will I even be alive to go to college, or get a job, or have babies?"

"You can't think that stuff," Teresa replied.

"But it's true, isn't it?" Then she looked at Papa, and with tears gushing out of her eyes, she cried, "Tell me the truth, Papa. It's true, isn't it???"

He just sat there, shaking his head and pressing his lips, trying his best not to cry.

Sami knew what that meant. "I'm not stupid, you guys! I have cancer, but I still have a brain! And I have dreams—big dreams—dreams like meeting my future husband, going on dates, and crying when he finally asks me to marry him! And I dream of wearing a beautiful white wedding dress, with a bouquet of pretty flowers in my hands, and I dream of you walking me down the aisle, Papa!"

SHE DANCED ME A STORY

"And I want babies too!" Samantha howled. "I want lots of babies, Papa! I want boys and girls, and I want to pick their names. And I want to feed them and change their diapers. And I promise to feed them the healthiest food, that way they can grow up big and strong like you—and I'll do my best to make sure they never get cancer!"

Samantha was crying so hard, she started to shake the bed. "And I want to get old, Papa! I want to be old and gray with tons of wrinkles all over my face! And I want to spoil my grandkids with presents on Christmas and their birthdays, too!"

Teresa looked at Papa, then reached beneath the pillows to find his hand. She hoped he'd have an answer (something, anything at all), but Papa never imagined this would happen—not like this, not today. Both of them were crying so hard, they could barely breathe. But that's when Papa looked at her, and with tears pouring forth from their hearts, they nodded to one another. It was an unspoken agreement, a covenant and life-long understanding that, no matter how painful it was for him to hear her words or for her to speak them, and no matter how hard it was to bear the weight of the others' mourning, there were things that had to be said, and things that had to be done. Most of all, that none of this was a mere matter of duty. It was an honor, even a privilege, to serve as a silent witness to the sorrows of Sami's dirge.

"I know bad stuff happens to good people," Sami wept, "but I promise to be a good girl, Papa. I won't ever be a liar or a stealer, either. And I'll always love people no matter what. And I'll work really hard to do my best all the time, and to never give up, and to keep on smiling-oh, God, I just want to keep on smiling!"

Then... she stopped.

Papa and Teresa just wrapped their arms around Sami, weeping as she wept. For even now that it was over, they knew that no words could possibly match or even speak to the pain that Samantha felt... or even of their fear they had that Samantha might be right. So, there they laid, surrounded by the sounds of two singing Swedish sisters, hugging and crying each other to sleep.

+ On the train back to London +

By the time the Bannisters arrived onboard, there were no seats left. So Mama sat in the space between the cars, running her fingers through Sami's soft hair, as she rested, fast asleep, on her lap. And Athan and Teresa played with their new Doctor Who figures on the floor, while Papa buried his nose in a newspaper, which, much to his satisfaction, exposed a conspiracy concerning the Freemasons and British leaders. But Ambrose sat in a corner, silently watching the rest of his family, scribbling down his final thoughts regarding their time in London. Trouble was, he had writer's block. He knew what he felt, and he was thinking about tons of different things, but he wasn't sure how to write it. Then, with his pencil crunched between his teeth, Ambrose thought to himself:

I KNOW MAMA AND PAPA WISH THEY COULD FIND A CURE FOR SAMI'S CANCER, AND EVERYONE IN THE FAMILY IS AFRAID THAT SAMI WILL DIE TOO FAST—OR EVEN WORSE, TOO SLOW—BUT IT'S OKAY THAT THEY DON'T HAVE ALL THE ANSWERS, YOU KNOW. THAT MAKES THINGS REALLY SCARY, AND I'M SO AFRAID WE'RE GONNA GET SO SAD, BUT WE GOTTA KEEP ON KEEPIN' ON.

Then he remembered all the fun they had, and how their home was always filled with music and laughter. And as the train entered the city, Ambrose looked one last time toward the London skyline, where his eyes caught a glimpse of a tremendous raincloud, which was doing its best to hide the daytime sun. Seeing this made him smile, and before closing his journal, he heard the fading sound of Mauro's flute in the whistle of the train, then wrote the words:

OUR FAMILY MIGHT BE SAD. BUT THERE'S ALWAYS HOPE! CUZ LOVE'S OUR SILVER LINING.

XXI

#NeverGiveUp
[On Christmas Eve]

"You did what?!?!" the kids screamed.

The family was furious—and for a very good reason.

"C'mon, you guys," Papa replied, "don't you think I know I messed up?"

"And on Christmas?!?!" Sami shouted.

"Okay, that's fair, so maybe I messed up BIG TIME!"

"There ain't no 'maybe' about this one, Papa," Ambrose said.

"Obviously, but that's what I'm saying, dude! And I feel terrible about it, okay? I just don't get why everyone is ganging up on me like this."

"Well, I hate breakin' it to ya, partner," Athan said with a Western drawl, then he twirled and re-holstered his toy cowboy gun, and snarled, "but you've been BUSTED!"

Ambrose shook his head, woefully. "More like super-duper-mega-busted."

Teresa had been quiet so far, but she was sitting in a bean bag near the tree, scooping marshmallows from the top of her hot cocoa, so she heard the whole thing. "Ho! Ho! Ho!" she said in the deepest voice she could do. "I'm Santa Claus, and I just wish everyone could get along and have a veeeery merry Christmas!"

Papa was so proud of his pretty princess girl, standing up to everyone like that. With a fatherly nod, he said, "Thanks, T-Bear. I love you, baby." Then he looked at all the kids, insisting, "See, that's what I've been trying to say all along."

"Sorry, Papa," Teresa replied, "but I was just practicing what I'll say to you next Christmas." And with an apathetic shrug, she added, "Cuz, yeah, you're *definitely* on Santa's naughty list this year."

Papa was in over his head, so he did what he always does when he was in a bind: he fell back on ol' faithful, begging and pleading for Mama to help bail him out.

"Sorry, sweetheart, but this is aaaaall you."

Mama was right, though. All of them were right! Truth is, he'd missed something very important, and it all revolved around a text from his friend at the United States Postal Service.

Papa's job connected him with all sorts of people, and one of them was a guy named John. He worked for USPS, and he was a real mover and shaker, which meant he knew a ton of people. So, when he learned that Make-A-Wish Michigan was sending Sami to the Doctor Who Experience, he got to thinking, *What can I do to make Sami's trip even cooler?* It didn't take long for him to figure it out, but it required a lot of work, so he made phone call after phone call, pulling as many strings as he possibly could, until, finally, he got the absolute perfect gift for Samantha.

"It was during the lead up to London, though," Papa complained. "And you guys remember how busy we were, right? I must not have seen his message, and I just forgot to get back with him, that's all."

"But he made it so that we could've met the actual Doctor Who!" Sami shot back. "We could've left the Doctor Who Experience and went straight to meet Peter Capaldi!"

"Well, it was Matt Smith, actually, but-"

"Matt Smith?!?!" the kids shouted in unison.

That revelation was so shocking that everyone just stood there, staring and glaring at Papa. Peter Capaldi was one thing, but Matt Smith? That was Sami's all-time favorite Doctor Who. And Papa knew it, too...

Sami was burning up over this, yet her glare was as cold and as sharp as an icicle. "Thanks for ruining Christmas, Papa..." she said in an uncharacteristically cruel voice. It wasn't shocking when she stormed out of the room, but everyone was blown away when she threw Papa's favorite ornament to the floor. And with tears streaming down her cheeks, turned around, and said, "... cuz it might be the last Christmas of my whole life."

No one dared say a word... that was, until Athan broke the silence with the ominous tune from Chopin's Sonata No. 2:

Dun-dun-da-dun-dun-dun-dun-dun-dun-dadun!

"Really, Athan?" Papa grumbled.

"And in B-Flat Minor?" Ambrose replied. "That's harsh." Ambrose shrugged, then tossed a fistful of tinsel on the tree. "Well, Teresa, you got that one right. Papa's *definitely* getting coal in his stocking this year."

Papa was so mad, mainly at himself, and he wanted to tell Sami he was sorry, but he was the last person she wanted to see right now, so he gathered his things and went up to the attic, where Mama found him, hours later, moping over his chessboard.

She sat down in the chair across the table, quietly evaluating the position of the pieces. And after she castled her queenside rook, she said, "You do realize that Sami knows you didn't mean to mess up on purpose, right?"

Papa let out an exasperated sigh, then shook his head as he advanced a pawn. "Nobody messes up on purpose, Ang."

"Well, you're wrong about that. People sabotage themselves all the time, and some people throw games on purpose." She re-evaluated the board, then moved her bishop to take the rook that Papa's move left unprotected. Papa looked at the board, surprised by the oversight, and moaned with exasperation. She figured it wasn't a sacrifice—he was too good of a player for that—but she couldn't help but chuckle at the irony. "You know, sweetheart, most of the time, mistakes like that are just honest mistakes."

Papa's eyes scanned the board as he processed Mama's words, then...

BAM!

His forehead slammed down on the table, and after an extremely exaggerated exhale, he mumbled, "You just put me in checkmate, Angela."

"Oops! Really?" Mama laughed. "Wow, I didn't even mean to do that."

"Uuuuugh," Papa groaned.

"Okay, Jeremiah, so, you made a mistake—"

Papa's head shot up from the table. "A mistake?" he scoffed. "Yeah, right. More like a super-duper-mega-big-mistake."

"Okay, a super-duper-mega-big-mistake. Still, so what? Would you change it if you could?"

SHE DANCED ME A STORY

"Obviously!"

"Do you really think Sami doesn't know that?" Papa didn't reply, so Mama reached across the table and took hold of his hand. "Things could be worse, ya know? I mean, it's Christmas. And Sami's cancer hasn't come back, so at least we know the chemo is working."

Mama let go of his hand and stood to her feet, then she took a moment to look at the pieces, then she leaned over the table and moved Papa's knight, which now protected his king. "Sometimes the situation isn't as bad as you believe, Jeremiah. And sometimes it just requires you to think... well, that, and maybe learning to take a little of your own advice every once in a while."

As Mama was leaving the room, Papa laughed, asking, "So, what advice is that, exactly, Mrs. Smarty Pants McKnow-It-All?"

She was already halfway down the stairs when she answered. "You could always start with #NeverGiveUp and #KeepOnSmiling."

So, Papa sat there, just thinking... and thinking... and thinking some more. Problem was, the more that he thought, the harder it was to think. It didn't help that the family was so busy, or that Christmas was big business for the Fun Spot, or even that the 2016 elections had his radio show in overdrive—and that didn't even include all the speeches that he and Sami were giving.

Add all of Mama's last-minute shopping and you would have a pretty good idea for the kind of crazy going on in the #TeamTinyDancer home.

"Papa!" Teresa shouted up the stairs in a really naggy voice, "Athan says his Power Ranger is prettier than my American Girl Doll!"

Oh, yeah, and don't forget, it was Winter Break, so the kids were home from school. And for reasons only children can possibly understand, they were doubling their ordinary output of absolutely annoying childhood nonsense.

"Papa! Ambrose says that calling the game Mario Brothers sounds cooler than calling it Mario Bros."

"Papa! Teresa says her joke about Count Mouseula is funnier than my funny joke about Julius Cheeser!"

"Papa! Sami says Thursday means Thor's Day when it really just means Thursday!"

+ Less Than One Week Before Christmas +

Papa was in the kitchen, and the sound of him slamming his MacBook shut could be heard throughout the house. Mama heard it the loudest, though, because she was grabbing some of Papa's cheese log from the fridge when it happened.

"Do you think you'll get fired from the radio station?" she asked as she sat in a chair next to him.

"Maybe..." Papa grumbled.

She spread some of Papa's cheese log on a cracker and tossed it in her mouth, saying, "Most of those weirdos celebrate Festivus, anyway, don't they?" she asked with a mouthful of cheese log. "I guess they can use that opportunity to air out all the ways you've grieved them with your conservative political beliefs this year, then they'll forgive you and forget all about it."

"Forgive?!" Papa laughed, sarcastically. "Atheist activists don't do absolution, and social media is basically the confessional from hell."

Mama rested her head on Papa's shoulder, and with a flirtatious voice, she replied, "Well, you know I'll always love you, even if you do get fired."

Papa rested his elbows on the table, and with his chin couched on the palms of his hand, he said in a very pathetic pouty voice, "Just another way I ruined Christmas."

"Ugh!" Mama scoffed as she slammed her hand on the counter. "I knew it, Jeremiah! I knew you were still stuck on all that. Seriously, get over yourself already. And while you're at it, stop thinking you ruined Christmas!"

"Ha-ha," Papa scoffed back. "How can I stop thinking about something you haven't even given me time to start thinking about?"

Mama shook her head, then grabbed the cheese log, and left the room. "Well, Jeremiah, now you can think all you want cuz your pity party is really getting on my nerves."

"At least you still have nerves left!" he shouted toward the door. "My last one quit weeks ago, and-Whoa! Wait! Get back here with my cheese log, you little stealer!"

"In your dreams, Mr. Grinch," Mama replied as she sat down in the rocking chair near the fireplace in the living room. "You ain't getting it back, either, not until I know you're done with all your boohooing."

Papa's nostrils flared like a bull as he scrambled for a zinger, but nothing came, so he did as other dads do in situations like that: he reached for whatever was nearby, hurrying his hands in an effort to convince himself that he was busy—and busy with something far more important than dealing with the argument he just lost to his wife. It didn't take long, though, before he realized that he'd been fumbling through a stack of papers. And this wasn't just any ordinary stack of papers on the counter. No, these were the kids' Christmas Wish Lists.

The children wrote them in crayon, which made Papa laugh a little, and the wishes made him smile. Athan asked for Legos and a Dirk Nowitzki "NBA FatHead" for his room, while Ambrose wanted Pokémon plushies, and Teresa asked for a big Barbie doll. Then, when he had reached the last page of the pile, he saw...

Sami's Christmas Wish List

1. DIARY WITH LOCK (THAT WAY THE BOYS CAN'T READ IT.)
2. FIVE NIGHTS AT FREDDY'S PLUSHIES
3. MINECRAFT (ASK THE BOYS, THEY'LL TELL YOU.)
4. MANGA ART BOOK
5. AN "ALL ABOUT ME" JOURNAL (LIKE THE ONE PAPA HAS.)
6. A TRIP TO NEW YORK CITY OR WASHINGTON D.C.

P.S. OH, AND I REALLY WISH THAT I CAN ONE DAY SKATE AGAIN.

Wow, Sam, Papa thought, *keepin' it simple, I see.*

Then, in a magical moment that may forever remain among the many mysteries of Papa's history, he saw something. Whatever he saw, no one knows for sure, but it must've been amazing because his eyes grew wide, and he shouted, "Aha! I got it!"

"What do you have?" Mama asked from the other room.

Papa strolled through the door, straight to the rocking chair, and grabbed the cheese log right out of Mama's hands, then turned around, and with an elvish grin that ran from ear-to-ear, he whispered, "Oh, you'll see. Trust me, you'll all see." Then he ran up the stairs, laughing like a maniac, saying, "All of you will see. All of you! Mwahahahaha!!!"

The weeks that followed felt offensively long, at least for the kids, so when Christmas Eve finally arrived, the house was alive with festivities. Sure, the kids loved their birthdays and Halloween, but Christmas was #TeamTinyDancer's favorite holiday. They treasured the symbols and the timbrels of holiday vigils, and they loved the sight of glittering snow through the nostalgic glow of candles in the window. They gorged themselves on festal foods, kickshaws like peanut brittle, gingerbread, and white chocolate peppermint bark, which they polished off with eggnog or apple cider—unless you were Papa, who was always guzzling Mama's homemade wassail. And the sound of Bing Crosby crooning their favorite carols was like icing on a fruit cake, which, for some weird reason (that the kids could *never* understand), always made Papa get mushy-gushy with Mama under the mistletoe. Even better, this year Papa agreed to let them open some of their gifts on Christmas Eve, that way they could play with them while he worked the holiday shift at the Fun Spot.

So, with no further ado, the family gathered around the fireplace, and Papa blew a year's worth of dust from atop his Gramma's old King James bible, then he read to his kids St. Luke's account of the Nativity. And when he was done, Papa closed the Bible for the upcoming year, and with a smile on his face, he said, "Merry Christmas," then unleashed the children on the piles of presents all around the Christmas tree.

Wrapping paper filled the air, and their eyes sparkled with surprise as they saw what Mama and Papa had bought. There were Legos, plushies, baby dolls, and art supplies. (Papa even bought Mama a gift card to Victoria's Secret, but that was hush-hush.) And once they were done, Papa loaded Sami's wheelchair into the trunk of the van, and with Christmas gifts in-hand, the family made their way to the rink.

+ At Byron Fun Spot +

The building was decorated with cutouts of snowflakes and stockings that were colored by the kids, and red and white Christmas lights were wrapped like candy canes around the rafters. And employees even hung icicles below the black lights.

"It's like the North Pole!" Sami exclaimed as Papa rushed to the locker room.

"It even smells like Christmas," Ambrose said.

"That's the smell of the pine trees," Kelly replied, proudly. "Well, that, and all the cinnamon pinecones."

"Wow!" Ambrose exclaimed. "Are the Christmas trees real?" Kelly tried to warn him, but it was too late. "Ouch!" Ambrose yelped. And with the tip of his finger in his mouth, he mumbled, "Yeah, them buggers are real, alright."

"So what are you guys doing here?" Kelly asked. "I figured you'd enjoy your dad's day off."

"Day off?" Sami asked with a confused expression on her face. "That's weird, he said he had to work tonight."

Kelly wasn't sure what he said, but it must've spooked Mama because he could see the whites of her eyes as she rushed over to him and started tugging on his sleeve. And in that voice parent's use when trying to distract or misdirect their kids from something they're trying really hard to hide from them, she said. "Oh, um, I guess he didn't tell you, huh? Yeah, well, you asked him to come in for, um, some Christmas Eve shoveling, you know, or something."

"Christmas Eve sh-OOF!!!"

Mama slammed her elbow so hard into Kelly's ribs, he almost lost his breath! "Nooow do you remember, Kelly?" Mama asked through her teeth.

Kelly might not have known what the heck was going on, but he knew what an elbow to the ribs meant. "Oh, yes!" he said, still rubbing his bruised ribs. "Of course, obviously! Our, um, Christmas Eve shoveling service. How could I forget about that?"

Mama smiled and winked at him, then rolled Sami over to her table near the DJ booth. The table didn't have her name on it or anything, but everyone knew Sami had cancer, and it broke their heart that she couldn't skate anymore. They loved that she helped, always working with her dad in the DJ booth, passing out candy during Limbo, and placing cones around the rink for Fast Skate. So, as far as the folks at the Fun Spot were concerned, that table was reserved, and it belonged to Sami and her family.

SHE DANCED ME A STORY

While Sami got situated, Papa's DJ friend Mark hopped on the mic and, directing everyone's attention to the center of the rink, he said, "Yo! Check it out! You won't even believe this, but Santa is at the Fun Spot RIGHT NOW!!!"

There he was, in all of his glory: Santa Claus! He wore thin, wireframe glasses, had wavy white hair, and a curly beard to match. His red coat was soft and silky, and he wore big black boots with beautiful silver buckles. Best of all, over his shoulder was a sack filled with gifts.

Children ran to gather 'round, showering him with hugs, last minute Christmas wishes, and questions, like, "Are you the *real* Santa Claus?!" He tried his best to answer them, and he gave everyone pieces of candy, but then he saw a little girl sitting alone on the other side of the rink, with her head hung low, and looking very, very sad. So, when he finished passing out candy, he waved for everyone to stand back, then he tiptoed toward the girl. And when he got there, he knelt near her feet, and in the most tender voice the girl had ever heard, said, "Samantha..."

JEREMIAH T. BANNISTER

Sami recognized that voice. "Papa???"

"Shhh..." he hushed with his finger pressed to his lips. Then he looked around to make sure no one was watching, and whispered, "I have something special for you, Sami."

"Really? Another present for me??" Sami could see Papa's smile through the white whiskers of his Santa beard as he reached deep into the sack, then pulled out a big and beautiful box. It was square, kinda heavy, and wrapped like a TARDIS, with a pretty pink bow on top. Sami put it near her ear and shook it a little, but she'd never heard that sound before. She even lifted it up to her nose, hoping the smell would give her a clue, but there was nothing. So, she carefully untied the pretty pink bow, peeled the tape from the wrapping paper, and slowly lifted the lid of the box. And once she realized what it was, she blushed, and tears of joy and sadness streamed down her face.

"They're roller skates!"

These weren't just any ordinary roller skates, either.

"They're low-riders," Papa said, as he got them out of the box.

"Papa?" Sami sighed.

"And they buckle over your shoes, so you won't even have to remove your brace or anything..."

"Papa??"

"And the wheels are smaller too, that way they won't wobble very much. Plus–"

"Papa!!!"

"Shhh!" Papa replied, looking over his shoulder to make sure no one heard her say his name. "You're gonna blow my cover, baby, so keep it down."

"Well, I've been trying to get your attention."

"I know, Sam, I heard you the whole time."

"Then why didn't you listen to me?"

"I am listening," he replied. Then he patted the skates, and asked, "So? Do you love these things or what?"

"Of course I like them. I love them, actually. And I love that you think of me like that, but..." With her head hung low, Sami sighed, and whispered, "Maybe you forgot, Papa, but I can't skate anymore."

"What?!" he scoffed, sounding very offended. "Who told you that?"

"My therapist told me that."

Papa smirked and shook his head. "Oh, yeah, I remember that." Then he cracked a half-smile, and asked, "But do you remember what I said when they told us that?"

"You said they needed to help me do exercises for balance and tumbling."

Papa laughed and thumped his King Kong. "You better believe I did!" Then he leaned in close, squinted his eyes all sneaky like, and in a mischievous whisper, he asked, "And did you ever wonder *why* I told them to do that?"

Sami thought for a second, trying to remember, but Papa never told her his reason. All he did was tell the therapist that's what he wanted them to do. "But why *did* you do that, Papa? Why did you make them teach me all that stuff?"

Papa raised the skates in front of Sami's face, and replied, "Because of what you're about to do, Samantha. Because *these* things right here demand it!"

"But therapists said it would be too dangerous for me to skate, especially because I'm on chemo, so if I ever fell down, I could-"

"You could tumble?" Papa interrupted. "I know, that was the whole point! And all you gotta do is the same stuff they taught you in therapy." He looked around for a moment, searching for something. "Well, I guess we forgot all the padding back in the therapy room, so if you're gonna fall—and we're crossing our fingers that you don't—then you're gonna have to fall on top of me. Sound good?"

"On top of you?" Sami scoffed. "How do you expect me to do that?!"

Papa held Sami's hands, and with a soothing voice, he said, "Because I'll never leave your side, Sami. I'll be right next to you the entire time. And I'll hold onto your arm, too. That way, you can feel safe, and I can know if you get shaky."

"You're *really* gonna skate next to me? The whole entire time?"

Papa laughed and pointed to his boots. "No way, Santa's gonna run. And you're gonna skate so fast, you'll make me work extra hard to keep up." He paused and looked out at the rink, then glanced back down at Samantha, and with his hand outstretched, he asked, "Do you trust me?"

Sami was really nervous, but then she saw Riley and Kelly jam skating. Athan, Ambrose, and Teresa were racing around the rink, too, and Dan was there with his wife and son. Everyone was having so much fun... skating.

There was a nervous quiver in her lip when Sami finally nodded, saying, "I trust you, Papa... I trust you with all my heart." Then she looked out at the rink one last time, and with a smile on her face, said, "Let's do this, Santa Claus."

"Oh, my gosh!" Dan said when he saw Mama setting up the tripod in the center of the rink. "This is really happening!" Then he skated as fast as he could, weaving in and out of traffic, and once he reached the DJ booth, he told DJ Mark what to do.

"Are you serious?!" Mark replied. "She's really going to—"

"Yes!" Dan interrupted. "And you gotta play the song—Sami's song!" The two of them looked over to Sami's table, just in time to see her stand up on her new wheels. Then they looked at each other, totally in shock, and Dan said, "You better make it quick too!"

Sami was nervous, and she moved her feet like someone learning to walk again, but Papa held onto her arm and let her wear his pea coat for extra protection... just in case. Right as Sami's skates crossed the border onto the floor, Mark turned on the mic, and told everyone, "We have a very special song request, and it's dedicated to a very, very special little girl."

"They're playing my favorite song!" she exclaimed. And it was just what she needed. So, Sami looked around one last time and then glanced back to the safety of her seat near the booth. She remembered all those times watching in envy as others rolled around the rink. She remembered all those fast skates cheering for others but wishing she was there, feeling what they felt as they soared through the air. And she looked at Papa, remembering all those times with him at therapy, learning how to balance and tumble, and thinking that all of that was for this very moment on Christmas Eve. So she closed her eyes, took a deep breath, and imagined that old Rainbow Road. When she opened her eyes, though, she found it more beautiful and aglow than ever before. Her Rainbow Road had been transformed, and it was alive, like the Bifröst, that radiant rainbow bridge that led to Thor's heavenly home in Asgard. And the floor bore an illustrious sheen, animated and a sparkle with LEDs and laser lights, as well as the roving lights reflecting off the disco ball. Then, with no warning at all, Sami burst out onto the floor.

Kids stood in awe as Sami skated around the rink, and parents cried at the sight of Santa Claus running by her side. Sami's siblings saw her, too, so they raced as fast as they could to catch up and skate alongside her, ensuring that no one could cut her off or knock her down. She wobbled here and there, which always gave Papa a scare, but Sami didn't mind, not one bit, for after a long nine-month hiatus, she felt the wind in her hair once again!

Papa was out of shape, but he ran himself to death that night. Resolved to endure any pain, any amount of exhaustion for Sami's dreams to come true, he ran, and he ran, and he ran some more... until, at last, the last song of the night ended, finally giving Papa and Sami some time to catch their breath at her table.

But Sami wasn't interested in catching her breath so much as wrapping her arms around Papa's neck and squeezing it as hard as possible. She wept like a baby, with tears and snot soaking into the soft fur of his Santa coat. "I skated today, Papa!" Sami exclaimed. "I really skated today! It's a dream come true! Oh, Papa, I love you! I really, really do!!!"

When the session ended, the family wished their friends a very "Merry Christmas," then returned home, where the kids fell fast asleep. That was perfect, too, since Mama and Papa used that time to stuff stockings and wrap gifts. Then, just before midnight, Papa grabbed the keys and put on his coat, trying his best, as he did every Christmas Eve, to sneak out of the house in order to attend Mass or Nativity Vigil. He pulled his hat over his ears, then wrapped the Doctor Who scarf around his collar and made his way to the door. But just before he was able to leave, he heard two angelic voices at the top of the stairs...

XXII

HAPPY B-DAY, BABY JESUS

"Why aren't you two asleep?" Papa barked in a whisper.

Sami and Teresa stood like silhouettes at the top of the stairs, as the multicolored bulbs from the Christmas tree and the nightlight in the upstairs hallway were the only things illuminating the stairwell.

"Me and Teresa want to go to church with you," Sami whispered back.

"It's 11:30 at night, Sam, and you'd still need to get dressed."

"We're already dressed," Teresa slurred with her thumb in her mouth.

"Hold up. Weren't you in your pajamas an hour ago?"

Teresa wiped her slobbery thumb on her pants, saying, "Yeah, but Sami said to me in the car that you were gonna try to be all sneaky and go to church, so we hid our clothes under our blankets, and—"

"Teresa!" Sami grunted, elbowing her in the shoulder.

"I mean... um, nevermind. Me and Samantha didn't know we were planning to sneak to church with you or nuffin'."

Papa scrunched his eyebrows, and his lips pressed together, but he kinda liked that his girls went to all that trouble to spend time with him—and deep down inside, he liked that they wanted to go to church with him. His first Mass was a Christmas Vigil, and as a Catholic, Christmas Vigils were always his favorite. But, he'd been an Atheist for nearly five years, and though he continued to go to the vigils, they had become very lonely. He'd sit alone, singing and signing himself with the cross, but he never really talked to anyone. That was easy for a while, as Catholic and Orthodox people in the pews shied away from the long-haired hippy guy with lip and nose piercings. But every once in a while, a priest would walk over to him, asking who he was and saying he hopes to see him again.

"I wouldn't bet on it, padre," he'd reply. To which the priest would always smile, saying something like, "Okay, then I'll pray. And, Lord willing, we'll see you again next Christmas."

All of that was well and good for Papa, but Sami was six years old the last time she went to church, and the family stopped attending services shortly after Teresa was born, so neither of them knew what they were in for—or even how to behave. Papa spent most of the ride describing what they should expect, but it was all so foreign to them, and they had tons of questions.

"What is an iconostasis?" Sami asked as she unwrapped a candy cane in the car.

"And why are we supposed to kiss the paintings?" Teresa wondered.

Papa tried to explain things as quickly and as simply as he could, and he struggled not to get lost in the weeds of technicalities (like the fact that icons are "written," not painted), but the kids didn't have the vocabulary for it, and there was very little in their lives that gave them a good point of reference.

"I guess it's just something you have to experience," he assured them as the van pulled into the parking lot. "And just follow my lead."

That was good advice, and he probably should've said it from the start. He enjoyed talking about those things, but all the words in the world wouldn't have prepared his girls for what they were about to experience.

"This church is so pretty," Teresa said. "It kinda reminds me of Aunt Curly's church."

"And look at all the angels!" Sami exclaimed. Then, pointing to the ornate dividing wall in the front of the church, she smiled at Papa, saying, "And that is the iconostasis thing you were talking about in the car."

SHE DANCED ME A STORY

The sanctuary was dim, lit only by chandeliers and prayer candles set in small boxes filled with sand, and the room was lined with rows of pews.

"Do you think people know we're strangers?" Teresa asked as Papa showed them how to greet the icon at the front of the church.

Papa signed himself with the cross, then whispered, "Probably, but they kind of expect strangers at Christmas time."

"It's kinda the whole Christmas story, isn't it?" Sami said, trying her best to sign herself with her right-hand.

Papa thought of answering her question, but the service started right as he was about to reply, so he grabbed a service book, and they rushed to find a pew to place their coats.

The All-Night Vigil is ancient and very active, involving a variety of movements and modes, all of which are intended, like the cloud of witnesses written in icons along the walls, to foster a sense—a very *real*, even palpable, sense—that the believer is beholding something both transcendent and immediate, universal and timeless, yet experienced in the here and now by each and every one. It was so mysterious, almost mystical, but Sami liked that, and so did Teresa. They felt the separation, knowing that they were strangers in the midst, and they wished it wasn't so, or at least that those thoughts and feelings they experienced that night would always remain. They loved how the service satiated all of their senses. There was the smell of incense, the sound of bells and Byzantine chant, the sight of the icons, the feel of their fingers pressed to the chest whenever they signed themselves with the cross, and the glorious taste of Artos Sweet Bread. They even enjoyed the homily, which told the story of an angelic messenger, the Blessed Virgin, and a baby with a birthday in a Bethlehem stable. But then came a final blessing, and the vigil came to an end. So, with the smell of incense still on their clothes, Papa and his girls grabbed their things and made their way toward the door.

"Hold on, guys," Sami said, just as they were about to leave. She'd noticed an icon near the door, and something about it grabbed her attention. It was an icon of Our Lady of Perpetual Help, and she stood there, gazing at it for a nearly a minute, then she raised her right-hand, awkwardly caressing the image with her fingers, then she leaned over, whispered something, then kissed the corners, crossed herself one last time, then waved to the icon and said, "Goodnight."

The ride home was quiet. Teresa had fallen asleep by the time they had arrived, so Papa carried her upstairs and laid her to bed, then returned to the living room where Mama and Sami were waiting...

"Did you have a good time?" Mama asked from her rocking chair near the fire.

"It was divine," Sami replied, giggling a little over her play on words. "Honestly, it was maybe the most beautiful thing I'd ever seen, and it kinda felt like a TARDIS."

"Like a TARDIS?" Mama laughed. "I've never heard anyone describe it like that before."

Sami shrugged, then looked up toward Ambrose's Nativity Scene, and said, "It felt really old and new at the same time, so it was like time traveling, but we didn't have to go anywhere. And even though it was a small church, everything felt really big, like the whole cosmos was there. Plus, with all the angels and music and God and stuff, it felt like we weren't even inside of space and time, so it sorta seemed like it was kinda bigger on the inside of the church than it was on the outside, the same as a TARDIS."

Papa draped his coat over the arm of the couch, then knelt near Mama. "Hey, Sami, I've wanted to tell you something for a while, but I've felt really nervous about it." Sami turned to face him, and there was a beautifully gentle glow from the star of the Nativity shining behind her. "I'm really sorry, Sam."

"Sorry for what?"

"I'm really sorry about ruining your chance to spend time with Matt Smith in Cardiff. It was my fault, and I've been beating myself up about it ever since, but I was too afraid to say anything to you." And with his head hung low, Papa sighed, "I'm just really sorry."

"Yeah, that was a big bummer, and I was really mad at you, but if I'm gonna tell you the truth, this Christmas has been totally awesome."

"So I didn't ruin Christmas?"

"Pfft!" Sami laughed. "No way, José! I mean, c'mon, just think about it for a second. I actually skated again, me and Teresa got to go to church with you, and my cancer is gone, too. So, okay, sure, it would've been awesome to meet Matt Smith—and if you ever get a chance like that again, you better not mess it up—but that didn't stop me from having the best Christmas of my life."

Mama yawned and got up from her chair. "And just think, Sami, you'll have even more presents in the morning."

Sami was excited, but after the day she'd had, she couldn't wait to go to bed. However, just before she reached the stairs, Sami turned back to face the Nativity, whispered something under her breath, then said, "Hey Papa, I know this sounds weird, maybe, but I want to know more about God and church and stuff."

"At 1:30 in the morning?"

"No," Sami laughed, "just that I do. I just want to know about their faith and why they do all that stuff at church."

"Hmm..." Papa hummed as he put out the fire.

"Yeah, Papa... later," she replied, and placing the ornament of Jesus into the manger, she whispered, "Happy birthday, baby Jesus," then limped upstairs to her room. She was frightened, however, by eerie sounds—and they came from the closet! She could've sworn that she heard something whimpering... or was it panting? Worst of all, it sounded like something was scratching at the door...

"What is that?!" Teresa cried from beneath her blankets. "It sounds like a bat!"

Sami wasn't sure, but she slipped out of bed, tip-toed toward the closet, and slowly reached for the handle...

XXIII

ANGELS IN THE VORTEX

Sami's shriek woke everyone in the house, and by the time Mama and Papa got to Sami's room, they found her and the kids sitting crossed-legged on the floor of the closet door, laughing and crying, and there was something in their arms.

"I put her in your closet when I saw the van come home from church," Mama chuckled. "Seriously, you guys can't even believe how hard it was to hide a puppy in this house."

This wasn't just any puppy, either. It was a long-haired purebred Saint Bernard.

Truth was, some of Sami's disabilities made her more vulnerable than the average tween, so Mama and Papa wanted a dog that would scare off any creepy weirdos.

"Trust me, Ang," Papa said as he dialed the breeder, "ain't nobody messin' with a girl who's got a St. Bernard by her side."

Sami named her Cocoa, and from that night on, the two of them were inseparable. Cocoa was more than just a puppy, though. She was an all-weather friend, and that is exactly what Sami needed, especially now, as she was really nervous about her upcoming MRI.

MRIs are standard fare for kids with cancer, and it wasn't like they'd seen anything out of the ordinary, but cancer is sneaky, and the signs can be really subtle. "Scanxiety" is real for both kids and their families, always living on-edge and wondering if everything is a-okay.

More than that, when Papa first saw Sami's Wish List, he was shocked by the kind of things she wanted, and with her sights set on D.C. and New York City, he knew they'd need more money-and that got him to thinking...

+ Days Later—Detroit Metro Airport +

"Why do you have to go to Palm Springs?!" Sami cried as Papa handed his luggage to the woman at the counter.

"Only for ten days," he said as he checked his ticket one last time, then waved for his kids to follow him. "Plus, Aunt Curly is gonna be there. Pa said I could work for him during a festival, that way we can make a bunch of extra money."

Teresa wrapped her arms around Papa's leg, crying, "But we're rich enough already!"

"And Christmas is over," Athan said, "so you don't need to buy any more presents until my birthday, but that's not until March."

SHE DANCED ME A STORY

"Yeah," Ambrose agreed. "Athan doesn't even need lots of presents this year, anyway."

That had Papa cracking up, especially when he saw Athan's reaction to the idea of a cheap birthday. He felt kind of guilty, though, because they didn't know the real reason he was leaving, and no matter how hard they tried, nothing in the world could change Papa's mind...

"But what about my MRI?" Sami whimpered. "And what about my chemo? How am I gonna be brave when they do my port?"

Sami's questions stung a little, and he was grateful for the interruption of the announcement over the intercom, but he saw those questions coming from a mile away. "Mama will be there with you," Papa assured her as he unlatched Teresa's arms from his leg. "And she helps you even better than I do." That was true, but Papa knew it wasn't the point, so he knelt down and sat Sami on his knee.

She lowered her head and said, "I just hate that you have to go, you know."

"That's one of the reasons we got you Cocoa for Christmas. It's all part of my super-secret master plan." She sighed and shook her head, so Papa held her hand, and said, "Trust me, Sam, everything is gonna be fine."

Now boarding Flight 217 to Palm Springs.

The family hugged Papa like they'd never see him again, then he stood up, kissed Mama goodbye, and turned to enter TSA.

"But what if my cancer came back?" Sami shouted.

Papa froze midstride. The words were jarring, and the thought was enough to send chills down anyone's spine... but Papa just smiled. He didn't believe a word of it—not one bit! Cancer is a sly old dog, but the family learned new tricks. And cancer already fooled him once, so he vowed it would never happen again—not in a million years. They were vigilant, keeping a constant eye on Sami, and they were trigger happy with the phone, never hesitating to reach out with questions about even the smallest and most seemingly insignificant of symptoms. So, he turned around, looked at Sami, and with the sound of absolute certainty in his voice, he shouted back, "There ain't no cancer, baby. Not even a little! You'll see, trust me!" Then he nodded, and reassured her, "Just trust me."

Everyone yelled goodbye, but seeing Papa disappear into the terminal made them cry even harder, so they raced to the window overlooking the airfield, where they waved and shouted to Papa's plane, watching and weeping until he vanished into the distance...

+ On Flight 217 to Palm Springs +

Papa had a love/hate relationship with flying, and Palm Springs was 1,882 miles from Detroit, but he had a window seat in a row all to himself, and after a glass (or three) of wine, Papa felt perfectly fine, biding the time with *Secret Formulas of the Wizard of Ads* and new entries in his journal. He wrote almost every day, filling it with page after page of aberrant artwork, rhythmic rambles, poetic parables, and paradoxical fables, all of them born in the bosom of bedlam and forlorn. And whether it was the fear of flying or the fruit of the vine flowing in his veins, he couldn't say, but he felt vulnerable, and he needed to be honest, even if only with himself...

+ The Chemo Clinic at Helen DeVos +

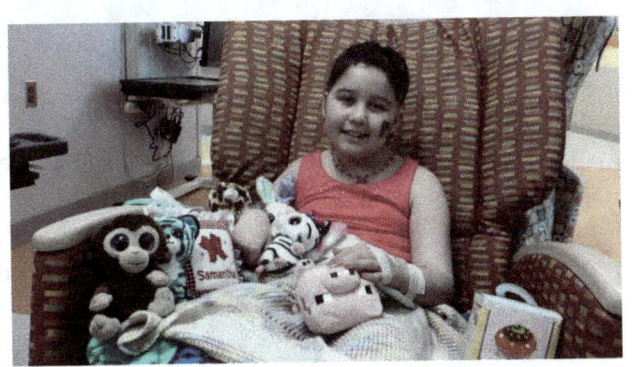

SHE DANCED ME A STORY

The chemo clinic was a conflicting display of spectacle and reality. There were slushies, pizzas, and a never-ending pipeline of Pop-Tarts, but behind the curtains were kids with cancer, and families afraid of death. Sami felt guilty being there, too, as she wasn't experiencing many of the symptoms the other kids struggled with. It baffled people, too, even the doctors, and that's tough because oncologists deal with cancer for a living, so by the time a new kid with cancer sits across from them, they'd seen the same sad story hundreds (if not thousands) of times, and they've come to anticipate a pattern:

"I'm really sorry you're in so much pain," Dr. Kurt said as the nurse gathered the things needed to access Sami's chemo port.

"Pain?" Sami giggled. "I don't have any pain. I mean, the port hurts a little bit, but not for very long, and then I'm fine."

The nurse rubbed a yellowish-orange disinfectant on Sami's chest, then she grabbed the Buzzy Bee. It vibrated, and when nurses put it on Sami's shoulder, it distracted her just enough to get her mind off what they were doing with her port. "Well, that's good," she said, "but I know it isn't any fun when your tummy hurts and you aren't eating very much."

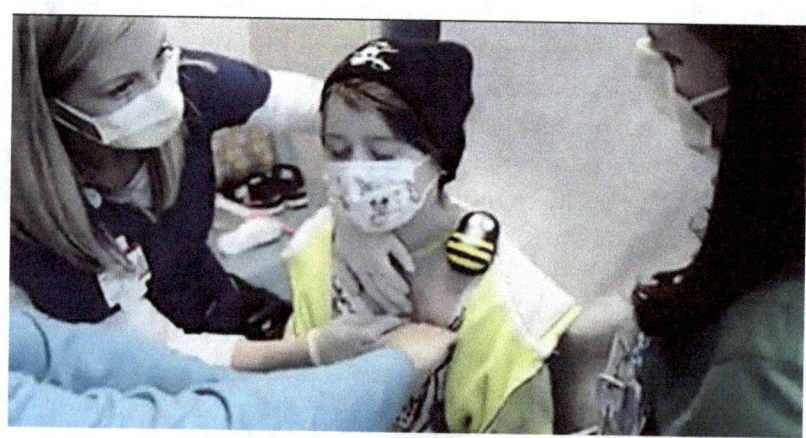

"My belly? My belly doesn't hurt. And I eat a lot of food every day." Then she looked at Mama, and with a wink, she said, "I have the munchies all the time!" Sami winced when the nurse inserted the Huber needle, but even if Buzzy Bee wasn't working its magic, the doctor's confusing questions were distracting enough.

"Hmm," Dr. Kurt pondered aloud, then she rattled off a litany of other things doctors have come to expect in situations like this. Surprisingly, Sami responded to each and every [otherwise reasonable] assumption with an assurance, not only that she wasn't experiencing those sad and scary side-effects, but that her experiences had been the exact opposite on every point.

"Hmm..." Dr. Kurt pondered aloud, "what do you think is helping you so much?"

No one had asked her about this before, and her parents never told her how to answer, so she looked back-and-forth half-a-dozen times from Dr. Kurt to Mama, until, finally, she looked at Dr. Kurt, and with a nervous expression on her face, she shrugged, and said, "Cuz 'Papa's meds'?"

+ Papa & Pa in Palm Springs +

Papa's dad had a tremendous tan, but with a whiskey barrel chest, desert sky blue eyes, and blonde hair that shined like the sun at high-noon, Pa and Papa were definitely father and son.

"You still ridin' the Valkyrie, huh?" Papa asked as Pa revved up the motorcycle.

Pa straightened his rearview mirrors, then tightened the straps of his helmet. "I'll always be a motorcycle man, son." Then he hit the kickstand with the back of his heel and pointed toward the passenger seat and told Papa to hop on.

"Oops, wait a sec," Papa said, hurriedly patting his pockets.

"You forgot something?"

Papa raised his phone to his ear, and said, "No, it's just the '80s calling. I guess they want you to give back that terrible Hulk Hogan fu manchu."

"Aw, man, c'mon!" Pa laughed. "Now hop on before I leave ya here, ya big goober."

Papa was born a trucker's son, and some of his earliest memories in that old Pennsylvania farmhouse were of his dad cruising in his mint-condition '62 Caddy or roaring down the road on one of his motorcycles. He'd owned a bunch of really cool bikes, too, like a mid-'60s Honda 90, a '74 Kawasaki 500 Triple (aka Widow Maker), an '81 Honda Gold Wing 1100 Interstate, and a number of '90s-era Honda Valkyrie GL 1500s, including a '99 he converted into a SuperValk. But, of all these, the Gold Wing was Pa's favorite.

SHE DANCED ME A STORY

"They're the Cadillac of motorcycles," he'd say, "like a convertible with the top down, and without doors."

It was gigantic, a luxury bike that purred like a puma, and its chrome pipes glistened like a jewel-studded tiara in the sun. And with a body painted majestic maroon, it really was a King of the Road. He rode it everywhere, including a 2,900-mile-trip from Dillsburg, Pennsylvania, to Los Angeles, California, to be a contestant on Press Your Luck, and the only thing better than riding was riding with his wife and kids.

That was nearly 30-years-ago, but Papa still remembered how he felt being a kid on the back of Pa's bike. The warm leather seats, the muffled sound of wind swirling around his helmet, and the butterflies in his belly whenever Pa leaned into a turn. Most of all, he remembered the sense of security, trusting with childlike faith that his dad was in control, that he knew what he was doing, that he knew where they were going, and that, no matter what, he'd do everything in his power to keep li'l Papa safe. Even now, as they cruised along the base of Mount Jacinta, surrounded by Golden Barrel cacti and multicolored Vincas interspersed through rows of Blue Hibiscus and Fan Palms bending in the wind, he felt so safe, so certain that things would be fine, that he let go of his father's waist, then stretched his arms like wings of a Golden Eagle, and with his eyes squinting up at the midday sun, he laughed at fear and death.

+ In Dr. Kurt's Office +

"I need a Band-Aid," Sami said as she wiped the blood from her finger.

Mama checked her bag, complaining, "You know, you wouldn't need a Band-Aid if you'd quit biting the skin around your nails."

Sami wasn't amused, but Mama had a point. She'd been biting her nails for days, worried about the results of her MRI. She remembered what Papa said at the airport, and Mama tried her best to keep Sami good and distracted, but they weren't the ones with cancer... and sometimes kids see big things in the little stuff parents tend to miss.

Plus, she just had another Pentam treatment, and Pentam was terrible! It always tasted so nasty, and the candies the nurses gave her to suck on never really made it any better.

knock-knock

Dr. Kurt wore a really pretty dress today, and her hair shone like gold under the lights in the room, but there was hesitancy in her hands, and her eyes looked especially sad.

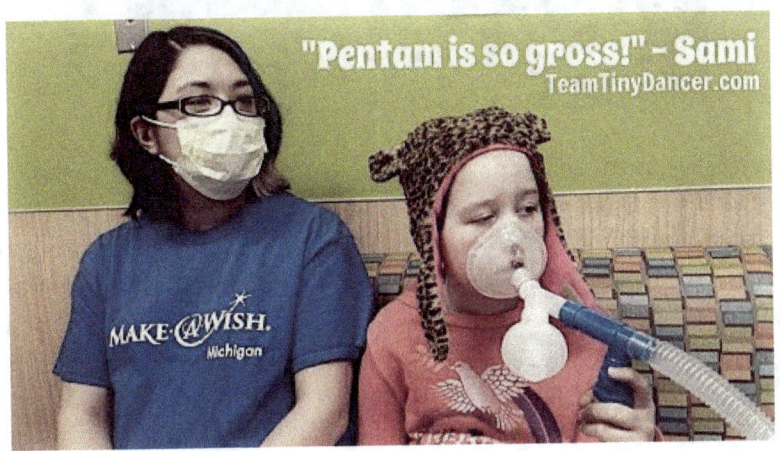

SHE DANCED ME A STORY

+ Back in Palm Springs +

"You should've seen it!" Pa laughed aloud. "Your face was as red as that tomato from Veggie-Tales! And you had tears coming out of your eyes!"

"It was crazy hot, man," Papa replied, eyeing the bottom of his medjool date shake. "For real, I think my mouth was on fire for over an hour."

Pa was laughing so hard that he could barely talk. "Oh, buddy, that's what you get eatin' the whole thing like that, seeds and all."

"Honestly, it was even hotter than the one I ate in Juárez, and they called that one *Diablo*."

Just then, Pa noticed Papa's phone vibrating on the table. He looked at the screen, and said, "Well, speak of the devil," then tossed the phone to Papa, whose eyes lit up the moment he saw who was on the screen. It was Mama, and he'd been waiting for this call all day...

"Hey, baby, hold on a sec," he said as he grabbed a few things and walked toward the RV. "I'm on a break with my dad, but I gotta grab a few things outside, so it's perfect timing." He could hear her talking on the other end, but the boxes in his hands were really heavy, and it made it hard for him to lift his shoulder to his ear. "Ugh, okay," he said as he grabbed a hold of the handles on the side of the box, "I got it." And with the phone to his ear, he said in a flirtatious voice, "Hey there, sweet thang, I've missed you!"

"Papa..."

"Oh, my gosh, Samantha?!" He was so embarrassed by the flirty words he just said, but he was so happy to hear Sami's voice.

"I have something I need to tell you..."

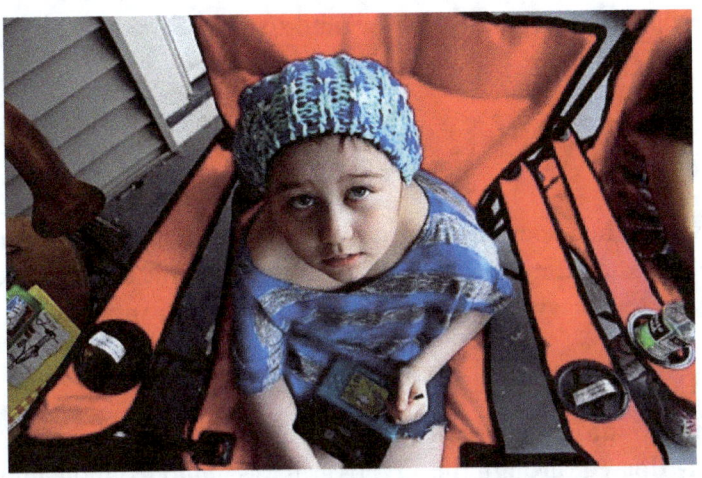

Papa listened, but there was something in this distance that caught his attention, and the sound it made was getting louder. So loud, in fact, that it became difficult to understand what she was saying, and his mind was tossed back-and-forth between them.

"Mama talked to Dr. Kurt today, and..."

He thought it was further away, that maybe it would change direction, or that they would have more time, but—

"She told us..."

It was closer than he realized.

"And now..."

It was wreaking havoc everywhere! Papers swirled through the air, and lawn chairs bounced like tumbleweeds through their site as

brutal bursts of wind kicked sand in Papa's face.

"Are you there?" Sami cried over the phone. "Are you even listening to me?"

The wind was so fast, though, and the noise from the debris was so loud that it was practically impossible to hear, and Papa still had that box in his hands, making it hard to press the phone against his ear! "Hold on, Sami! Don't go nowhere, I just got something crazy goin' on, so you gotta give me a sec!"

"Papa!" Sami yelled through the phone. "Just listen to me! Please! It can't wait!"

He rushed toward the RV as fast as he could, but he stumbled a little climbing the stairs, and when he finally stabilized himself on the step, he pressed the phone to his ear, just in time to hear Sami scream through the phone:

Papa! My cancer is back!

Papa's eyes shot open, and his mouth dropped open with devastation, but before he even had time to respond, a gust of wind hit the RV like a freight train, causing the heavy metal door to come unlatched, and—

BAM

It slammed into Papa's arm, causing his phone to fly high into the sky as Papa's body floated through the air. His arm was numb from the impact, and it tingled like he'd slept on it wrong, but his back wasn't numb, so when he finally hit the ground, it hurt so bad, he feared he had broke a rib, and he cried aloud in pain. It was excruciating, and for a moment he thought he was going to puke as everything started spinning, but then, from his bed on the ground beneath the clouds of sand storming inches above his face, he heard a small *click-clack* near the left-side of his head. It was his phone, and he could hear Sami screaming:

"Papa! Are you okay?! Paaaaaapaaaaaa?!?!"

He grunted as he reached for his phone, and his arm moved like someone with severe nerve damage. His fingers weren't any better, either, so he struggled to grab his phone, but when he finally had it in his hand, he pulled it tight to his ear.

"I don't know if you can hear me, Papa, but I love you, and I want you to come home! I need you! I promise to trust you with all of my heart, just promise you'll never stop fighting for me! Papa? Papa?!"

Suddenly, the screen went black. It said Sami ended the call, and he wondered why she hung up, but it didn't really matter. He was in shock, and with his heart racing closer and closer to 200bpm, he knew he was in the middle of a panic attack... so he was grateful when the tunnel vision started, and at peace when everything went to black...

He'd had panic attacks like this before, so he was surprised by how quickly he opened his eyes. Even stranger, the storm was gone, and all he could hear was the hoot of an owl and the sound of rushing rapids. He stumbled as he stood to his feet, and he was shocked to find himself high atop a cliff. There were sand dunes as far as the eye could see, and sunset was on the horizon line, but he couldn't see the owl, and there was no sign of the rapids.

That's when he felt a tug on his hand...

It was Samantha. The sunlight sparkled like diamonds in her sweat, diamonds that twinkled like shooting stars as they trickled down her temples. And she giggled as she tossed something into the darkness of the gorge at the edge of the cliff. She got on her tip-toes, leaning over the ledge to watch the objects fall, and once they were out of view, she put her hand to her ear.

"Shhh..." she said with her finger to her lips. "Listen..."

Papa tried, but all he could hear was the dreadful sound of the rapids. Then he saw the white of her eyes, as though she'd heard what she was listening for. And with a nod of satisfaction, she looked out at the sunset, then grabbed hold of Papa's hand, and with a pretty flap of her eyelashes, she looked at him, and asked, "Are you ready for this?"

Then, just as he was about to answer, Sami pulled him as hard as she could, and the two of them went flying off the cliff, straight into the abyss! They were in freefall for what felt like forever, and the deeper they got, the further away they were from the light, and the louder the sound of the rapids became.

"Hold on, Sam!" he cried, gripping tightly to her hand. "I got you!" But he couldn't see or hear her anymore, and her grip started to slip. "Don't you dare let go!" he shouted. "You'll be okay, just don't let go!" His fingers slid from her wrist, down to her palm, and then to her fingers. Hope was slipping, so he locked his last finger like "friend" in American Sign Language, screaming as he held on for dear life.

But then she slipped away!

He cried out her name, but the rapids were so loud, he couldn't even hear his own voice... and that's when he felt the mist on his face.

SPLOOSH

Papa plunged beneath the surface. It was bitter cold, and conflicting currents came at him from every direction, making it tough to hold his breath. He opened his eyes, searching for Samantha, but the substance was dark, and all he could see was a mountain, upside-down, with its top buried beneath the ground, and it was spinning like a whirlpool. He struggled to swim to the surface, feeling like he was wading through mud. And once he reached the open-air, he knew why: it wasn't water at all, it was sand, midnight black, and it was spinning like a record.

THUD

Something hit him from behind, and when he turned to see what it was, he was aghast to see that it was the same magical mirror from the dream on his chessboard during Sami's big surgery. It was trapped in the sand, and half of it was beneath the surface, but he saw himself in the reflection, and he was laying lifeless on the ground. He spun around, searching for Sami, but all he saw was a sea of familiar objects, items like his diary and fountain pens, roses and redwood trees, even roller skates and disco balls, as well as chess pieces and curious wooden beads—and all of them were being sucked into the center, but none of them were Sami.

And with the roar of the rapids in his ears and the mist of the mysterious sand in his face, he closed his eyes real tight, then focused on his heartbeat...

... the silence...
... and the solitude...
... to see, ever clearly...
... her pretty handwriting...
... her name, signed in cursive...
... with sighs & ink only he could read...

"Papa!" Sami cried.

He opened his eyes, and there she was, but she was too close to the vortex, and no matter how they tried or how loudly they cried, the distance between them was always divisible, and the harder they swam—crying, begging and pleading for one another—the deeper the two of them sank into the sand.

There was a whimper in the quiver of Sami's lip as she wept, "I love you, Papa!" Then she smiled, and, with waves of sand rising to her lips, she reached out her hand, and tried to tell him something... but the rapids were too loud, and before she could try again, the murderous waves whirled around her face, and the daunting deep dared death, suffocating Samantha beneath the crushing crash of its sandy crest.

"No!!!" Papa screamed, and he tried swimming faster toward the center, but the cyclone seemed satiated, full from feasting on the sorrows of Sami's sacrifice. The waves continued to whirl, but not nearly as fast, and for a moment he thought of escaping, but all of these objects lingering in the sand were all he had left of her, and he was lured by the lullaby of their lamentation, mourning the madness of love and love lost. The whole thing was hypnotic, so he failed to see an angel peeking out from the vortex. It captured Sami's final breath and cupped her parting words in its hands, then raised them up to its lips, and with a breath benign, it blew them into a westward wind. Her sentiment sailed like sound waves through the air, then bounced like musical notes atop the spinning record of the sand, until, at last, they reached Papa's ears, and his heart was made happy by the sound of her song...

"You're wrong, Papa... this isn't what you think... it's all upside-down and inside-out..."

He didn't understand why she said that, and he had no clue what it meant, but he trusted her, so he closed his eyes, exhaled every ounce of his breath, then stretched out his arms, allowing himself to be drawn into the vortex. All of the objects were sucked along with him, and there was terrible pain in the end, but with the sound of rushing rapids fading into the distance, he was back in a freefall, and entirely at peace...

+ On the Flight Back to Detroit +

The booze made Papa sleepy, and he must've passed out because his pen slid across his diary, leaving a huge streak of ink across the page. He was a perfectionist when it came to his journal, and part of him wanted to tear it all out, but something about it felt tragically fitting. He'd been thinking about his time in Palm Springs and Sami's week back home, as well as the radical realignment of retribalized men in Marshall McLuhan's "Global Village."

And Papa thought about God...

Did McLuhan divine (like Nietzsche did) that deities would be dethroned by the demons of our Digital Age, leaving us disordered & deranged in the here and now? (Methinks it's true...) But what's a discontent to do? Must we be glad, whistling as we stagger, drunk as a skunk, past the graveyard of gods and the groups that called on their names? Or may we be sad, mourning over the misadventure of magic and myth in a world gone maniacally mad? Or ought we hold fast to the Golden Mean, the Wisdom trapped in the thicket of extremes, between the twin rocks of shipwreck known as indignance and indifference? The world is teeming with different answers, but who's to say?

(Ay, they shoot horses, don't they?)

He felt so stupid writing these things, and he was glad his diaries were private, but for the first time in years, he felt like a kid longing for a Christmas gift on display in a stained-glass window. He felt there was a strange malaise in the modern Secular Age, and he resented how it had made his family feel so alone and out of place. He used to say he didn't know what to do,. but pride is tough, and sin is a heckuva drug

When the plane prepared for landing, Papa buckled his belt and gazed out the window. It had only been ten days, and from this height, Detroit still looked the same, but differences were all around. And when the plane parked, people stood up from their seats, and Papa imagined his family waving and weeping in the window. He smiled, then uncapped his pen, and there, at the bottom of the page, he wrote:

Everything (and everyone) is changing... even...
Sincerely, Me.

Onward & upward in 2016!

XXIV

50 FIRST DATES
[aka Love—Into A Million Pieces]

New London, Connecticut, was like a land trapped in time. Even after all these years, everything looked and felt just as it had when Mama and Papa lived there many years before. Papa had enlisted in the Navy on September 11, 2001, and after basic training, he was stationed at Naval Submarine Base New London. He met Mama during leave, and they tried doing the whole long-distance thing. Mama soon packed her bags and moved to New London, where she boarded a room in a mansion, the same mansion wherein they were married just a few months later.

"You guys really lived here?!" Sami asked.

"Oh, we didn't just live here," Mama replied, "we got married here." Then she leaned over Sami's shoulder, whispering in her ear, "And it's where you were conceived."

SHE DANCED ME A STORY

"Ew! Gross, Mama!" Teresa scoffed with an icky face.

Maybe it was TMI, but it was true, and deep-down, it's why Mama insisted that they return. Sami was her firstborn, which meant that Sami was connected to all sorts of firsts for Mama: the first time she noticed her pregnant belly in the mirror, the first time she felt a kick, the first time she felt the pangs of birth, and first time she saw her firstborn child, bloody but beautiful, and crying to suckle at her breast. All of those firsts were connected to Samantha. Mama cherished the memories, storing them in her heart for all these years, which made this trip a lot like the mansion itself: more than simply a place, but rather the season of their lives that were lived there.

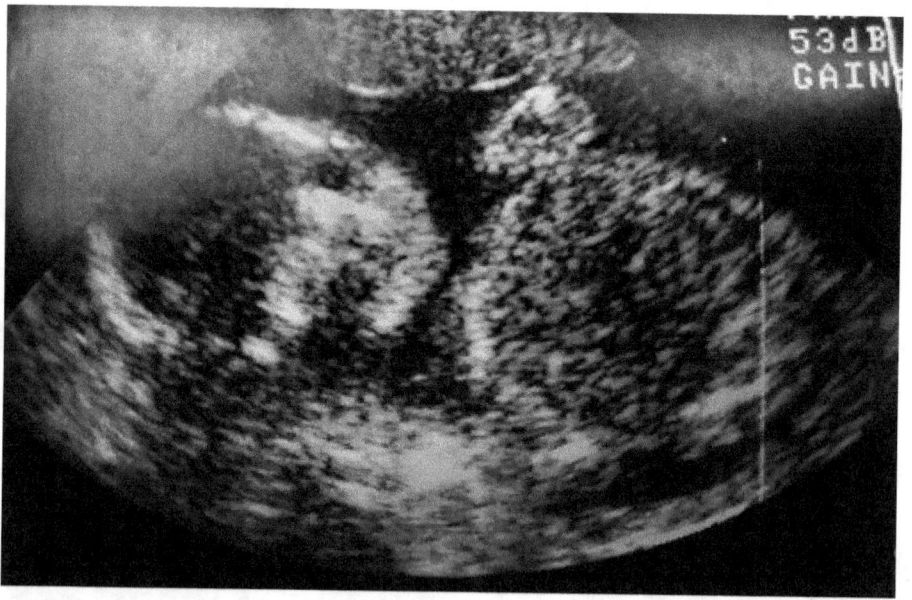

Mama smiled with pride as the kids ran around outside, and she was relieved to see that Sami loved the house. She gazed up at the pillars, still enthralled by how tall they were. She always loved that about this home, considering it perfectly fitting, not only that her firstborn was conceived in a mansion near the sea, but that the pillars stood atop a Stairway to Heaven, serving as a sort of Jacob's Ladder, connecting the mystery of the heavens to the majesty of the home.

"And you weren't kidding about these stairs," Ambrose said, tired and out of breath. "They're definitely divine, but my legs feel like I just climbed up a million steps or something."

There were only thirty, and thirty is a far cry from one million, but there really was something more than meets the eye about those stairs, and by the time you reached the top, you were likely quite winded. So after the week they had just spent wheeling Sami around Washington D.C. and New York City, neither Mama nor Papa were looking forward to schlepping Sami's chair up the stairs. Sami's cancer had gotten worse, though, so she struggled to walk, even with a cane, and found herself increasingly dependent on her wheelchair.

"I'm really sorry, Papa," Sami said as Papa knelt to lift the front of her chair. He said it was fine, and he tried his best to hide it, but she saw the wince in his eyes when he lifted the chair, and she noticed in New York how his arms would shake, and how he was always asking Mama to massage his shoulders. Even now, she could feel the tremble of his legs as he walked backward up the stairs, and she watched as sweat beaded up on his brow and trickled down his temple. She felt so bad, and she hated that she had so little to offer. When they reached the top, she kissed his cheek, and wiping the sweat from her lips, she fluttered those extra-long lashes, and with Precious Moments sparkling in her eyes, she smiled, and told him in a lyrical, even sing-songy voice:

"Papa / I love you / with all of my heart / into a million pieces!"

The kids were already racing around when Mama pushed Sami's wheelchair into the common room. They were in awe, gazing up at the artwork on the walls.

"This is the most prettiest house I've ever saw in my whole entire life!" Teresa exclaimed. It was gorgeous, with illustrious paintings, classical sculptures, and an antique interior. "It's like a Barbie mansion, but even better."

Mama sat down on the leather couch, looking up at an old painting that hung over the fireplace. It's where they had gotten married, and it felt like nothing in the room had changed since that November day. "It's a home for writers, artists, and musicians," she said, "so most of the stuff around the house was made by people who have lived here."

"Did you or Papa make any of this stuff?" Athan asked as he ran his fingers along the curves of a bronze sculpture of Aphrodite.

"Pfft! I wish!" Mama laughed. Then she scowled at Athan and swatted his hand. "This stuff is obviously really expensive," she said, silently wagging her finger at him. "So keep your hands off, okay."

The family continued fluttering around the room, fawning over all the fancy things, when Sami saw a series of doors. One was open, and it led to a long, dark hall. The other stood at the opposite end, and it was closed, but there was a bright and beautiful light shining through its keyhole. She looked back at her family, just to make sure that no one was watching, then she grabbed her cane and silently sat up from her chair, then limped into the inner darkness that led to that mysterious outer light.

The hallway was scarier than she imagined, with creaking floors and walls covered with a curious collection of canvases. She beheld rabbits in the wilderness, a fire casting shadow puppets on a wall, and two lovers kissing on a tree swing in a garden. And there were images of a family praying over food, and of a mother blowing out a candle on the nightstand near the bed where her daughter laid fast asleep. But what captivated her was a mysterious door at the end of the hall. Where did it lead?

"Whatcha lookin' at, baby?"

"Oh, my goodness," Sami shuddered. "You scared the daylights out of me, Mama!" Papa and the kids weren't far behind. Once they caught up and were all together again, Sami slowly raised her right hand and pointed her curled fist toward the door. "Can you tell me what's on the other side?"

What Sami didn't know was that this was Mama and Papa's favorite part about living at that house, and they'd been looking forward to showing her all day. "I'll do better than tell you," he said. "I'll show you." Then, as he reached for the door, Sami wrapped her arm around his, and said, again, in that same sing-song voice:

"Papa / I love you / with all of my heart / into a million pieces."

He froze for a moment, and there was a conflicted expression on his face, almost like he was going to cry, but then his chest expanded with a slow, deep breath, and—

Sunbeams burst through the doorway like gusts of wind through an open window, and the light was so bright, that Sami had to close her eyes. "Isn't it heavenly?" Mama asked. Sami used her hand to block the light, then slowly opened her eyes... It was the most beautiful garden she'd ever seen, filled with trees of willow, oak, and apple, and with colorful flowers as far as the eye could see.

"Look, you guys," Ambrose said as he rushed into the light, "there's a path!"

"It's more like a labyrinth," Athan replied, trying to catch up with his brother.

"Or maybe even a maze!" Teresa said in a chirpy little voice, but nobody heard her. She thought about running to catch up with the boys, but then she got distracted by two stone statues guarding the gate to the garden. They were angels, beautiful to behold, and they were weeping. And with her thumb still in her mouth, she said, "I wonder who built all this?"

The family made their way through the garden, stopping every now and again to stare at a statue or to smell a pretty flower. But the deeper they went into the maze, the more consumed they became. Sami wondered if it was heaven, and she worried that it would end, but just when she thought she'd seen and smelled it all, she beheld a path, hidden from plain view by the saddest of weeping willows.

SHE DANCED ME A STORY

"What's back there?" Sami asked.

"That," Mama said, "is the heart of the home."

The four of them walked toward the path, and once they got there, Papa grabbed a bundle of those weeping branches, then slid them aside like drapes of a canopy, revealing the mystery that lies behind the veil.

Sami gasped! For there, hidden by the weeping willow tree, was a garden within a garden. It was circular, entirely surrounded by pines, pillars, and park benches. Angels and gargoyles were stationed round about, and in the middle was a wishing well.

"Stargazer lilies!" Teresa shouted. "Those are Sami's most favoritest flowers in the whole wide world!" Then she ran with Mama into the flowerbed, plucked two of prettiest Stargazers they could find, then hurried them back to Samantha.

Sami wasn't sure what to do with them, though, so Papa grabbed the flowers from her fist, then turned her body to face him. "Alrighty, Sam, let's see if this works," he said, tucking the flowers behind her ear. Then he stepped back to get a good look. And with a Chef's Kiss to his fingertips, Papa exclaimed, "Bellissimo! Bellissimo!"

Sami felt so special, so pretty, and so loved in that moment, and she couldn't help but to blush. Her heart was an avalanche of thoughts and emotions, but there was only one thing on her mind, and it was all that she could say...

"Papa / I love you / with all of my heart / into a million pieces."

It was the third time she'd said that sentence since the family first arrived- and it was the exact same each and every time! She'd flap her lashes, gaze at Papa with Precious Moments in her eyes, then sing of her love for him.

Always the same facial expressions...

Always in that lyrical, singsong voice...

Always the same cadence and inflections...

And they were always the exact same words...

But that was nowhere near the worst of it, for Sami had been doing this since Washington D.C... and she'd already said it nearly 50 times before.

JEREMIAH T. BANNISTER

+ Reason Rally—Washington, D.C. +

Sami sat beneath an umbrella that was connected to her wheelchair, looking around at all the people. There were thousands of them, mostly Atheists and Agnostics, and they came from all over the United States. Dozens of her Facebook friends and followers had made it to the event, and their bright and colorful #TeamTinyDancer shirts made them easy to find—but Sami was looking for something... a *little* different.

"Hey, Papa," Sami asked, "why are there hardly ever any other kids at atheist events? And why are mostly only white people here?"

Papa used a newspaper to block the sun from his eyes, then he took a look around. "I dunno, Sam. It's kinda messed up a little, huh?"

"Yeah, it's even more messed up than that guy on the stage who told a really gross joke about sex and killing babies."

"The comedian?" Papa replied.

"I don't think so, but if he was, I feel really bad for him, cuz there were only, like, three or four people that laughed at any of his jokes."

These complaints were only the tip of the iceberg, though. Sami's frustration with Atheism ran deeper and wider than gross jokes by unfunny comedians. Like Mama and Papa, Sami was more traditional than the unbelievers at Reason Rally, especially about kids, families, and things to do with culture. She missed church, too, or at least what she remembered of it. She had told Papa she wanted to attend, just to see how they worship and learn why they believe the way they do. And she had hoped that a few of the groups Papa worked with were kind of like a church, but none of them were—and that often made Sami feel alone and out of place.

Sami looked up at Papa and used the back of her hand to block the sun from her eyes. "This really isn't our scene, you know..."

"Huh?" Papa replied. "What do you mean?"

Sami scrunched her face and looked around. "I dunno, this just isn't us." She squinted her eyes, looking out as far as she could, then shook her head. "These just aren't our people." But then she glanced over at an entourage of men and women wearing #TeamTinyDancer shirts, and with a huge smile, she said, "Now, *those* people? Those are *my* people."

The rest of that day was spent relaxing with her "entourage," which included a family friend who was an Army veteran that helped push Sami in her wheelchair throughout the day. The day concluded with an evening filled with fancy food and popular Atheists dancing the night away.

The following day involved a woman named Brandy and a tour of the White House. It was Brandy's birthday, and someone from the Secret Service gave her tickets as a gift, so the tour was even better, as it included special (and super-secret) areas, as well as the Press Briefing Room in the West Wing.

But her favorite part of the trip to D.C. was the tour of the U.S. Capitol.

Sami loved the United States, so she always enjoyed learning about its history, especially when the history could be seen through the lens of paintings, sculptures, music, and even architecture. That made The Capitol a practical goldmine. Sami ran her fingers along the Amateis Doors, studied the scene in Chapman's painting of the Baptism of Pocahontas, and reflected on time while gazing at the elegant Car of History Clock.

"My favorite, though, was the Statue of Freedom," Sami said as Papa read a plaque about the Whispering Gallery. "She's strong but beautiful, with gorgeous feathers, stars on her helmet, and the prettiest dress in all the world." She smiled and looked up at an American flag, saying, "She's what I think of when I think about America."

Papa wanted to see if the Whispering Gallery was real. Apparently, the half-dome produces an acoustical effect that makes it so that, in certain spots, people standing far apart can be heard more clearly than the people standing nearby. He pushed Sami's wheelchair to a particular spot, then told her to say something when he gave her the signal. He then ran across the room, looked around to make sure he was standing in the right place, then cupped his hand around his ear and gave her the signal.

Sami was about to say something when there was a weird twitch in her eye, and she felt dizzy. It didn't last long, so she thought nothing of it. And, then, with a smile on her face, she cupped her hands around her mouth and whispered...

Papa waited, but not for long, for there, in the mix of all the other sounds competing for his attention, he heard a gentle whisper.

"Papa / I love you / with all of my heart / into a million pieces."

It happened a second time at the 9/11 Museum. The whole experience was hard for Papa, and by the end of the exhibit, he was broken, weeping and on his knees, surrounded by his children. So Sami repeating that she loved him with all of her heart didn't come as a surprise. In fact, her words were fitting, and she said it so pretty that it turned out to be just what Papa needed in order to smile and get back to his feet.

The third time happened outside Trump Tower, after the family got a picture with Ivanka.

The fourth was at the Statue of Liberty, by which time Mama and Papa were getting concerned, wondering why Sami was repeating herself this way. But then it happened again on the subway, and multiple times on their walks and rides throughout the city, and then again that night in Time's Square.

Each time was harder than the last, and the family felt so helpless, unsure of what to do or what to say. And that's when Mama told Papa she'd be right back, then walked to an alleyway, where she dialed the doctors at Helen DeVos.

"How often has this happened?" Dr. Kurt asked.

"At least a dozen times!" Mama replied.

"Oh, no..."

She didn't say anything for a while, but those words (and that silence) said more than enough. Truth is, Dr. Kurt didn't need to tell Mama what was going on with Sami, as she only called to confirm what her heart already knew:

Sami's cancer was progressing rapidly...

Mama almost spoke up when Dr. Kurt broke the silence. "Have you ever seen 50 First Dates, Angela?"

"With Adam Sandler and Drew Barrymore? Yes, of course."

SHE DANCED ME A STORY

Dr. Kurt sighed. "That's what you need to do. You need to treat it like every time is the first time she's ever said it... and like it might be the last time you'll ever hear it. I know this is a lot to ask, but you have to love her like you've never loved her before." Dr. Kurt could hear the bustle of Time Square in the background, but no amount of commotion could conceal the sounds of Mama sobbing. "And please don't let her know," she said. "Sami's mind is like a broken record, but she doesn't know she's skipping, so it's like she's singing a song for the very first time every time she says it."

"And she's singing it over and over, Dr. Kurt!" Mama cried.

"I know, Angela, I know... and I'm so, so sorry." Dr. Kurt paused for a moment, just long enough for Mama to catch the silver lining in her voice when she returned to the phone, saying, "Then just be glad that *that* is the song Sami's singing, and cherish the fact that her heart has it locked and on a loop."

The walk back to the car was hard, but Mama and Papa were glad to be pushing Sami's wheelchair, as it allowed them to walk behind her, weeping together as Sami sang—

+ Back in the Garden +

"Papa / I love you / with all of my heart / into a million pieces!"

Now, with the family leaning over the edge of the wishing well at the center of the secret garden, Sami saw the sunset, and it cast her family in a whole new light. There was a glow around their heads, necks, and shoulders, which made them appear like silhouettes, but she could see the devotion in their smiles, and their love in the water of the well from the tears that fell from their eyes...

XXV

A VERY STORMY FOURTH OF JULY

+ July 4, 2016, at Home in Grand Rapids +

Life got hard when they returned home from New London. Sami struggled to hold down her meds, and she'd cry out every morning, begging for help, but by the time Mama and Papa arrived, Sami was already sitting in a puddle of her puke. They tried all sorts of things, but nothing seemed to work (or at least nothing that they weren't too scared to try)... but all of that was about to change today.

"Close the door!" Papa yelled.

"I'm right here," Mama laughed. "But why do you want the door shut?"

Sami looked up at her from her seat on the bed. "Papa's teaching me how to use a bong."

"Shhh!" Papa griped. "Be quiet. And shut that stinkin' door!"

Sami looked at Mama, who was just as confused as her. "Um, Papa, we're in our house, you know?"

"And we're the only ones home," Mama laughed.

That was true, and he felt kind of silly for being scared like that, but this was serious. She'd been taking those capsules for over a year, and they worked like a charm. She had no pain, no nausea, not even depression, and she was able to eat and sleep exceptionally well. Best of all, she hadn't needed any medications from Helen DeVos and Mary Free Bed. But she could no longer down her capsules, so she needed something more... and this was something more.

Papa showed her what it was, explained how it worked, and held the torch while she vaped the wax. Sami coughed so hard she almost puked, but she tried again... and again. Each time was easier, and within a few minutes, she was relaxed, without pain, and with no more urge to puke.

SHE DANCED ME A STORY

"Wooooow, that helped soooo fast," Sami said as she laid back on the bed, already high. "It's way different from the capsules, too, because those take, like, a half-an-hour or something to even work—and that was definitely waaaaaay tooooo long."

That bong became attached to her hip, and it worked for a week or two, but it was harder to gauge than the capsules, so she would get extremely stoned, and that always made her really tired... so tired, that the urge to puke became the only thing that got her out of bed. But after a while, even that wasn't enough, so Sami needed a puke bucket, and she never spent much time alone.

Adding insult to injury, this made it tough for Sami to leave the house. They tried one time to go out to eat, and Emilie tagged along, but Sami was so tired, and she lost all the color in her face. The waitress seated them in the corner, but Papa feared that she was going to get sick... a fear which was confirmed seconds later when Sami retched all over the table. Making it even worse, the place was packed with people—and everyone saw it.

Mama talked to the manager, who was very understanding, and the waitresses kindly helped Papa and the kids clean up the mess. And Gladys took care of Sami, wiping the puke from her face and hands before wheeling her to the car. Papa was fuming mad, though. He saw the way the people stared, and he heard the disgust in their whispers. Some complained, "We lost our appetite!" while others demanded refunds, but most of them just looked with disgust at Sami, grumbling about the audacity of "that family" in the corner. And of all these, there were two that made Papa especially mad.

A rotund mother and her even pudgier son were devouring their third or fourth helpings when it happened. The son started making fun, while the mother grumbled and covered the boy's eyes with her gnarly hands.

"Why did they come here?" she grumbled with a mouthful of food. "I mean, just look at that girl. She's obviously sick, probably with the flu or something bad like that."

"I bet she's contagious, too, mommy!" oinked her pudgy son.

"Mm-hm, and now she probably spread it to everyone here!"

Every syllable coming out of their mouths made Papa angrier and angrier, but then the woman looked straight at him, and said, "That poor girl. Her mom and dad clearly care more about themselves than they do about her and the health of everyone here."

"My daughter is dying!" Papa shouted for everyone to hear. Then he looked straight at the woman and her son. "And thank God her brain cancer isn't contagious..."

Everyone stared at him, aghast at the words spilling out of his mouth. And he would have said many more, rambling on about childhood obesity and the obscenity of a woman only a few sweets away from a bed-ridden state complaining about anyone else's health, but he had a sick (and very embarrassed) daughter waiting for him in the van.

Then came the Fourth of July...

This holiday was always festive, but this year was a ruckus. The fireworks and music started around 7 a.m. (if they ended the night before at all), so their booms, cracks, and bangs never seemed to end. Cocoa hated it, and Lion did too, but everyone loved to sit outside and watch as people from their neighborhood lit up the sky with a colorful glow... that is, everyone except for Sami.

She'd been sleeping seventeen-hours-a-day for nearly three weeks, and even more as time moved on. She wasn't eating, either. Helen DeVos had exhausted their options, and barring a miracle, Sami was going to die. Mama and Papa searched around, looking up treatments online, and Paul made some calls, but every answer they gave had the same ending:

"This study is in another country..."
"We currently have no spots available..."
"Your daughter is too young for this study..."
"This treatment isn't for anaplastic astrocytoma..."

It felt so hopeless, and the family feared that Sami could die at any moment. Then, around 11:30 p.m. on the Fourth of July, the lights went out.

The family wasn't sure what caused it, but the whole block was without power, so the only light came from cellphones, candles, flashlights, and the fireworks blasting off in the nighttime sky. Mama thought it would be fun to have a bonfire as the neighbors were putting on a firework show that was choreographed to all different kinds of music. She figured that would keep the kids busy while the city figured out the electricity. So, Papa gathered some wood, lit a fire, and got the kids started with hotdogs. He then went inside to check on Sami.

He heard his phone ring as he walked through the door, so he knew he left it back at the fire, but it was late, and if it was important, he was sure Mama would pick it up, so he just kept walking. The house was pitch-black, but he didn't mind. He'd been up these steps a thousand times, and he knew how many strides it took to reach Sami's room. But as he approached Sami's room, something felt off, just different. It was quiet. It was unsettling, at least for the Fourth of July, as the world was so loud and colorful outside. It just didn't seem right... not tonight.

The knob was cold to the touch, and the door made a creepy creaking noise as it opened, but it was the stillness that bothered him. It was eerie, as the only light came from the occasional firework, which glowed through her blinds in a harrowing array of distressing reds and blues. And the fireworks were jolting, too, bouncing like thunder off the walls and hardwood floor. Worst of all, were it not for Lion and Cocoa, Papa would've felt like he was the only living soul in Sami's room. For a moment, he was surprised that Sami could even sleep, but she'd been like this for a week, and today was definitely the worst.

Sami had only woken up once that day to brush her teeth and take some meds, but the rest of her day was spent in bed, quiet, alone, and fast-asleep.

"Sami," Papa whispered as felt around on the bed. He felt her shin through the blanket, so he knew she was there, but she didn't say anything, and she didn't move. "Come on, sleepyhead, you should get out of bed for a little... Mama and the kids are making hotdogs... and you gotta take your meds, anyway... so... Sami?... Sami?? Sami, are you okay???" He tried again and again to wake her up, and his voice got louder and louder with each and every plea. But there was nothing! No movement, no sound, and now he wished he'd brought his phone. He yelled for Mama, but a firework went off at the same time. The explosion was huge, and it happened closer to the ground than anyone expected. People gasped in fear and wonder, marveling over how dangerously close it had come to them. The light from the explosion shined through the blinds, and for the first time since he arrived, Papa saw her...

... still as a statue, pale as a ghost!

He lunged toward her, putting his ear up to her lips. She was breathing. "Sami!" Papa cried. "Wake up, Samantha! C'mon, baby! Don't do this to me— not now, not yet!"

Still... nothing. Not a peep, not anything at all...

Papa grabbed her by the shoulders, shaking her harder and harder, but nothing could wake her up. In a panic, he climbed atop her, straddling her waist, looking to where he knew would be her face. Wagner's *Ride of the Valkyries* soared through the speakers outside when Papa grabbed hold of Sami's shirt, lifted her body toward him, and screamed in her face as loud as he could:

"SAMANTHA!"

BOOM

The grand finale of the fireworks show sounded like a war zone as hundreds of fireworks blasted off in the air, and the multicolored explosions flashed like a strobe light in the room while Papa screamed over and over again. "Wake up! Wake up! My God, why won't you just wake up!!!" Then he collapsed on top of her, with his ear pressed down on her chest, and he wept... but that's when he heard her heartbeat and the air filling up in her lungs. It sounded so peaceful, and then—

Sami moved!

Papa gasped and bolted back up on the bed. "Sami! You're alive! Are you okay?!"

"What do you want, Papa?" Sami groaned, exasperated (and apparently in pain). Papa laughed and cried at the same time, and he hugged her like there was no tomorrow, weeping harder than he's ever wept before.

But all of that came to an end when the power kicked on and they heard Mama calling their names as she raced up the stairs...

XXVI

FOURTH DOWN & SUNSET
[A Hail Mary at Beaumont]

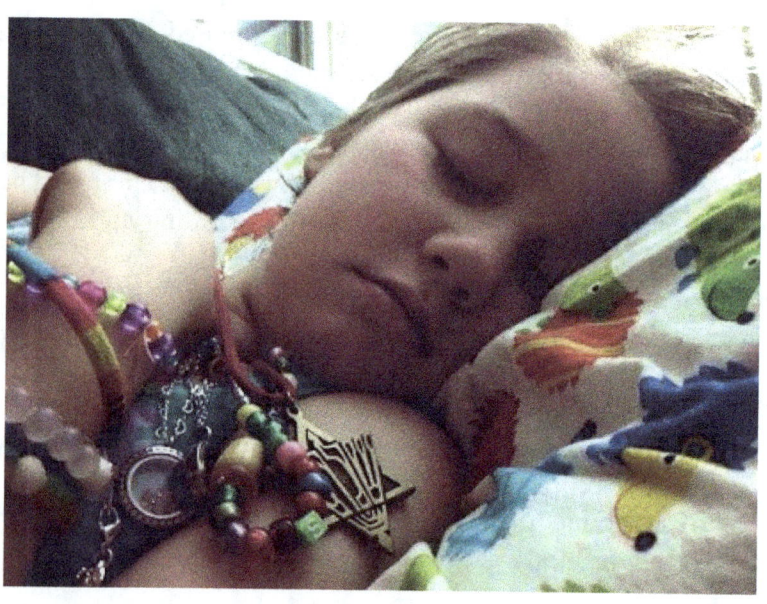

+ The Morning of July 5, 2016, +

Morning couldn't have come fast enough...

"Pull the car up to the house," Papa shouted as he tossed the keys to Mama. Then he raced back to the house to help Sami. She was laying on the couch downstairs, where she'd been most of the night, so he reached his arms beneath her body, picked her up, and declared, "I'll take care of you, Sam. I got you."

Sami knew he didn't get any sleep, and she could tell that his back hurt from having laid on the floor near the couch, but she knew that none of that mattered, not right now, not to Papa. She felt the trembling of his injured arm, but she wasn't afraid that he'd drop her. In fact, for the first time in days, she wasn't afraid of anything at all. As they crossed the threshold of their front door, Sami nuzzled her nose into the shirt atop his shoulder, and whispered, "Papa…"

He paused for a moment. "Yes, sweetheart?"

She knew that he was scared by the timbre of his voice, but she gazed up at him, and with a tender twinkle in her eyes, she told him that she loved him. "And please never stop fighting for me, Papa." He nodded his head, but his jaw was clenched, and though he pressed his lips, she could hear the hyper-focused cadence of his breathing. Papa was weeping inside as Sami smiled and fell back into the strength of his shoulder.

Mama buckled her in, and Papa shut the door, but as he was about to hop in the car, he saw his neighbors. Many of them were standing outside. Some were crying, busying their hands, while others covered their mouths in disbelief.

The ride was long… and very quiet. Mama wondered whether Papa wanted to listen to music, and she almost turned on the radio, but she could see in his eyes that music was the last thing on his mind. He hated commercial radio, anyway, especially when he was trying to think—and after last night, thinking was all that he could do.

+ The Night Before—After the Grand Finale +

Mama raced up the stairs, crying out for Papa and Sami, and by the time she reached Sami's room, she was all out of breath. "You guys won't even believe this," she said between breaths.

"What is it, Mama?"

Mama held out her hand. She was holding Papa's phone. "We got a call from a doctor at Beaumont. His name is Dr. Chen, and he's the one who does that PULSE radiation stuff." She paused, and with a deep breath through her nose, she stood up straight, and told them. "He said yes."

"Seriously?!" Sami cried. "Dr. Chen said he can help me?!"

Mama nodded, and with a beautifully hopeful smile on her face, she told them, "He not only said he could. He said he would!"

Unfortunately, there were problems with this plan: first, Dr. Chen couldn't see her for another week. And, second, Sami was fading—and faster than the family even realized. For a mere 30 minutes after the situation at Sami's bed, Sami was standing up, walking around the house, even up and down the stairs without assistance, and she talked like everything was fine.

"Look at this!" Sami exclaimed as she raised her right-hand right up over her head. "I can do it no problem, Papa!" It was true, she could—and she proved it repeatedly. It was so surreal, so entirely inexplicable, that Mama and Papa quietly wondered whether it was a miracle. She hadn't raised her hand like that in over a year. "And, look," Sami said, pointing at her leg, "my limp is gone!" She even jumped up and down. "I have so much energy right now!" she laughed. "I just want to go on a run or something! Can we go on a run? Please?!"

But then, as quickly as it had come, this extraordinary energy simply went away... and then came back... then went away again... and on and on this went, back-and-forth and back-and-forth for hours and hours on end. When it was going, it was going strong, and Sami was powerful, on top of the world, feeling like she could do anything and everything she wanted. But when the energy disappeared, it left her high and dry.

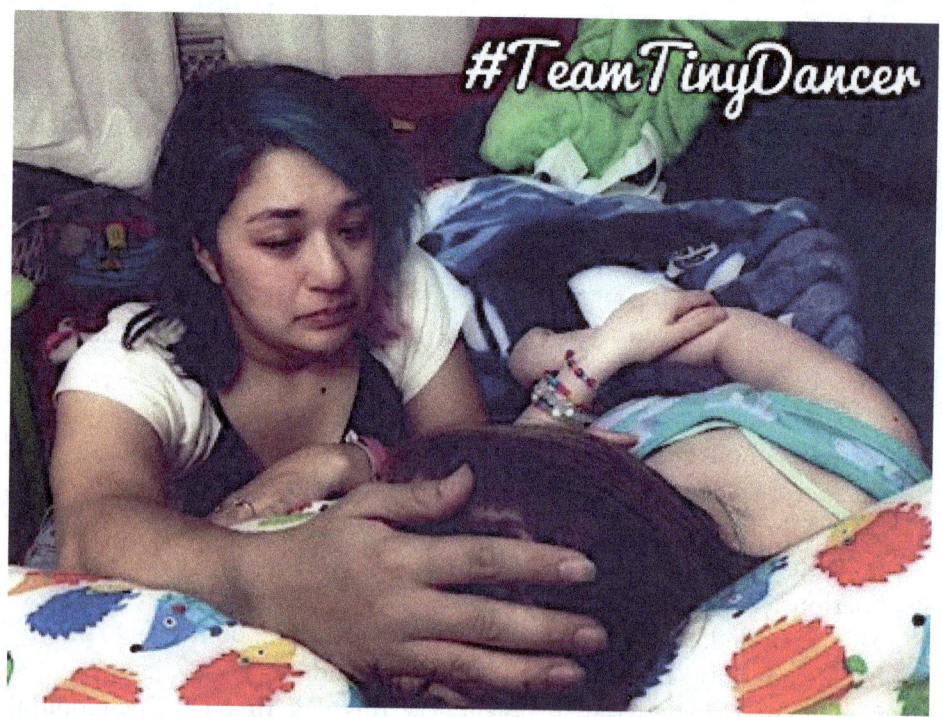

Turns out, Sami was re-experiencing those hypothalamic storms, kind of like the ones she had at Helen DeVos, only this time her brain wasn't healing from surgery... it was entering the throes of death. Eventually, that energy overwhelmed her, leaving her laid out on the couch, twitching and trembling like she was having seizures. And when the storms had all passed, she was silent, still, and unresponsive, just as she was in her room earlier that night.

Mama spent the rest of the night on the couch with Sami, crying assurances that they would get help in the morning, while Papa paced the room, making calls...

+ Three Hours After Leaving Grand Rapids +
+ At Beaumont—Near Detroit +

SHE DANCED ME A STORY

Papa carried her through the front door of the Beaumont ER. The spectacle got everyone's attention, and when the nurses realized she was dying of cancer, they rushed her to the first available doctor.

"This place looks kinda boring," Sami said. "Like, ugh, bleh." She glanced at all of the furniture and the paintings on the walls. "They don't even have one fun picture, and there's just a bunch of boring adult stuff all over the place."

Aesthetics were the least of their troubles, though, for no sooner had they arrived, than they faced some serious obstacles. Honestly, most of those were Papa's fault. He knew that their dramatic entrance into the ER would allow Sami to "leapfrog" over the others in the Waiting Room, but it also created a lot of chaos and confusion—two things you definitely don't want to deal with when you're racing against time. And while it was obvious that Sami needed help, she lacked the proper papers, so nurses didn't really know how to handle it. Making matters worse, her condition was dire, which meant her case was urgent, but that required that people hurry, and people in a hurry make a lot of honest mistakes.

All of this came to a head with the medics manning the MRI.

"These aren't your ordinary images," Papa insisted. "This is an experimental treatment, and Dr. Chen required a very specific set of scans."

"We hear what you're saying, Mr. Bannister, but this is our job, so you should trust we know what we're doing."

But they weren't really hearing him—and they definitely didn't know what they were doing...

"What are these?!" Dr. Chen complained as he flipped through images. "They're useless! All of them!"

They *were* useless, *all of them*, and by the time the new batch of images was reviewed, Sami had been at Beaumont, without Dr. Chen's treatment, for nearly five days...

...and her cancer was progressing unrestrainedly.

Most of the symptoms were things she'd dealt with before, only now much worse. Sami's right-arm was completely paralyzed, so feeding herself was a slow and sloppy struggle. On one occasion, Mama noticed Sami scraping her spoon atop her soup.

"Are you going to eat that," Mama asked, half-jokingly, "or are you just gonna play with it?" The problem was, Sami wasn't playing with her food.

"It's like being stuck on repeat," the nurse whispered in Mama's ear. "Sami probably doesn't even know it's happening."

Suddenly, Sami stopped. And with her eyes still facing downward, she sighed, "I do now." Mama and the nurse felt so ashamed. They didn't mean for Sami to hear them talking. "I'm not deaf, you know?"

Nothing, however, compared with the horror everyone felt whenever Sami complained about the pain. It was excruciating and unpredictable, causing her to toss and turn in her bed, and doctors tried all sorts of meds—they even tried increasing the dosages—but nothing worked. Making matters worse, when Sami was finally scheduled for her first round of PULSE radiation, the treatment required her to remain still and calm. So in a last-ditch effort to pacify her, the doctors prescribed a sedative. ("Just something to take the edge off.") And it worked.

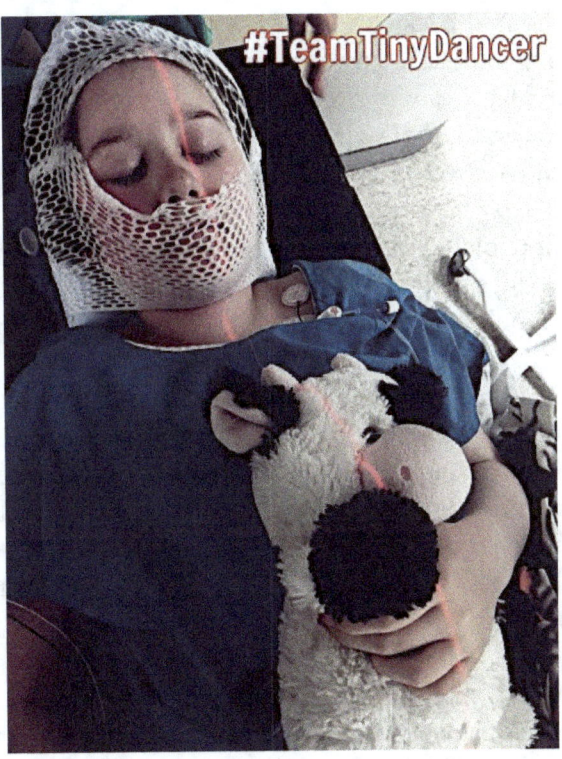

"She did great!" exclaimed the nurse escorting Sami to her room. Then she handed her two balloons, and said, "Welp, one down, only thirteen left to go."

Everyone was so relieved, so happy and filled with hope. Mama was elated, laughing and crying at the same time, and Papa reveled in the idea that this could afford the family more time. After all, that was what they had been fighting for. Yet, in the middle of all their merriment, Sami sat in her little pink wheelchair, balloons in-hand, gazing gloomily toward the ground. Unlike them, she felt neither happy nor hopeful, and she was no longer sure even what it was that she was fighting for—in fact, she was finding it hard to feel or be sure of anything at all...

She listened for a while longer, then she raised her head conspicuously high, and turned her eyes toward Papa...

He looked magnificent and mighty—as bold and as brave as the day she was born. She gazed at the silver in his golden hair, and pondered the crow's feet that creased across his temples. Time and tragedy had taken their toll, and yet there he stood, strong as a sequoia, and just as old—in some ways, maybe even older. And she thought back to her life as a toddler, always trying to climb the heights of his long and sturdy trunks. And she recalled the twelve years spent under the cover of his canopy, where she took respite in the shelter of his shade... and she never tired of swinging on his limbs.

How do you say goodbye to a redwood tree? she wondered. *It'll still be here when I'm dead and gone... standing tall and strong, even when I'm done dancing.*

Papa was still rejoicing when he looked down at her, and with a sparkle in his smile, he nodded, silently assuring her that everything would be okay. Sami smiled, too, but only out of love. For deep down, a sorrowful sigh had swallowed Sami alive, and she was so, so sad.

The sun was fading below the skyline by the time they returned to Sami's room, so they ate a celebratory spaghetti dinner and settled in for the night. Papa was excited, and he wanted to update friends and followers on Facebook about Sami's first day of radiation, and Sami was lying in bed, talking on the phone with a family friend who'd recently been diagnosed with cancer. But Mama, she could barely keep her eyes open. She'd been living off Starbucks and cat naps since they'd arrived, so she needed a good night's sleep—and in a nice, warm bed.

"Is that okay?" Mama yawned.

"I don't mind," Sami replied as she fidgeted with something on her lap. "And aren't Nana and Uncle Isaac with the kids at the hotel, anyway? I bet they all miss you like crazy, Mama."

Mama knew Sami was right, but she was still reluctant to leave. Sure, she was tired, but she dreaded the idea of not being there for her daughter, especially if something went wrong. So Papa closed his laptop, helped Mama to her feet, and gave her a kiss, and promised her that everything would be fine.

"Nothing bad is gonna happen," he said as he handed Mama her purse. "And we promise to stay right here, won't we, Sami?"

"Mm-mm," Sami replied, mechanically, with her eyes still locked on her lap.

Mama laughed, then kissed Papa on the cheek. "Fine, but you guys better call me if anything happens, you hear me?"

Papa watched Mama walk down the hall, and right as she reached the exit, he yelled, "Trust me, baby, nothin' is gonna happen." But when the exit door was shut, he turned around, and wrung his hands. "Yeah, nothing but an awesome night of Pillow/Blankets! Mwahaha!"

He raced back to Sami's bed, where he quickly crawled under the blanket, and cuddled up beside her. He was so content, just lying there, resting his head on Sami's shoulder. "I just wish they had *Super Friends*," he said.

"Me too," Sami mumbled with something in her mouth.

Papa propped himself up on his elbow. "Hey, what are you eating there?"

"Skittles..."

"Skittles?" Papa complained. "Where'd you get those?!"

No sooner had Papa asked that, than Sami started fidgeting with something on her lap. And with her thumb pinched tightly to her middle finger, she slowly and awkwardly raised her hand to her mouth. "You gave them to me."

Papa's eyes opened wide with fear, for not only had he not given Sami any Skittles, but there were no Skittles on her lap at all. He was so scared and confused, especially because Sami had been doing this for nearly twenty minutes. But, he had to remain composed, so he did what he had always done and played along. It hurt his heart so badly, and he wanted to scream and cry, but instead, he smiled, and replied, "Oh, yeah! I remember now. But I didn't want you to eat all of my Skittles, I just wanted to share a little." He pretended to peek into the invisible bag Sami was eating from. "So, um, what flavor are you eating there, Sam?"

"Red..."

"Mmm... the red ones, huh?"

"Yeah, they're my favorite."

"Oh, wow," Papa exclaimed, "what a coinkidink! They're my favorite too!" And in a super-sly voice, he said, "You know, you should totally hook me up with one of those..."

Sami tossed a fistful of fake Skittles in her mouth. "No way," she said, still moving her mouth as though she was chewing. "You're gonna have to buy your own bag."

"What the—?" Papa laughed. "And why is that?"

Without skipping a beat, Sami tossed an invisible Skittle in her mouth, then motioned her hand like she was crinkling the wrapper, then threw it toward the floor, and said, "Cuz I just ate the last one."

"How dare you, Sami Lee! What. A. Jerk." Then he snuggled his head against her chest, and said, "Well, I guess I'll forgive you... this time. But don't think I won't remember this. Oh, trust me, Sami, I'll definitely remember this." He hoped for a laugh, or even a half-hearted chuckle, but there was nothing...

Sami's voice got very serious all of a sudden, and with her eyes still facing downward, she asked, "Hey, Papa, can I tell you a secret?"

"A secret, huh?"

"Yeah, a secret... and please promise you won't get mad..."

Papa sat upright in the bed, then turned to face her. He wanted her to see that she had his full attention, and to prepare himself for whatever it was that she wanted to say. "You can tell me anything," he assured her in a gentle, fatherly voice. "I promise."

Sami just sat there, staring at the bed. She then took a very deep breath, exhaled, and said, "I want to go home, Papa..."

Fear gripped his heart. "But we—"

"Please!" she interrupted. Then she calmed back down, quietly asking, "Please, Papa, just promise you'll take me home..."

"Okay, but what about—"

"Please!" she interrupted again. "I just miss it, okay. I miss fat lil' Lion! I miss his scratchy tongue and whippy tail—and I miss the way he always purrs me to sleep. And I miss petting Cocoa, with all her fluffy fur! I miss Nana and Aunt Curly! I just want them to play with my hair and paint my nails!"

"Yeah, but—"

Sami slammed her hand on the bed, and lifting her head curiously high, she looked down her nose at Papa, and cried out, "Don't you see??? I just want to go home!!!"

Papa sat there, stunned by what he'd failed to see: Sami's eyes, they weren't just facing downward, they were "sunset"—and he knew what that meant! He'd read about it in a book Dr. Kurt had given him. It's a partial paralysis of the eye, caused by an increased amount of intracranial pressure that drives the eyes downward... and Sami's were setting hard, with her pupils half-hidden under the cover of her lower eyelids. It meant there was a chance Sami was going blind. He was afraid to ask, and he was so angry at himself for failing, yet again, to see the signs and symptoms of Sami's sickness, which made him unable to appreciate (or even to understand) the real reasons for her sadness.

"I promise, Samantha... and I promise I'm listening... and I'm starting to see." His mind raced with fear, and his heart broke with the specter of defeat, but he knew what he had to do. "I promise to take you home, baby. I promise." He was falling apart inside, and he struggled not to cry, so he tried to lighten the conversation, even for a moment. "You'll have to introduce me to this 'little' Lion, though, because our Lion, back at home? He's a total fatso."

Sami chuckled. "He is pretty fat, huh?" It was small and fleeting, but it was the first time Sami laughed in days. "You really mean it, though, Papa? You'll take me home, for real?"

"I won't take you back home, for fake, if that's what you're asking."

"Hmm," Sami hummed with delight. "You're good at that, you know..."

"Oh, yeah, and what is that?"

Sami smiled. "You're good at being a good dad, Papa." Then she pointed to the balloons that the nurse gave her earlier that evening. "I want you to have it, Papa. A gift from me to you, and I want you to keep it forever."

"Your balloons?" he asked.

"Yeah, but mainly the one that says 'Good Job' on it. The heart balloon is still for me."

Papa turned and grabbed a hold of the balloon... a balloon that read, "Get Well!" Papa's heart broke when he read it. He looked at her once again, and he saw that she was sighing again, so he told her how much he loved the "Good Job" balloon, and with a solitary tear streaming down his cheek, he promised to text Mama before bed. "I'll let her know that we're taking you home."

With that, Sami gazed up at the ceiling, and with the prettiest little voice anyone ever heard, she said, "Yaaaaaaaaay," then closed her eyes and faded deep into the drowsy dusk of sleep.

XXVII

THE SWORD OF MANY SORROWS

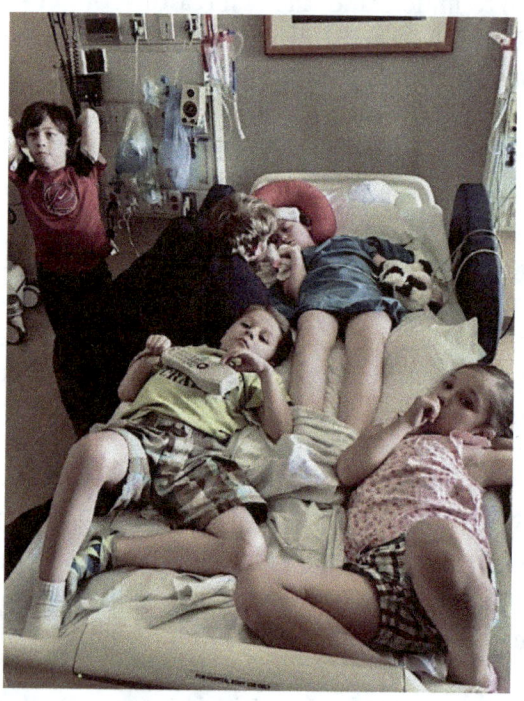

+ 12:36 A.M., JULY 14, 2016 +

CREEEEAAAK... SHUNK

Papa heard the sound of the nurse slowly shutting the door, but his eyes were glued on the balloons. He'd been sitting in silence for nearly two hours... and he still hadn't texted Mama. *What if it's just a big misunderstanding?*

he wondered. *And what if Sami changes her mind? I mean, would she have said that if Mama was here?*

"Oh, Mama..."

He rubbed his thumb over the face of the phone, tapping and untapping the passcode. *It's difficult enough to be devastated,* he thought, *but it's a living hell to be helpless.* Paradoxically enough, Mama was the very definition of helpless right now: fast asleep, in a nice warm bed, surrounded by children, far away from the tragedy in Sami's room.

Papa sat up straight, closed his eyes, and took the deepest breath he could. His lungs filled up like hot air balloons, and his mouth puffed out like chipmunk cheeks. He knew it was naive, even childish, and he could only imagine what he looked like, but there was something about this that felt safe, like a toddler covering their eyes so the monsters can't see them... or that after holding his breath for so long, he'd start seeing stars.

Exhaling was cathartic, but he hated opening his eyes. Then he saw Sami. She was wide awake, but her eyes were still sunset, so he scooched down the bed, just far enough that they could see each other's eyes. "Hey, sleepyhead," Papa said, as he hurried to hide his phone. "You must've been tired, huh? You didn't even wake up for vitals."

But Sami just sat there, staring...

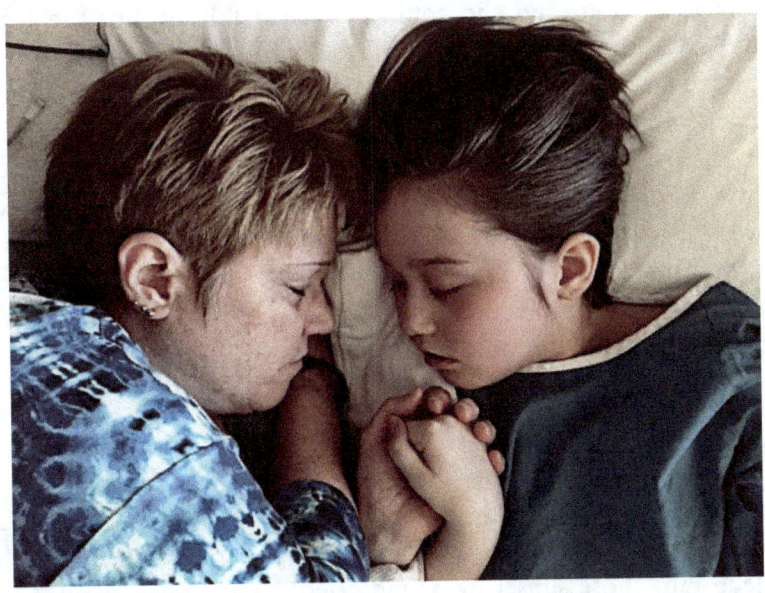

Papa reached for the TV controller, then looked up toward the TV. "I thought you'd wanna stay up and watch something with me," he said. "They don't have *Super Friends* or anything cool like that—trust me, I checked—but they've got reruns of Doctor Who..."

Still... silence.

Papa was so happy, and with a smile on his face, he turned to face Sami... but when he did, he saw that she was crying. And suddenly-

BEEP-BEEP-BEEP-BEEP-BEEP-BEEP-BEEP

Sami's monitor squealed like a siren.

Papa leapt from the bed and frantically pressed the alert button. "Hold on, Samantha!" he cried. "You'll be okay, baby. Someone's comin'! I promise, they'll be here in a minute, okay!" But no one came. He smashed that button so many times—harder and harder and harder—but no one was there to help. He started to panic, and the buzzing was getting louder and louder and louder! "Sami???" he begged, crying frantically. "Can you hear me, baby?!?! Please, you gotta say something, Sam!!! SAMANTHA!!!"

But there was nothing... only silence.

BEEP-BEEP-BEEP-BEEP-BEEP-BEEP-BEEP

Her face was flat, and she couldn't turn her head, but the tears kept streaming, so Papa knew she wasn't dead. Still, he had to find a way to communicate-but how?!?!

That's when he saw her fingers moving. He knelt by the bed and put his finger in the palm of her left hand. "Squeeze once for YES," he said. "And squeeze twice for NO. You got me?" It was a decent idea, and it worked, but not for very long. "Don't go nowhere, Sami!" he shouted. "Just let me think... I just gotta think!" Papa's mind was spiraling out of control, and his heart was cussing at the help that never came. "C'mon, Jeremiah!" he screamed at himself. "You just have to think!!!"

Then, she blinked...

"Of course!" Papa laughed, anxiously. "Precious Moments, baby! Give me those Precious Moments eyes one more time!" Scrambling by her side, he stared deep into those sunset eyes, and cried, "Same rules, okay? One for...

wait, no, that won't work!" The whole idea was so confusing, and he was racing against time, but he knew the changes he had to make. "All right, Sami, listen good!" He held up a peace sign, and said, "Okay, I need you to blink TWO TIMES for YES. You understand me? Blink TWO TIMES for YES!"

blink... blink...

"YES!!!" Papa howled. "Now we're talkin', Sam!" His heart was racing, but he tried to keep cool, and for a moment he felt he was making some progress. More importantly, he knew he was the only person in Sami's world right now, and the last thing she needed was to watch in horror as her dad crumbled into pieces right before her eyes. *There would be plenty of time for that later, anyway.* So he faked a smile and promised to stay by her side. "I'm not going anywhere, sweetheart. I'm with you forever, baby girl!"

Papa's words made Sami cry even harder, and her belly started to tremble...

BEEP-BEEP-BEEP-BEEP-BEEP-BEEP-BEEP

But the blinks were so hard to read, and things were only getting worse! *Did she blink on purpose? Was that half-a-blink?? Is the long pause because she's thinking???* And those long pauses got longer and longer, making it practically impossible to know what she was thinking—or whether Sami was even thinking at all.

Papa ran back to the button "Where are you?!" he growled, slamming his hand against the wall. He thought he might have broken his hand, but he didn't care—Sami was dying, and they were running out of time! And that's when he heard a noise on the other side of the room. He turned to look, so relieved that someone had finally come... but it wasn't the door that made the noise, it was Sami, and she was shaking her foot as hard as she could.

Papa dashed to the end of the bed, then knelt low to the ground, far enough to connect with Sami's sobbing sunset eyes. He grasped a hold of her foot and spread his fingers wide, hoping he wouldn't miss even the slightest shift of her foot. "I need you to listen. Promise me, baby! Promise you'll listen like never before!" Then he pressed her foot to the side of his head, and said, "You gotta PUSH for YES and PULL for NO. Show me, Sam! Show me you can still hear me!"

Sami pushed with her foot...

"Ahhhh!" Papa cheered. But he needed to be certain that Sami's YES was YES and her NO was surely NO, so he decided to do something strange: he tricked her. "Mama said you told her you don't want to watch *Super Friends* anymore? Is that true?"

Sami didn't like that one bit, so she pulled her foot, angrily, toward her...

He laughed a little, admitting his trick, but his mind was flooded with the millions of things he wanted to ask and the billions of things he still had left to say. But the grains of time in the hourglass of Sami's life were running low, and he felt the cold of The Reaper's shadow, as he stood, patiently waiting and whetting his scythe at the foot of the bed.

BEEP-BEEP-BEEP-BEEP-BEEP-BEEP-BEEP

Suddenly, Papa reached over his head and ripped the scythe from The Reaper's hands, then plunged it deep into the heart of his mind, where men divide the wheat of needs from the chaff of human greed. And from that threshing floor, two questions emerged...

"Are you scared, Samantha?" Papa asked in a deadly serious voice.

Sami pulled her foot...

"NO..."

Papa pressed his lips and shook his head, for though his heart was crushed between rocks of hope and despair, he now found himself caught between the wolf and the precipice... and with only one question left. So he gnashed his teeth, and with tears rolling like rivers down his cheeks, he cried, "Do you trust me, Samantha? Do you trust your Papa?"

Sami's foot slid against the side of Papa's face, her soul gliding across the lamb's wool curls of his beard... and his eyes grew wide with fear.

"YES!"

Sami pushed so hard, it practically knocked him over, and a flood of tears poured all over the place... but then her foot went limp, and a dead stare crept over Sami's face.

BEEP-BEEP-BEEP-BEEP-BEEP-BEEP-BZZZZZ

Papa lunged onto the bed, crying out to her, but there was nothing. He shook her as hard as he could, shouting her name over and over again, but, again, there were no movements, no sounds, no nothing at all. Sami was in a coma.

"Help us!" Papa screamed. He wrapped his arms around her, holding her tight, and with the sound of his heartbeat in her ears, Papa cried out, "Please, someone—ANYONE—help us!!!"

Alas, the door swung open, and nurses poured in from every direction, whirling around the room, hustling and bustling and barking their orders, while Papa sat in the eye of the storm, calmly and quietly holding Sami in his arms.

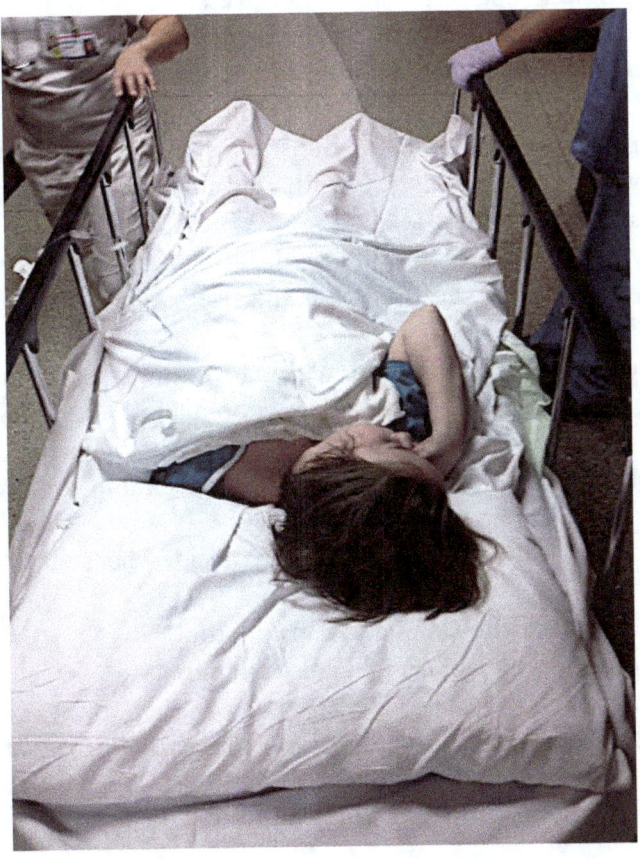

SHE DANCED ME A STORY

✦ 6:02 P.M., JULY 14, 2016 ✦

"Sami's cancer is in her spinal cord..."

Papa heard the words, and he knew he needed to listen, but he had been awake all night, and his mind was still racing, trying like mad to make sense of the scene. There were doctors, maybe eight of them, a mix of men and women, various ages, different faces, all of them vested in their Sunday best and bright white lab coats; but their faces were a blur, lost in a blend of helpless words and hopeless eyes. And there was Mama. She sat there, silently, slumped in her chair, screaming in a whimper, with tears of her worst fears flowing down her flushed-pink cheeks. It was pure agony, and it followed on the heels of fun and games, like a snowball fight with friends that ended in an avalanche of unexpected farewells and bittersweet goodbyes...

"There's nothing we can do, Mr. Bannister," the doctor said.

His words were jolting, but this didn't shock Mama, who still sat there, gazing at the illuminator on the wall, scanning the results of Sami's MRIs. She had a million questions on her mind, but she didn't have the heart to ask them, for she knew they were telling the truth, and there was nothing in all of the world that anyone could do.

"Can't you give her steroids?" Papa pleaded. "What about surgery? There has to be some kind of medication she hasn't tried. And why can't we continue with the radiation?"

He was digging deep, hoping something would stick (anything at all) but the more he begged, the more he saw the doom and the gloom in the room. Mama, her heart shot through with swords of firstborn sorrows, and the doctors, most of them with children at home, imagining the dread of tables being turned and Sami being one of their own.

"Mr. and Mrs. Bannister, you will need to decide where Sami will spend her final days..."

Mama gasped, but she knew, and Papa did too.

"Promise me something, Ang," Papa whimpered.

"Anything... anything at all."

Wiping his tears with his shirt, he asked, "Just promise me you'll never hate me..."

Mama tried to talk, but she was crying too hard, so Papa held her hand, and the two of them wept together, nodding to assure one another that things had to be this way, as it would forever mark the day of that dreadful decision that no parent ever wants to make. With their hearts and minds aligned, they held tight their swords of sorrow, and in one fell swoop, plunged them deep into their hearts, declaring, as one, that their daughter would die at home.

XXVIII

ZOMBIES & QUIET ZONES

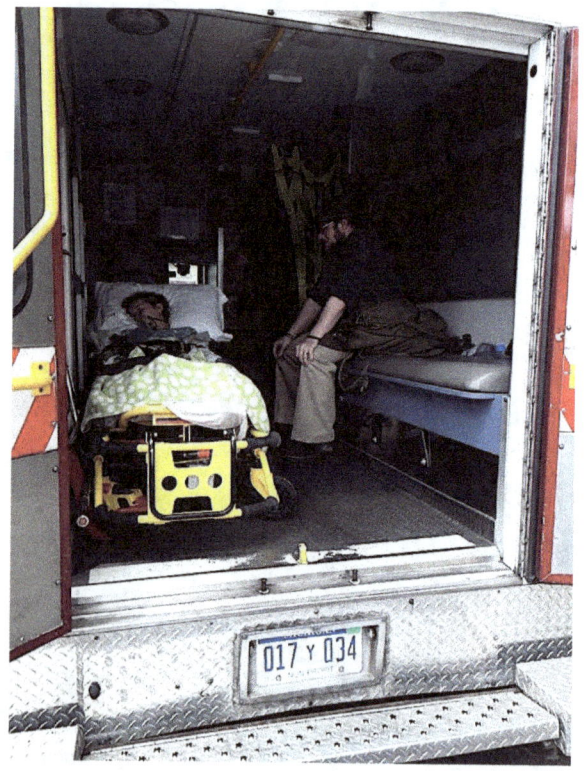

+ The Next Morning—Leaving Beaumont +

Doctors said to be careful, to choose his words wisely, as people in comas may still be able to hear. "They may even be able to sense the emotion in your voice." It was a dreadful contemplation, and Papa didn't know if it was true, or if it was, whether it was true of Sami, but none of that mattered because he had very little to say, at least not now, anyway. Instead, he contented himself with tearful kisses and fingers through her hair, offering only the occasional assurance that, even now, in the silence and darkness of the ambulance, she was brave and beautiful, and that the family would never, ever leave her side.

Outside the ambulance was an entirely other world. The interstate was teeming with traffic, and the lights above the vehicle were spinning round and round, twirling in time with the sound of the sirens. And a motorcade had assembled. Thora from BlackRock came up with the idea, but others were quick to join, including someone named Skull Basher. He was with the U.S. Zombie Outbreak Response Team, and when he heard that Sami was heading home, he called an emergency meeting, where members voted to make Sami a certified Junior Zombie Hunter, then spent the next few hours decking out their suburban with green emergency lights and a litany of encouraging words. It was an attention-grabber, which made it a perfect pace car, but people are weird, and with places to go and people to see, they carried on as though nothing was wrong… at least until two truckers saw what was happening.

They saw the lights and the words on the Zombie car, and their hearts were torn asunder, thinking of their kids back home. It upset them that no one seemed to care, so they pulled up alongside one another, blocking all the traffic coming through from behind them, and with a wave and a blast from their horns, the road home belonged to Sam.

SHE DANCED ME A STORY

People lined up all along the sidewalk, and many held signs, crying out, "We love you, Princess Sami! We love you, #TeamTinyDancer!" Others sat in their cars, watching from a distance, unable to bring themselves to come any closer. And some just sat on the porch, chain-smoking cigarettes that bounced up and down from the quake of their quivering lips. And Dr. Kurt was already inside, while Hospice Care prepared for Sami's arrival.

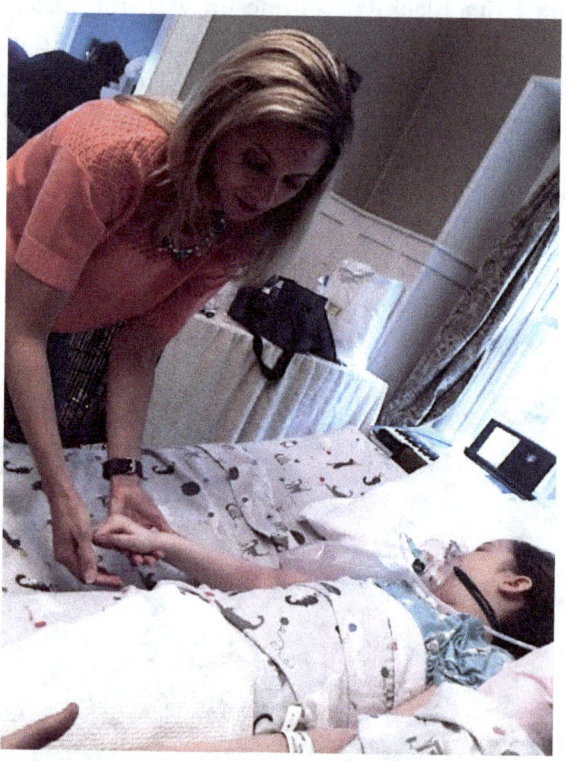

Aunt Curly held the door for the EMTs as they wheeled Sami's bed up the front steps, and Papa led them through the house, while Mama and Nana prepared the room where Sami would die. Cocoa whimpered at the foot of Sami's bed, as Lion licked Sami's hand as hard as he could, and the Hospice Care nurse gave the family their final instructions...

"We have to administer Morphine every three hours?!" Mama cried.

"Sadly, yes, you'll have to, since Sami can't swallow on her own anymore."

"But if she can't swallow, how is she supposed to take the medicine?"

The nurse sighed, then said in a hushed voice, "It's liquid, Angela, and you'll just need to administer it every three hours."

"Every three hours?" Papa asked. "Is hospice gonna help with that?"

"And why can't we have it on a drip through an IV or something?" Mama asked.

The nurse gathered her things, then stood near Sami, gazing down at the sleeping beauty on the bed. "There is no hospice for children in Michigan," she said.

"We'll do it!" Aunt Curly replied. Then she grabbed Nana's hand, saying, "We can do this, right, Mommy?"

Nana wiped her tears and nodded. "There'd be no greater honor in the world." Then she looked at Aunt Curly, and said, "This is God's gift to us."

The nurse talked with them about what their duties would entail. They found a notebook to record every time they administered her medications, checked her vitals, or there were notable changes in her status. They also agreed to take it in shifts, that way the other could get some sleep. And they needed it, too, because the next few days would be some of the busiest of their lives.

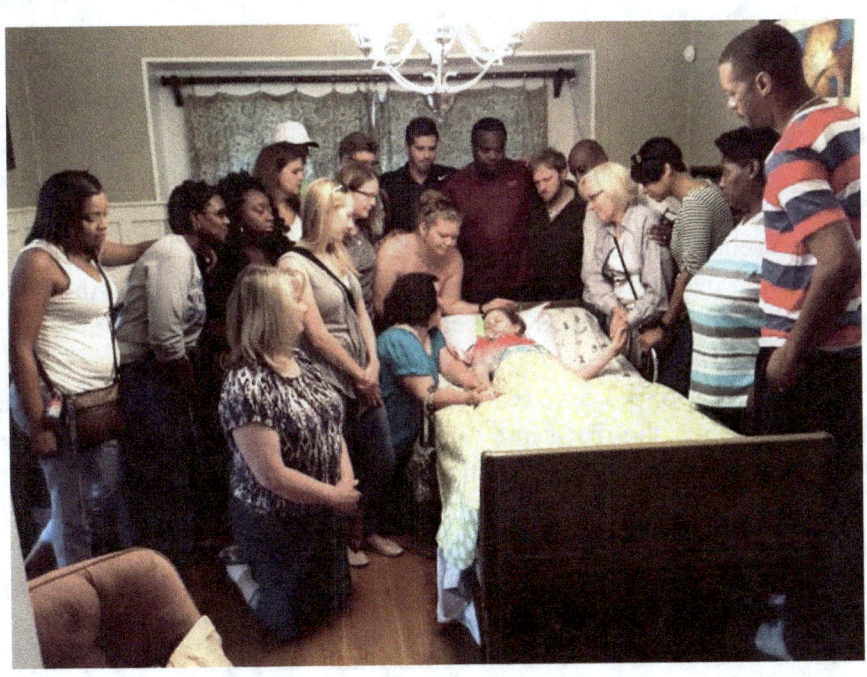

SHE DANCED ME A STORY

People flooded in from all over the place, and all of them had stories to tell. There was a family from Canada, and another from Mexico, as well as some from Tennessee. Papa's dad flew in from California, and Papa's friend from Indiana stayed with them for the duration. Family from Battle Creek helped Mama and the kids, while CFI cooked and delivered the food.

It was a well-oiled machine, and all the parts were constantly moving, but no one rested from morning to night, as hundreds of people made their pilgrimage. The rooms were packed with teachers and students, and the halls were a flurry of kids from the rink, whereas the backyard was flooded with people from BlackRock, and there were no parking spots for blocks!

"I was homeless," one man that came to visit Sami said, "and I'd go into the public library every day. But then I saw this story of a little girl with cancer, and she told people to 'dream bigger thoughts.' I felt so guilty, so ashamed! I'd been through hard times, but then I stopped even trying. Not no more! I got a job a few weeks after that, and now I even got my own apartment."

"I was addicted to heroin," a woman added, "and I was living in a tent in the middle of the woods. It was scary, especially at night, but if I was awake, I was either on heroin or looking for heroin-and I was willing to do anything for my next fix. But I was with my friend one time, and we were scrolling on her phone... that's when I saw Sami, and she was wearing those little rabbit ears, talking about people doing whatever it takes to live the life they want, and doing whatever they gotta do to do the things they love. It made me think about my son. I was all messed up, so the state took him when he was just a baby. I decided right then and there that I'd get him back. No one thought I'd really go back to rehab, and it was definitely the hardest thing in all the world, but I just kept thinking of that little girl and my little boy..." Then she laughed and cried, looking down at the boy in her arms, saying, "And I've been clean for 352 days."

A little boy also spoke up, telling everyone how he'd been a bully. "I even bullied Sami when she first came to school. I hurt people, and I was always getting in trouble. But then she wasn't in school anymore, and our teacher told us she had cancer. I saw her on TV, too, and our principal had us write letters to her in the hospital. It made me feel so bad for all the stuff I did, and not just the mean stuff I did to her, either. I felt bad for all the ways I hurt everyone! And I remember when Sami came back to school. She had to use a wheelchair sometimes, and sometimes she used a crutch, and that made it hard to carry her stuff, so I helped her every day. And whenever kids talked behind her back about the way she walked or held her hand, I always stuck up for her." The memories made him cry. "She never judged me or nothin'—not even one time—and when I asked for forgiveness, she said I changed, and that she forgave me before I even asked her to."

"We were on the verge of divorce," said a couple from Colorado, who'd been listening on the couch. "All we had left were papers to sign. But we saw Sami's story and her hashtags..." Then they looked at their teenage kids, and said, "That night, right at the dinner table, we vowed as a family to make it work; to Never Give Up and Keep On Smiling, no matter what."

The kids cried and wrapped their arms around their parents, saying, "And that was over a year ago! We're still a family because of her!"

People told story after story of how they'd been transformed by a little girl they'd never met, a little girl with bunny ears, battling brain cancer... the little girl now dying in the other room.

They didn't just want to tell their stories, though, they wanted to be heard. And they wanted to hear about the weeks that Papa went silent on social media. He posted the day the doctors said it was over, and again on the Fourth of July, when he told everyone that it was now the fourth quarter, and that if they wanted Sami to live, it would take a successful Hail Mary at Beaumont. After that... radio silence. And it stayed that way for nearly two weeks. People were glued to their screens, checking every time they got a notification, but there was nothing... that was, until now.

Papa told (and retold) the stories of Sami's final weeks to a room that never had fewer than twenty-five people—and whenever one person would leave, two more would come in! This went on for hours, and again the next day, starting when Papa came down the stairs at 7:30 a.m., only to find that there were nearly thirty people standing on the sidewalk, patiently waiting for him to open the doors to Sami's home. But that second day got really overwhelming, and everyone started to wonder if Papa had even eaten—or if he even cared about food anymore. Sami was quickly declining, and people started to worry that they wouldn't get to see her. Some even argued about who was next to go in, so Aunt Curly made a sign that said, "Quiet Zone: Please Wait To Be Let In," and taped it to the door. Everything was put on hold, though, when Emilie, Gladys, and Clara showed up.

SHE DANCED ME A STORY

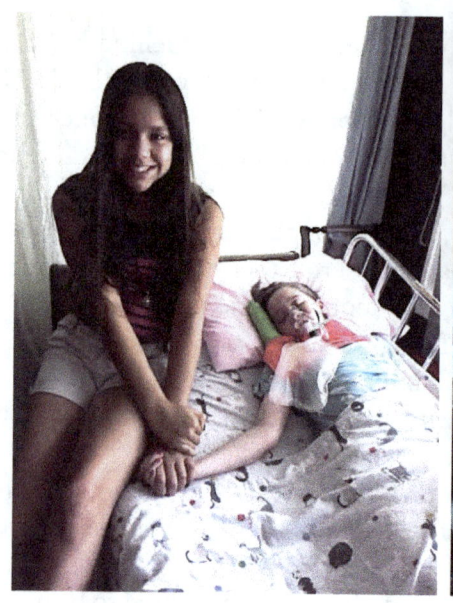 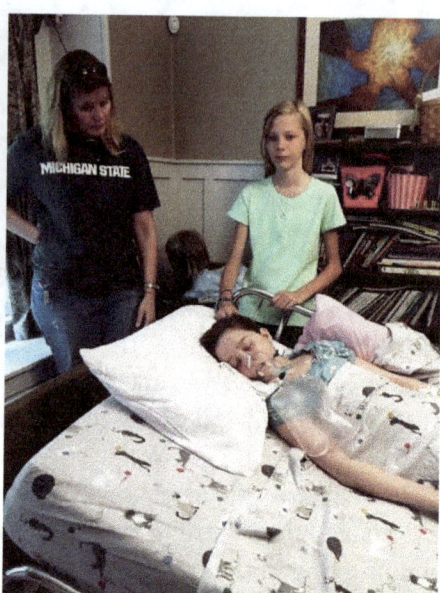

Clara wept, and she was confused, as an evangelist at their church had prayed for Sami's healing. "And it was a powerful prayer!" Clara insisted. "I thought it worked, I thought that's why her cancer went away. I just don't understand, Mr. B." Clara just sat there, shaking her head, repeating the words, "I really thought it worked..."

Emilie stood by Sami's bedside, but she wasn't listening to Clara. She was too busy staring off into the distance, with her hands held out like a beggar, pleading for an answer that no one seemed to have.

And Gladys sat on the bed, holding Sami's hand, crying and smiling, doing her best to keep her composure. She told Sami she was beautiful, and that she was the best friend anyone could ask for. "I love you so much," she said, "and when my family found out what had happened, my dad called the elders of the tribe, and the leaders did something really special... They made you an honorary warrior, Sami. They even gave you a name. You're Anungooqua, which means 'Star Girl.'"

Then she perked up, and said, "Oh, and I brought you some gifts." Gladys went to the door, where she grabbed her purse and something on a hanger that had a bag over it. From her purse she removed little copper cups, a pouch filled with tobacco, and a feather from the tribe. "And there's this," she said as she removed the bag from over the item on a hanger. "It's the dress I wore in our princess competition." Gladys started to cry, saying, "It's really beautiful, and I love it a lot, but I really think you should have it because you're a princess in my heart, and I love you like a sister..." Then she draped her arms over Samantha, and cried aloud, "I really don't want you to go, Samantha! I love you so much!"

Everyone in the room cried as Sami's Peter, James, and John gathered one last time around her bed, weeping on her shoulders, whispering into her ears, and hugging her goodbye.

As the sun set, people started heading out, and when the final one said goodnight, Mama and Papa joined the family in the Quiet Zone. The room was dark, lit only by an oil lamp, and the kids sat on Sami's bed, snuggling up with her beneath the blankets, while Nana played with Sami's hair, and Pa told silly stories of Papa as a kid. Everyone laughed at Papa's expense, but he didn't care—in fact, he felt it was kind of fitting, as those were always Sami's favorite stories. And once or twice, Papa wondered if he'd heard Sami laugh. After a while, the kids fell asleep, so Papa carried them to bed, then he hugged Nana and Curly goodnight, and slowly made his way up to the cold, lonely dark of the attic.

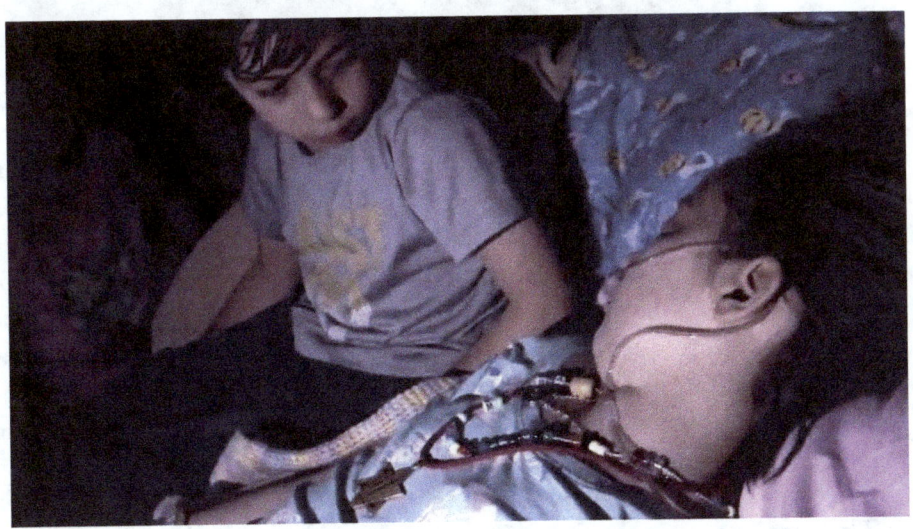

Nana and Curly had work to do, though, and they stuck to their shifts... until around 3 a.m., when Sami stopped breathing.

SHE DANCED ME A STORY

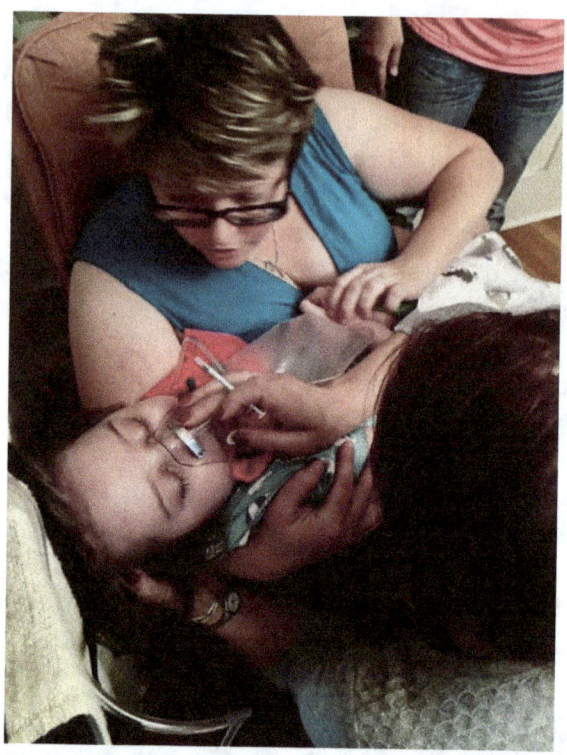

Nana was in the bed with Samantha while Aunt Curly was attempting to sleep on the floor next to them. The absence of Samantha's breathing jolted Aunt Curly awake. She pressed her head against Sami's chest and heard the faint beating of her heart. And then, after what felt like an eternity *gasp* Sami took another breath. The hospice nurse had warned them that Sami's breathing pattern would change, and it quickly became apparent that the episodes of apnea, known as Cheyne Stokes respirations, were going to continue increasing in both frequency and in length. So, they lifted the side rails of the hospital bed and carefully sandwiched themselves on either side of Samantha.

At that point, they decided that continuing to record in the journal was no longer necessary. Curly and Nana spent the next hours peacefully praying, twirling Samantha's hair, and reminiscing.

That small space in the Quiet Zone became a sanctuary that night. Sami's bed was the safest of havens, and her night was filled with all of the love Nana and Curly could offer. And then came one of the stillest and most beautiful mornings...

At 6:53 a.m., in the soft glow of the dawn coming through the windows of the Quiet Zone, the women kissed Sami's cheeks as Aunt Curly's husband took a picture.

The instant of that shutter will forever mark the moment Sami's heart beat for the final time.

"The sweetest girl was just received into paradise, Mommy," Aunt Curly said in a gentle voice. "We just joined in the work of angels and delivering Samantha home." Then, after a few silent, dreamlike moments, the two of them began to weep.

Nana combed out her granddaughter's hair one last time, as Curly finished praying the Orthodox prayers for the departed. They stared out the Quiet Zone window at the TARDIS, lit up in the light of sunrise. Curly dreaded what she had to do next, but she knew that it was hers to do... and that the thirty stairs dividing the Quiet Zone from the cold, lonely dark of the attic would be some of the gravest she would ever ascend.

tap-tap "Jeremiah..." *tap-tap* "Please wake up, Jeremiah... please..."

Papa's eyes snapped open as he sprung up from the ground. He'd only been asleep for a few hours, but he was wide awake now. Curly looked at him, but she didn't have to tell him why she was in the attic, as there was only one reason in all of the world why she'd dare to wake him up like this.

Papa shook his head defiantly, and snarled, "No, Curly! No!! Please, God, no!!!"

The hurt in Curly's heart poured through her eyes as she whimpered the words, "It's time, Jeremiah... your family needs you... downstairs... right now..."

XXIX

ELLE EST BELLE EN BLEU
["She is Beautiful in Blue"]

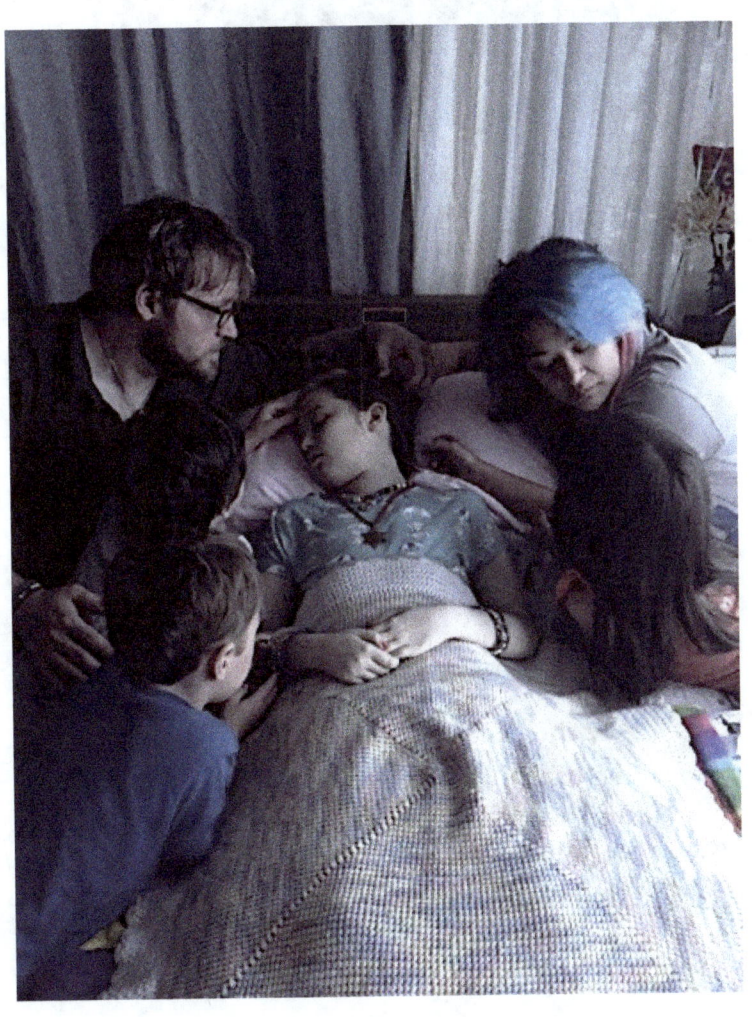

SHE DANCED ME A STORY

Weepers wailed as Papa soared down the steps
— the sound of creaking sighs, a perfect storm —
to a shipwrecked crew, showing their respects
for a life, an artform, defeated by a swarm
of sirens, taunting, "see what lies beneath..."

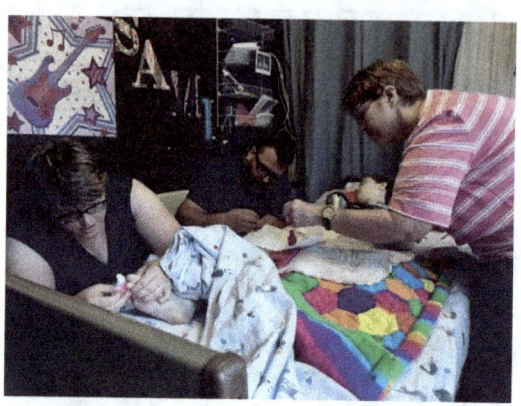

Papa donned Fury like a uniform,
and he wore Rage like a crown wound of wreath.
His parents pled, "Son, you must cast away
Anger's sword, lest it be Hatred ye unsheathe,"
but their pleas were foam & spray
from crashing waves of a downward spiral.
And Fury & Rage, how they longed to stay,
to rip & roar, wreak havoc for a while...
that's until he beheld where Sami laid.

A star, beautiful in blue... with a smile?
His roar, now a sigh—oh, the price he paid
for Anger looking Love right in the eyes.
"Ecce homo!" he cried. "God, see what You've made:
This humble home Your heavy hand has tried—
My wife & kids, now mourning and adrift.
Ah, we laughed & cried... then today, she died."

JEREMIAH T. BANNISTER

She's soft in rigor—ripe for God to sift.
In despair, Papa cried, "Mea Culpa,
Mea maxima culpa!" Then, to lift
her, in his arms, at home in the umbra
of his shadow on her swaddling clothes,
technicolor quilts for freezing tundra.
But memories kindled embers of ice,
for Papa's heart grew cold with every thought—
and the Inferno overwhelmed his paradise.
My girl! She lived & died as she ought!
But this? Abraham's sacrifice? We've lost
an angel! Now where's that Lamb of God I fought?
Life ate the cake, but Death consumed the frost.

SHE DANCED ME A STORY

Aghast, Mama watches, and her heart breaks,
remembering joy and mourning the cost.
Love, why my firstborn? Loss, a mere token?
She nearly screams, "She's only 12-years-old!"
but some words are better left unspoken...

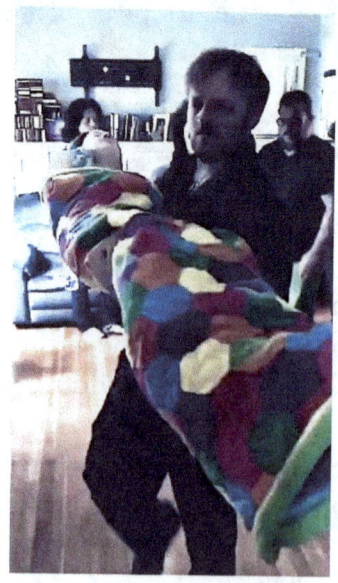

Their friends wept and family rushed to hold
the door for Papa, if only to bless
the bride, asleep, crossing the threshold,
gowned in a dress fitting Papa's noblesse.

JEREMIAH T. BANNISTER

Papa strode in silence, too torn to speak,
much less to face what he ought to caress.
Lo, his heart, it ached! And his arms were weak
as he relived the day Sami almost quit,
when her hope ran dry from an outlook bleak.

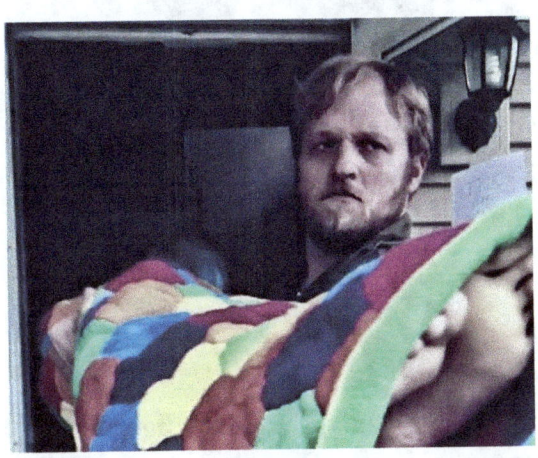

"I give up," she cried, "cancer won't permit
me to be, me with dreams—wild & free!"
"Please, don't!" Papa pled, "You must recommit:
to never quit! To keep smiling! Memento mori!"
But now, with Sami's hearse in view, he sighs,
"As I am, you were. As you are, I'll be."
He longs to die, to join her, fast asleep,
but that, their calling... and this, his destiny:
the hell-bound mission creep of *amor fati*.

Overhead, Brother Sun sang litanies—
painfully pretty songs, of rinks to skate,
art to draw, and *Super Friends*' serenity.
And Wind's warm fingers brushed her hair—*Too late!*
My daughter, she's dead, and I, anointed,
dancing tip-toed the devil's descent to Hate.

SHE DANCED ME A STORY

Toward a gurney, the Gravedigger pointed
to where she'd cast off on the damned River Styx,
where the body and soul are disjointed.
Her family stood with weeping eyes affixed
on Tiny Dancer and her crying clown:
Dead Alive & Dead Inside—a full eclipse.

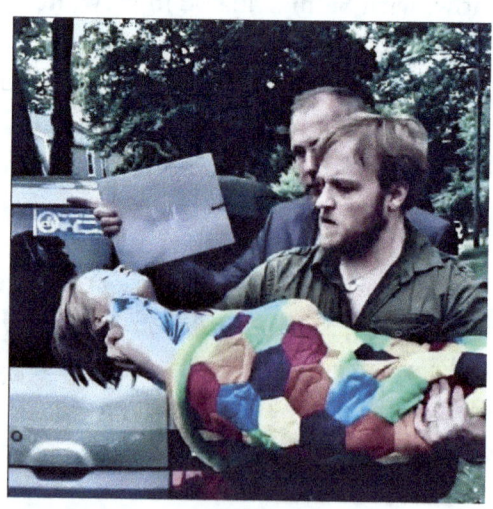

JEREMIAH T. BANNISTER

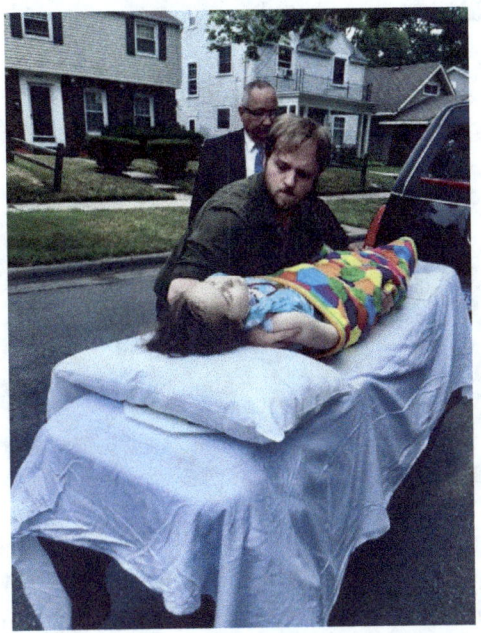

He laid his princess down, kissed her icy crown,
then friends & family baptized her with tears
born of disquiet deep enough to drown.

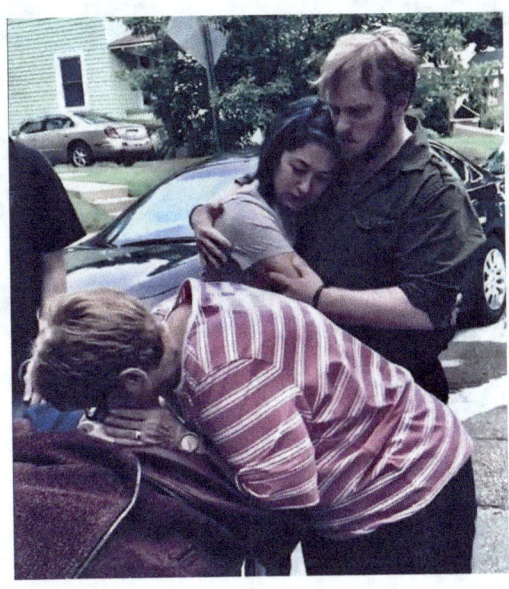

SHE DANCED ME A STORY

The hearse door, now shut, failed to assuage their fears,
so Papa stood tall, saluting a supernova
while the team envisioned coming years,
For, with the catafalque gone, Sami's dance... was over.

section iv:

A WORLD WITHOUT END

**THE BITTERSWEET:
+ LIFE & DEATH +**

XXX

BIRTHDAY CANDLES AT A FUNERAL

+ Outside Fountain Street Church +

"ARE YOU REALLY GONNA GIVE THAT HEARSE A TICKET?"

The scene outside the church was tumultuous, with people screaming and shouting at a parking inspector.

"A 12-year-old girl died of brain cancer!"

"Her casket is inside the church right now!"

"And her funeral is supposed to start in five minutes!"

Papa heard the whole thing, and some people took pictures and video, especially when the officer shrugged a "meh" before ticketing Sami's hearse. The whole thing was outrageous.

It was total pandemonium, and it bordered on bursting into a full-blown mosh pit—which, to be honest, Papa felt might be fitting, maybe even appropriate given the circumstances—but he didn't really care. In fact, he wasn't even *there*, for his eyes were locked on the charcoal skies lurking along the horizon line. He feared it would form a dreadful storm, even a wicked twister... and he worried it was destined for them.

+ Inside Fountain Street Church +

Kids in costumes ran through the halls while their parents reminisced, and pall bearers prepared the procession of Sami's casket. The pastor didn't like the idea, but Papa had the final say, and that's the way he wanted it. Sure, it was a little old-fashioned, but Papa felt it was fitting, even appropriate, especially in a church like Fountain Street. It was neo-Romanesque, with tapestries, mosaics, and stained-glass windows all around. And with Byzantine-styled effigies and Mercer-tiled floors, it was a beautiful cloud of witnesses, featuring the likes of Plato, Lincoln, Jefferson, and Darwin, even Erasmus and Leonardo da Vinci. It seemed well-suited for Sami's funeral, even for Papa's eulogy, which echoed the sentiments felt at Fountain Street nearly 100 years before, when Alfred Wishart and Clarence Darrow sparred over whether "belief in a general purpose of the universe is rational and justified." From where Papa stood, it still seemed like both sides had a point.

The organ peeled like thunder, and people stood to their feet as bearers carried Sami's casket down the aisle. It was white, graffitied with colorful notes, names, and drawings from many of those who knew her, and it was covered in stargazer lilies. Through the throng of people, Mama saw Papa's smile and his fist raised high in the air. She couldn't help but cry, for in that moment, Mama beheld the symbols that their family worked so hard to provide. They envisioned a wedding—and it felt like one too—when subjects would stand to honor the virgin vested in wedding-day white, with her father, the King, right by her side, while her Queen Mother wept to be letting her go.

Singers sang of thorns and roses, and people wept as minstrels plucked their heartstrings, and poets preached such pretty things, telling tales of days of dancing and nights under comet-covered skies. And the tears, they rained, when Papa vented his pain before them all in eulogy, revealing a litany of bittersweet mysteries shrouded by the veil of Sami's final days. His heart danced on the edge of an active volcano, and the heat of his words caused a clamor, like an old-time revival, with people weeping and wailing in the pews. Some were so sad, they fled the room, even if only to breathe! And when the eulogy ended, the bearers returned to take hold of the poles alongside Sami's casket, and walked toward the back of the church, lamenting the fact that every step brought their Tiny Dancer one step closer to that ticketed hearse that was parked outside, patiently awaiting her arrival...

Row after row stood to their feet as Sami passed them by. Some bowed, others saluted, and everyone was wiping their tears as Thora sang the farewell song from BlackRock:

Kind kin and companions, please join in this rhyme,
To cry out with voices in chorus with mine!
And raise your glass to our fallen friend,
As we may or might never hail our Princess again!

As she was singing, nearly thirty people stood from their seats to make their stand beside her. There were Mad Vikings, peasants, pirates, and dukes, even queens in royal blue. With tears in their eyes, they stomped their feet to the ground, raised their goblets high for one last toast, and sang with all of their might:

Sami's boat lies at anchor, she is ready to dock.
I bid her safe sailing, kept safe from the rocks!
And if again I greet her, on bended knee,
I'll sing in praise of her kindness to me...

And no sooner had the bearers left the building when thunder crashed, lightning cracked, and sheets of celestial sorrow rained down from heaven!

+++

Everyone then gathered in the Fellowship Hall, where the kids scampered 'round, and a DJ played consoling music for those in mourning. It was beautifully tragic, and everyone wanted to talk to Papa, but something kept him preoccupied, and he was constantly glancing around. That was until something caught his attention, and with little more than a nod, he slunk from his seat and snuck to the stage, where he signaled to everyone that he had something to say...

"Mama," he said, with his hand outstretched. "I need you up here with me."

Mama was stunned by the sudden (and unwanted) attention, and she had a sneaking suspicion that Papa had something up his sleeve, but she wasn't one to make a scene, so she stood from her chair and walked toward Papa at the front of the room. But no sooner had she reached him when—

CLICK

The room went dark, with the only light now coming from a disco ball shining brightly overhead. It startled her, and she looked, nervously, around the room, but all she could see were the silhouettes of friends and family sitting in their seats.

"What are you doing?" she whispered, hoping no one would hear her. But she spoke straight into the mic, and everyone started laughing. The whole thing was embarrassing, and she just wanted to run, to get away and hide from this miserable, God-forsaken day.

... That was, until she looked at Papa.

He was smiling, but the bags beneath his eyes were black with lack of sleep, and his unkempt hair was wet with sweat. It was a good front, but his heart cried out through those bright blue eyes: he was tired and broken, and in his deepest moment of need, his heart reached out for her. She wanted to hug him, just to cry into his chest, but before she could make a move, Papa knelt down on one knee. His chin quivered, and with tears welling up in his eyes, he told her he was sorry. "I hate that things turned out this way, and I wouldn't wish a single bit of it on my worst enemy!" Then he took a hold of her hand. "But it's something we had to do, so I'm just glad I had to go through it with you." Mama started to cry, and she tugged on his hands, hoping he'd stand up, but he still had something to say.

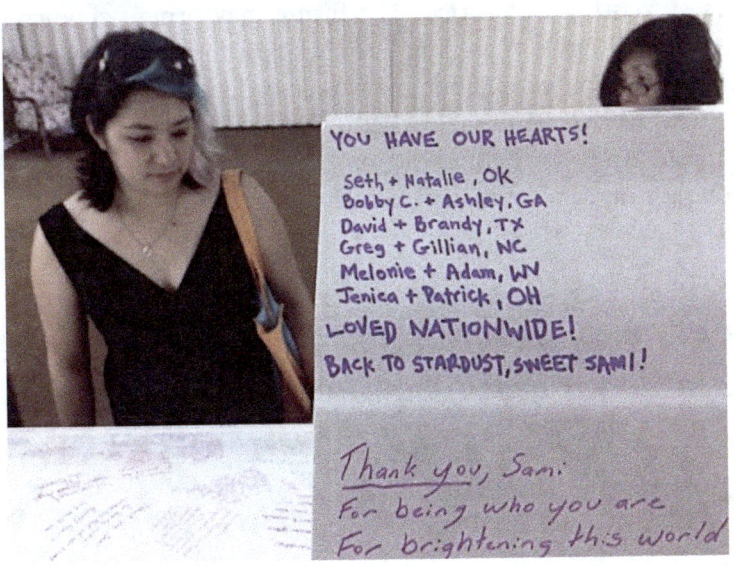

"And I just wish Sami's funeral didn't have to be on your birthday..." People shuddered at the thought, and gasps were heard around the room. Hardly anyone knew, but Papa thought about it the entire time. "Sami's death has been hard on so many people, but you?!?! You're her Mama—and she was your first-born! She'd known you from the moment of her conception, and she cried for you when she was born, loving nothing more than to rest in your arms. And the things you did for her when she needed you most—those are things that legends and dreams are made of..."

"... But now, for the rest of your life, your birthday will be bittersweet." Then he stood to his feet and wiped the tears from her eyes. "And that's why I want to promise you—right here, right now—that I'll always love you. I'll love you 'til the day I die, Angela Lee. And the kids and I mean it when we say that the Bannister family will always be #TeamTinyDancer."

"Forever and ever!" someone shouted.

A few Christians even cried, "Amen!"

And friends and family rose to their feet for a standing ovation.

Then, when the clapping came to an end, everyone sang *Happy Birthday* to Mama, and the DJ dedicated a dance to the family.

It didn't take long for others to join them, and as fast as the room went quiet and black, it came back to life, lit up by the lights of love and laughter. There were kids in costumes, giggling and buzzing about, and adults raised their glasses, toasting to whatever the future may bring, while couples held hands and danced together, gazing into those infinite moments that glistened in the pupils of their eyes. And the Bannister kids ran up to their parents, wrapping their arms around their waists, where they swung and swayed as one with the music. And, yet, behind the guise of their smiling eyes was the sound of a sorrowful song, and lyrics that lamented aloud:

Here's a health to our Princess, we served her so well
—For kindness and laughter, no girl could excel!
She smiled at death, now her soul flies free
—But there's no family as heartbroken as we...

JEREMIAH T. BANNISTER

XXXI

TO LIVE (AND DIE)
[Beneath the Waves]

+ North Carolina—One Month After the Funeral +

    The wind blew through Teresa's hair, causing it to fly in front of her face, but she could still see Papa standing at the ocean's edge, gazing at the waves that rolled beneath the sunset. He'd been walking up and down the beach for over an hour, but he kept to himself, and he'd barely said a word.
    "Do you guys think Papa's gonna be okay?" she asked.

Athan dusted some sand from a shell, then squinted his eyes to see what Papa was doing. "Yeah, he's fine," Athan replied. "He's just sad cuz of Sami."

Teresa scrunched her nose, unsatisfied with Athan's answer. "We're all sad, though, ya know, but he's not even talking to anyone or nothing."

"Don't judge him about it," Ambrose said.

"I'm not judging Papa!" Teresa scoffed, angrily. "I love him just like you guys, and I—"

"No, no—" Ambrose interrupted, "I wasn't trying to say that in a mean way or anything. I'm just saying that he's trying hard to do his best, so we just gotta be patient, that's all."

"Mama and Papa did everything they could," Athan said as he dropped a pile of shells and rocks to the ground. Kneeling, he started writing something in the sand, then he looked at a cracked seashell in his hand, saying, "But now Sami's gone, and that's basically the worst thing that could ever happen to a mom and dad, so their hearts are just broken really bad..."

Teresa tucked her hair behind her ear, then watched as Papa walked further away from the group. "I just hate how he looks so sad all the time."

Ambrose raised a piece of quartz near his eye, then peered through it, saying, "Trust me, I know how sad he is." Then he skipped the quartz as hard as he could, watching as it bounced atop the waves, and when it finally dropped into the ocean, he sighed, "I hear him cry through the vents every night."

+ At the Shoreline of the Atlantic +

The tide flowed over Papa's feet, splashing against his ankles like waves crash against the rocks, and he could feel the sand shift beneath his soles as the tide dragged the waters back to sea.

The weeks before and after Sami's death took a toll on the family. The gravity of childhood cancer pulled hard on almost every area of their lives. They'd lived in Sami's orbit for sixteen months, so her death wasn't just tragic, it was cataclysmic. Even in the midst of an enormous outpouring of support, the family was spiraling, unhinged and unmoored through the deep space of life after death. That's a dangerous place to be, and for more reasons than may be obvious, as it is there, in the chaotic void caused by the loss of a child, that marriages and families often fall apart.

One of Papa's friends, Greg, thought it might be good for the gang to get away, to head out-of-state for some much-needed R&R. He was one of the few Atheists who knew that Papa was more conservative and traditional than most Atheists. Though they often disagreed—debating late into the night—he loved the family, and Sami had transformed his life, even inspiring him to pursue his dream of becoming a pilot.

He and his fiancé opened their home near North Topsail, North Carolina, to #TeamTinyDancer and Sami's entourage from Reason Rally. Some of the family's favorite friends were there, so this trip was exactly what all of them needed.

Papa was conflicted, though. On the one hand, he was a very vocal unbeliever, the host of an Atheist radio show, and a board member for one of the largest secular non-profits in Michigan. So, he was neck-deep in a very secular humanist Atheist community, and Sami's death seemed to have cemented his skepticism. Yet, on the other hand, he was a family man with many traditional values. No matter how much he lashed out against God, he couldn't shake the way Sami challenged his Doubt, and he hated the possibility that she was now nothing more than bones in the ground, food for worms and creeping things.

So much of Papa's life had been consumed by ruminations regarding death and destruction, even despair. The devil on his shoulder chalked it up as having been born a boy, but that devil is a liar, and Hades hungered for men and women alike-even little children like Sami. That devil wasn't entirely wrong, as Papa's fear of (and fascination with) death probably began before he cut his teeth. But barring the whole who, what, where, when, and why of how it all began, this much may be said as a matter of fact: most of his days had been devoted to a dialogue (and Dionysian dance) with Death.

It wasn't all doom and gloom, though. There were Kairos moments, transcendent through and through—and curiously enough, many of them took place near beautiful bodies of water. Papa returned to these memories all throughout his life, always trying to retrace where he was while being who he'd been... and whom he'd been with while he was there...

... and that's what he was doing on the shores of North Topsail.

He recalled standing near a rail at Seattle's Elliott Bay, where he first observed the power and majesty of the Pugit Sound. The rhythmic back-and-forth of container and supply ships was dreadfully delightful, even hypnotic, as the boats swayed from port to starboard like a mother rocking her baby to sleep. He remembered the stroll on the boardwalk of the Mermaid Quay at Cardiff Bay, where the winter winds of Wales cut across the crashing waves, conjoining in chorus to create a truly serendipitous symphony of sound. He re-envisioned that dreary day with Sami in New York Harbor, as they saluted Lady Liberty from the deck of a water taxi sailing all too fast and far too slow. And here, with his family, mourning on the Carolinian shoreline, he watched as whitecaps danced in the distance. He was reminded of the snow-covered peaks of Wyoming's ancient and awe-inspiring Grand Tetons reflecting off the calm and quiet waters of Lake Solitude. But, as it was with Sami on the Jubilee Bridge overlooking the River Thames, he was hit by an undeniable truth. For it was then, while honing in on the coastal horizon of North Topsail, that he felt the salty sea splash between his toes... gently reassuring him that, soon enough, everything will come to an end, leaving little more than a high-water mark, rapidly fading in the wake of its return from whence it came.

To dread the deep and the dark.
To worry over the winds and the waves.
To lose themselves in the lullabies of life and liberty.
That Hades, in time, swallows heathens and heroes alike.
Death was a diabolical dirge, deserving to be despised... defied...

... and, if at all possible, to be defeated.

These were terrible truths seen in the sea, but he saw them through the rose-colored glass of his godlessness, and like the distant storm looming over the Atlantic, Sami's death had always been in view, always been approaching, yet seemingly safe and far away... until, alas, that dreadful day when, for Sami, the scythe of Death finally came.

"What do you see out there?" Mama said as she laced her fingers through his.

He didn't see her coming, but he was glad that she was there, and his heart melted when she rested her head on his shoulder. "A bunch of S-words," he replied. "Stuff like Sami... the sea... sand... the saints—"

"Saints?" Mama asked.

"Well, St. Cyprian, but his name starts with a C, so I just ran with saints." Then Papa scratched his head, and said, "There's another guy too, but his name is really weird, and I always forget how to pronounce it."

"What possessed you to think of stuff like that?" Mama asked.

"Just some things they said, I guess. I dunno, like, the whole idea of being born with a halter around our neck, that every step brings us closer to death, and that all the power in the world couldn't convince the Reaper to spare us even an hour."

"Wow," Mama exclaimed, "that's pretty dark stuff, sweetheart..."

Papa sighed, and with his eyes set on the horizon, he replied, "Yeah... pretty dark stuff..." Truth is, he could've said other S-words like sin, salvation, sanctum, and sarcophagus, or even sentimental, but for nearly six years, their world was supposed to be one of science and secular-humanism. All the religiosity seemed kind of silly... or at least it would have, were Sami still alive, and if there hadn't been a scary storm hovering over the horizon. Part of him wondered if it was the same storm as the one he saw at Sami's funeral. It seemed to be following them across the country, and he couldn't shake the feeling that it was slowly closing in on him and his family.

"Well, no more sulking," Mama said, patting him on the chest. Then she took his hand and led him back toward the bonfire, where his kids had been patiently waiting...

+ With the Kids—Near the Bonfire +

"SURPRISE!" the kids shouted as they ran out to greet them.

"Whoa!" Papa laughed, almost getting knocked over by the kids, who were smothering him with hugs and kisses. "You guys are acting like you haven't seen me in forever!"

Teresa hugged him with all her might, and with a huge smile on her face, she said, "That's because we made a present for you."

"Really?" Papa said. "You guys made a present for me?"

"Technically, it was mostly me," Athan boasted, "but I guess they helped a little bit."

"No," Teresa scoffed, angrily, as she led Papa across the beach. "We helped a lot, you little liar! Plus, Ambrose did one part all by himself."

Then they stopped...

Papa glanced around, wondering why he was there, but then he looked to the ground and saw something that made him cry. There, written with rocks collected from the beach, were the words:

#TeamTinyDancerFOREVER

"Adding the 'FOREVER' was Ambrose's idea," Mama said with a smile.

Papa just stood there, shocked and in awe of all they'd done. "What made you think of that?" Papa asked, wiping the tears from his face.

"Well, you used to always say we were in Sami's orbit, and I loved the way that looked in my mind when I thought about it. But since Sami died, you don't say that anymore..."

Papa sighed, "I know, bro. It's just hard, ya know..."

"Well, you asked a question the day after Sami died, and I've thought about it a lot ever since."

"What question was that?" Papa asked.

"You asked me, 'What are we now? Who are we now that Sami is gone?'" Then Ambrose smiled and pointed toward the ground. "Well, that is exactly what we are: #TeamTinyDancerFOREVER."

Papa gazed at them, blown away by the joy radiating from their faces. And for the first time in weeks, Papa was happy too. But then a frown came over his face. "I dunno," he said, nervously shaking his head. "Something just doesn't seem right." The kids panicked, and Ambrose almost cried when Papa knelt to the ground. And with one last look around, Papa pressed his hand into the sand. "There, that's more like it." Then he looked at his kids, and with a mischievous smirk on his face, he said, "Now, if only I could find four more hands, I think it would be perfect."

The kids laughed a sigh of relief, then raced to Papa, where each of them pressed their little hands into the sand. Each of them, with tears in their eyes, pressed as hard as they could, allowing the emotions they'd stored inside to flow from their hands like the tide. And when they were done, they sat by the fire, crying, laughing, and listening to Papa strum on a six-string banjo. The strings jangled aloud with heartfelt vows to accept whatever kind of death life was pleased to send them, with all of its pains, penalties, and sorrows... so long as through it all, they remained united as one, always revolving in Sami's orbit, as #TeamTinyDancerFOREVER.

As the night wound down, the wind picked up, and lightning struck over the sea. Mama hurried to put out the fire while the kids packed their bags, and Papa ran to grab the van. It was a long drive back to where they were staying, but with the smoke of the smoldering fire still in view, the rain began to pour, and the tides roared, sweeping over the family's hands in the sand. Each ebb and flow took more and more, until, alas, there remained only permanent things… the name of a family… written in stones.

Tempus Fugit
[IN THE FOG OF WAR]
Part IV of IV

+ Upward Spiral Turnpike—Ride Home after the Rink +

55 MPH...

The drive home from the rink was difficult, but the reasons ran much deeper than the pain in Papa's back. He thought of those things that led him there—the very forces that threw him to the ground. He knew them well, for they had haunted him all year, serving as gentle reminders that he'd been living a lie, or at least the farce of a well-intended facade. Worst of all, it centered around one tricky little question:

JEREMIAH T. BANNISTER

"Do you still *feel* Sami, Jeremiah?"

60 MPH...

Kelly asked it in a livestream shortly after Sami's death, and at that time, Papa replied, "Of course I do. I've got her writings and all her artwork, too. Not a day goes by where someone doesn't share some picture or video of her. Some people even have stories I've never heard—and it's these things, these million pieces of her, that keep Sami alive to me." But he knew full-well that he was wrong, and though he tried, he couldn't hide from the questions and quandaries that tore at his heart.

And that is why he was alone, why he had driven out to the Fun Spot, and why he had asked the deejay to play *Tiny Dancer*. He knew he would cry, but he had to let it out, and he knew of no better place in all the world than Sami's Garden of Eden.

Tears had poured down his face, and his eyes began to burn. Papa had soared like the wind, skating faster than he'd ever skated before, and he wept aloud as he weaved and wound his way throughout the crowd. He was a tempest—within and without—and for a minute he felt on top of the world, but all of that changed the moment he saw Sami's face on the floor.

Her smile, her eyes, her long flowing hair—all of it was there—and her body floated like a phantom in the glistening glare of lights whirling atop the wax of the maple floor. He was terrified but also inspired, and he loved the way she made him feel so playful, without a care. He chased her, pushing faster and faster—as fast as he could—surging to the sounds of the song. But round and round and round they went, and no matter the crazy and dangerous things he was ready and willing to do, it seemed as though she was always and forever just barely beyond his reach.

When Elton John sang the final chorus, Sami's hands reached through the floor! It intrigued him, and he was tempted to take a dive face-first into her arms, but he only dared to reach out his hand, straining to connect with the living dead. And just as their fingers were about to touch, a little girl with golden blades swerved in front of him—

CLICK-CLACK-CRACK!!

Papa had slipped and fallen to his back on the floor—

70 MPH...

Now, on the narrow stretch of a country road leading to Upward Spiral Turnpike, Papa rolled down his windows, listening to the raucous sound of the silence in the wind. He was rattled out of his mind, and the vision at the rink caused his whole body to shake. With the steep and winding road ahead, Papa squeezed the steering wheel, and pressed the pedal to the metal. Wind poured through the windows from every direction, swirling around him like a tornado. Papers from his backpack whirled through the air and out the windows as his hair flew in front of his face. And the faster he drove, the faster he felt himself losing control.

75 MPH...

+ Back in the Quiet Zone +

The balloons in the room grazed against the ground, and the sound scratched like nails on a chalkboard—a slate, once cluttered with verdicts and vows, now dusty from erasures and time. The pain was overbearing, and Papa trembled in fear, but he knew that the end was near, even if the battle had only begun. Lightning cracked as he grit his teeth and winds beat against the house when he stood to his feet, yet there he was, with head raised high and shoulders squared, watching as the last breaths of life bled from the balloons. And once it was done, he opened the door to death and despair, unleashing the beast of WAR—ever-hidden but always there, crouching, quietly and in wait, at that station of life where love and loss kissed and waved, then bid farewell, and parted separate ways.

WAR flashed its talons, and blood dripped from its fangs as it lunged through the air—crushing and clawing, gashing and gorging, pulverizing Papa for two whole weeks! And he cried, aloud, "No mercy, Sami! No mercy!" Then he collapsed to his knees, where he was mauled by the memories—so many feats of astounding betrayals and vengeance arising from the ashes of defeat!

JEREMIAH T. BANNISTER

+ Back in the Upward Spiral +

When the speedometer hit 80 mph, everything went haywire. Papa was frantic, thrashing about like a rabid wolverine, slamming his hands like sledgehammers on the steering wheel. His breathing was erratic, and he was on the verge of a panic attack, but he was sick and tired of pretending—and he just couldn't live the lie anymore. Something had to give—anything at all—and it was here something happened that hadn't happened in years...

Papa Prayed.

"God! Where are you? Are you even there?? Do you even care??? Tell me she's not just rotting six feet deep! Promise she's more than little bones buried like a treasure chest in the ground!" He shook his head furiously, and his body rocked violently. "I can't believe it—I won't! Death is for chumps—for sinners like me—but for Sami? She was a saint!"

Spit splattered on the windshield as foam flew from his mouth, and his eyes bulged out of his head. The van veered back and forth on the road as he flailed and thrashed about. He was like a man in the throes of death, but the turns were getting tighter, and he was drifting dangerously close to the edge of the road on the mountainous Upward Spiral.

"I hate myself—I get what I deserve. But you? You believed my every word! And why? Because you said I never lied! Oh, Samantha, I'm a labyrinth of lies, and I fake it all the time, swearing up and down, 'Oh, I'm good. Oh, I'm fine.' But I'm not—it's all a lie! And I wear a fake smile, like some crying clown, but I'm a wigwam of sin always caving in, and my heart is full of hate. Vanity after vanity—nothin' but a life of dirty rotten lies!"

His vision bled coxcomb red, and the moon melted like butter as stars rained down from the sky, lighting up the landscape with fields of fire and mushroom clouds of brimstone.

He growled and shouted to heaven. "Tear away what's gotta go! Take out what shouldn't be there! I don't care if it hurts—I want it to kill me—just tell me the truth—O God, let me know it's You! Tear my guts out, smash me to pieces—do whatever you gotta do. Just promise you'll never heal my lonely broken heart..."

85 MPH...

Within days, Papa's world was falling apart. Trials and tribulations seemed to come out of nowhere, hitting him from every direction like cars at a Demolition Derby, each one stripping away, piece by piece, the work he had dedicated his life to.

"What's wrong with you?!" screamed the outraged mobs.
"The board decided you're done at CFI, Jeremiah."
"I am not friends with old-fashioned freaks!"
"Jeremiah, Teresa is getting held back..."
"Your sons are struggling emotionally..."
"We've canceled your 9/11 speech about Sami."
"Effective immediately: your radio show is off the air."
"Team Tiny Dancer is canceled... canceled... canceled!!!"

"AUNT CURLY HAS TERMINAL CANCER!".

A Great Horned Owl flew high overhead, then swooped down to glide beside the van. It peered through the window, watching with pity as Papa shamed himself to pieces. At 90 mph, Papa saw a sign for the end of this spiraling toll road, and with a death wish in his smile, he shifted into overdrive.

At 95 mph, Papa reached the top, and there, he saw the end. It was dreadful, like a drawbridge or ramp with nothing on the other side. He thought about turning around to wind back down the hill, but there was something alluring about the clouds and open air, about the mystery ahead. And though he couldn't see where his van would land, he felt convinced that, somehow, someway, he'd be okay. And with his world in flames, he felt he had nothing more to lose. So, he took a deep breath, squinted his eyes, and imagined the family, full of life, and cancer-free. Then he squeezed the wheel as hard as he could, and, pressing the pedal of his van to the metal, he shouted with all his might:

"Save me, Sami Lee!"

His wheels kissed and waved goodbye to the world below as the van flew over the hill. For a moment he felt like the Dukes of Hazzard, flying in a freefall, alive and adrift in an endless sea of tranquility. But it was there in midair that he saw something strange in the distance. And as the van sped toward the ground, Papa pumped his brakes, but all for naught, and he feared he'd collide with whatever was below. Then, when the van finally slammed on the ground, Papa smashed his feet on the brakes, and—

SHE DANCED ME A STORY

95 – 75 – 45 – 25 – 10 –

His wheels squealed as they skid down the street, leaving long black trails under plumes of smoke billowing in his wake. And the smell of burning rubber filled the air as the van came to a stop. Papa sat there, quiet and still as a statue with its eyes wide shut, sensing the new reality 'round about him...

The violent winds didn't whirl through the car anymore, and the noisy papers were on the floor. The fire that burned hot on his face was replaced by a springtime chill, and the sounds of stars crashing to the earth were replaced by the hoot of a Great Horned Owl and the whisper of leaves in the breeze. He opened his eyes to see what had scared him, but only a moment too late, for all he saw were the comb-like serrations of the horned owl's pinions racing up and out of view. His heart became sad, but only until his eyes caught sight of the street sign, which placed him and his overheating minivan at the intersection of Confession and Catharsis...

+ Back in the Quiet Zone +

These memories played like movies on the film of his smoke, reeling, rewinding, and replaying repeatedly for months on-end. The life they'd made, the story that Sami danced for him, crumbled like a sandcastle in the palm of his hands. All that work, all that time, gone in the blink of an eye. It felt so unreal—almost otherworldly—to be boxing at shadows and chasing the wind. But the harder he fought, the less he would win, and he always lost even more in the end.

Then came the comfort of quiet and calm, when the fog finally faded away, and though his world had been upended, he still had those balloons, and he knew his family was on their way. So, he grabbed the balloons, then folded them like an American flag, securing them as a soldier at retreat, and with his cane squeezed tightly in his hand, Papa marched with a limp, duty-bound to descend, deflated from defeat, into the blinding light of darkness at the bottom of the basement stairs.

Moments later, Mama and the kids walked through the door, and they were excited to see Papa, so they ran toward the sound of the Song of the Siren, but when they got to the door of Papa's office, they discovered that he was nowhere to be found.

"Really, baby?" Mama said as she entered his room. She lifted the needle from off the record, and her nose scrunched in disgust at the smell of marijuana, so she knew that Papa had been there… and that he was sad. She'd seen the calendar, though, earlier in the day, so she knew the reason why. Then, just as she turned to leave the room, she saw Papa's book, opened and face-down on the floor, so she picked it up, and there, where Papa left off, she beheld the upward spiral of Mount Purgatorio, as well as a handwritten letter, that read:

Has it really been ONE YEAR since the day you died?!?! O my, Samantha Lee, how time flies (in the fog of war) …

XXXII

THE SAVING SOLITUDE OF SILENCE

+ Moments Later—After Leaving the Quiet Zone +

The click from Papa's flip of the switch at the bottom of the basement stairs shot through the room, followed by the buzzing surge of electric light. The house was old, and the bulbs were too, so they flashed and flickered a little, but Papa didn't mind. In fact, he preferred it. There was something fitting about being depressed in a dimly lit dungeon. And he appreciated the symbolism, as if light were fighting the tides of wear and tear, and that its aim was not only to overcome the gloom, but to eradicate the darkness, exorcizing it through absorption, leaving something in its stead that was better and brighter than the dark night of the soul before.

All around him were fragments of his favorite and least favorite things. There were stacks of books, family photos, and folders filled with his written work, as well as a bunch of boxes, each of them packed with an enormous assortment of clutter and keepsakes. It was daunting, and his heart scampered for any excuse to turn back and walk away, but the books gave him looks and the boxes cried out:

There's a ton of work—no doubt, it's true—
and it might take months, but it's yours to do.
So enter Great Silence—that all-weather friend—
and never give up, you'll read why in the end.

And so it began...

Papa spent the next week venting, all ahuff and apuff as he untied and unpacked the bags. There were mountains of them—and these didn't include the stacks of books and boxes that towered toward the ceiling. His heart pounded at the sight, and his mind raged with blame as he did his darndest to disconnect from the disaster. He tried to conjure an age-old trick, waving a magic wand and laying the blame on everyone and everything around him. It was a cheap move, and he knew it wasn't true, but it helped, even if only to pretend that the buck didn't really stop with him. The beads of sweat above his brow betrayed a certain truth, though, and a curious kind of shame—that primordial remorse rooted in the fear of what (and of who) he'd find through cleaning the room.

Little by little and bit by bit, Papa picked away at the mess. He spent days and nights alone, stewing in the silence of sadness and solitude, and he rarely ever took a break. There was something quite cathartic, though, about tearing into bags, and to work all day without saying a word—he didn't even listen to music. And the more he worked, the more he discerned, and the more he discerned, the more he learned to divide the wheat from the chaff. His basement was a threshing floor, and just like his life, it had become a total wreck, so there was something therapeutic in his labor. And, though, at first, his cleaning appeared to make things worse, he was sure it was bound to only get better.

And it did get better.

He worked his way through tons of trash. Teresa had her Barbies and her Bratz with missing arms and tangled hair; and the boys had their plushies, with buttons gone and fluff falling out of their ears. And then he found Mama's red and blue dress, the one she wore before they got married. It didn't fit anymore, but it was always his favorite, and he was happy that it still smelled like Mama's old perfume. And there were Sami's things too, like sandals with red blinking lights that didn't work anymore, and Caboodles jam-packed with handmade jewelry. He even found that big yellow book and statue of Our Lady of Mt. Carmel from Fr. Sirico. And after sifting through those things he neither needed nor wanted, he found himself surrounded by a fortress of nostalgia.

When the final bag was taken to the trash, Papa stood there, admiring his accomplishments. The room was still a wreck, and with all the heavy lifting Papa did, he was afraid he had hurt his back even worse, but something was different, something worth so much more than the sweat and risk of injury...

... for, the basement began to breathe—and for the first time in months, so did he.

Books came next, and there were dozens of boxes to go through, but Papa didn't mind—not one bit. In fact, he'd looked forward to it. He was a book nerd, the kind that enjoyed smelling the pages. He thought of his library as a collection of comrades and companions, friends (and even enemies) found along the way. And just like he did with songs, so he did with books, viewing them like lampposts in a timeline, landmarks used to cue memories (both good and bad) of places he'd been, people he'd met, and thoughts and feelings he'd experienced throughout the odyssey of his life. His favorites were those written long ago, so most of the authors were dead, but he always said he preferred it that way, as their words were trapped in time, ever-present and always well, even if only in the melancholic mania of his bipolar mind.

He took his time with each one, running his fingers along the spines and covers, and he opened the oldest to see if they still had that antique aroma he loved so much. Then he divided them up. It took a long time, but he loved getting lost in the ritual. He had a stack for political economy, another for history and culture, and others, still, for philosophy and psychology, science and religion, and graphic novels too, as well as for poetry, art, music, and chess. It was here, however, that Papa came to a realization—and what followed was a first for him...

Somewhere along the line, he developed a deep-rooted disinterest in certain books, or at least for certain subjects. He wasn't sure when or even how it began, but he felt like a man who'd fallen out of love, having now only to wave and walk away. He feared he was being impulsive, even purely situational, but after rehearsing the reasons he'd have to keep them on his shelves, he couldn't evade that gnawing feeling that there was a very good reason for finally letting them go... and that is just what he did.

It felt relieving, like a burden being lifted from his chest, making it easier— even exciting—to get rid of even more. Then, when he had dwindled it down to one last box, he took the books he wished to keep and set them on the shelves, tossing throwaways near the bottom of the stairs, then returned to his seat, where he gazed with wonder at the weeks-long work of his hands.

Papa was delighted, and he rather enjoyed patting himself on the back, but he still had that one box left. He was reluctant to peel off the tape, and he was slow to open the flaps. For he knew that, there, in that last and lonely box, was an assortment of special items that once belonged to Sami. They were heirlooms, relics that parents who'd lost a child would die for.

He thumbed through photos, tumbling through the years like someone fumbles through a pack of football cards. It felt surreal, so fake and yet so real, to see Sami, young and beautiful, alive, yet forever trapped in the grainy film of time. His chin quivered beneath a bittersweet smile at the sight of Mama, with the blood of childbirth speckled on her cheek, smiling and half-dazed with her firstborn child swaddled on her chest.

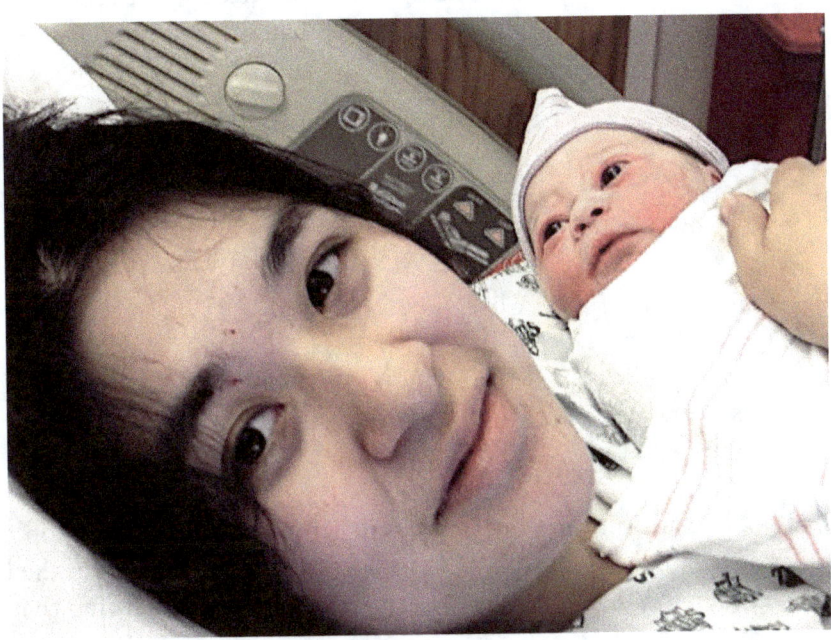

It felt so good to remember, to recall the days when weeks felt like years and years felt like forever, but all of this came crashing down when a shiver shot up his spine. For, there, beneath the photos, were Sami's diaries.

These weren't just artifacts, they were sacred treasures, and he trembled when he touched them, fearful of what he might discover inside. But Sami had been gone for a year, and he hated that her life was hermetically sealed, leaving him with nothing new to see or hear from her. He had to read it! He needed to see—he needed to feel her again. Then, just as he was about to open her diaries, he broke his weeks-long silence...

"Forgive me, Sam," he sighed. "I hope you'll understand."

Page after page were goldmines of memories, and he read them like theologians study Scripture. There was art he'd never seen, and there were stories he'd never heard—tales of boys and betrayals fit for a queenly tween—as well as cute and adorable things about her siblings. He took his time, knowing that every turn of the page was one page closer to the end. That end of her chronicles eventually came, and he was heartbroken... until he saw that there was one last item at the bottom of the box.

There was a letter attached to it, and the letter featured cute little manga characters that Sami had drawn, so he knew it was written toward the end of her life. And there, alongside the little girl, was a poem she'd written ...

The poem made him cry, but most were happy tears, and he couldn't help but laugh at Sami's perfect timing. With this joy in his heart, he set the letter to the side, then looked back into the box, where he saw something that took his breath away...

There, at the bottom of the box, was the Pokémon mask that Sami wore during radiation. It was eerie, with jet black circles drawn for eyes, and the targets were still taped onto the sides. None of that mattered, though—not to him—because that mask bore something he thought he'd lost forever: it was the exact size and shape of Samantha's face!

He groaned, "O God!" It came from the pit of his stomach, and with tears gushing out all over the place, he pressed Sami's plastic face tightly to his chest, and shouted, "Why, God? Why??"

Mama was cooking in the kitchen when she heard Papa's cry, and she feared he was hurt. She ran as fast as she could, but halfway down the stairs, she looked across the room, where she saw her husband, weeping and laughing as he hugged and kissed the cheeks and forehead of Sami's mask. It felt like something sacred, so Mama tip-toed down the rest of the stairs. Before her feet hit the floor, she bumped into the pile of books that Papa planned to throw away. She knelt and glanced at the titles and was baffled by what she saw: all of the books were written by Atheists.

What is he doing? Mama wondered.

She was so confused, but then she raised her eyes and beheld the bigger picture. For, there, in the tears and the laughter, was Mama's heartbroken husband, surrounded by the iconostasis of the culmination of his efforts. His bookshelves were covered in garland, Christmas lights, and frames of their family's favorite photos. There was a glass jar filled to the brim with Catholic sacramentals, a big yellow book, and the statue of Our Lady. This was his library, but it told a story of its own. She'd wondered whether Papa had written it, or if he'd been like an archeologist, brushing away debris, allowing the excavation to speak for itself. Either way, the silence and solitude had sifted her husband, and the foundation beneath their feet had shifted, leaving little more than the unfinished business of an unfurnished room. Even more, she wondered whether Papa could read the writing on the walls or if he'd been sitting too close to see any of it at all...

XXXIII

BATTLE ROYALE: IN THREE ACTS
[The One vs. The Many]

+ One Month Later—In Ambrose's Room +

Papa sat alone on the edge of the bed, left sorely confused by the Cat O' Nine Tails his kids had just whipped him with.

"It's a conspiracy!" he grumbled with a clackity-clack of his cane to the floor. "Or maybe some moron is manipulating my kids!" He knew that wasn't likely, and he feared it wasn't true, but he was furious out of his mind, and whatever (or whoever) was to blame for this, there were at least three things that were certain:

1. *Papa had no need for the God hypothesis...*
2. *The Church would never be part of his equation [again]...*

SHE DANCED ME A STORY

3. *The problem began about a month or so ago...*

The questions started rolling in shortly after Papa finished purging the basement...

Act One: Ex Nihilo Nihil Fit
[Out of Nothing, Nothing Comes]

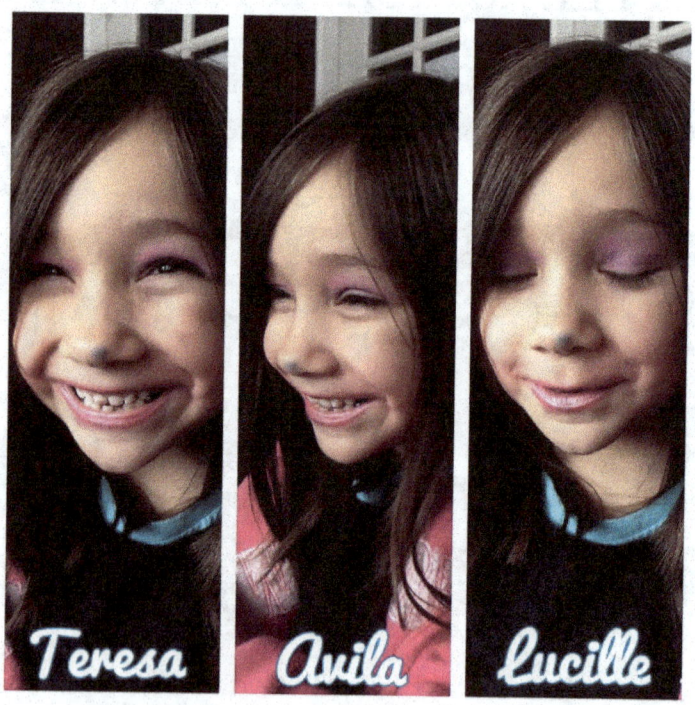

The first encounter happened when Teresa got a present in the mail. One of Papa's friends had bought her a tea set, which included a crown and silky gloves, so Teresa dressed up like a princess, brewed a batch of Papa's favorite Kool Aid, then wrote a cute letter with pink and blue crayon:

Dear Papa,

You're my dad. And you're the bestest #1 dad in the whole wide world, so, would you please come to my Pretty Princess Tea Party?

She even included choice boxes at the bottom of the page.

☐ YES ☐ NO

Pick YES or NO but just promise me you'll go. Oh, and NO BOYS ALLOWED. ONLY YOU!

Papa tried his best to dress up nice and fancy, and the two of them enjoyed hours sipping sugary "tea" while playing with LEGOs on the floor.

"Can I ask you a question?" Teresa said as she worked on her LEGO home.

"Of course you can, T."

"Okay, so, like, I've kinda wondered for a little while if maybe you could tell me who built the builders."

Papa handed her a bright blue LEGO door, and chuckled, "The builders of what?"

Teresa shrugged. "I dunno, like, just the builders of the universe and stuff."

SHE DANCED ME A STORY

"The universe?" Papa replied, nearly spitting his "tea" out on the floor. "Like the sun and the moon and the stars? All *that* kind of stuff?"

"Yeah, who built the builders who built all that stuff?"

Papa sat up on his elbows and looked at Teresa. "Why would you think that the world has a builder? Do you think it needs to or something?"

She stopped what she was doing and looked out the window. "Well, yeah, cuz how else would stuff in the universe get here?"

Papa did his best to try and explain, but Teresa followed every answer with a question, questions that always involved a variation of that age-old nuisance of "Who (or what) made this (or that)?" On and on and on this went—and it could've gone on forever—but Papa disliked the non-answer of an infinite regress, so he sat up straight, and with an air of confidence in his voice, he declared, "*Nothing* built the builders, T."

"NOTHING?" Teresa gasped. Then she squinted her eyes to look at the LEGOs, closely inspecting their design. "It sounds really silly cuz it doesn't make sense, but maybe I'll learn how nothing does all that stuff when I get bigger like you."

The two kept playing with the LEGOs, and they talked about many other things, but Papa could tell that Teresa didn't like his final answer. What she didn't know, though, was that Papa didn't like that "nothing" answer, either. That was tough, too, because it put him at odds with most of his Atheist friends. But he called it a copout, a fideistic fallback that religious people rightly decry as the "Science of the Gaps." And he'd heard it a million times. "One of these days," they'd say, "science will answer once-and-for-all that age-old nagging question of 'Who built the builders (and stuff)?'" Most people didn't buy the line, but Atheists didn't care—they wore it on their sleeve. And though they couldn't tell you what that answer would be, they were certain the answer would not (because it cannot) be God.

The front door flew open and the kids came rambling into the room.

"Hey, Papa, check it out!" Ambrose shouted. "Someone sent me a letter in the mail!" He tore open the envelope and pulled out a card. "I knew it!" he exclaimed. And with the card pressed hard against his heart. "It's from my godmother!"

It's wild how tiny and unexpected things can change a situation, but that piece of mail put an end to T's conversation about causality and cosmology. Papa was relieved to be released from that rigamarole, but the better part of him felt bad that he was glad that their conversation had ended—and that it ended in that particular way. He was pleasantly surprised, then, that when all the LEGOs were put away, Teresa hugged him, and said, "You made me have the best party today, Papa. And even though you don't know who built the builders, I still think you're my favorite #1 dad."

Act Two: Sine Qua Non
[On God & Moral Animals]

It was just a week or two later when Athan came bursting through the door. "Get back here, Athan!" Mama yelled as she followed him into the house.

Papa sat there, totally confused, in his chair. "What the heck? You guys just left!"

Athan heard Papa, but he didn't care. His emotions were off the charts, and by the sound of it, he had a lot more talking left to do. "You're just being rude!" he shouted. Then he threw his bag against the wall, and said, "And you never listen to me, Mama—NEVER!"

"Oh, I listen to you, all right. I heard every word you said! Why do you think we drove back home?"

Papa waved his hands in the air, and shouted, "Enough!" then slowly lowered his hands like he was turning down the volume in the room. "Seriously, what the heck is wrong with you guys? And why are you even home right now?"

Athan crossed his arms in protest. "I dunno, probably because Mama tells me to shut up all the time."

"That's a lie!" Mama replied, now with her finger in his face. "I told you to do something, and you disobeyed me. So I warned you, 'If you don't shut up, I'll drive you back home and make you talk to Papa.'"

Athan rolled his eyes and looked at Papa. "See, I told you that's what she said."

By this point, Teresa and Ambrose had walked through the door, and neither of them wasted any time before providing authoritative explanations for what *really* happened in the van. It wasn't a full-blown fight (not yet, anyway), but they definitely disagreed over the details, and they'd clearly been debating them for a while.

"Stoooooooooooooop!" Papa shouted. It wasn't loud or angry enough to scare the kids, but it was clear to everyone that Papa had had more than enough.

"Wow," Athan said, sarcastically, "looks like someone is having a bad day."

(Okay, so almost everyone.)

Papa scowled and told the kids to get back in the car. "Except you, Athan." The plan in Papa's mind seemed like a perfect idea until Athan executed his rather brazen one. He flew off the rails, ranting and raving about his personal opinions regarding the real reasons for all the chaos in the car.

According to him, things went down like this...

(And lest anyone doubt the authenticity of this story, please rest assured that the author went to extraordinary journalistic lengths to confirm each and every detail—details that, much to his surprise, matched up perfectly with what really went down on that miserable Monday morning.)

Just as the family was leaving for school, Athan dashed out the door and raced to the van, then hopped in the front, and hurried to buckle in. Teresa saw what he was doing, though, and that made her mad. So mad, in fact, that she started screaming at the top of her lungs (at 7 a.m. in the front yard, no less). And what was the charge? That Athan was a "sneaky little stealer." Stealer, you ask? Well, that is one way of putting it. Turns out, the kids had come up with a system, and Athan was skipping turns. The whole thing was absurd, and not a one of 'em kept a written record, so every day was Groundhog Day, with every morning starting with fights over who sat where and when.

Even so, Teresa knew for a fact that it wasn't Athan's turn. "He was definitely double-dipping—and Mama knew it too!" And that explains why Mama told Athan to let Teresa sit in the front, which, of course, made Athan angry, not only because he was the first one in the seat, and not even because Teresa was gloating over the fact that she was right and he was wrong, but because the entire order just so happened to trigger a memory. Contrary to the claims of everyone else involved, Athan "missed a turn last week," and he "definitely remembered that it was Teresa" who deprived him of his turn.

Teresa disagreed, of course, and was appalled by Athan's accusation, so she shot back by calling him a big fat liar. This infuriated the daylights out of Athan, which made Teresa fight back even more, which is why... well... let's just say that it went on like that for a while, with the two of them supposedly recalling the ridiculous details of the most mangled memories that anyone had ever heard. Arguments like these are an arms race, though, and these kids were going nuclear, accusing each other of being "the real liar of the whole entire family."

SHE DANCED ME A STORY

Trouble emerged, however, when it became obvious that Athan's claims boiled down to a simple "he said/she said," and with Mama being on Teresa's side, he was sure to lose. So he did what any clever nine-year-old boy would do and called in Ambrose as an official eye-witness. It was an age-old trick, and it typically worked, as Ambrose tended to side with his brother. But, Ambrose didn't remember Athan missing any turns. In fact, just hearing those two debating the topic made Ambrose remember at least two or three times where he ended up missing turns. "And that's because Athan and Teresa are always selfish about stealing everyone's turns all the time!"

At this point, we must remind the reader that Mama was in the car the whole time, and the kids had fried her last nerve before they had even left the house. And though it might be hard to imagine how this situation could possibly get any worse, every time Mama tried to interject or calm things down, "The kids just wouldn't stop arguing!"

And this is where things reached a breaking point, for when Athan feared that the mission was lost, he threw down the gauntlet, claiming that, "everyone steals my turn every time!" It was a desperate move—I mean, c'mon, *every* time?—and it caused quite a ruckus, with the kids insisting they never skip turns, while Mama blasted death stares at them and beat her hands against the steering wheel.

"And that," Athan said with an air of accomplishment in his voice, "is the 100% true story of why Teresa and Mama made us late for school."

Papa just stood there, stunned and staring in total disbelief of what he'd heard—not so much that the nonsense in the van actually happened (he was quite sure that it did), so much as by the fact that he was forced to hear a single word of it. Then, after a few moments of silence to commemorate the stupidity of the situation, Papa asked what he felt was an obvious question:

"But Mama told you to move, right, Athan?"

"Yes, but—"

"And she's your Mama, right, Athan?"

"Um, obviously, but—"

"Obviously but nothing, bro. Seriously, man, I don't mean to be rude, but who the heck do you think you are, talkin' to Mama like that?"

"Mama isn't always right, though, you know?"

Papa chuckled, nervously, then scratched his head, and said, "No, Mama isn't always right, but she's still your mom. It's why you gotta listen to her, man, and if she tells you to do something, you just gotta do it."

Athan scoffed, then turned his back on Papa, and mumbled something mean beneath his breath.

"Look, if you've got something to say, Athan, you better say it to my face."

Athan spun around, and with an icy stare in his cadet-gray eyes, he snarled, "Who says I've always gotta do what Mama wants?"

Papa pointed to himself. "I do!"

Athan rolled his eyes again, and replied, "Yeah, that's what bullies say. And what if you're wrong, Papa? Would I have to do those things too?"

Papa's eyebrows raised so high in astonishment, they practically flew off his face. For, as Athan knew full-well, if anything upset Papa, it was when people rolled their eyes at him. He said it demonstrated that they didn't take him seriously, and at this point in the conversation, that is exactly how he felt. But he knew better than to lose his cool, so he took a deep and calming breath, and said, "You gotta do what we say because it's the right thing to do, and it's the right thing to do because you're supposed to honor your mother and father."

"Hmph," Athan grumbled. And with his arms crossed in defiance, he squinted his eyes, and said, "Yeah, that's convenient—for you and Mama. And who came up with that rule, anyway? Oh, right, let me guess..." then he stared, accusingly, at Papa.

Athan knew he'd messed up, and he thought (and even hoped) that Papa would fight back, so he was surprised when Papa just stood there, silently looking out the window.

Papa could see far enough ahead to know that the only way he'd "win" this argument was to hide self-incriminating details. Papa was an Atheist, after all, yet there he was, trapped in a thicket, invoking the Fourth Commandment (or the Fifth Commandment for non-Catholics). Knowing as much was bad enough, but beliefs are a little like a game of Jenga, and one piece pulled or placed in the wrong spot threatened to trigger a total collapse of the tower. And that's what happened...

Papa was overwhelmed by an avalanche of Biblical beliefs and values. He hid them in the shadows, those ancient caverns reserved for things that everyone takes for granted—that canon that forms the very core and foundation for how and why people live, move, and have their being. All of these were hand-me-downs, mere residue from his life as a Christian, but they were cherished, and their influence could be seen and felt in almost every detail of their lives, touching on topics like sex, gender, love, marriage, birth control, abortion, and as it turns out, parenting.

Sure, Papa knew he could make the case without a mention of the Lord—he'd been doing that for years—and Athan wouldn't have a clue... but Papa would. He'd never forget how he twisted the truth, manipulating the moment like Play-Doh in his hands. And for what? To make Athan obey? Maybe. But deep down inside, the Atheist in Papa knew that, without God, he was stuck right back at the beginning. He would be left with nothing more than, "Because I think it's right," backed by the circularity of an old parental power-play: the brute force of the common refrain, "Because I told you so."

Papa continued to gaze, quietly, out the window, watching leaves as they fell from the trees, and in a soft and resigned voice, he asked, "Please, Athan, just listen to Mama." And with an unconvincing smile, Papa nodded, and left the room.

Act Three: Ubi Amor, Ibi Dolor
[Et Oratio]

+ Several Month Later—Fall of 2017 +

Mama played with Cocoa while Papa raked the leaves, and Teresa and Athan were riding bikes. Ambrose pretended to play with his puppets, but once the kids and their bikes were out of view, he made his move. He tip-toed across the yard to Papa, and just as he got close, he crouched low to the ground, and whispered, "Pssst... Papa... I need to talk to you."

"What's up, buddy?"

"Shhh!" Ambrose'a puppet replied, looking around like the two of them were afraid that someone would see them. "You gotta be quiet... and follow us."

Papa was about to ask why they couldn't talk, but when he turned around, he saw Ambrose being sneaky and using his puppet arm's to wave for him to follow.

"Oooh," Papa said, "it's *serious*, huh?" Ambrose smiled, nodding his and his puppet's head up and down. Then Papa looked around, just to make sure that no one was watching, and whispered for Ambrose's puppet to lead them to somewhere that they could talk in private. It was all in broad daylight, so there was really nowhere to hide, and Papa looked silly trying to be sneaky with his cane, but the two of them moved like ninjas through the yard, then crawled into the house and crept up the stairs, and when they reached the boys' bedroom, Ambrose used his puppet to shut and lock the door.

"Whew!" he sighed in relief, using his puppet's hand to wipe the sweat from his brow.

Papa used his cane to move some stuffed animals, then sat on the edge of the bed and started spinning Athan's Rubik's Cube. "All right, Ambrose, I think we're safe."

Whatever the reason, it appeared to be serious because Ambrose stopped smiling. "Will you promise me you won't get mad?"

"I guess that sorta depends," Papa replied as he struggled with the Rubik's Cube. "If you did something bad, then I might get mad, but I don't even know what this is all about."

Ambrose bit his lip and shuffled his feet as he hemmed and hawed with his hands. But after a few seconds, he gulped and took a breath, and when he'd exhaled, he looked deep into Papa's cerulean eyes, and said...

"Papa... I pray to God."

Silence consumed the room. Ambrose's words cut to Papa's core, and for a few moments, he just sat there, staring blankly at his son. He hated the thought of Ambrose in prayer, crying in a closet to a God who wasn't there (or who simply didn't care). And for a split-second, the devil within got the best of him as he turned his head in shame. Ambrose sighed at the sight, feeling bad for making Papa mad. But Papa wasn't really mad, or if he was, he wasn't mad for long. Ambrose's sigh soared across the room like sounds plucked from David's harp, soothing Papa no less than it soothed the sorrowful soul of old King Saul. He was hurt—there was no doubt about that—but Papa loved his boy, and he *was* only eight-years-old...

"So who taught you how to pray, Ambrose?"

"No one, Papa."

"No one taught you how to pray?" Papa laughed. He didn't believe it, but he knew that, while Ambrose was many things, he wasn't a liar. "What *do* you say, then? Are you just making up words on-the-fly?"

Ambrose blushed bashfully and replied, "No... I mean... well, okay, maybe." Then he chuckled, and said, "Honestly, I don't really know how to do it right, and sometimes I think I'm probably messing it up, like, maybe I'm just saying stupid words or something."

"What kind of words do you say?"

"Nothing very big, Papa. I really just ask God to help our family because Sami died, and now everyone misses her a lot." Ambrose paused for a moment, analyzing the patterns of the Rubik's Cube in Papa's hands, thinking through the various ways he could say what he was about to say next. For it was the heart of the reason he wanted to talk to Papa—and to talk to Papa alone. "I always ask God to help our family," he said, nervously, "and I pray for you the most every day before I say amen."

"Me?" Papa asked, pointing at himself.

"It's just that you look really tired a lot, and sometimes when I go to bed, I can hear you crying through the vents on the floor." Little tears welled-up in Ambrose's eyes. "And it makes me sad because I can't help you, and it's the saddest sound in the whole wide world, so I cry with you too, and then I ask God to help us to never give up and keep on smiling, because I know that's what Sami would do... I mean, if she was still here, you know?"

Papa used his anger to fight back the tears. His conscience scolded him for being hypocritical, as it wasn't long ago that he himself had cried out to God.

But that was different, he thought. *I cried out in fear and self-loathing—and at least I know what it means to pray, as well as how to do it right—but Ambrose? He prays like Nana and Aunt Curly: like someone who believes that God is really there, anxiously waiting for us to dial His number or flash the Bat Signal in the air... and he trusts that God cares.*

"And what makes you think Sami would pray, anyway?" Papa asked.

Ambrose shrugged, and with a half-smile, he wiped away his tears. "It's because I feel like God tells me that Sami is already in heaven and that she prays for us all the time every day. She loved you the most in all the universe, though, so I know it makes her really sad to see you cry so bad, and maybe that's the reason why she prays... you know, that way you can get all better... and so you can see her again in heaven after you die."

Papa's heart roared with rage, and his mind was a fiery furnace, but going scorched-earth wouldn't help anyone, much less his son. So, he bit his tongue, asking only why Ambrose thought that God said any of those things at all. "I mean, do you really feel like God talks to you?"

Ambrose and his puppet were appalled. "Talks to me?" He and his puppet laughed, and with his fireman buddy pulled close to his face, the two of them shook their heads, and said, "It's not like God is talking to me in my ear or something. Sheesh!"

The two of them were still laughing as Ambrose walked to the door, but just before he grabbed the handle, he stopped, went silent, then turned around, and in the most serious and sympathetic voice Papa had ever heard, he said, "But I still think it's the right thing to do, Papa." And with that, Ambrose closed the door, leaving Papa with his unsolved Rubik's Cube, stunned, and now alone.

"TIME OUT!"

Papa yelled so loud that all the neighbors could hear him, and he was so furious when he flew down the stairs, he almost forgot his cane.

"FAMILY MEETING—NOW!"

XXXIV

SOMETHING (OR SOMEONE)
[Greater Than the Sum]

+ Emergency Meeting—A Few Days Before Christmas +

    Mama and the kids were already on the couch when Papa limped into the room. None of them knew why Papa looked so mad, but he started pacing around the room, stopping every now and again, each time looking like he was about to say something. But then he'd just shake his head, huffing and puffing as he returned to angrily pacing the room.
    "You guys think this is really funny, don't you?" he snarled. "Just a bunch of fun and games, I bet. Well, religion isn't a game, and none of this is funny!"

Mama always gave him the benefit of the doubt, but this had her completely confused. "Are you including me in this?" she asked, pointing to herself.

"Should I?" Papa barked back. "I don't even know what to think anymore!"

Mama was almost offended, but the whole thing sounded silly, and Papa was acting peculiar, so she just crossed her arms and waited to see what all the fuss was about.

"For real, have you guys been talking behind my back or something?" he asked. "Or is someone talking to you about this stuff? Seriously, I wanna know!"

The kids looked at each other, and they wanted to giggle a little, but they were afraid it would give Papa the wrong idea. None of them dared to talk, either, and for exactly the same reason. But Papa wasn't playing around, and he expected someone to answer, so Athan bit the bullet and took the lead.

"What are you talking about, Papa?" he asked, nervously.

"Don't give me that, bro. Someone put you guys up to this, didn't they? Was it one of your friends? Was it Nana? Aunt Curly??"

"What did we even do?" Teresa asked.

"What did you do? What did you do?? All three of you goin' on about 'Who built the builders, Papa?', 'Who makes the rules about right and wrong, Papa?'" Then he looked at Ambrose, and said, "'Oh, and I forgot to tell you, but, yeah, I pray, Papa.'"

Everyone looked at Ambrose, who sat there sheepishly, with cheeks now blushing with embarrassment.

"You pray?" Mama asked.

"And who said anything about building builders?" Athan wondered aloud. "What is that even supposed to mean?"

"Oh, c'mon already!" Papa scoffed, pointing at Teresa. "She's asking who created the universe!"

"Ah, okay, I've wondered that too," Athan replied. Then he looked again at Ambrose, and said, "Seriously, though, you pray, Ambrose?"

"I pray, too, sometimes," Teresa said, "but only when I'm really scared, like when we had a tornado, and that one-time Papa was scared trying to catch that bat that was flying all over the house."

"I remember that!" Ambrose said.

"Papa was so freaked out," Athan laughed, pretending to bite his nails. "Do you remember how he was all, like—"

"STOP!!!" Papa yelled. He was frazzled, practically pulling his hair out, and somehow the situation was now even worse than when it started. Through all the chaos of their confusion and contradictory answers, it became painfully obvious to Papa that his kids were clueless as to the conspiracy theories whirling around in Papa's head. And with that, the room returned to its previous silence... until Ambrose asked:

"Papa... are we Catholic?"

Papa raised his eyes toward the ceiling and held his breath, then slowly exhaled as he dropped his chin to his chest and wiped the exhaustion from his exasperated eyes.

"I wondered that too, sometimes," Teresa said. She grabbed her doll and began to brush the knots from her hair, saying, "People always ask me if I'm Catholic whenever I tell them my name."

"Same with me," Athan said. That kind of startled everyone, as it was a rare moment of agreement between Athan and his sister. "But it's true. I mean, I'm the only Athanasius any of my friends have ever known."

Papa scoffed, shaking his head at the thought of Athan's friends, most of whom were Christians, having no clue who St. Athanasius was. "Figures," he mumbled under his breath. "Christians don't know jack about their past." That was terribly uncharitable, of course, and it wasn't anywhere near being true, but it was definitely true for his kids—and he knew it for a fact. "Are you Catholic?" Papa sighed. "Yes and no. On the one hand, all of you were baptized in the Catholic Church. To Catholics, you're Catholic, and with names like Isaac Athanasius, Ambrose Louis, and Teresa Avila Lucille—"

"Those are *really* Catholic names," Mama said.

"Is there a St. Samantha Lee?" Teresa asked.

"Duh!" Ambrose scoffed. "Of course, Sami is a saint."

"Actually," Papa corrected him, "Sami was named after the actress from Bewitched."

"And *that* was all Papa's idea," Mama laughed.

"But Sami will definitely be a saint one of these days," Athan said, "that's for sure."

"That's what I meant," Ambrose said matter-of-factly. "I mean, obviously."

"No!" Teresa grumbled. "You don't even know what you're talking about, Ambrose."

"Ugh!" Papa groaned. "Teresa is right, you guys. None of you have any clue what you're talking about."

"See?" she said. Then she started to braid her doll's hair, and scoffed, "You guys are just like little babies making things up."

"No! I-I mean, yes," Papa stammered. And with his hand over his face, he groaned, "you guys are just conjecturing. You don't have a clue what the heck you're even talking about."

"But that's why we're asking," Athan replied.

Ambrose nodded, adding, "Yeah, and that's why I told you guys I wanted to go to my godmother's church on Christmas Eve."

"Wait. What?" Papa shot back. "You never said anything about Christmas Eve! And you don't even know what it means to have a godmother, bro."

Mama had that *Uh-oh, I'm in trouble!* look on her face. "Okay, see, so maybe I forgot to mention this, but when I was talking with Marijo recently—"

"Wait!!" Papa replied. "You talk to Marijo?"

SHE DANCED ME A STORY

"Of course. She accidentally sent Ambrose a duplicate piece for his Nativity, so I gave her a call."

"That dang Nativity..." Papa mumbled under his breath.

"I had her on speaker phone. Ambrose overheard her asking what we were doing on Christmas Eve, so he rushed in and started begging to go."

"I know what a godmother is, anyways, Papa," Ambrose insisted. "They're really pretty Italian ladies who tell Mamas and Papas that they need to be the best parents they can be." Then he took the figurine he'd been holding in his hands and pressed it against his cheeks. "And they always send nice cards and Christmas ornaments to their godsons in the mail every year." Like everything else thus far, that wasn't entirely true, but it was true of their experience. Marijo was all of those things, and she really did send Ambrose ornaments every year. In fact, the Nativity Scene on the mantle was her gift to him, and she sent little figures to add to the scene every year. "This year she sent me another Little Drummer Boy." Then Ambrose's smile turned into a frown, and in a sad and grumpy voice, he complained, "Godmothers always invite their godsons to go to church on Christmas Eve, too, but some papas are meanies and always say no."

Athan glared at Papa, adding, "Yeah, and then he just goes all by himself when we're all in our beds."

"That is, unless you're T-Bear and Sami who are all sneaky and stay up past bedtime," Ambrose added.

The conversation went on like this for a while, and the deeper it got, the closer they approached the question Papa knew they'd eventually ask. At this point, though, it was practically inevitable... and it came much quicker than he imagined it would.

"Papa, can you show us what church even looks like?"

He was clever, though, and in the debates between Atheist parents and their inquisitive kids, he was one step ahead (or so he believed). So, he agreed to show them. He grabbed his laptop and looked up different kinds of religious services.

First, he showed them the Hari Krishnas, followed by Islam, and then some enthusiastic videos of the "The Holy Ghost Bartender," the Fundamentalist Mormons, and some old tyme Appalachian snake-handlin' services. He probably would've gotten away with it, too, except that none of the kids could imagine Nana, Pa, or Aunt Curly doing anything like that at their churches.

JEREMIAH T. BANNISTER

Part of him thought about throwing his family under the bus, playing on his children's naivete, but Mama ruined that scheme before it even started.

"Show them videos of the church we used to go to in Battle Creek," she said. "That's where my mom goes to church, and it's the same kind of church Great-Gramma Bannister goes to." It didn't end there, either. Oh, no, Mama rattled off several Protestant churches the two of them had attended over the years. Worse yet, she'd point out people they knew, talking about things like children's church, youth group, and Vacation Bible School. The kids loved the stories, of course, and they were even kind of jealous.

"Atheist families don't really have very much stuff like that," Teresa said. Then she wrapped a hair tie around the braid in her doll's hair, and said, "It's like they don't even believe in making babies and raising families or something."

"Yeah," Athan said, "but this still looks kinda boring. And why is everyone just sitting there listening to some guy in a suit tell them his opinions."

Whew! Papa thought to himself. *That was getting too close for comfort.* Papa was proud of his boy, taking the lead like that, so he smiled and mussed Athan's hair...

That was until Athan said, "But those aren't even Catholic, anyway, are they, Papa?"

"Yeah, I've seen Aunt Curly's church before," Teresa said, "so I know it's really pretty with big fancy drawings all over the place."

Papa glared angrily at them, then he mumbled under his breath as he typed, "Eastern Orthodox Divine Liturgy and Roman Catholic Latin Mass." He chuckled when he pressed enter, though, imagining how the kids would find it all so foreign, with its smoke from swinging censers, curiously colored vestments, and strange lines of people being fed bread and wine on a spoon. But, he was wrong yet again, for there they sat, silently watching, entirely enthralled by the sounds and the spectacle of the ceremonies. Sure, they were young, and they were unquestionably curious kids, but this was cataclysmic. They were spinning Papa like a dreidel, threatening to flip his little Atheist empire inside-out and upside-down.

It was clear to Papa that something (or Someone) greater than the parts of #TeamTinyDancer was at play, and whatever (or Whoever) it was having a heyday, watering and shaping his children like clay. It was all fate or formality by this point, but, alas, when the videos ended, the kids looked at him with their pleading beady eyes and begged him to take them to church on Christmas Eve.

SHE DANCED ME A STORY

He looked to Mama for help, but she just witnessed the same thing he did—and by the sound of it, she was closer to their position than she was to his—so he glanced one last time at the kids, and with nearly a decade's worth of reluctance in his heart, he sighed, "Fine, we can go to Midnight Mass with Marijo."

The kids jumped up and down, dancing and prancing like maniacs around the room, childishly chanting, "We're gonna go to chur-urch! We're gonna go to chur-urch! And we're staying up past mid-night!"

There was no more talk of God and church for the rest of the evening, but when Mama put the kids to bed, she went back downstairs, where she found Papa rummaging through an old box of DVDs in the living room.

"What are you looking for?" Mama asked as she sat in the rocker and started to knit.

"Aha!" Papa exclaimed. "I knew I didn't throw them away!" They were DVDs of old Feature Films for Families, with movies like Rigoletto, On Our Own, Buttercream Gang, as well as the Christmas episode of McGee & Me.

Mama laughed, "Wow, baby, really? What's next, Psalty the Singing Songbook?"

He paused for a second, wondering if he even had old Gerbert episodes, but then he snapped out of it, and said, "Wait, Psalty? No way! But these? These are classics."

Mama never understood what he saw in those movies. Papa loved them as a Christian kid, and continued to even as an Atheist adult. He often complained that there weren't very many good, wholesome family-friendly films anymore. "Not like Veggie-Tales or Davey & Goliath," he'd say, "but also not like the mindless crap you see on TV and the Internet all the time." He'd typically follow this up with some nostalgic childhood memory about—

"Little House on the Prairie! What do you think, Ang? Do you think Teresa would love all those stories about Ma and Pa and their adventurous little girls?"

Mama couldn't help but laugh. "You surprise me sometimes, Jeremiah, ya know that?"

"Really? Why's that?"

"I dunno, just that you said we could all go to Midnight Mass with Marijo, and now you're finding a bunch of Christian stuff for the kids to watch. I guess it's just not what I would expect from you."

A cunning grin crawled across Papa's face, and there was a mischievous look in his eyes. "Can I tell you a secret?" he whispered.

"Don't you even, Jeremiah," Mama said with a shake of her head. "You better not say you were lying to the kids. It would kill 'em—if they didn't kill you first!"

"Lie?" Papa scoffed. "Why, I nevuh!"

Mama laid her knitting needles on her lap, and with a deadly kind of seriousness in her voice, she said, "Jeremiah..."

"No, of course I wasn't lying to them." Then he scrunched his lips, and with a shrug of his shoulders, he added, "But lie is such a strong word, isn't it?"

"Jeremiah! Ambrose already called Marijo and told her we'll be there! Are you really going to take that back now? And of all the days, you'd take it back on Christmas Eve?"

"No, Ang, you're missing the point. I just happen to know something that the kids don't know." Mama was not impressed (at all), and she was nervous about where this was going, but Papa was proud of the scheme that he had devised. "Okay, so hear me out. Marijo lives in Kalamazoo, so her church is an hour away, and if Christmas Eve is like it normally is, there's gonna be tons of snow, so that'll make it even longer, and there's no way we're driving a three-hour round-trip for church, especially not for a Midnight Mass on Christmas Eve. I mean, c'mon, that would have us gone from 10:30 at night until about 3 in the morning. And there ain't no way they'd go for that, especially not on Christmas Eve."

"And why is that?" Mama asked.

"Because Christmas is in the morning, and what kid wants to sleep in on Christmas? No way, they want to wake up as early as they can, that way they can open presents."

Mama just smiled and resumed her knitting, rocking back and forth in her chair.

"What? You aren't gonna say anything?"

"What's there to say, Jeremiah? You thought this one through, didn't ya."

He heard the sarcasm in her voice, but he didn't care. "It's pure genius, Ang," he said, bragging like he'd cracked the code to Fort Knox. "Best of all, I can just tell them we'll go some other time, and they'll forget or get all wrapped up with other stuff, so we won't need to worry about it for a whole other year!"

SHE DANCED ME A STORY

"Aw, darn," Mama said, looking at the scarf she was knitting. "Missed something."

"What did you miss?" Papa asked as he put McGee & Me in the DVD player.

"Oh, I didn't miss anything. You did."

"Me? Pfft! Yeah, right. Like what?"

"Oh, nothing big, just that Marijo moved to Grand Rapids years ago... and they go to Sacred Heart, which is, I dunno, about 10 minutes up the road from here."

Mama didn't look up from her work, but she could see Papa out of the corner of her eye, and there was something charming in the helpless tone of his "ugh" and sweet in the sound of the thud from his forehead falling flat atop the cardboard box of Feature Films for Families.

XXXV

THE CRUX AT THE CROSSROAD
[Christmas Eve 2017]

+ 11:59 p.m.—Standing Outside of Sacred Heart +

So there he stood, smack-dab in the heart
of the crossroad where his faith & reason parted ways,
robed (as he'd hoped) in ghostly hues of winter blues,
gazing through the pane of a stained-glass window
that streamed with the tears from frostbit years
now a melt in the warmth of an ember's amber glow.

He recalled the Precious Moments in her eyes
when her heart, alive & aflush, punch-drunk with love,
burned through the blush in her candy-apple cheeks
painted perfect and pure over ivory white
with strokes from the brush belonging to the One
Who set the star in the sky of Christmas Night.

'Twas so long ago in a land locked away
when days of sadness shined, and laughter reigned
over Rainbow Roads of hard maple wood floors
that flowed like ink from the tips of fancy pens
drawing out monsters that compose the song of the siren
lulling mankind with disparaging words to sleep. And then-

Kling-klang! Kling-klong! rang the ancient song
chanted by cherubim enthralled by the rapture of the bells
that groan & grind in mystical measures of liturgical time,
forever advancing by harkening back to that prophetic past,

SHE DANCED ME A STORY

where Love foretold of war, daring the Fates & Furies
to not duplicate the day Darwin's darling daughter died...

"Please, Papa," Mama cried, "don't let your heart divide."
And with his head bowed, Papa sighed, then walked inside.

XXXVI

A Godmother's Sacred Heart
[World Without End]

+ Moments Later—Inside Sacred Heart of Jesus +

Papa opened his eyes in the darkness, deep within the quietude of prayer. Mama led the kids toward a pew near the narthex, where the children read through hymnals while Papa thumbed the wooden beads of his chaplet—the one Marijo gave him when she talked about her son who had died.

Other families shuffled in, and Papa hoped to find Marijo, but it was dark, and everyone was shrouded by the shadow. He heard them, though, in the chattering of their teeth from the cold of the world beyond the walls, and for a moment the church was abuzz with the sound of children stomping the snow from their boots. Everyone hustled and bustled to find a seat, and just when the last shadow sat down, the sacristy bell rang, and the choir in the loft sang...

Of the Father's heart begotten,
Ere the world from chaos rose
He is Alpha; from that Fountain
All that is and hath been flows;
He is Omega, of all things,
Yet to come the mystic Close,
Evermore and evermore.

Everyone stood as the altar boys made their procession, and the fragrance of frankincense and myrrh saturated the sanctuary. Papa loved that smell, and he still burned incense in his home, but this was top-shelf resin, the sort of thing one offers to the gods. The shadows of the procession danced along the walls, but the shrouding smoke that filled the air made it hard to see, especially from his seat near the center aisle. It wasn't long, though, before the young men turned the bend at the back of the church, then made their way toward the altar, which was aglow with an otherworldly bluish-gray haze from the flickering flames of candelabras shining like stars in the night.

The whole thing felt ancient, even primal—like a timeless tragedy, as somber and as sorrowful as the wilderness, and there was a disquieting desolation in the silhouettes of the servers. And, it was right then, while admiring the embroidery on the lonely white of their surplices, that Mama and Papa saw a ghost!

"Isn't that the priest that prayed for Sami?" Athan whispered.

"Yeah," Teresa said in a voice too loud for church. "He's the one who called her Fire Toes." Then she raised her eyebrows, and said, "He used fancy words when he prayed."

Papa was too shocked to reply, and by the look on Fr. Sirico's face when the two of them made eye-contact, Fr. Sirico was just as surprised to see him.

JEREMIAH T. BANNISTER

"Whodathunkit?" Ambrose whispered to Mama. Then he tugged on Papa's arm, and with a chuckle gleaming in his eyes, he said, "I guess there is some sort of a conspiracy goin' on around here."

And the choir sang:

At His Word the worlds were framed.
He commanded and 'twas done
Earth and sky and boundless ocean,
In their threefold order one;
All that sees the moon's soft radiance,
All that breathes beneath the sun,
Evermore and evermore.

A young man emerged from the darkness, and he brought with him a book. The readings were rhythmic, telling tales of people walking in darkness through lands of doom and gloom, of how they'd seen a tremendous light, one that brought abundant joy, and how every boot that trudged in battle, every cloak rolled in blood, will be burned as fuel for flames. For at the end of an ancient line, a child will be born, and his name shall be Emmanuel.

"I know that story," Teresa said as she hugged Papa's arm. "You read it to us on Christmas, and that's what they read at the church we went to with Sami."

Whether it was the scene or the song or the readings and remembrance, Papa couldn't say, but something sparked within him, and his heart began to melt. He tried to deny it, but nothing worked, so he distracted himself, pressing even harder on the beads between his fingers, but the harder he pressed, the more they rattled. And, the more they rattled, the tighter he'd squeeze them—so tight, it awoke the angels in the architecture, who now droned with ghostly tones:

He assumed this mortal body,
Death and sorrow here to know,
That the race from dust created
Doomed by law to endless woe
May not henceforth die and perish
In the dreadful gulf below,

SHE DANCED ME A STORY

Evermore and evermore!

He looked at his children. They had been moved by the meekly maiden and her mild child, and they were mesmerized by the stories told through the gleam of stained-glass windows around the church. They witnessed scenes of angelic annunciations, shepherds in stables, and greetings from a kinswoman who hailed, "Our Lady, full of grace!" And Mama looked so bright, so hopeful, like a lost girl who'd found her way home.

What is happening to us? Papa cried inside. *What do they see that I don't see??*

Something beneath the building shook, and he trembled at the sight of the priest as he strode to the other side of the altar. His movements were gradual, even glacial, like a man gliding up a mountainside; and when he reached its peak, everyone stood to their feet.

On his feet, Papa saw something previously hidden from view, and it came through a twinkle from the corner of his eye. It was light from a star shining down atop a family, abandoned and alone in a humble home, yet surrounded by furry animals and a little boy beating on his drum.

But for what? Papa wondered. *To quell man's fear of death?? To mend the Bifrost broken by iniquity???*

Teresa tugged on his sleeve, then took her thumb out of her mouth, and pointing at the manger at the center of the stable, she smiled, and said, "Happy birthday, baby Jesus."

gling-gling-gling

The knell of the bells rang aloud, and everyone collapsed to their knees as Fr. Sirico raised his hands in prayer. Sign after sign of the cross felt like arrows in Papa's flesh, each of them tearing deeper and deeper into the callous of his heart.

And the angels sang the thunderous lines:

Let the storm and summer sunshine,
Gliding stream and sounding shore,
Sea and forest, frost and zephyr,
Day and night their Lord adore;
Let creation join to laud thee
Through the ages evermore,
Evermore and evermore.

Lo! Veils lifted like a drawbridge from over Papa's eyes, and time slowed to a halt when, for the very first time since crossing the threshold of those large arched doors, Papa beheld the church for what it truly was:

The pillars? The smoke?? The ancient marble altar??? Even the heavy wooden kneelers! It was the nave from his dream the day of Sami's surgery. *But if all of those are here, then what about—*

He gasped, and his eyes were wild, frantically searching the pews for her face--for any trace of her at all--but it was still too dark. *Where is she?* he moaned. He felt like a Quaker, shaking as he fought tooth and nail against the light that burned within, but he was losing that fight, evidenced by the click of those wooden beads and the clack of him gnashing his teeth. Then--

GRRRRRR...

It was the deepest and darkest grinding growl he'd ever heard, and the ground rumbled beneath his feet. He wiped his tears, hoping to see someone, anyone who'd heard and felt it also—but his family just sat there, silent and starstruck, and for the first time in years, appearing utterly and entirely at peace...

SHUNK

Papa covered his face with his forearm as light burst forth from a golden crown high above the altar. It was enormous, radiant like the sun, and stood at the center of a dome, which was blue and shot through with trees of copper and sparrows with gold leaf flecked through their wings. Then the dome began to spin. At first, it was slow, like a merry-go-round getting started on a playground. Then it began to go faster, the patterns bled into a blur, and the birds began to fly. They flew right off the dome, which had now turned dark as night. The branches where the birds were perched had disappeared, having transformed into galaxies, while the birds that remained, and leaves that hadn't blown off became planets and moons, all of them orbiting the sun of that radiant golden crown. But even these things flew faster, and the world within the dome spun wildly out of control. Planets and galaxies collided, causing enormous amounts of dust and debris, making the whole scene impossible to see, until—

BOOM!!!

A supernova! Its blast blew everything to smithereens. Stardust rained down like glitter from the dome, and angels and demons emerged, all of them swirling about in the glittery glow of the storm. Bolts of lightning flashed from the clash of their swords, and thunder rumbled as they tumbled through the air, but in the midst of that tremendous tumult, Papa finally saw her...

There Sami was, before his eyes, descending ever so gently from the eye of the storm. She was clothed in an amaranth dress, but she looked nearly ten years older than the tiny dancer in his dream. He wondered if it was even her, but she limped with a pretty pink cane, and there was a yellow brace wrapped around her waist. Her wrists were even covered in Sami's hand-made jewelry, and she was wearing the skates that she had received for Christmas. Papa sobbed with such joy as Sami pulled her furry bunny ears down over her head, and his heart cheered when she began to skate around the ledge of the dome encircling the golden crown.

The limp in her leg made it slow and clunky, and her right-arm still looked like a bird's broken wing, but she was doing it—and all by herself! He gasped, though, when the demons lunged at her, and he was inspired as the angels fought them back, wielding their swords with all of their might to protect Princess Sami! But the demons, they hissed, so malicious and conniving, and they ducked beneath the wings of the angels, then soared with flashing fangs toward Sami, bound and determined to destroy her. But every time they swung their swords, they missed! They tried and tried and tried again, but they missed her by an inch every time, and though they nipped and bit at her heels, they were always left hungry. They looked like dogs chasing Rhosgobel rabbits, which almost made Papa laugh. But then he saw a guileful demon lying like a lion in wait, and his heart practically stopped when Sami lost her balance!

He watched in horror as saliva dripped from the tips of the devil's fangs, and when the demon pounced at Sami, Papa squeezed the beads of Marijo's chaplet as hard as he possibly could, and cried aloud in his heart to God:

"Glory be to the Father, and to the Son, and to the Holy Spirit, as it was in the beginning, is now, and ever shall be, world without end. Amen!"

Sami didn't lose her balance, though. She was crouching to the ground, and just when the demon's sword was about to cut her through, she leapt through the air, twirling and whirling so fast that she became a blur of effervescent light. Her cane soared through the air, and so did everything else—her belt, her skates, her bracelets, and bunny ears, even disco balls and chess pieces. Everything flew in different directions, each thing aimed directly at an evil, heartless demon! One demon after another howled in pain, screeching and squealing as they were vanquished by the symbols. The blur ceased when she landed on the crown, and, at last, Papa saw her clear as day!

She had long, brown, flowing hair, and her wedding garment gleamed and glistened. She danced wild and free, in ways he'd never seen, and her limp was gone. She stood in a perfect fifth position, her grand jeté and pirouettes were flawless, and her double-barrel calypso was stunning. Then, with a chassé, she stepped and brought her feet together, then leapt through the air, and with her back arched, she executed a perfect Firebird leap! Once she landed, she curtsied and held out her lovely hands. Stargazer lilies poured like a waterfall from her palms, and Papa watched in awe as they fell like feathers toward the ground—

SHE DANCED ME A STORY

𝔤𝔩𝔦𝔫𝔤-𝔤𝔩𝔦𝔫𝔤-𝔤𝔩𝔦𝔫𝔤...
𝔤𝔩𝔦𝔫𝔤-𝔤𝔩𝔦𝔫𝔤-𝔤𝔩𝔦𝔫𝔤...
𝔤𝔩𝔦𝔫𝔤-𝔤𝔩𝔦𝔫𝔤-𝔤𝔩𝔦𝔫𝔤...

The chime of the bells harkened time back to speed, and with thousands of pedals descending from the stardust in the dome, Fr. Sirico raised his golden chalice. And just when it appeared that the pedals would reach the wine, the clouds parted, and the moon beamed through the stained-glass window, illuminating the Sacred Heart that had been hidden in the shadows behind the altar. Then, just when it seemed that the pedals, wine, and Sacred Heart were about to converge, a blinding light swept over the sanctuary.

And the angels in the architecture of Papa's livened heart began to sing:

Thee old men, Thee young men,
The boys in chorus sing;
Matrons, virgins, little maidens,
With glad voices answering:
Let their guileless songs re-echo,
And the heart, its music bring,
Evermore and evermore!

When Mass ended, the kids were invited to get some candy from a basket, and the family searched for Marijo. They found her near the baptismal font, admiring the manger while talking with Fr. Sirico.

"Merry Christmas, Marijo!" Ambrose cheered as he ran to greet her.

She knelt down and wrapped her arms around him. "You made it!". Then she glanced up at Papa, and with a look of concern that only good godmothers could give, she said, "Honestly, Jeremiah, I didn't think you'd come."

"Oh, trust me," Mama replied, "he tried getting out of it."

Marijo laughed, then mussed Ambrose's hair. "Well, I guess baby Jesus had different plans for you then, huh?"

The family talked for a while with Fr. Sirico, while Marijo took some pictures with the kids. It was getting late, and everyone was exhausted, so they made their way toward the large arched doors at the back of the church. Just as they were leaving, Fr. Sirico called to Papa, and in a fatherly voice Papa would never forget, he said:

"Welcome home, Prodigal Son."

SHE DANCED ME A STORY

    Papa nodded, and he wished him Merry Christmas, but with the door separating the sacred from the secular quietly closing behind him, he found himself back in the bitter cold of Christmas morn, thinking about an old magnet his mother had on their refrigerator. It featured a housewife with dinner in her hands, and words over her curly red hair that read: *Home is Where the Heart is*. He always loved that magnet, and he believed those words now more than ever. But that meant he wasn't quite home, at least not yet, but he was close... and his heart knew what needed to be done.

XXXVII

SETTLING SCORES
[On Warped Chessboards]

+ Back Home—Fifteen Minutes Later +

    There was a clumsy cadence in the clip-clop sound of Papa's wingtips as he limped up the stairs, and the clickety-clack of his cane bounced like ping-pong balls off the attic walls. He trembled from exhaustion, and the groaning of the steps gave voice to the radiating pain in his back. But, he felt compelled, like a snowflake dancing in the wind, duty-bound and driven by the swirling eddies of yearning and despair. He had avoided that room for nearly two years, paralyzed by a menacing fear... the fear of what he might think and feel, and of what he would be forced to relive in that long-abandoned attic. So, when he reached the top of the stairs, he stood there, eyes closed, listening to the lingering sound of his breath, then turned to face his fate.

Midway across the room stood Sami's lamp, now placed atop the table... the table with the chessboard. Both the source and reflection burned with an almost otherworldly glow, radiant as a double rainbow in the dark.

"How long have you been on?" Papa said to the lamp as he draped his coat over the back of the chair. "We're lucky, you know. The whole house could have burned down." Then he looked around the room, where he saw posters of Batman & Robin, Muhammad Ali, and a forever young Marilyn Monroe. Every poster brought back so many memories, but none of them as profound as the poster of Sami's exploding TARDIS. She bought it in Cardiff, and it was her favorite, bursting with color and painted in the style of Vincent van Gogh. Papa kissed the tips of his fingers, then touched the poster with his hand. And with tears streaming down his cheeks, he drew a heart with his finger over the core of the blast, then closed his eyes, and said:

"I love you, Samantha, with all of my heart... into a million pieces..."

Opening his eyes, he sat down in the chair where the two had played their final game. He stared at the pieces, trying his best to reimagine the occasion... but he couldn't. It had simply been too long. And adding insult to injury, someone had moved the pieces.

"Kids..." he grumbled under his breath.

Part of him was angry, wondering why things couldn't just be left as they were. But the better part of his heart found the whole fiasco kind of funny. He imagined the kids sneaking up to the attic, tip-toing barefoot through the room, then mindlessly moving all the pieces, and giggling as they ran back down the stairs, reassuring each other with playful whispers,

"Don't worry, Papa will never know."

"And what the heck?" Papa said, shaking his head in utter disbelief. "This endgame is the most rigged thing I've ever seen in my entire life!"

It looked ridiculous, and it was most certainly rigged as the kids had left Papa's lonely king trapped on a corner square, now forced to duke it out alone against Sami's king, queen, rook, and three pawns. These kids weren't playing by-the-book, that's for sure, but Papa took one last look, scanning the squares for any way out, even if it meant the stalemate of a draw. He played it out in his head, thinking through all sorts of variations, but every sequence always ended the same:

"Checkmate..."

Exasperated, Papa leaned over and grabbed an object from off the floor. He intended to throw it, but then he realized what it was: Sami's old, checkered pillow, the one she had in her hands on their very first night of Pillow/Blankets. And he remembered... there was a music box inside.

He turned it over and wound it up, and with the sound of *Jesus Loves Me* ringing in his ears, he closed his eyes and reclined in the chair. It was bliss, but it didn't last long, for when the song came to an end, he opened his eyes to the optical illusion of Sandro del Prete's "Warped Chessboard." He beheld that age-old battle between black and white (and the gradient of grays in between), as well as all the ladders connecting then and there with here and now. For the first time in years, he saw what he had tried so hard to suppress... and he knew what he was destined to do.

Sitting up in his chair, Papa reached for his king...

"Papa?" Mama asked from the bottom of the stairwell. "Is everything okay up there?"

"Yeah, I'm just settling old scores."

SHE DANCED ME A STORY

"Well, hurry up. The kids are waiting to open their presents."

Mama started to walk away but then turned back and yelled up the stairs, "Oh, and if you see Sami's lamp up there, just grab it and bring it down. We can use her light for the living room."

Papa assured her that he would, and then he looked at the board a final time. He smiled, and with his finger pressed down upon the king, he said:

"Sometimes, you lose to win…"

… then he toppled his king, casting his crown to the ground.

As he was leaving, he turned back toward the room, and, with Sami's lamp in-hand and red-checkered pillow pressed tightly to his heart, he saluted the exploding TARDIS and wished Princess Sami a very Merry Christmas. Then, in the quiet and dark of his attic, he rewound the dial on Sami's musical pillow, and with the melody of *Jesus Loves Me* dancing through the air, he emerged from the darkness, where, with the smell of incense from Sacred Heart still on his clothes, he descended into the light of love and laughter now bursting with life at the bottom of stairs.

#TeamTinyDancerFOREVER

Princess Samantha Lee Bannister is buried at Fort Custer National Cemetery in Augusta, Michigan. Annual Panikhidas are served at her graveside.

If you have experienced anything life-changing, miraculous, or otherwise inexplicable that you believe is directly related to Sami and the #TeamTinyDancer family... YOU ARE NOT ALONE. Please share your story with the family by emailing:

TeamTinyDancer@gmail.com

JEREMIAH T. BANNISTER

ACKNOWLEDGEMENTS

I want to thank all the people who patiently (and impatiently) waited for me to complete this project. Their support (and constant nagging) helped me through some terribly tumultuous times. Many of you were quoted in this book, but your words or actions might have been attributed to one of the story's few dozen "composite" characters. I thank you in advance for recognizing this to be my heartfelt (and painstaking) effort to incorporate as many people, words, moments, and memories as possible.

I'm grateful for the assistance, advice, and encouragement Diane Baum, Timothy and Whitney Flanders, Phil Gonzalez, Luke Getz, and Chad Lutzke provided throughout the process. More than these, I'm thankful for my sister, aka Aunt Curly. Her tea-fueled late-nite editing sessions over the phone, finely-tuning (and toning down) the text made this book what it is today. In fact, here's a free Easter egg: the powerful ending of "Zombies & Quiet Zones" is almost entirely derived from my sister's written account of her and Nana's memories of that fateful summer morning in July of 2016.

Most of all, I'm forever indebted to my wife and children. Angela, for her patience, love, and long-suffering. And our kids, for their kindness, creativity, and comradery. I hope and pray that you will always cherish our family's story, that this book will help you to never forget the sister you loved and lost as little children, and that you will forever find in these pages the heart of a father who loves you more than you'll ever know.

Lastly... Samantha Lee. You taught me many things, like biding time and the best way to die. You blazed a trail for me, living out what it means to never give up and keep on smiling, especially when life has us dancing on the edge of an active volcano. And you challenged me to never hate, to dream bigger thoughts, and to live and love with all of my heart... *into a million pieces.*

Jeremiah T. Bannister
March 27, 2023
[My 45th Birthday]

www.ingramcontent.com/pod-product-compliance
Lightning Source LLC
Chambersburg PA
CBHW070747230426
43665CB00017B/2284